No. 886
$12.95

# THE HANG GLIDER'S BIBLE

### BY MICHAEL A. MARKOWSKI

## TAB BOOKS
Blue Ridge Summit, Pa. 17214

FIRST EDITION

FIRST PRINTING—JUNE 1977
SECOND PRINTING—MARCH 1978

Copyright © 1977 by TAB BOOKS

Printed in the United States
of America

**Library of Congress Cataloging in Publication Data**

Markowski, Michael A
   The hang glider's bible.

   Bibliography: p.
   Includes index.
     1. Hang gliders. 2. Hang gliding. I. Title.
   GV764.M37        797.5′5         77-5600
   ISBN 0-8306-7886-7
   ISBN 0-8306-6886-1 pbk.

30, 747

This book is dedicated to Mom and Dad, and to all hang glider pilots throughout the world with the hope that it will foster safety in all aspects of our new flying sport.

In an effort to make this the most comprehensive book of its kind, the author has gone to great lengths to present representative material from all hang glider manufacturers. Most manufacturers were very cooperative and generous in supplying information. Thank you very much.

In order to keep this book the most current in the industry, all manufacturers are requested to send periodic updates on their latest products and developments (brochures, drawings, 8 × 10 glossies, etc.) and news releases to the author at: P.O. Box 4371, Harrisburg, Pa, 17111.

The author would really appreciate hearing from homebuilders and experimenters, too. You could contribute greatly to the advancement of hang gliding. Please send glossy photos, drawings, etc of your latest hang glider projects to the author. Perhaps you will find your ideas published in the next edition of this book.

I'd like to extend a special thank you to my wonderful wife, Roberta, for diligently deciphering my "writings" and typing the manuscript. It was quite a task.

# About The Author

Mr Markowski's life literally revolves around flight. He is a graduate aerospace engineer and licensed private pilot who, since 1971, has devoted considerable time, study and effort in developing low speed and motorless flight vehicles. He was instrumental in initiating hang gliding in the eastern sections of the country and began his writing career in 1972 as editor of the original **Skysurfer Magazine**. Since that time, he has designed more than 30 different hang gliders, co-founded two hang glider manufacturing companies, co-managed a hang gliding school, taught hang gliding theory on an adult education level, and is considered a competent authority on foot-launched flight.

He has lectured to numerous groups, including the two International Symposiums On The Technology and Science Of Low Speed And Motorless Flight held at M.I.T. in 1972 and 1974. He was also responsible for the Forum On Foot-Launched Flight at the 1974 and 1975 Annual Convention and Fly-In of the Experimental Aircraft Association. He has appeared on national television shows and has also written many magazine articles including a cover story for **Scientific American**.

In addition to designing, writing and flying, Markowski is an aeronautical consultant and holds memberships in The Soaring Society Of America, Experimental Aircraft Association and United States Hang Gliding Association.

# Foreword

Ever since I can remember, I've always wanted to fly. As a babe in arms, I oohed and aahed at anything that suspended itself "mysteriously" in mid-air, seemingly defying the law of gravity. Airplanes, birds, and even clouds held an unbelievable fascination for me: a fascination that's been growing and growing ever since.

From the time I was "wing-high-to-a-seagull," I have built and flown model airplanes of all descriptions. Since I was too young to be a pilot, I did the next best thing. Often though, while climbing trees and hills, I thought how "neat" it would be to be able to leap and fly, landing gently in the field below. I used to sit and daydream for hours at a time, watching how easily the birds did it. I often thought, why can't I?

As time went on, I read every book I could get my hands on related to flight. I wanted to learn as much as I possibly could about the mystery of flight. Eventually, I graduated from college with a major in aerospace engineering and got my pilot's license. But after all that, something was still missing. Sure, flying an airplane was really great, but something was lacking.

It didn't really "feel" like I was flying. Strapped to a cushion of vinyl inside an aluminum and Plexiglass shell, I simply couldn't "taste" flight. I couldn't touch it. I wasn't a part of the air. Figure I-1 shows the pilot, exposed to the elements, flying free like a bird.

Then one day while working on supersonic design, I stopped to daydream for a while. I thought about my boyhood and how I wanted to fly like a bird. Now I had the knowledge to design my own wings. Wings so light, I could pick them up. Wings so light, I could run with them down hill, lift off and fly, landing gently in the field below. I was convinced. I couldn't wait any longer; I would do it.

Ever since that super daydream during the winter of 1970-71, I've been deeply into foot-launched flight, or hang gliding as it is popularly called. Since then I have designed,

Hang Gliding: The most natural form of human flight. Bob Gray knows what it's all about.

built, flown and observed many hang gliders fly, and taken a few notes along the way so that I wouldn't forget what I did, felt, heard and saw.

It is my intent to write down some of the things I have learned about flight so that you too may realize your childhood or current dreams of flying; so that you may experience the true and total freedom that only foot-launched flight can provide; so that you may learn to fly yourself more easily, quickly and safely than was possible for me.

I'd like to wish you well in your quest for flight. Be cautious and conservative in your approach to learning and practicing. Develop safe habits from the very beginning. Learn to walk before you run and jump before you fly. I know that sometimes your emotions will try to overpower your sense of good judgment, but think before you leap. Respect the wind, and observe the limitations of your glider. In the words of the late Wilbur Wright (both he and his brother, Orville, were superb hang glider pilots): "For the purpose of reducing the danger to the lowest possible point we usually kept close to the ground. Often a glide of several hundred feet would be made at a height of a few feet or sometimes even a few inches. It was the aim to avoid unnecessary risk. While the high flights were more spectacular, the low ones were fully as valuable for training purposes. Skill comes by the constant repetition of familiar feats rather than by a few over-bold attempts at feats for which the performer is yet poorly prepared."

Michael A. Markowski

Illustration Credits

Aeronatical Annual 1897: 1-18, 1-19, 1-20
Airmart Hardware Digest: 8-3, 8-15
Allen, W.A.: 2-19, 2-24, 3-16, 7-24
Author (Michael A. Markowski): 2-10, 2-31, 2-35, 3-12, 3-13, 3-14, 3-15, 5-1, 5-2, 5-8, 5-9, 5-10, 5-11, 6-1, 6-2, 6-3, 6-6, 6-7, 6-8, 7-2, 7-3, 7-4, 7-5, 7-6, 7-7, 7-8, 7-9, 7-10, 7-11, 7-13, 7-14, 7-18, 7-19, 7-20, 7-22, 7-26, 7-27, 8-2, 8-5, 8-6, 8-7, 8-8, 8-9, 9-12, 9-27, 9-28
Bennett, Bill: 1-46, 2-6, 2-9, 2-11, 2-12
Bibliotheca Aeronautica: 1-2
Buckley, Jack: 5-3
Chanute Documents: 1-21, 1-27
Clarke, T.K.W.: 1-25
Conover Products: 1-24
Dwiggins, Dom: 1-47
Dwyer Instrument Co.: 6-5
Eipper-Formance, Inc.: 2-3, 2-14, 2-36, 2-37, 2-38, 2-39, 9-1, 9-2, 9-7, 9-10, 9-11
Electra Flyer Corp.: 9-23
Free-Flight Systems, Inc.: 2-3, 2-5, 2-32, 2-33, 3-5, 3-6, 9-3A, 9-4, 9-5, 9-8, 9-13, 9-14, 9-17, 9-22
Gray, Bettina: 2-17
H.A.S.P. Catalog: 8-19, 8-20
Hoerner, Dr. S.F.: 7-12, 7-15, 7-16, 7-17
Industrial Fasteners Institute: 8-5
International Nickel Company: 8-3, 8-4
Jensen, Volmer: 1-45, 2-20, 2-21, 2-22, 2-40, 2-41, 2-42, 2-43, 2-44, 2-45, 6-21, 9-15, 9-19, 9-20, 9-24, 9-26
Kiceniuk, Taras: 3-11
Loos and Co.: 8-22, 8-24
Manta Products, Inc.: 2-2, 9-16
Ministry of Defense (Philip Jarret): 9-18
Mountain Green, Inc.: 2-30, 2-46, 2-47, 2-48, 5-12
Musee De L'Air: 1-6, 1-7, 1-8, 1-9, 1-10, 1-12, 1-17, 1-22, 2-23
NASA: 7-21, 7-23, 7-25
Peerless Chain Co.: 8-21
Phantom Wing, Inc.: 2-1, 2-7, 2-8, 2-13
Rogallo, F.M. (NASA): 1-33, 1-39, 1-40, 1-41, 1-42, 1-43, 1-44
Roughley, T.C.: 1-15, 1-16
Simons, Martin (Australian Gliding): 1-31, 1-32
Smithsonian Institute: 1-1, 1-23, 1-26
Spurgeon, James: 1-4, 1-5
Stimpson Co.: 8-25
Sunbird Gliders, Inc.: 9-25
Sunsail Corp.: I-4, 1-50, 2-18, 3-10
Trampenau, Robert: 2-34
Ultralight Flying Machines, Inc.: 2-23, 2-25, 2-26
Uveges, George: I-1, I-2, 1-48, 3-6, 3-7, 3-9, 5-4, 5-5, 5-6, 5-7, 9-3B, 9-6, 9-9
U.S. Government Printing Office: 8-4, 8-6, 8-7, 8-8, 8-9, 8-10, 8-14, 8-23, 8-26, 8-27
ISM Corp.: 8-11, 8-12, 8-13
UP, Inc.: 2-15
Van Dusen Aircraft Supplies: 8-16, 8-17, 8-18
Wellsman, S.F.: I-3, 3-3, 3-4, 3-8, 8-18
Whenham, S.F.: I-3
Wills, Wings, Inc.: 2-16
Wolf, William: 2-27, 2-28, 2-29

# Contents

# Introduction

"With each advent of spring, when the air is alive with innumerable happy creatures; when the storks on their arrival at their old northern resorts fold up their imposing flying apparatus which has carried them thousands of miles, lay back their heads and announce their arrival by joyously rattling their beaks; when the swallows have made their entry and hurry through our streets and pass our windows in sailing flight; when the lark appears as a dot in the ether and manifests its joy of existence by its song; then a certain desire takes possession of man. He longs to soar upward and to glide, free as the bird, over smiling fields, leafy woods and mirrored lakes, and so enjoy the varying landscape as fully as only a bird can do." (a quotation from Otto Lilienthal, Father of hang gliding).

How many times has one looked skyward and seen the effortless flight of a soaring bird? How many times did this person envy the bird as he floated gracefully on the wing, swooping and turning, climbing and diving? How many times has one desired to experience the true freedom of bird flight with his own personal wings, but didn't believe it possible? Well, today it is possible...by hang gliding (see Fig. I-1).

The purpose of this book is to be an up-to-the-minute comprehensive presentation of what is fast becoming today's most popular new sport! It is planned to appeal to general as well as particular interest. For, while thousands are

Fig. I-1. The birds have nothing over me now.

"getting-into-it," there are few experts. It is written in an easily understood, layman's language with no engineering double-talk.

The book is divided into two parts: an informative introduction to hang gliding for the beginner, and a more technical presentation of theory for the more experienced flyer, as well as builder. Part One gives a brief history of hang gliding, types of hang gliders and techniques of hang gliding for the beginner. Part two gives the theory of flight and explains hang glider components and materials.

Why hang glide? There may be several reasons. A few could be: 1) One has always marvelled at the beauty and effortless flight of the soaring birds and often wished he could be as free. 2) One has some theories and designs of his own that he'd like to try without being bogged down with great expense and government regulations. 3) One's friends hang glide and he'd like to share in the experiences of flying and the social activities of their group. 4) One has always read about being a pioneer and imagined how great it would have been to fly with such flyers as Lilienthal, Chanute and the Wright Brothers. 5) One would like to get into private flying or soaring but just doesn't have either the time or the bucks. 6) One plans a career in an aeronautical field, be it an engineer, pilot or executive.

What are the basic requirements for becoming a hang glider pilot? First is a genuine desire to fly, which you obviously have or else you wouldn't be reading this book. Devoting some time to flight instructions is another. (Most folks pick up the basics in a half-day session at the slope.) And finally, is the understanding of the basic principles and theories of flight.

The desire needs to come from deep within. Assuming one has it, he can proceed by studying this book and then joining his local club. Go to their meetings and flying sessions. Watch, learn, then do.

Hang gliding is the only prominent sport that hasn't been fully developed. The field is wide open. People ski, swim, run, bicycle, etc., but until now very few people have really flown, in the true sense of the word. Hang gliding is an age-old dream come true.

A word must be stated about the types of hang gliders one may be flying. The standard, basic hang glider, is called the Rogallo wing "kite." It's name comes from the man who invented it for NASA'S space program. Ironically, man had to walk on the moon before he awoke to the potentials of self-flight. The Rogallo wing was researched and tested a great deal by NASA. They spent millions of tax dollars to develop a space craft recovery system to replace the parachute.

As one may know, a parachute generally descends straight down; it doesn't fly. The Rogallo wing, however, can glide. In fact, it goes 4 feet forward for every foot it drops. In addition to its gliding ability, the Rogallo is extremely portable. It folds easily for car-top/ski-rack transport and generally weighs between 35 and 45 pounds, depending on size. It is most likely the first hang glider one will learn to fly.

Fig. I-2. Some hang glider schools use "dual" kites for instructing.

In the sport of hang gliding, the Rogallo is most often referred to as a kite, primarily because it looks like one (see Fig. I-2). So the name stuck. In fact, Dr. Rogallo's original patent was for a kite. At any rate, the kite is generally considered as the first hang glider one ought to fly.

Other types of hang gliders range from the more "conventional" looking monoplanes with a wing and tail, to the flying wing types without a tail. These hang gliders give higher performance but are also considered more difficult to master. They normally employ weight shifting and/or aerodynamic controls for steering.

In case one hasn't yet decided, the "flexible" Rogallo wing kite is by far the most successful hang glider today, despite its low performance level. This is mainly because the kites are foldable, portable and extremely convenient. The simplicity of the design outweighs its lack of performance. Most high performance gliders are too complex and time consuming for the average enthusiast. However, those seeking a greater challenge might find it in these higher performing gliders.

The first cost, that of purchasing one's own hang glider and accessories, will be the highest. Once it's paid for, however, the rest is up to the individual. There are countless hills from which to launch and ski lifts have a small charge that is well worth it. One probably already owns most of the necessary clothing, except perhaps a good helmet, which he must use!

## Moral Aspects?

As with all sports, there are certain dangers involved in hang gliding. Basically, one must study and understand flight and the atmosphere thoroughly! Most importantly, he must develop a deep respect for the wind. The *wind* is the *boss*! It can be friend and foe alike. If used wisely it will allow one to have the greatest experiences of his life. If used foolishly, it can maim or even kill. Of course, there's a danger involved, but as in all sports, if approached conservatively, it can be done with minimum risk on your part.

Some folks are fearful of flying and I suppose someone somewhere is afraid of something sometime. This is human nature. But ultimately fear is nothing more than a habit. It can be overcome. The fear on my first hang glider flight was overcome by the excitement, the exhilarating feeling, the freedom from gravity.

Like all human activities, hang gliding has various limitations: limitations of the glider, the atmosphere and the pilot. Learn them and observe them.

Now let's take a trip to a local hang gliding site, and get more acquainted with some actual flying.

## A Typical Scene

Upon arrival at the site, one will most likely find a variety of hang glider types and sizes. Most however, will probably be of the "kite" configuration in a wide array of beautifully colored sails. If the wind is steady, and blowing at 15-20 mph, one will be able to witness sustained flight, in all its beauty, as hang gliders chase after birds, imitating their maneuvers.

Locate the person in charge at the site and state the desire to learn more about hang gliding. He will be most happy to show the "flight line" and explain the various gliders and their basic differences. One will, most assuredly, be very welcome, as those into hang gliding are eager to share their new found freedom and increase their numbers.

Along about this time, if one isn't quite ready to take his first leap, he might wish to watch some more flying or perhaps pick up some literature to take home to study before deciding if one is ready to begin to learn hang gliding. One may even sign-up for lessons and perhaps begin that same day, if the operator's schedule permits.

Before one starts though, he will be advised to read over and study some of the basics of flight, so he knows what to expect while learning the art of the birds. A book, such as this, should give one an adequate working knowledge of what hang gliding is all about.

Most sky schools have the same basic outline for training of the novice, with variation as to cost, types of training gliders, hours available for instruction, etc. In general, one may use two basic plans. First is a pay-as-you-go set up in which the hourly cost of the glider and instruction is stipulated and one pays for each hour of instruction and for the use of the instructor and/or glider. Once one has learned the basic maneuvers, he can simply continue renting the glider alone, and sign on with the instructor as needed or to learn the more advanced techniques. If one tires of renting, he may wish to buy a glider for his very own, either as a do-it-yourself kit, or a ready-to-fly package.

The second basic plan, and perhaps the most economical in the long run, is to buy a complete "package deal." In this setup one may purchase the glider with instructions on flying it included.

To become a good hang glider pilot, one must practice, practice, practice until he develops the instinctive-like skills and reflexes he will need to conquer the great ocean of air

Fig. I-3. One with my kite.

around him. Follow the sequence and techniques presented in this text and one should do well in starting his self-flight experiences. One should consult an instructor whenever he wishes to progress. He's trained and experienced to help improve flying skills in as safe a way as possible. The skilled pilot's poised body is shown in Fig. I-3.

Assuming one has made his first few successful straight-out and gentle turning flights, and the instructor feels confident that he can control the craft sufficiently in "ground skimming" flight, he will probably have one go the operating slopes to gain more experience and skill. During one's practice sessions of ground skimming and gentle turning, always remember to be courteous and follow the rules of the slope. In general, gliders lower on the slope have the right of way, as do those engaged in landing. After one is sure no gliders are in his

Fig. I-4. Hang gliding is a joyous, beautiful experience.

path or expected landing area (and some distance all around it), he may begin the takeoff run. When landed, he must remember to remove himself from the area as quickly as possible. Don't forget, others are waiting at the top of the slope for one to clear the area. He has the right of way but should not abuse it.

Peering into the future, one can look forward to some of life's most fantastic experiences (see Fig. I-4). The sheer joy, freedom and thrill of hang gliding will be each person's to enjoy and share with his friends for a life time. Happy Hang Gliding!

# Chapter 1
# Hang Glider Progress

**HANG GLIDER PROGRESS**

Man's past is full of fantasy, fiction and fact of his desire to fly like the birds. The Garber model of da Vinci's Wing-flapper, illustrated in Fig. 1-1 is one of these examples.

To gain a better insight into what hang gliders are all about, it is helpful to study how they developed. It is important to look at history and what has already been done in order to avoid mistakes previously made. There's really no practical use for repeating errors, though some may wish to duplicate past designs and events for an even deeper under-standing of the hang glider. For most people, this historical chapter should provide a good review of what has already been done and give them a good idea of how hang gliding developed.

The sport of modern hang gliding is certainly the most unique happening in all of aviation history. Originally conceived in ancient times and practiced extensively in the

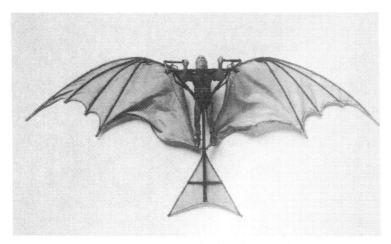

Fig. 1-1. Garber model of da Vinci's wing-flapper.

1890s by some enterprising experimenters, the art was dropped when the Wright Brothers successfully flew their power flyer. Indeed, a handful of men had thought that hang gliding would develop into the most exhilerating sport which one could practice. However, as soon as power was applied, mankind viewed the hang glider as merely a step in the pursuit of progress. On December 17, 1903, almost all hang glider progress came to a screeching halt.

Primitive people most likely dreamed of flying as soon as they could think. They watched the birds fly and envied their freedom and ease of traveling. This dream of "flying like-a-bird" has persisted down through the ages. There's probably not a single person alive today who hasn't at least thought of himself flying.

To begin our study of hang glider history we must disregard such tales as the ancient Greek myth of the flight of Daedalus and the fall of Icarus as depicted in Fig. 1-2. This famous story was probably dreamed up by some flight-fancying Greek scholar who wrote that Icarus fell because he flew too near the sun and the wax of his wings melted allowing the feathers to fall out. There is however perhaps some moral to the story: hang glider pilots beware! Don't fly too near the sun. We must also disregard the "tower jumpers'' who are too numerous to list. Needless to say, most of these brave fools didn't live to talk about it. A word to the wise is sufficient. At any rate, don't jump from towers, whatever you do.

## LEONARDO DA VINCI

The first really significant personality in the history of hang gliding is none other than Leonardo da Vinci, that outstanding fifteenth century architect, engineer, artist and scientist.

The mysteries of flight were a natural for this inquisitive mind to probe, and so he did. This greatest of the world's geniuses applied himself to the problem of the ages. He wrote of bird flight: ''A bird is an instrument working according to mathematical law, which instrument it is within the capacity of man to reproduce with all its movements, but not with a corresponding degree of strength, though it is deficient only in power of maintaining equilibrium. We may say, therefore, that such an instrument constructed by man is lacking except the life of the bird, and this life must needs be supplied from that of man. The life which resides in the bird's members will,

Fig. 1-2. A very old woodcut illustrating the flight of Daedalus and the fall of Icarus.

without doubt, better conform to their needs than will that of a man which is separated from them, and especially in the almost imperceptible movements which produce equilibrium. But since we see that the bird is equipped for many apparent varieties of movement, we are able from this experience to deduce that the most rudimentary of these movements will be capable of being comprehended by man's understanding, and that he will, to a great extent, be able to provide against the destruction of that instrument of which he himself has become the living principle and the propeller." (*Codex Atlanticus*)

Based on his observations of large birds, da Vinci concluded that a relatively small amount of power was actually required to fly. He therefore deduced that man could also exercise enough strength to fly. He further wrote: "A man, when flying, shall be free from the waist up, that he may be able to keep himself in equilibrium as he does in a boat, so that the center of gravity and of the instrument may be set itself in equilibrium and change when necessity requires it to the changing of the center of resistance."

There are statements that da Vinci himself actually flew, but no proof. Later on however, one Paolo Guidotti, of Lucca, constructed some wings of whalebone ribs and feathers, after da Vinci's ideas. It seems as though he actually did make a few glides of up to several hundred yards, but eventually made a bad landing on a rooftop and broke a thigh bone.

Da Vinci did make some model helicopters of wire and paper that actually lifted. He also invented a basic sort of square parachute.

## SIR GEORGE CAYLEY

Sir George seems to have been the first person in the history of the world to have done practical experiments in hang gliding. Prior to these however, he carried out a long series of experiments with models to determine the lifting qualities of surfaces when moved through the air at inclined angles. His studies led him to suggest the use of tail surfaces that could be pivoted up and down, for pitch control. He also indicated that lateral, or sideways stability could be gained by giving the wings a slight dihedral angle as viewed from the front.

Futhermore, it would be impossible to overemphasize the importance of the conclusion he reached regarding the curved surface and its superior lifting qualities over that of a flat plane. This concept is perhaps the most profound in all of aeronautics.

In 1809, Cayley constructed his first full-sized hang glider. He describes it, in one of his notebooks:

"I made a machine having a surface of 300 square feet, which was accidently broken before there was an opportunity of trying the effect of the propelling apparatus, but it would sail downwards in any direction according to the set of the rudder. Its weight was 56 pounds and it was loaded with 84 pounds, thus making a total of 140 pounds, about 2 square feet to the pound. Even in this state, when any person ran forward in it with his full speed, taking advantage of a gentle breeze in front, it would bear upwards so strongly as scarcely to allow him to touch the ground, and would frequently lift him up and convey him several yards together."

Forty years were to pass before Sir George built his first true man-carrying glider. It had a wing area of 330 square feet with the wings set at a dihedral angle for lateral stability. A rudder and elevator were connected by cords to a tricycle landing geared nacelle, in which the pilot rode and steered. Two levers located vertically in front of the pilot were also connected to a pair of smaller flapping wings, each of 6 feet span. This setup was to be used to observe the small wings' adjustment on the gliding angle.

The man-carrying glider was successfully flown at Brompton Hall unmanned, with ballast, and also flew several yards with a ten year old boy on board during two separate occasions. Its empty weight was 138 pounds.

In 1853, Cayley built a third glider closely resembling the 1809 glider, but with the latest refinements. It was probably a triplane configuration. This craft had a total surface area (wing and tail) of 500 square feet and weighed about 165 pounds. The center of gravity was placed far enough ahead of the center of lift to give a gliding angle of five or six degrees. It is reported that Cayley persuaded his coachman to make the first known manned gliding flight in history. It covered a distance of some 500 yards across the small valley at Brompton Hall, the Cayley family seat near Scarborough, York.

One cannot help but conclude that Cayley, in fact, "invented" the airplane. His place in hang gliding cannot be over emphasized. He conceived the horizontal tail for longitudinal stability, the elevator for pitch control, wing dihederal for lateral stability and the vertical fin and rudder for directional stability and control. His work, however, was done in secret because he would have been scorned by his contemporaries. It was not "discovered" until 1927! Think what might have happened, if....

## LOUIS PIERRE MOUILLARD

Mouillard was a French writer and aeronautical experimenter who published the aeronautical classic, *L'Empire de l'Air*, in 1881. He observed bird flight continually and professed that man would be able to soar indefinitely without power, by using natural wind. He actually carried out hang gliding experiments in Egypt and was issued a US patent in May 1897. In his famous book, he wrote of some observations:

"The most stirring, exciting sight (the word is not too strong) is to stand in the vulture roost on the Mokatan ridge near Cairo, and to look upon the tawny vulture passing within five yards in full flight. All my life I shall remember the first flight of these birds which I saw, the great tawny vultures of Africa. I was so impressed that all day long I could think of nothing else, and indeed there was good cause for it was a practically perfect demonstration of all my preconceived theories concerning the possibilities of artifical flight in a wind. Since then, I have observed thousands of vultures. I have disturbed many of the vast flocks of these birds and yet, even now, I cannot see one individual passing through the air without following him with my eyes until he disappears in the distant horizon....

"The vulture's needs are few, and his strength is moderate. To earn his living he but needs to sight the dead animal from afar;

and so, what does he know? He knows how to rise, how to float aloft, to sweep the field with keen vision, to sail upon the wind without effort, till the carcass is seen, and then to descend slowly after careful reconnaissance and assurance that he may alight without danger, that he will not be surprised and compelled to precipitous and painful departure; and so, he has evolved a peculiar mode of flight; he sails and spends no force, he never hurries, he uses the wind instead of his muscles, and the wing-flap occasionally seen is meant to limber up rather than to hasten and rough the air. The true model to study is the vulture—the great vulture. Beside him the stork is as a wren, the kite a mere butterfly, the falcon a pin-feather. Who so has for five minutes had the fortune to see the Nubian vulture in full sail through the air, and has not perceived the possibility of his imitation by man is—I will not say of dull understanding but, certainly inapt to analyse and to appreciate."

## F.H. WENHAM

In June of 1866, the newly founded Royal Aeronautical Society held its first meeting. It was here that the well-known engineer, F.H. Wenham, presented a paper on aerial locomotion. Of utmost importance is the fact that he expounded on the virtues of both the high aspect ratio (or long and slender wing) and the idea of superposing or stacking a number of wings together on a biplane or triplane configuration (Fig. 1-3). The high aspect ratio was seen on the soaring birds and indicated greater flying efficiency while the superposing principle allowed for greater lifting force in a small space. Wenham wrote:

"Having remarked how thin a structure is displaced beneath the wings of a bird in rapid flight, it follows that, in order to obtain the necessary length of plane for supporting heavy weights, the surfaces may be superposed, or placed in parallel rows, with an interval between them. A dozen pelicans may fly one above the other without material impediment, as if framed together, and it is thus shown him two hundred weight may be supported in a transverse distance of only ten feet."

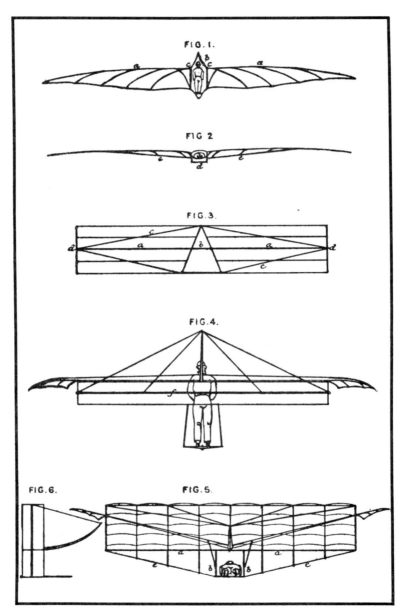

Fig. 1-3. Diagrams used by Wenham to illustrate his 1866 lecture on the value of multiple planes.

He went on to speak of the graceful albatross:

"One of the most perfect natural examples of easy and long-sustained flight is the wandering albatross—a bird for endurance of flight probably unrivalled. Found over all parts of the Southern Ocean, it seldom rests on the water. During storms, even the most terrific, it is seen now dashing through the whirling clouds, and now serenely floating, without the least observable motion of its outstretched pinions. The wings of this bird extend fourteen or fifteen feet from end to end, and measure only eight and a half inches across the broadest part. This conformation gives the bird such an extraordinary sustaining power, that it is said to sleep on the wing during stormy weather, when rest on the ocean is impossible. Rising high in the air, it skims slowly down, with absolutely motionless wings, till a near approach to the waves awaken it, when it rises again for another rest."

Wenham then conducted a series of experiments for the Society on the lift and resistance of wings and other shapes.

### JOHN J. MONTGOMERY

John. J. Montgomery first became interested in flight in 1860, when he was but a boy. It wasn't until 1883, however, that he managed to construct his first flying machine: an ornithopter or wing flapper. Montgomery's 1883 hang glider is shown in Fig. 1-4. Needless to say, this design didn't work out

Fig. 1-4. A model of Montgomery's 1883 hang glider by Jim Spurgeon.

too well. So, in 1884-85 he began experimenting with fixed-wing hang gliders, three in all. The first one proved the value of the curved wing which he copied from a seagull and with it he flew 600 feet. (Today there is a $1,500 prize offered to the first person to duplicate the event.) His second hang glider used flat wing surfaces, and proved to be totally useless. His third hang glider incorporated wing warping (twisting) of the wings for lateral control.

Montgomery's first hang glider models were tested in a very novel way. A cable was suspended between two hill tops in California, and the gliders were dropped from them. He was able to give them such stability that they could even themselves after being launched upside down, and glide smoothly to the ground.

He himself made a number of flights with the assistance of some cowboy friends, but stopped when he put his foot in a squirrel hole on one landing and hurt his leg.

Then, in 1893 at an aeronautical congress in Chicago, Montgomery gave a paper based on his aeronautical work. One of his observations was very important: "A current of air approaching an inclined surface is deflected far in advance of the surface, and approaching it in a gradually increasing curve, reaches it at an abrupt angle."

It wasn't until 1905 that Montgomery again entered the scene. This time we find him with an improved hang glider with two main wings: one placed behind the other in a tandem arrangement. His new glider weighed 45 pounds and had controls for steering. Engaging the intrepid parachute jumper, Daniel Maloney, many descents were made from 4,000 feet above the Santa Clara college grounds. The glider was attached to the bottom of a manned balloon and cut loose when at a sufficient altitude. Maloney was able to perform the most graceful flights anyone could imagine: figure eights, hair raising dives ended by abrupt stalls, spiral and circling turns. At times the speed of the glider was estimated at almost 70 miles per hour, and yet Maloney was still able to land at a predetermined spot on his own two feet. This was truly remarkable to a flight skeptical audience.

Montgomery also employed two other glider pilots, Wilkie and Defolco. Unfortunately, Maloney was killed in an accident and the act was discontinued. Montgomery describes the fatal accident as follows.

"The ascension was given to entertain a military company in which were may of Maloney's friends, and he had told them he would give the most sensational flight they had ever heard of. As the balloon was rising with the aeroplane (glider), a guy-rope dropping switched around the right wing and broke the tower that braced the two rear wings and which also gave control over the tail. We shouted to Maloney that the machine was broken, but, he probably did not hear us, as he was at the time saying, 'Hurrah airship' and as the break was behind him, he may not have detected it.

"At all events, when the machine started on its flight, the rear wings commenced to flap—thus, indicating they were loose—the machine turned on its back and settled a little faster than a parachute.

"When we reached Maloney he was unconscious and lived only thirty minutes. The only mark of any kind on him was a scratch from a wire on the side of his neck, the six attending physicians were puzzled at the cause of his death."

Fig. 1-5 portrays one of Montgomery's gliders after being released from a balloon.

Montgomery did quite a bit of research in the use of curved lifting surfaces and the movement of air all around them. He had intended to carry out much more experimentation, but the great San Francisco Earthquake prevented it. It wasn't until 1911 that he again started gliding, but unfortunately he was soon killed in a fall in one of his gliders. In October, while in the air, he was struck by an unexpectedly violent gust of wind, which sent the glider crashing into the ground. He hit fairly hard and injured his head and hip. At the time he did not think he was severely hurt, but later on he complained of severe pains. These continued to get worse, and stayed with him until death.

Montgomery graduated from St. Ignatius College in San Francisco in 1879. He is often referred to as a Professor, though it is believed he didn't have a PhD. He was the son of a former assistant attorney-general of the U.S. Two of his

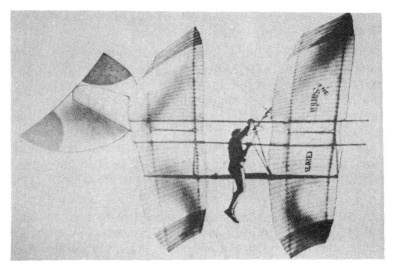

Fig. 1-5. Montgomery's 1905 "Santa Clara" after being released from a balloon.

college classmates were James D. Phelar, mayor of San Francisco (1896-1902) and Rev. R.H. Bell, well known for his work in wireless telegraphy.

## HORATIO PHILLIPS

While not connected directly with hang gliding as such, Mr. Phillips contributed an interesting article on aeronautics to the magazine *Engineering*, 1895 in England. He extensively investigated the problem of properly curved wing sections, this being the most serious work to that date. He also produced a series of multiple winged models with tremendous lifting power. They looked like venetian blinds. His studies led him to the theory that the upper surface curvature of a wing caused a partial vacuum, thus creating lift.

## LILIENTHAL

Not enough can possibly be said about the great pioneering work of Otto Lilienthal and his brother Gustave. In fact, an entire book could and should be written about Otto, the father of hang gliding. It is to him that we can directly trace our beginnings in foot-launched flight. Indeed, on May 23, his birthday, hang glider flyers all over the world pay homage to him. Otto is depicted flying his 1892 glider in Fig. 1-6.

Even when they were school boys, Otto (1848-1896) and his brother Gustave (1849-1933) began experimenting with flapping-wing model flying machines. However, it wasn't until years later that they became serious enough to construct a full-size, man-carrying hang glider.

Before they began real hang gliding however, they conducted an extensive and thorough study of bird flight. Unlike so many other bird watchers, the Lilienthals looked at the details of how birds fly. They learned precisely what a bird does with its wings: how it alters dihedral for changes in stability and how it varies wing curvature to change lift and drag characteristics in a given flight situation. During those observations, they evolved the "theory of flight" which is the foundation for the modern science of aerodynamics. Then, in 1889, Otto published his classic book, *Bird Flight as the Basis of Aviation*, which covered the Lilienthal's observations and theories. The book appears to have been read by nearly everyone who had a serious intent in building and flying heavier than air craft.

During his studies and observations of bird flight, Otto realized the tremendous importance of curved wing surfaces.

Fig. 1-6. Lilienthal's 1892 hang glider.

He also made many other interesting aerodynamic observations, among them, the generation of upward components of air in a natural wind—an explanation for the soaring flight of birds.

Furthermore, he found that even in the absence of the so-called upward components of wind, the lift in a natural wind was still superior to that in a strictly uniform air flow. This effect has only been recognized in recent times due to cross-velocity gradient (different wind speeds and directions) which generally prevail in natural winds, especially in air near to the earth's surface. The type of soaring done under these conditions is called "dynamic soaring."

All that the brothers thought, however, was not sound. In fact, they had one rather nebulous "theory." They had devoted much thought to the possibility of creating negative drag (i.e., propulsion) by designing a suitable airfoil shape. Needless to say, this idea violates the basic laws of physics. You can't get something for nothing! Regardless of this, several years after Otto's tragic death, Gustave actually published a "theory" for negative drag, which didn't really accomplish much.

Otto Lilienthal built his first hang glider and began leaping from hills in 1891. It had a slightly dihedraled wing of some 23 feet span and was made of willow wands covered with waxed cotton cloth. Flight path control was accomplished solely by weight shifting and proper body movements. In flight, his weight was supported by a parallel bar arrangement in the center of the wing. In its entirety, the emply glider weighed only 40 pounds, thus enabling Otto to launch himself into the air by running down a hillside.

Before he began jumping from hills, he relied on a spring board in his backyard! Then, in a short while, he began jumping from mounds in the nearby fields. It was here he discovered that wind gusts could become too much for his first pair of wings. Therefore, he added a tail to aid directional stability. His best flights that year were 80 feet long from a 20 foot high mound.

In 1892, Otto set up a base of operations at a hill top near Steiglitz, including a shed to house his operations. He even went so far as to make his hang gliders foldable for more compact storage.

After a year, Otto began to look for a more suitable location where the prevailing winds would be to his advantage in experimenting. He found his new site in the Rhinow Mountains, near Rathenow. Now, up until this time, he had experienced no serious accidents, but, here on one test flight, he was caught by an unexpected gust of wind which sent him crashing into the ground from 60 feet. The glider had been moving along at 35 miles per hour! Fortunately, he escaped with only minor injuries: a sprained left arm and a flesh wound on the side of his head.

Lilienthal's drawings for his 1893-94 hang glider are depicted in Figs. 1-7 and 1-8.

Lilienthal moved once again, in 1894, to a hill he had constructed from canal diggings especially for hang gliding, near Berlin. At the base of the hill was a storage space for his gliders.

While experimenting at this location, he came to the conclusion that a biplane configuration offered greater stability. He experimented with some models and then built a full-sized version. It had 194 square feet of wing area. During some practice sessions, he was able to glide distances of up to a quarter mile in length and 75 feet high! The biplane was

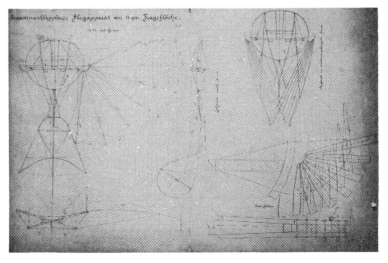

Fig. 1-7. Lilienthal's drawings for his 1893-94 hang glider.

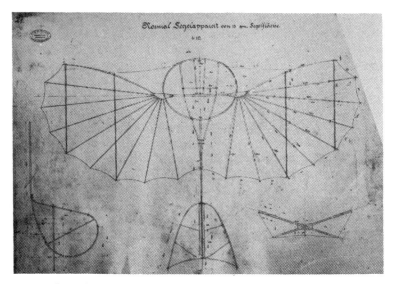

Fig. 1-8. Lilienthal's drawings for his 1893-94 hang glider.

finally built and flown in 1896, after a succession of various monoplane versions. Otto's 1894 monoplane is shown in Figs. 1-9 and 1-10. Fig. 11-11 shows his 1896 biplane. The 1895 monoplane hangs today in the Musee de L'Air in Paris (Fig. 1-12).

Fig. 1-9. Otto's 1894 monoplane weighed less than 40 pounds.

Fig. 1-10. Spectators are captivated by Lilienthal's hang gliding. The 1894 model had a glide ratio of 8 to 1.

Still in search of better ways to control his hang gliders in the wind, Otto fitted an elevator to the tail of his latest biplane. It was connected to his head by a line and could be controlled by a simple nod. Lateral control was still done by the side to side swinging of his legs, however. At about this same time, 1896, Otto was planning to fit a 2 1/2 horsepower carbonic motor to his latest biplane. It was connected to the wing tips and was controlled by hand operated valves. Figs. 1-13 and 1-14 show Lilienthal's patent for one of his flying machines.

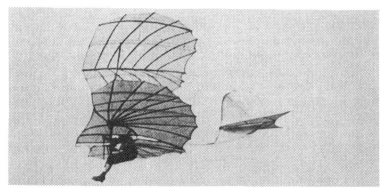

Fig. 1-11. Otto claimed his 1896 biplane had more lift than the monoplane.

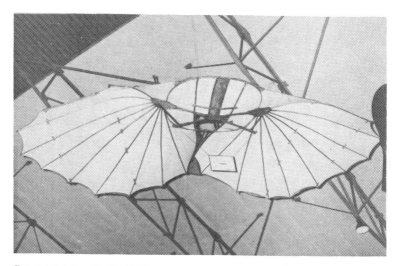

Fig. 1-12. Lilienthal's 1895 monoplane as it hangs today in the Musee de L'Air in Paris.

True to his methodical, conservative way of doing things, Otto tested everything on the ground before he ventured aloft. Unfortunately, he never got to fly his new machine. During a practice session in one of his monoplane gliders, near Stollen, he lost control and fell to the ground from a height of 50 feet, on August 9, 1896. He had broken his spine and died the following day. Before he passed away, he uttered these immortal words: "Sacrifices must be made."

Otto made over 2,000 glides of up to a quarter mile in length in winds as high as 22 miles per hour. Though originally a firm believer in the monoplane and the ultimate attainment of true soaring flight, he died testing the biplane he was to power. Nonetheless, he had learned more than any other man in history about flying. He proved that human flight was possible by designing, building, testing and actually flying through the air with his own hang gliders. His visions, insights, observations, theories, modifications dictated by flight experience, and a willingness to share his findings with others, most definitely give Otto a special and most important place in the history of hang gliding. No wonder he is called "the father of the airplane."

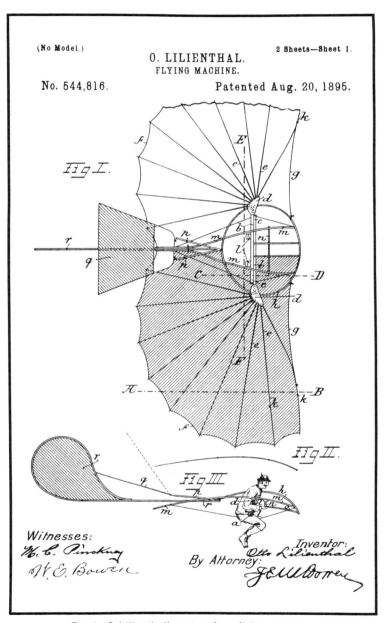

Fig. 1-13. Lilienthal's patent for a flying machine.

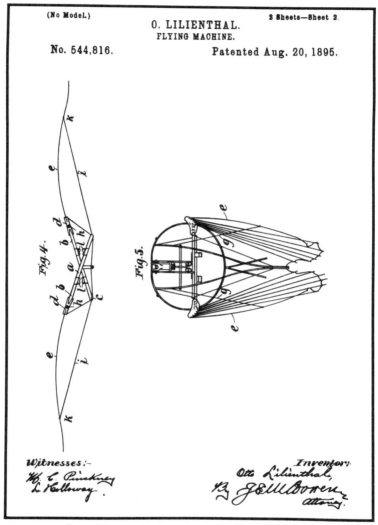

O. LILIENTHAL.
FLYING MACHINE.

No. 544,816.

Patented Aug. 20, 1895.

*Fig. 4.*

*Fig. 5.*

*Witnesses:-*
H. C. Pinckney
L. Halloway.

*Inventor:*
Otto Lilienthal,
by J. Ell. Bowen
*Atty.*

Fig. 1-14. Lilienthal's patent for a flying machine.

## LAWRENCE HARGRAVE

An Australian, Hargrave deserves mention here because of his invention of the box kite (1894) which served as an inspiration for some early biplane designs. Figs. 1-15 and 1-16 reveal some of Hargrave's kite designs.

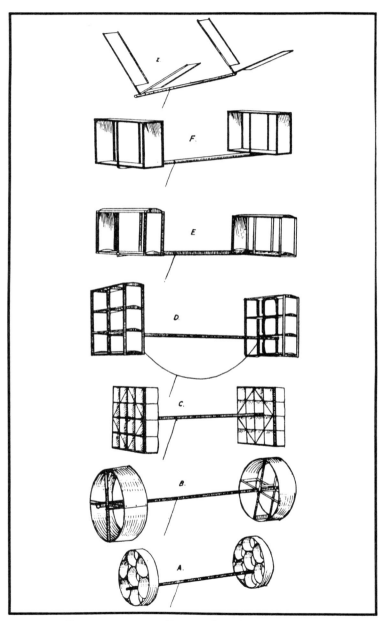

Fig. 1-15. Lawrence Hargrave's earliest kites. 1893.

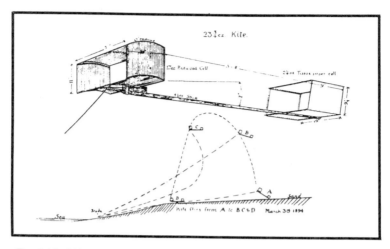

Fig. 1-16. A Hargrave soaring kite and the course taken in its flight. 1894.

## OCTAVE CHANUTE

The following is a quotation from *The Sunday Journal,* September, 1896:

"It is claimed that at last a machine which will really fly and carry a man without danger has been constructed. [Fig. 1-17 illustrated Chanute's 1896 biplane.] The inventor is Octave Chanute. former president of the Society of Civil Engineers, and a scientific thinker of pronounced ability."

"At first glance the Chanute airship looks very much like a ship with all sails spread. There is a resemblance to a ship, too. in the details. The frame, which supports a man, is of willow and spruce, shaped in a general way like a canoe, save that there is a greater curvature of deck plane and keel. Made as it is, this frame is light, though rigid to a degree, and sufficiently strong to support a man above the average weight."

"Extending from the boat-shaped frame there are six pairs of wings. The ribs for these are of willow, covered with light silk. saturated in a preparation of gun cotton sufficiently strong to prevent penetration by either water or air. Each wing is curved on a parabola of one-twelfth of its width of two feet. and each is seven feet long, thus furnishing a surface of something over fifteen feet square. The outside ends of the wings are connected with a width of prepared silk, acting as a keel to the airship. (Chanute's biplane with a swing seat is shown in Fig. 1-18.)

"But the important improvement claimed for the Chanute flying machine, above other and similar inventions, is an automatic regulator which keeps the wings at an angle with the plane of air current through which the machine is carried, and is so arranged that the direction of the current has no effect. [Fig. 1-19 is a drawing of Chanute's 1896 hang glider. Fig. 1-20 is a triplane hang glider of 1896.]

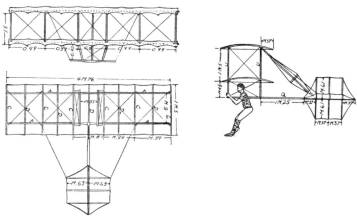

Fig. 1-17. Chanute's 1896 biplane at Warren Dunes Park, near Chicago. Three-view drawing of Chanute's biplane which had so much influence on the Wright Brothers.

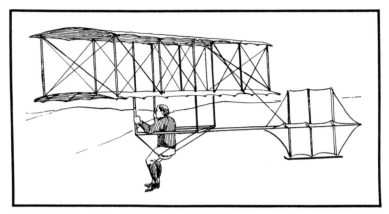

Fig. 1-18. Chanute's biplane with a swing seat.

"It is the success of this regulator which means the success of the flying machine. The machine is fourteen feet in width, fifteen feet in length and weighs thirty-six pounds.

"The first experiment made was using the new machine as a 'skimmer,' that is, without motor or propeller, with the intention of literally studying the subject of 'aspiration' (the ability to sail straight in the face of the wind without the slightest motion of its wings).

"A run was made by experimenter Avery along the side of a hill, by jumping into the air and governing the apparatus in the wind gusts. The first flight carried the operator fifty feet, and never less than two feet above the ground. [Chanute's 1902 triplane is depicted in Fig. 1-21.] This was considered an astounding result, considering that absolutely no motive power beyond the wind was used. It also demonstrated that the idea of the automatic regulator was correct in principle.

"After that first skim, the two assistants of Mr. Chanute made between 150 and 200 jumps, all without the slightest accident, either to themselves or the machine. These jumps varied in length from 50 to 100 feet, and each one proved beyond a question of doubt that the apparatus was perfectly manageable, automatically stable, and strong enough in every part.

"In confirming these early experiments to jumping with the machine, Mr. Chanute has followed the line which he has long

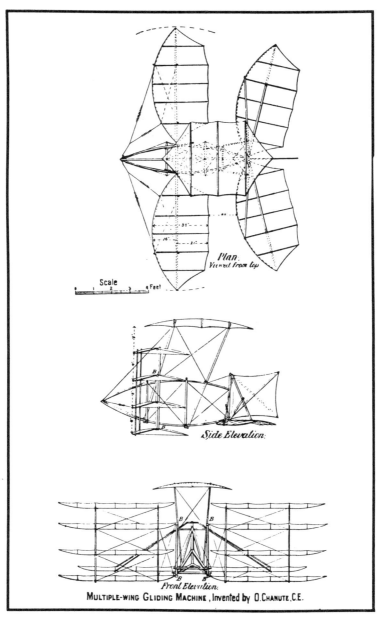

Fig. 1-19. Octave Chanute's multiple-wing hang glider of 1896.

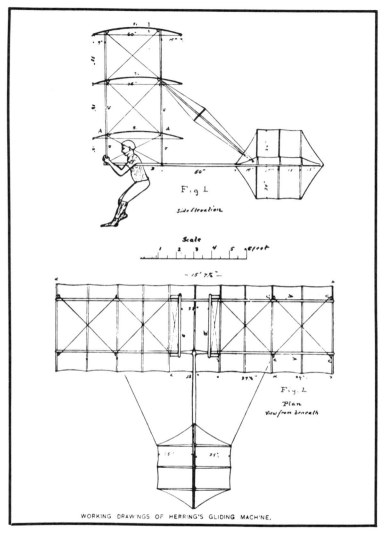

Fig. 1-20. Herring's (Chanute assistant) triplane hang glider of 1896, built under Chanute's direction.

advocated, that the chief problem which is to be solved before man can hope to fly in the air is that of safety.

"He holds that this must first be worked out in a full-sized apparatus, mounted by a man and exposed to the vicissitudes of the wind, before any attempt is made to soar or to apply a motor or propelling instrument."

Under the series of planes which constitutes his machine were two paralled bars [see Fig. 1-22]. Mr. Chanute supported himself below the machine like a pendulum, by putting his arms over these bars so that they were under his armpits. In this way he was able to change the direction of the machine while coasting through the air, by altering the position of his body.

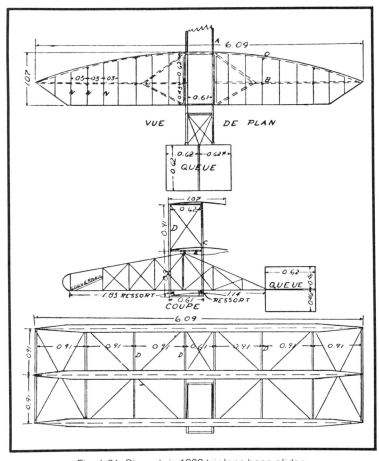

Fig. 1-21. Chanute's 1902 triplane hang glider.

Fig. 1-22. Chanute's famous 1896 biplane today, as it hangs in the Musee de L'Air.

He made journeys of 300 feet, reaching at times a height of 30 feet, and has alighted as easily and gracefully as a bird. When starting from the top of the hill the operator ran a few steps when the machine rose and proceeded swiftly through the air in an almost horizontal position. When he wished to stop he tilted his body so that the wings were inclined upward. This checked the speed and the airplane coasted slowly to the ground.

The flights were made in the direction from which the wind was blowing. As the most reliable air current in that section came from the north, most flights were in that direction and toward the lake (Michigan), which is only about 200 feet from the sand dune from which most of the flights were made. On several occassions the men miscalculated their speed and sailed too far, and fell into the water.

After a few such accidents had occurred, the experimenters were more careful, as involuntary baths were not to their liking.

## PERCY PILCHER

At the time of his death in an accident in September, 1899, Percy S. Pilcher may have been very close to the realization of powered flight. Drawings had been prepared for an engine to power his most successful machine, THE HAWK, and the construction of the engine, for use that winter, was in hand.

His sister, Ella Tidswell, recalled her brother's experiments in the *Aeronautical Journal*, July, 1909:

··From Pilcher's earliest boyhood he was entirely wrapped up in the idea of flying, and from the time he was thirteen, when he joined the Britannia, he made small experiments. I remember when he was fifteen, a cadet in the Royal Navy, his explaining to me what he believed would be the shape and working of the flying machine of the near future.

··At nineteen he left the Navy, worked through Elder's Shipbuilding Yard at Goven, Glasgow, and afterward went to the University of London. In 1893, when he was assistant Lecturer in Naval Architecture and Marine Engineering at the University of Glasgow, he began his experiments in aeronautics.

··During the winter of 1892-1893 he built the machine we called the Bat. The body piece was, as far as I remember, 11 feet 8 inches long and 2 feet 3 inches wide.

··The area of the wings was 1/2 square foot to the pound weight, the machine being constructed to bear, including its own weight from 180 to 200 pounds. The machine itself weighed 45 pounds.

··The wings were laced to two rather heavy spars crossing a triangle in front of the machine, and guyed by wires to the triangle which reached 2 feet 6 inches below the body piece and about the same distance above it. When the lacing to the front spars was undone, the wings folded back like a fan.''

··It was necessary to have it so, in order that it would pack easily, as Pilcher was obliged to live in the town on account of his work. In Glasgow he had the loan of a large room under the roof as a workshop, while we had to go down to the country for the experiments.

··In his first experiments the wings of the Bat were very much raised—almost v-shaped—and the rudder in this instance was shaped like the outspread tail of a crow, with a small vertical rudder to keep the machine head to wind, the horizontal rudder working up and down on the vertical one.

"The very first day of the experiments, which were made in the beginning of '93 near Cardross, from a slight elevation and against a slight wind, Pilcher was raised twelve feet from the ground, where he hovered without any forward movement for between two and three minutes, and then descended by tilting the machine forward quite successfully."

"But the next time he rose the wind caught the machine sideways, and his weight being insufficient to restore the equilibrium, it tipped forward and sideways in landing, breaking one of the front spars.

"After this he lowered the wing tips and had some very good results, such as from 30 to 40 yards about 10 to 15 feet from the ground, starting from the top of a hill and gliding against the wind, the angle we reckoned, being approximately 1 in 10."

"He also altered the rudder, which was now made of two round disk sails, one vertical and the other horizontal, really formed of two large hoops covered with sail silk, each of about 15 feet in area, the vertical one being fixed, and the horizontal one working on it."

"We took a farmhouse with a very large, empty barn at Cardross, on the Clyde, where we got nice, clear wind on the hills, and he was able to practice almost daily, his longest soar with no motive power being about sixty yards, and greatest height about twenty feet.

"At Cardross he built two more machines. One was never quite finished as the framework, which was built to carry an engine proved too heavy for soaring. It was a monoplane, the wings being very square cut, and the body piece much the shape of the Bleriot short-span flyer."

"He then went rather to the other extreme, influenced, no doubt, by a month of very light winds, and the Gull was built with a wing area of 1 1/2 feet to the pound weight, and was so light as to be cumbersome and impossible to use for practice, except with the very lightest breeze."

"The Hawk—the most successful of all—was the last machine that Pilcher built. The Hawk was built at Eynsford, in Kent, with a wing area of 3/4 foot to the pound weight, and was estimated to carry one man and an engine—about 250 pounds. [Figs. 1-23 and 1-24 show Pilcher's Hawk.]

Fig. 1-23. England's hang glider pioneer, Percy Pilcher, with his successful "Hawk".

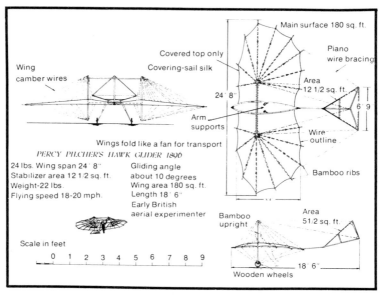

Fig. 1-24. Percy Pilchers HAWK glider 1896.

''The ribs of the wings are of pine wood, each rib slipping into a long pocket, and the sail lacing on to the body piece.

''The curve of the wing is 1 in 20, and the apex of the curve about 1/3 from the front of the wing.

''The wings are guyed to two uprights, and the machine runs on very small bicycle wheels.

''With this machine Pilcher had many very successful flights, notably one at Eynsford, from the top of one hill to the top of the next across a valley, when as a substitute for power, he had a light rope attached to the machine, which was hauled in on a pulley on the far hill.

''This flight was over 250 yards—nearly 300 yards—and of course, in this case, across the valley, the flight was a high one.

''The balance was perfect, and so was the steering gear. The machine rose high, making a great upward curve from hilltop to hilltop, and landing beautifully.

''Pilcher had hoped to add a motor engine to this machine the following winter. Drawings for it had been made, and the work of construction began at his works—Wilson and Pilcher,

54

Ltd., Westminster—when his career was cut short in this thirty-third year by the fatal accident at Stamford Hall, Yelvertoft, caused by the snapping of one of the rudder guys during a flight, after a heavy rain, on September 30, 1899.''

The construction details of Pilcher's Triplane hang glider are shown in Fig. 1-25.

## THE WRIGHT BROTHERS

Wilbur and Orville became interested in aeronautics during boyhood when their father brought home a small flying toy powered with rubber bands. They were fascinated by its ability to flutter about the room, and were introduced to the elements of aviation when they tried to repair it and make others of similar type. Orville became particularly clever at building and flying kites, and later, about 1885, when he and Wilbur were young men, they read of the unusual success being achieved in the design and use of gliders by Otto Lilienthal of Germany. They thought of the pleasures of coasting on the air and decided that they too would take up

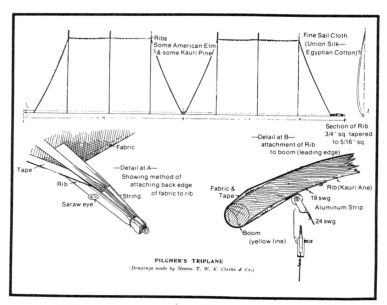

Fig. 1-25. Construction details of Pilcher's triplane hang glider.

gliding as a sport. The experiments in aerodynamics and with model aircraft then in progress by Prof. Samuel P. Langley, third Secretary of the Smithsonian Institution, were being described in newspapers and magazines of that day, and in May 1899 the brothers decided to write to the Smithsonian Institution and request information for their own study and experimentation. Soon they received several Smithsonian pamphlets describing the efforts by Mouillard, Langley, Lilienthal, and others, and suggestions for related reading of Chanute's *Progress in Flying Machines*, Langley's *Internal Work of the Wind*, and *Experiments in Aerodynamics*, and James Means' *Aeronautical Annuals*. The latter contained not only accounts of contemporary efforts but also reprints of historical accomplishments. Chanute's book was a nearly complete review of efforts of the nineteenth century. He had supplemented his research by the design, construction, and testing of several types of gliders. Upon writing to him, in Chicago, the brothers received additional suggestions.

At their shop in Dayton, Ohio, where the Wright Brothers conducted a business of making and repairing bicycles, they constructed a glider-kite with which they tested some of their first ideas for support and control, but realized that better conditions of terrain and wind were needed to provide more informative results. Following correspondence with the Weather Bureau they believed that Kitty Hawk, N.C. would be well suited to their experiments. This opinion was confirmed when they received a letter from W.J. Tate, of that little village, describing the large sand dunes and steady winds at that remote area situated on a sandy stretch between Albemarle Sound and the Atlantic Ocean.

There, on the porch of the Tate home, the brothers assembled their first large glider. It was a biplane of about 17 1/2 feet span and had 165 square feet of surface including the elevating plane in front of the lower wing. From their computations the brothers believed that this glider would support the weight of a man in winds of 15 to 29 miles per hour, but such winds were infrequent during their stay at Kitty Hawk that fall, and they did not have many opportunities for testing it with a man aboard. They did, however, learn some things about its performance by flying it unmanned, as a kite, operating the controls through cords manipulated from the ground.

The brothers returned to Dayton and, hoping to obtain more lift by an increase in size, planned their next glider with a span of 22 feet and an area of 290 square feet—somewhat larger than the gliders of previous experimenters. When, during their next vacation at Kitty Hawk in 1901, this glider was flown, it was apparent that it had greater lift than the 1900 glider. In free gliding it would support the pilot when winds of medium velocity were blowing. These tests gave them some experience in operating their control system from aboard the glider, by moving the front elevating surface to control altitude and manipulating their wing-warping controls to counteract sideward gusts.

At this point it is helpful to understand the elements of aircraft control. Whereas an automobile needs only to be steered from left to right, an airplane has three axes of turning: right and left as for an auto, up and down for climbing and descending, and sideways tilting for maintaining balance. Some previous experimenters with gliders had tried to control steering, elevation, and balance by shifting the weight of their bodies or swinging the legs, but this was not too effective. The Wrights devised a better means of effecting control by manipulations of the surfaces. Thus the front elevator of their glider could be moved up or down by a handle to control climb or descent. For lateral balance they twisted or warped the outer ends of the biplane cellular wing through wires so that a tendency for one wing tip to fall was corrected by warping it to present a greater angle to the air, thus elevating it. At the same time, though interconnecting wires, the other wing tip was twisted to a negative angle and thereby depressed.

In some ways, however, the experiments of 1901 were a disappointment to the brothers. The curvature of their wings, fore and aft (camber), was a bend of about 12 to 1. Experimenters had long known that a curved wing was better than a flat kited-like surface, and Lilienthal had preferred a relationship (camber) of 12 to 1. The Wrights copied this in their second glider but felt that the results were less efficient than with their first glider, which had a shallower curve. They

Fig. 1-26. Wilbur Wright flying prone in the 1902 glider. This was the most sucessful flying machine to that date because it used the Wright-invented aerodynamic controls.

therefore added some sticks and wires that flattened the curve of the ribs, and were gratified at the better performance. At times, however, the wing-warping system did not produce expected results. They thought that a vertical keel at the rear might improve this and decided to add such a surface to their next glider, but the difficulties encountered with control and design were so discouraging that for a while they wondered if the numerous problems would ever be solved.

There were many other factors in aircraft design that the Wrights pondered over, such as the proper relationship between span and width of wings (aspect ratio), amount of gap between the wings of a biplane, whether three surfaces were better than two or if one was best, and whether wings should be above or behind each other.

They decided to devote their winter to investigating these and other problems. Two methods of testing could be used: the shape under test could be moved through the air, or the object could be supported on balances and air blown past it. The latter provided better opportunity for study. Accordingly, Orville rigged up a small box and placed two different surfaces

58

within it to study their relative action as air was blown through it. This test led to the construction of a larger wind tunnel about 6 feet long and 16 inches square. The wind was generated by a pair of fan blades mounted on a grinder head driven by a belt from the line shaft in their shop. During that season they tested over 200 different shapes at many angles and in various relationships. This scientific laboratory work provided them with a reliable set of figures and tables from which they could design their next glider with more confidence.

The third glider was 32 feet in span but not much greater in area than its predecessor because its wing was narrower (i.e., higher apsect ratio), in accordance with their wind-tunnel findings. This new design had a vertical tail surface, and a better system of operating the wing-warping wires—using a hip cradle instead of foot pedals. As the bicycling season drew to a close and the brothers could afford to take another vacation, they went to Kitty Hawk, assembled their craft, and were ready for tests by mid-September.

It was soon apparent that their new glider was much better than any other. Fig. 1-26 shows Wilbur Wright flying the 1902 glider, and Fig. 1-27 is a drawing of this glider. They made over a thousand gliders, some in winds as high as 30 miles an hour and more, and for distances exceeding 600 feet.

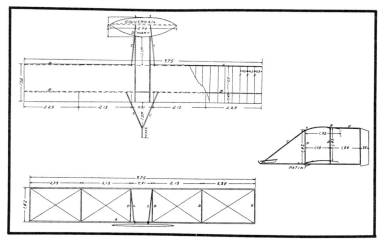

Fig. 1-27. Three-view drawing of the Wright's 1902 glider.

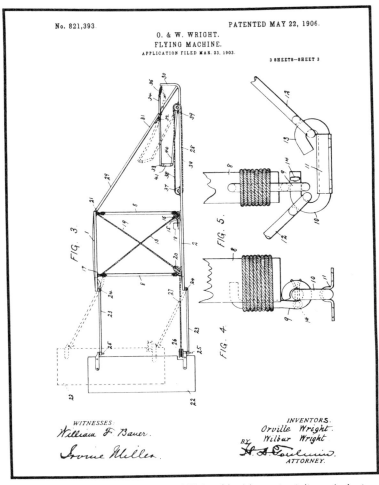

Fig. 1-28. Wright Brothers original Flying Machine patent. Its main feature was aerodynamic controls.

Again, however they noted that at times the lateral balance did not function as intended. They finally traced this fault to the vertical tail at the rear, and after detailed study decided to change this from a fixed surface to a hinged rudder. To counteract the tendency of a low wing to drag, they combined the rudder action with the warping system, so that one movement by the pilot operated both. This method of control proved to be remarkably efficient. It was incorporated in the patent for which they applied (see Figs. 1-28 through 1-30) and is one of the greatest inventions in the history of air transportation.

## WILLI PELZNER

The following is an excerpt from *Australian Gliding*, Martin Simon, Editor:

"With your wings outspread from your shoulders, a mild breeze flowing up the slope in front of you, take a deep breath,

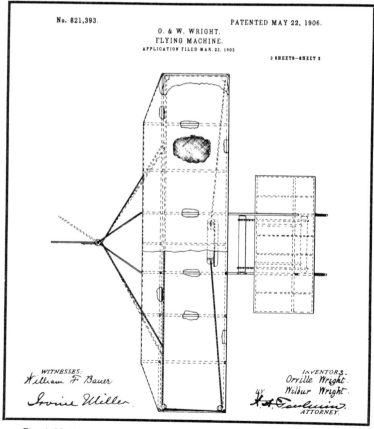

No. 821,393.

PATENTED MAY 22, 1906.

O. & W. WRIGHT.
FLYING MACHINE.
APPLICATION FILED MAR. 23, 1903

3 SHEETS—SHEET 2

WITNESSES:
William F. Bauer
Irvine Miller

INVENTORS:
Orville Wright.
Wilbur Wright.
BY
ATTORNEY.

Fig. 1-29. Wright Brothers original Flying Machine patent (details).

O. & W. WRIGHT.
FLYING MACHINE.
APPLICATION FILED MAR 23, 1903

3 SHEETS—SHEET 1.

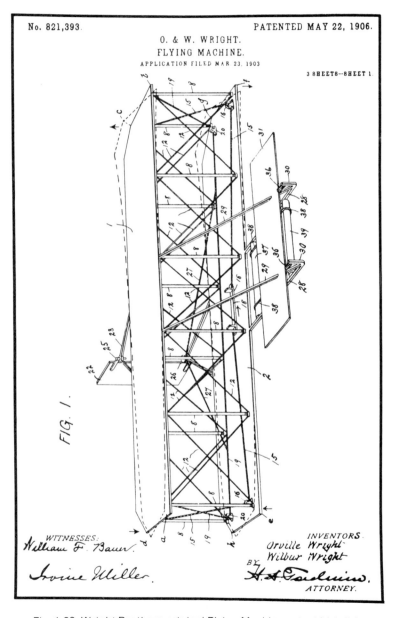

*FIG. I.*

WITNESSES:
William F. Bauer.

Irvine Miller.

INVENTORS.
Orville Wright
Wilbur Wright
BY
H. A. Toulmin.
ATTORNEY.

Fig. 1-30. Wright Brothers original Flying Machine patent (details).

run forward a few paces and leap into the air. Steer yourself by swinging your body gracefully this way or that; legs back to raise the wings to a greater angle of attack, forward to pitch nose down, left to turn left, swing right to pick up the wing again, skim down the hill a few feet up, swerve to avoid a bush, tuck your feet up to clear a hummock and float out over a gully. For a few moments you are fifty or perhaps even more feet above the ground, every movement of your body reacting against the air, flying just like a bird. Then suddenly you see your own shadow, dark and batlike, getting close and closer as the slope flattens ahead, legs dangling, knees flexed, body pushing aft to stall the wing and you alight gently on two feet, totter forward, stand, and the flight is over. You turn to look up the hill to where your friends and admirers wave and cheer. Then you carry your biplane hang glider back up to the top and do it again. How long was the last flight? Twenty eight seconds, 300 meters? Next time try for thirty and 350. You might even manage 40 seconds and a half a kilometer distance—if you are as good as Willi Pelzner was in 1921.

[Figure 1-31 shows a drawing of Pelzner's hang glider.]

"Pelzner came from Nuremburg to the first Rhon gliding meet in '21 and '22. Contemporary accounts of these meetings classified each aircraft as an Eindecker, Doppeldecker or Dreidecker according to the number of wings, and then as a Sitzgleiter. From Lilienthal, Pilcher and Chanute, there was the Hangegleiter, from which the pilot literally hung, legs trailing, from supports under his elbows or armpits. Pelzner was the great maestro of the Doppeldecker Hangegleiter. In 1921 and 1922 he carried off many prizes. He built all his own craft and developed a simple structure that proved strong enough to carry him safely on flight after flight without serious mishap, yet light enough from him to control flight by bodily movements, changing the center of gravity to trim the aircraft and overcome the upsetting effect of gusts or turbulence. Pelzner's gliders were also astonishingly cheap; even in a time of desperate financial trouble and inflation in Germany they cost him less than 20 marks to build. Derigged, they were small enough to be loaded onto a passenger train as traveller's luggage at no extra charge; the parcel measured about 2.7

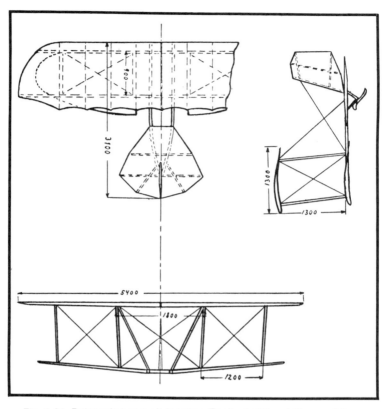

Fig. 1-31. Pelzner's hang glider plan. The last of the old hang gliders.

meters long and 1.3 meters high, but only 50 centimeters thick.

"The various Pelzner gliders differed a good deal in size and detail, although all were built roughly to the same basic scheme. The earlier models were built smaller and very light; 5.4 meters span with total wing area about 14 square meters. They weighed less than ten kilogrammes. The later types spanned up to 7 meters with areas of 16.5 square meters, and weighed twice as much. Probably as Pelzner's skill improved he was able to control bigger and somewhat more efficient gliders.

"The framework was good. Two tapered longerons, a shoulder width apart, ran fore and aft with the lower wing main spars running cross wise and attached with bolts. At the rear these two main members were drawn together to support the tail unit, and from the tail to the upper end of the main wing struts two diagonal members ran. This basic framework was of oval or streamlined sectioned timber, 2.5 centimeters by 4 centimeters in cross section where the loads were greatest, thinning down to 2 by 3 centimeters elsewhere. The upper and lower wings both had two spars, the front spars being 4 centimeters by 0.5 centimeter section, the rear spars 3.5 centimeters by 0.8 centimeter on the lower wing and 3.6 by 1.1 centimeter on the upper. Light curved ribs were bound to the spars, and the two wings were joined by light vertical struts, the outer ones being spindled in section to save weight. The whole structure was braced with wire.

"Pelzner covered his surfaces with oiled paper, glued onto the underside of the ribs of wing and tail. The leading edge of the lower wing was formed by the front spar, but the upper wing apparently had a light front member of wood or wire which gave a stiff entry to the primitive aerofoil. Some models had double thickness paper covering around the leading edge. The earliest models had no movable control surfaces at all, but later Pelzner fitted a rudder which he controlled by means of a sling around his right hand—a forward movement for a left turn, a backward push for a right hand turn.

"To manage these craft Pelzner worked out an athletic style of flying which excited much admiration. At the 1921 meeting he accumulated a total flying time of 38 minutes, higher than that of any other pilot. He did this in a total of 62 flights averaging over half a minute each, some of them covering 400 and 500 meters distance at his best glide ratio of about 6 to 1. In cash prizes he paid for his gliders hundreds of times over.

"But of course, Klemperer's demonstrations in the Schwarze Teufel and Blaue Maus showed clearly where the future lay, although, in 1921, it was only after Pelzner had folded up his paper aeroplane and put it on the train for Nuremburg that the Eindecker Sitzgleiter began to realize its potential [see Fig. 1-32].

"Pelzner played little part in the subsequent development of gliding, he somehow never seems to have taken to the

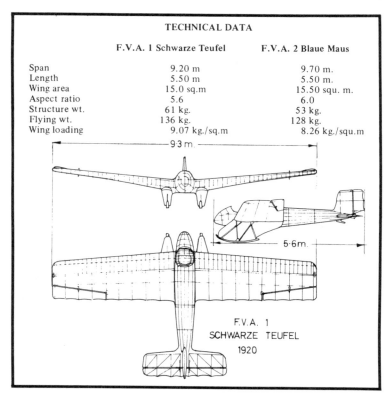

| TECHNICAL DATA | | |
| --- | --- | --- |
| | F.V.A. 1 Schwarze Teufel | F.V.A. 2 Blaue Maus |
| Span | 9.20 m | 9.70 m. |
| Length | 5.50 m | 5.50 m. |
| Wing area | 15.0 sq.m | 15.50 squ. m. |
| Aspect ratio | 5.6 | 6.0 |
| Structure wt. | 61 kg. | 53 kg. |
| Flying wt. | 136 kg. | 128 kg. |
| Wing loading | 9.07 kg./sq.m | 8.26 kg./squ.m |

Fig. 1-32. The glider that caused hang gliding to cease in 1922 at the Wasserkuppe.

Sitzgleiter. But in 1970, at the Wasserkuppe again, he took part in the Commemorative meeting fifty years after the first Rhon.''

### FRANCIS M. ROGALLO

In 1919, when Rogallo was seven years old, an airplane flew over his town (Sanger, California) and he decided to make aeronautics a career. Rogallo is pictured, in Fig. 1-33, flying his original kite, and the patent for this kite is depicted in Fig. 1-34. Around 1925 when he was 13, he saved enough money to buy a ride in a dilapidated Curtiss Jenny in Fresno without first discussing the possibility with his parents. Today he probably wouldn't fly in the same airplane if it were free.

In 1933 and about 1937 he applied for the U.S. Army Air Corps flight training program but was turned down. The Navy turned him down around 1934 because a childhood accident had eliminated the two largest toes on his right foot.

In 1946 Rogallo spent several days in Lock Haven, Pennsylvania, helping the Piper Co. build an experimental airplane with a full-span slotted flap and plug-type spoiler aileron (one of his earlier inventions). Shortly, Meyers, a Piper pilot, gave him about 10 hours of dual instruction and he got a student permit to solo. He had done most of his flying in a

Fig. 1-33. Francis M. Rogallo, the inventor, flying his original all-flexible kite.

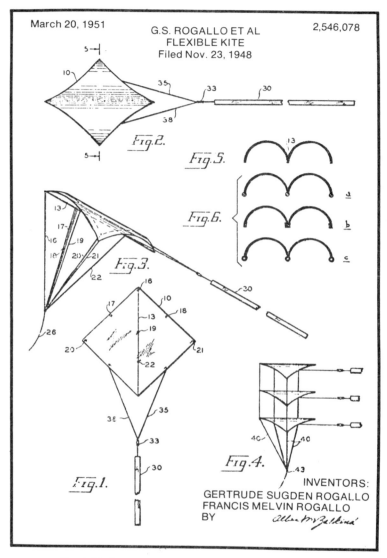

March 20, 1951

G.S. ROGALLO ET AL
FLEXIBLE KITE
Filed Nov. 23, 1948

2,546,078

Fig. 1-34. Rogallo's original flexible kite patent of 1951.

prototype Supercruiser with a 125 hp engine and was going to solo in it on the day before he was to leave Lock Haven. When he arrived at the field he found that the assistant chief engineer had gotton there a little before and had gone for a flight in the airplane he was to use. The airplane caught fire in the air and crashed, killing the pilot, who was alone. Because of the resulting great confusion following the accident, Rogallo did not solo before leaving Lock Haven and he never got around to soloing any powered aircraft, although he has flown several since then.

Figures 1-35 through 1-38 illustrate a selection of later Rogallo patents and the patent for this kite is depicted in Fig. 1-34.

His first solo flight in a glider was in Tom Purcell's Flight Sail about 10 years ago.

Several years ago, Rogallo (everyone calls him "Rog") designed and built four variations of the all flexible wing, each of about 300 square feet of cloth area. He has flown these on an anchor line on the sea shore and also glided them from the top of the big dunes at Kitty Hawk. Three of his four children and one grandson have also had flights. These wings are marvelous for storage and transportation, and they are unbreakable, but the glide ratio is less than 3 to 1 and it would be difficult to self-launch one. He hasn't flown this type of wing since he got his "standard Rogallo" a couple of years ago with which he has made over 300 flights.

Several Rogallo models are illustrated in Figs. 1-39 through 1-44. In 1945 at the close of World War II, Rogallo and his wife Gertrude thought the NACA should initiate research that would give the average citizen a better opportunity to fly his own airplane by developing a more practical and less expensive airplane. The NACA decided not to undertake such a project, so Gertrude and he decided to work on it at home in their own time. One of their goals was to develop an inexpensive, rugged wing that could be folded easily when the aircraft was on the ground—like a bird or a bat folds its wings.

The March 1951 *Ford Times* story and the November *Ground Skimmer* cover shows one configuration of wing they developed in 1948. There were many others, varying in shape and structure. This work has had much influence on the design of kites, gliders, and parachutes and may someday also influence the design of powered aircraft.

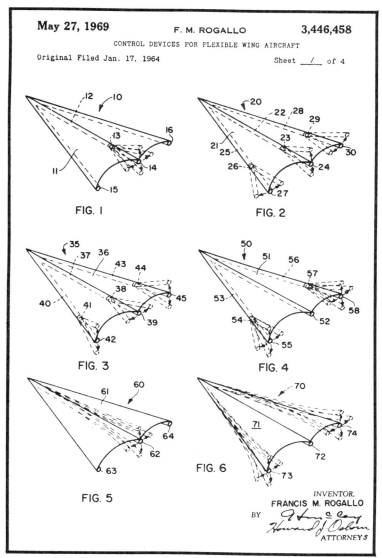

Fig. 1-35. A selection of later Rogallo patents.

## RECENT HISTORICAL DEVELOPMENTS

After Pelzner did his flying at the Rhon meeting, all hang
gliding came to a complete halt. The fantastic performances of

the Schwarze Teufel and Blaue Maus proved the superiority of the gliders with a seated pilot in an enclosed fuselage and monoplane wings. The future of gliding was obvious. It was longer, further, faster and higher.

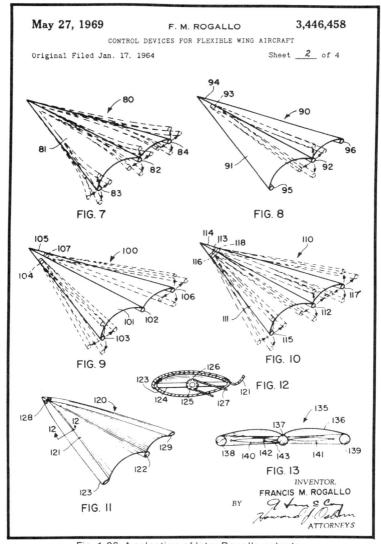

Fig. 1-36. A selection of later Rogallo patents.

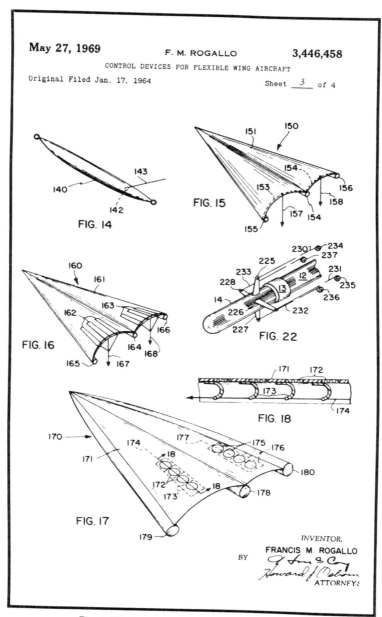

Fig. 1-37. A selection of later Rogallo patents.

72

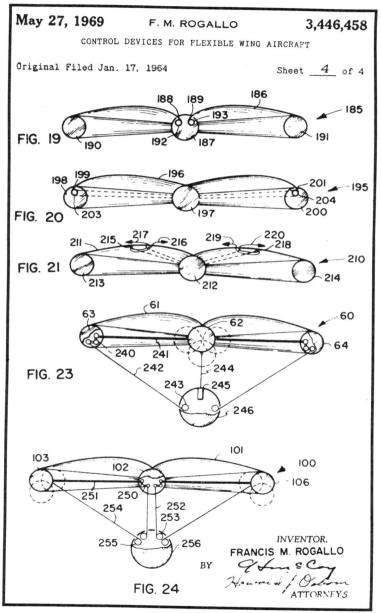

CONTROL DEVICES FOR FLEXIBLE WING AIRCRAFT

Original Filed Jan. 17, 1964        Sheet __4__ of 4

FIG. 19

FIG. 20

FIG. 21

FIG. 23

FIG. 24

INVENTOR.
FRANCIS M. ROGALLO

BY

ATTORNEYS

Fig. 1-38. A selection of later Rogallo patents.

73

Fig. 1-39. F.M. Rogallo and his flexible wing model with metal keel and leading edges, but no cross bar in the Langley 7 × 10-foot wind tunnel.

It wasn't until 1941, when the United States placed a wartime ban on civil flying near the coast, that pilot Volmer Jensen became frustrated enough to build a hang glider. It was a Chanute-type with one major difference: it replaced the archaic weight shifting method of control with full three-axis aerodynamic controls (see Fig. 1-45). Mr. Jensen then managed to pacify himself until after the war. Nobody could stop him from hang gliding. After hostilities ended, Volmer went on to build more conventional, powered aircraft that could be built by the enthusiast. It wasn't until 1971 when he came out with his beautiful swingwing that hang gliding would hear from him again.

Then, in 1951, a patent was issued to a Mr. and Mrs. Francis M. Rogallo for a kite they had invented three years

Fig. 1-40. A powered wind tunnel model of a Rogallo wing utility aircraft.

Fig. 1-41. A 1/12th-scale, radio controlled dynamic research model of a Rogallo supported dummy Saturn booster. 1961.

Fig. 1-42. A 50-foot, inflated keel and leading edges Rogallo for space craft recovery. 1961.

Fig. 1-43. A high aspect ratio cylindrical Rogallo in the Langley 7 × 10-foot transonic wind tunnel.

earlier. It wasn't an ordinary kite either. In fact, it was so revolutionary that the United States government decided to annex Rogallo into the NASA space program. It was thought the new kite could be used to replace the parachute then in use for spacecraft landing. The Rogallo could glide forward and be directed to land at an airport. As it developed however, the project was "scrubbed" during the mid-sixties, after the government had spent millions on wind tunnel research and prototype development. Even so, the Rogallo flexible wing concept worked and several full-size, man-carrying examples were built and successfully flown. It was all so very simple. The kite aircraft could be folded for transport to the airport, opened up like an umbrella and flown away. Man could have flown centuries ago....

Fig. 1-44. An all-flexible, tension structure Rogallo with Apollo spacecraft in the Langley 7 × 10-foot wind tunnel. 1965.

Fig. 1-45. Volmer Jensen's 1941 three-axis, aerodynamically controlled hang glider, the VJ-11 "So-Lo".

In 1957, Bill Bennett, an Australian, became involved with water skiing and kite flying, in association with Bill Moyes and John Dickenson. At first, Dickenson was, in the words of Bennett, the "Dr. Cyclops" of the trio and did not fly. That was up to Bennett and Moyes. By 1964, Moyes was actually building the new Rogallo tow kites for sale as they were quite superior to the old flat sail kites. In 1967, Moyes managed a tow record to 1,000 feet while Dickenson became a proficient flyer and set a duration record of over 3 hours in 1970.

Meanwhile, back in the United States, things were starting to happen. During the period from 1961 to 1963, Barry Palmer of Phoenix and friends, made hundreds of hang glider flights using the Rogallo concept. The flights ranged in length up to 200 yards, altitudes of 80 feet, and overall glide ratio of 4.5 to 1. No injuries except for minor skin lacerations were recorded. The glider had a wing area of 280 square feet and was never flown in winds above 10 mph.

In 1964, a man named Richard Miller, past president of the SSA (Soaring Society of America) and a very literate soaring writer, was vacationing on Cape Cod's great sand dunes and seized the Rogallo idea for his own. "It would be great to skim over those dunes just like the Wright Brothers," he thought.

After he returned to his California home, he teamed up with his good friend, Bruce Carmichael (SSA's aerodynamics chairman) and built a hang glider version of the Rogallo wing. That was in 1966.

The structure of the glider was bamboo with the permanent joints bound and fiberglassed. For assembly the bits and pieces were tied with cord, rope, twine or strips cut from inner tubes, whichever was handiest. The sail was either 4-mil or 6-mil polyethelene sheeting with rows of grommets along the edges and down the center to provide holes for lacing to the keel and leading edges. Its total weight was about 20 pounds and it cost around 40 dollars to build. The glide ratio was only about 3 to 1, but it flew and was it ever fun! Later the glider was improved by using aluminum tubing for increased performance and durability.

Miller and Carmichael let several other people try their hand at flying the new fun flying machine but nobody else took to it. Beach bums, surfers, etc. gave it a whirl but went back to their thing after it was over. The time wasn't right for a movement to begin.

Back in Phoenix again, 1967 finds one Emil Kissel starting to publish a two page, bi-monthly newsletter called *Low, Slow and Out of Control*, devoted to foot launched gliding concepts. This was at the urging of our friend Richard Miller. After four issues the editorship was transferred to Robert Wister, also of Phoenix. By the sixth issue, the little newsletter contained ten pages but then died after reaching a circulation of 100.

In 1969, Bill Bennett went on a vacation with his water-skis kite and gave an exhibition at the National Ski Championships held at Berkeley, California. Here, he met Dave Kilbourne, a water skier, who offered to tow Bennett aloft with his own boat. Bennett accepted and then taught Kilbourne how to fly, who went on to become the first person in history to soar a kite for over an hour, in 1971. After the meet, Bennett went to the east coast and managed to fly over and land at the base of the Statue of Liberty—on July 4, 1969 (see Fig. 1-46). He was promptly apprehended by authorities but the demonstration drew a lot of publicity. Bennett then went to California to settle where he set up manufacturing the ski kites and now hang gliders as well.

Fig. 1-46. Bill Bennett introduces the Rogallo tow kite to the United States on July 4, 1969.

The February 1971 issue of *Soaring* Magazine published a letter from Joe Faust called "A Different Drummer". It was about hang gliding and created quite a stir. Faust was resurrecting the old Phoenix newsletter into a 20 pager called *Low & Slow*. At about the same time, the Spring 1971 issue of *Sport Planes* carried a story about an outrageously inexpensive airplane: "The $24.86 Airplane" proclaimed the cover. In fact, Richard Miller was shown flying the glider (see Fig. 1-47), which was dubbed "Hang Loose." Plans were quickly thrown together and Jack Lambie, the designer, sold thousands at $3.00 a set.

According to Lambie, it all started one day while he was trying to teach his junior high school students about aerodynamics. Well, they didn't dig all those formulas so Jack (a pilot himself) asked the kids if they'd like to build and fly their own airplane and learn by doing. Well, the response was obvious. That did it. The hang gliding movement was about to begin.

Then, sometime during the early spring of 1971, Lambie and Faust teamed up and sponsored "The Great Universal Hang Glider Championships". It was held on Sunday, May 23, in honor of Otto Lilienthal's 123rd birthday. It was unbelievable. Thirteen gliders showed up: a majority of some Rogallos, and a flying wing, by Richard Miller. The "Conduit Condor" is shown in Fig. 1-48, with designer.

Faust was immediately contacted by the Merv Griffin TV talk show, the London Times and CBS as well. The FAA also asked to be kept posted on such future happenings. The twenty page *Low and Slow* newsbooklet began to grow. People all around the world were subscribing. It was coming together. Hang gliding was here to stay.

That first meet contained a potential for danger. "Don't fly higher than you care to fall," became the watchword. While

Fig. 1-47. The original "Hang Loose" with designer Jack Lambie hanging on. Fall 1970.

Fig. 1-48. Richard Miller and his "Conduit Condor," the highest performing hang glider at the first Universal Hang Glider Championships of May 23, 1971.

the majority of flights were semi-controlled crashes, some lasted as long as 19 seconds and covered 800 feet. Compared to other active sports like skiing, surfing or football, bruises were few. By the end of the day everyone was talking about "the next time." The "Otto Meet" as it was called, has been held annually ever since, not to mention many, many more all over the country.

By June of 1971, 25 people banded together to form the Southern California Hang Glider Association, under the direction of Dick Eipper and Lloyd Licher. Their newsletter, *Ground Skimmer* has since grown to a magazine and the SCHGA has developed into the USHGA (United States Hang Gliding Association) with about 15,000 dues paying members.

Over on the east coast, things were starting to happen as well. In the summer of 1970, Robert G. Mixon of Miami, Florida built and flew a Chanute-type biplane based on a plan found in a 1909 *Popular Mechanics*. The local paper ran a front page headline "Those Magnificent Men In Their Flying Machine" on June 15, 1970. A local TV station even took some footage of a cliff launch. Mixon said he did it out of frustration due to the high cost of conventional flying. Later, he even offered plans, because of a large number of requests for his story which appeared in the February 1971 issue of *Sport Aviation*.

Going north, to the ski areas of New England, we find Terry Sweeney (see Fig. 1-49) of New Hampshire experimenting with some Chanute type hang gliders. He and some friends made many, many flights, learned much and had a lot of fun. Their gliders replaced the older airfoils with more modern versions.

Since then, the sport has spread to the interior of the country and around the world. Two full-color magazines have appeared on the scene, giving hang gliding a real professional look. First came *Hang Glider* in the fall of 1974, then *Wings Unlimited* in the winter of 1975. Records of all kinds are being made almost daily. Distance is now held by Rick Poynter of New Zealand who flew a ridge for 50 miles. Altitude drop is held by Dennis Burton who was released from a hot air balloon

Fig. 1-49. Terry Sweeney flying his "Ariel" in New Hampshire. 1969.

**83**

Fig. 1-50. A modern Rogallo wing hang glider.

22,500 feet above the Mojave Desert for a flight that lasted 35 minutes and covered 26 miles. Mark Clarkson went up 5,700 feet above his takeoff point in 1974, for the altitude gain record. The duration record is now more than 15 hours.

Hang gliding is coming of age, too. A modern Rogallo wing hang glider is pictured in Fig. 1-50. In February of 1975, the CIVV (International Soaring Commission) met and decided not to take on hang gliding as a division but to recommend it for a full and separate commission status of its own. Then in June of 1975, the CIVL (International Hang Gliding Commission) held its first meeting. Thirteen countries were represented and a poll taken of the hang gliding activity worldwide. The results indicated that there were almost 40,000 hang glider pilots and over 42,000 hang gliders throughout the world. The USA reported figures of about 25,000 and 30,000 respectively.

In September 1975, a general conference of the FAI (International Aeronautical Federation) which governs world-wide aviation sports, met in Ottawa and gave hang gliding its full commission status. Hang gliding is now an official aviation sport which will be governed by the CIVL and FAI. In the United States it will come under the office of the NAA (National Aeronautic Association), the country's aero club, while other countries have similar organizations.

# Chapter 2
# Typical Hang Gliders

## TYPICAL HANG GLIDERS

The material presented in this chapter is intended to provide information concerning the basic types of hang gliders that are available today. No support of any particular design is intended or implied. Such items as performance, stability, control, construction, portability, weight, along with three-view drawings and photographs will aid one in selecting a hang glider for his particular needs. This information should not, however, decide one's ultimate choice, but should lead a person in the right direction. One should go out and see the gliders fly first and, if at all possible, take an introductory lesson on the most interesting type of hang glider.

It should be emphasized that most modern hang gliders are not difficult to construct or operate, once one learns how. One does not have to be an expert machinist or woodworker, either. Instead, the construction of a hang glider requires

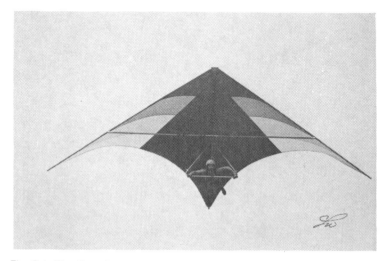

Fig. 2-1. The Rogallo wing is the most typical of all hang gliders. This example by Phantom Wing.

much care and attention to detail. There is no room for error when in the air. There's no place to pull aside and park.

As for operation, the *basic* techniques can be learned in an afternoon for the simpler Rogallo wings (see Fig. 2-1), while the higher performance gliders are another matter. However, the actual movements involved are more often subtle than forceful. One should also possess a cool head and a reasonable sense of daring.

The most important items in the design of a hang glider include a good stable configuration, adequate control throughout its expected operating range and, of course, structural integrity. In the case of the so-called standard Rogallo wing. (Fig. 2-2 shows a standard Manta wing.) These items have been practically spelled out by the HMA, at least minimally. In the higher performing hang gliders, however, no "standards" exist. In any case, a reputable firm with a competent staff should be looked to for a good design. It will have been both analytically and, most importantly, flight test proven.

The first several flights with a new or unfamiliar design should always be done in the lightest of winds on a slope that is equal to about 75% of the maximum glide ratio. The novice should stay low to the ground and practice straight and level flight first. He should also become accustomed to his design's response in pitch and get a general feel for its overall handling, including ground work. Then he is ready to begin "working his way up the hill."

## STANDARD ROGALLO WINGS

The "standard" flexible, Rogallo wing "kite" is, by far, the most popular hang glider in use today (see Fig. 2-3),

Fig. 2-2. Prone flight in a standard Manta wing.

Fig. 2-3. A "Flex-Flyer" being soared prone.

comprising roughly 95% of the market. These simplest of
flying machines offer excellent portability, light weight and
convenient assembly, with no tools. If used in the proper
conditions, they can provide a lot of fun and have forgiving
flight characteristics. The stall is very gentle and the nose can
be prevented from dropping by parachuting vertically to the
ground. Kites can also be "dynamically" stalled by an abrupt
pitch-up of the nose just before touch down, eliminating all
forward and vertical speed. Most people are introduced to
hang gliding with this type of craft.

The biggest, single limitation in operating a Rogallo is the wind. Flying in winds up to about 12 mph is reasonably sane, while winds of 20 mph and up should be considered extremely dangerous. Most gusty conditions are also dangerous to the Rogallo and other hang gliders as well. If the sail is caused to luff (either by high winds and/or gusts) the longitudinal stability is lost and the kite will enter a dive that it may not be possible to recover from. This is extremely important to keep in mind. Check with the manufacturer's recommended top flying speed, too.

A Free-Flight standard gives a good view of its planform in Fig. 2-4.

The typical Rogallo wing hang glider is constructed of aluminum alloy tubing which is braced with aircraft cable including special fittings (see Fig. 2-5). It is held together by aircraft hardware and has a sail made of stabilized Dacron sailcloth which weighs anywhere from 3 oz. to 4.5 oz. If properly maintained, it should last for several seasons of normal use. Corrosion and mildew are potential maintenance problems, but only minimally, depending on the local climate. A canvas bag is normally employed in covering a folded kite for transport and storage. The pilot is suspended in a swing

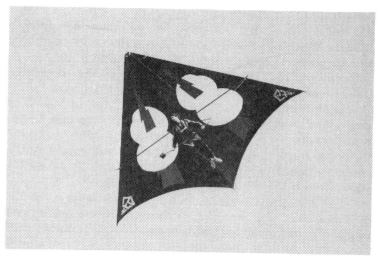

Fig. 2-4. A Free-Flight standard.

Fig. 2-5. Pete Brock soars along the beach.

seat or harness and control is maintained solely by a weight shift/trapeze bar arrangement.

Since there are currently more than 30 different manufacturers of standard, conical, Rogallo wings, no attempt will be made to feature them all. Furthermore, they all fly with about the same characteristics, while possessing differences in design detail and construction. Glide ratios and sink rates may vary from kite to kite depending upon sail cut, billow and pilot body position. Figures 2-6 through 2-9 are representative of a typical, equal-length keel and leading-edges Rogallo, now considered to be the original standard configuration. To get more information on a particular design, write directly to the manufacturer for details.

The primary differences in performance between 80° and 90° kites are as follows: For a given length keel, the 90° nose angle kite has a sail area almost equal to the sail area of the next larger 80° nose angle kite. For example, a 17 foot long 80° kite has the same wing area as a 16 foot long 90° kite. This means that the smaller keel length 90° kite will provide for the same wing loading as the larger 80° kite. The basic criteria for selecting the correct size kite is based on a wing loading of one pound per square foot of projected sail area.

Theoretically, the 90° nose angle kite can yield a glide ratio slightly better than the 80° (4.74 versus 4.47 in the prone position). The 80° kites are also, theoretically, minutely more stable in pitch (because of their greater sweepback), all other variables remaining the same. Stability is also affected by the center of gravity (CG), pilot position, and sail billow. The lower the man is, the more stable the kite. The more the billow the sails have, the more stable the kite, but the less the L/D or, glide ratio. The average billow today seems to be about 4°, a reasonable compromise between stability and glide angle. The quiet operating sails are shaped, or cambered, instead of being

Fig. 2-6. Bill Bennett leaves Dante's View for Death Valley's floor a mile below.

Fig. 2-7. A Phantom II flyer shows good form.

cut with straight seams. This technique also improves performance both aerodynamically and esthetically. In many cases, however, body position and pilot skill can make the critical difference in performance.

## THE WORLD CUP STANDARD

The new standard Rogallo, the World Cup Formula, was drawn up in order to really make hang gliding meets a test of the pilot's actual flying skills. With all designs practically the same, aerodynamically and structurally, the entrants will have an equal opportunity, or common denominator by which to perform. The World Cup Formula configuration is based on many years of actual flying and designing experience and is the "ultimate" standard Rogallo in terms of today's technology and art. One thing has not changed, however, that being the instability that occurs when the sail luffs and collapses. Then too, the minimum billow for the World Cup is specified as only 3.5°, certainly not a super stable sail. Battens, however, which are allowed in the World Cup Formula, do appear to improve the stability over an un-battened sail.

The World Cup Specifications are as follows:

1. Nose Angle—90° maximum
2. Billow—3.5°minimum
3. Aspect Ratio—3.5 maximum
4. Main Tubes—4
5. Top Cables—4

Fig. 2-8. The seated position offers more comfort on longer flights.

Fig. 2-9. Dick Boone lifts off in his "SkyTrek."

**Table 2-1. Dimensions for Original Standard Rogallo Wings ($AR_{80°} = 2.58$, $AR_{90°} = 2.82$)**

| Keel Length | Wing Span 90° Kite | Wing Area 90° Kite | Wing Span 80° Kite | Wing Area 80° Kite | Pilot Wt. 90° Kite | Pilot Wt. 80° Kite |
|---|---|---|---|---|---|---|
| 15 ft | 21 ft-3 in. | 159 sq ft | 19 ft-3 in. | 144 sq ft | 120 lbs | 100 lbs |
| 16 ft | 22 ft-7 in. | 181 sq ft | 20 ft-7 in. | 164 sq ft | 140 lbs | 120 lbs |
| 17 ft | 24 ft-0 in. | 204 sq ft | 21 ft-9 in. | 185 sq ft | 160 lbs | 140 lbs |
| 18 ft | 25 ft-5 in. | 228 sq ft | 23 ft-2 in. | 208 sq ft | 185 lbs | 160 lbs |
| 19 ft | 26 ft-10 in. | 255 sq ft | 24 ft-5 in. | 232 sq ft | 210 lbs | 185 lbs |
| 20 ft | 28 ft-3 in. | 283 sq ft | 25 ft-8 in. | 257 sq ft | 235 lbs | 210 lbs |

**Load Factors**
These vary from about +4, −2 to +6, −3 ultimate, depending upon the diameter and wall thickness of the main tubing.

96

6. Lower Cables—6
7. Outriggers (Deflexers)—2 maximum
8. Keel must not be longer than leading edges.
9. Battens: There may be up to four (4) per sail cone, but they must be flexible (not formed) and of the same thickness and width. They must be unsupported and not over $1/4'' \times 1''$ in cross section.
10. Camber Cut: not allowed
11. Wing Loading: 0.9 pounds per square foot (psf) minimum
12. Drawing a line from the wing tip, the sail, keel and lower cables may not venture above this line toward the nose.

See Table 2-1 for the dimensions of the standard Rogallo Wings and Table 2-2 for its performance factors.

A comparison of basic Rogallo wing planforms and performance is shown in Fig. 2-10.

## PHOENIX

The Phoenix (see Fig. 2-11) is a medium-aspect ratio Rogallo hybrid with a "fan tail" sail cut, and cable tensed semi-cylindrical leading edges. It is controlled solely by means of weight shifting.

The Phoenix will perform better than a standard, but not as well as a high apsect ratio kite. It is characterized by a "fan tail" cut trailing edge that is reported to increase the aspect ratio, provide for greater stability and eliminate sail flutter. It incorporates a typical trapeze bar and can be flown either seated or prone, depending on the arrangement of the lower

Table 2-2. Rogallo wing performance factors.

| Performance (W/S = 1.0 psf) | 80° Nose | 90°Nose | World Cup | World Cup* |
|---|---|---|---|---|
| Stall Speed ($V_s$) | 16 mph | 15.7 mph | 14.8 mph | 14 mph |
| Min Sink Speed ($V_{r/s\ min}$) | 18 mph | 17.7 mph | 16.8 mph | 15.9 mph |
| Cruise Speed ($V_{L/D\ max}$) | 24 mph | 23.6 mph | 22.2 mph | 21.1 mph |
| L/D at $V_{r/s\ min}$ | 2.53 | 2.73 | 2.99 | 2.91 |
| L/D at $V_{L/D\ max}$ | 4.47 | 4.64 | 5.21 | 5.21 |
| r/s at $V_{r/s\ min}$ | 421 fpm | 397 fpm | 344 fpm | 326 fpm |
| r/s at $V_{L/D\ max}$ | 472 fpm | 438 fpm | 375 fpm | 356 fpm |

* at W/S = 0.9 psf.

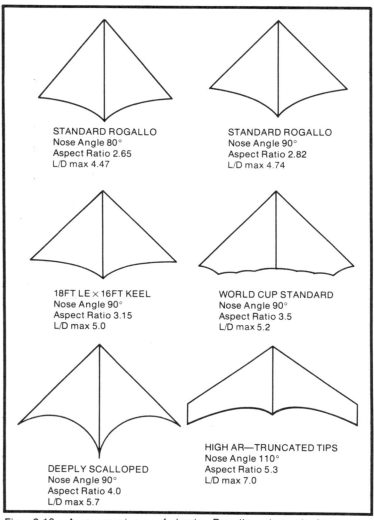

STANDARD ROGALLO
Nose Angle 80°
Aspect Ratio 2.65
L/D max 4.47

STANDARD ROGALLO
Nose Angle 90°
Aspect Ratio 2.82
L/D max 4.74

18FT LE × 16FT KEEL
Nose Angle 90°
Aspect Ratio 3.15
L/D max 5.0

WORLD CUP STANDARD
Nose Angle 90°
Aspect Ratio 3.5
L/D max 5.2

DEEPLY SCALLOPED
Nose Angle 90°
Aspect Ratio 4.0
L/D max 5.7

HIGH AR—TRUNCATED TIPS
Nose Angle 110°
Aspect Ratio 5.3
L/D max 7.0

Fig. 2-10. A comparison of basic Rogallo wing planforms and performance.

longitudinal cables. Prior flight experience in a standard should be had before learning to fly this design. Its wing loading is about the same as a kite's which, coupled to the increased aspect ratio, adds up to a lower stalling speed and a higher top end. The manufacturer claims "excellent penetration...even in high winds." It is also claimed to have greater pitch control and stable response.

Takedown/setup times are on the order of 5 minutes, and the Phoenix may be folded and transported just like a standard. The Phoenix is self-launched.

Figure 2-12 is a drawing of the Phoenix which shows its design.

The following are the aircraft specifications:

### Dimensions

| | |
|---|---|
| Wing Span | 28 ft-10 in. |
| Wing Area | 205 sq ft |
| Aspect Ratio | 4.1 |
| Keel Length | 17 ft |
| Leading Edge | 19 ft-6 in. |
| Nose Angle | 95.5° |
| Billow | 4° |

Fig. 2-11. The Phoenix was designed by Dick Boone of Delta Wing.

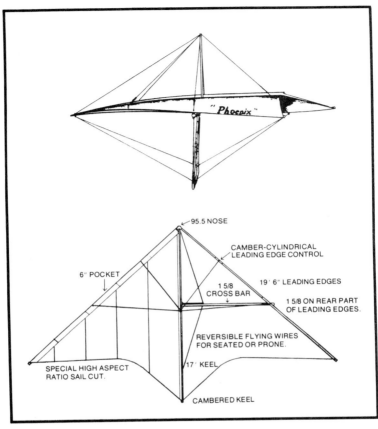

Fig. 2-12. Phoenix plans.

## Weights and Loadings

| | |
|---|---|
| Empty Weight | 42 lbs |
| Max Flying Weight | 282 lbs |
| Useful Load | 240 lbs |

## Performance (at 215 lbs)

| | |
|---|---|
| Best L/D | 6-to-1 |
| Min Sink | 300 fpm |
| Stall Speed | 16 mph |
| Cruise Speed | 24 mph |
| Max Speed | not given |

## SCORPION

The Scorpion (see Fig. 2-13) is a high-aspect ratio Rogallo hybrid with tip extensions (also referred to as truncated tips), a deeply scalloped trailing edge, finite aft sail extension, and tapered leading-edge pockets. It is controlled solely by means of weight shifting.

The Scorpion will fly with the best of the hybrids. It is characterized by a unique finite aft sail extension which ought to mean improved longitudinal stability. It also has what the manufacturer calls a "keel sail equalizer" that allows for the sail to adjust under the changing air pressure distribution in a turn. A typical trapeze bar/harness arrangement is used, but special training should be taken before attempting to fly it. Its wing loading is about the same as that for a standard Rogallo, thus, coupled with the greater efficiency of the high aspect ratio wing, it has a very low stall speed. This may limit its speed range somewhat. At the stall, one wing tip will tend to

Fig. 2-13. The Phantom Scorpion has a deeply scalloped sail.

drop. Pitch and roll response are reported adequate just above stall.

Takedown/setup times should be within 10 minutes, and the Scorpion may be folded and transported much like a standard. It is a self-launched glider.

The following are the aircraft specifications:

### Dimensions

| | |
|---|---|
| Wing Span | 32 ft |
| Wing Area | 200 sq ft |
| Aspect Ratio | 5 |
| Keel Length | 16 ft |
| Leading Edge | 19 ft |
| Nose Angle | 110° |
| Billow | 2 3/4° |

### Weights and Loadings

| | |
|---|---|
| Empty Weight | 47 lbs |
| Max Flying Weight | 242 lbs |
| Useful Load | 195 lbs |

### Performance (at 210 lbs)

| | |
|---|---|
| Best L/D | 7-to-1 |
| Min Sink | 254 fpm |
| Stall Speed | 14 mph |
| Cruise Speed | 24 mph |
| Max Speed | not given |

## CUMULUS V

The Cumulus V, pictured in Fig. 2-14, is a high-aspect ratio Rogallo hybrid with tip extensions, shaped keel and large, tapered, leading-edge pockets. It is controlled solely by means of weight shifting.

The Cumulus V performs with the best of the hybrid Rogallos. It is characterized by a higher wing loading and a faster cruise speed than for a standard Rogallo, giving it improved penetration. Although it incorporates a typical trapeze bar/harness arrangement, its higher performance warrants special training. More planning will be necessary in setting up the approach to a landing. Some prior standard Rogallo flight time is definitely an asset to the would-be Cumulus pilot. The longer wing span will make it slower in roll as compared to a standard. The stall is described as being gentle, with the nose dropping through at about 16 mph. Pitch response should be quicker than for a standard. The tightly billowed sail and large nose angle suggest that the longitudinal stability might be less than that of a standard.

Fig. 2-14. The Eipper-Formance Cumulus features truncated tips and a short keel.

103

Takedown/setup times should be within 10 minutes and the Cumulus V may be folded and transported like a standard Rogallo. It is definitely a self-launched hang glider.

The aircraft specifications are:

## Dimensions

| | |
|---|---|
| Wing Span | 29.5 ft |
| Wing Area | 165 sq ft |
| Aspect Ratio | 5.3 |
| Keel Length | 12 ft |
| Leading Edge Length | 18 ft |
| Nose Angle | 109° |
| Billow | 2.5° |

## Weights and Loadings

| | |
|---|---|
| Empty Weight | 39 lbs |
| Max Flying Weight | 240 lbs |
| Useful Load | 201 lbs |

## Performance (at 215 lbs)

| | |
|---|---|
| Best L/D | 7-to-1 |
| Min Sink | 250 fpm |
| Stall Speed | 16 mph |
| Cruise Speed | 25 mph |
| Max Speed | not given |

## DRAGONFLY

The Dragonfly (see Fig. 2-15) is a high-aspect ratic Rogallo hybrid with tip extensions, shaped keel and applied leading-edge pockets. It is controlled solely by means of weight shifting.

The dragonfly's performance will enable the hang glider pilot to fly when the standard Rogallo will not. It requires about half the wind of a standard and yet is capable of being flown faster. Flight near the stall is claimed to be super stable with no tendency to drop a wing, even in a 40° bank. For maximum approach control, it is recommended that the pilot extend his body in a vertical position for drag to degrade the glide ratio. The uncambered, 3° sail billow helps give the wing a very low stall speed. Control is said to be sensitive, and standard Rogallo pilots tend to over-control the glider

Takedown and assembly times are longer than for a standard, but the Dragonfly may be transported like a standard. One must have a USHGA "Hang Four" rating or equivalent or be recommended by at least three flyers of known ability to the Professional Flyers Association or Ultralite Products. Optional "soaring windows" are available for flying in high traffic areas.

The following are the aircraft specifications:

### Dimensions

| | |
|---|---|
| Wing Span | 31.09 ft |
| Wing Area | 202 sq ft |
| Aspect Ratio | 4.79 |
| Keel Length | 11 ft |
| Leading Edge Length | 20 ft |
| Nose Angle | 102° |
| Billow | 3.0° |

Fig. 2-15. The UP "Dragonfly" over Point Fermin, California, rigged supine.

### Weights and Loadings

| | |
|---|---|
| Empty Weight | 43 lbs |
| Max Flying Weight | 238 lbs |
| Useful Load | 195 lbs |

### Performance (at 218 lbs)

| | |
|---|---|
| Best L/D | 6.5-to-1 |
| Min Sink | 258 fpm |
| Stall Speed | 12 mph |
| Cruise Speed | 22.5 mph |
| Max Speed | 38 mph |

## SUPER SWALLOWTAIL 100B

The Super Swallowtail is a high-aspect ratio Rogallo hybrid with battens, roached sail, shaped keel, tapered

Fig. 2-16. The Wills Wing Super Swallowtail uses tip battens instead of tip extensions for an improved taper ratio.

leading-edge pockets and anhedraled cross spar, as illustrated in Fig. 2-16.

The Super Swallowtail performs with the best of the hybrids and is reported as being very stable. According to the manufacturer: "It is easy to pull into a dive, yet hard to keep it there. It can be flown hands-off for minutes at a time—even in turbulent air—returning to straight and level flight on its own after a gust upsets its glide path." This situation seems to be typical of the high-aspect ratio kites, i.e., more sensitivity, but more stability as well. This may be attributed to a large extent to the greater sweepback angle of the quarter chord line. These Rogallo types also generally possess a broader speed range than the standards.

Takedown/setup times are under 10 minutes and the Super Swallowtail may be transported like a standard. Although the manufacturer didn't state so in his literature, it would probably be wise to have a "Hang Four" rating before attempting to fly this glider.

The aircraft specifications are:

### Dimensions

| | |
|---|---|
| Wing Span | 34.1 ft |
| Wing Area | 210 sq ft |
| Aspect Ratio | 5.54 |
| Keel Length | 16 ft |
| Leading Edge Length | 22 ft |
| Nose Angle | 100.44° |
| Billow | 1.92° |

### Weights and Loadings

| | |
|---|---|
| Empty Weight | 44 lbs |
| Max Flying Weight | 244 lbs |
| Useful Load | 200 lbs |

### Performance (at 218 lbs)

| | |
|---|---|
| Best L/D | 7-to-1 |
| Min Sink | 250 fpm |
| Stall Speed | 16 mph |
| Cruise Speed | 22 mph |
| Max Speed | 40 mph |

## SUN IV BC

The Sun IV BC (see Fig. 2-17) is a high-aspect ratio Rogallo hybrid with an "S" shaped keel, fully battened sail and finite tips. It is controlled solely by means of weight shifting.

The Sun IV BC is the latest offering in the Sun Line of quality hang gliders and it offers top level Rogallo performance. This hang glider is reported as having a slow take-off speed and it will soar in wind conditions under 15 mph, depending on terrain, of course. Like other high aspect ratio

Fig. 2-17. The Sun IV, high aspect ratio kite has double deflexers.

Fig. 2-18. The latest version of the Sun IV, the "BC", is fully battened which improves stability and performance.

kites with truncated tips, the Sun IV BC should exhibit greater stability and be more responsive in pitch. Some available options are: soaring windows, aerodynamic streamlining, custom sail patterns, and a variometer. It is reported as having cross-country flight and thermaling capabilities.

Takedown/setup times should be less than 10 minutes and the Sun IV BC may be transported like a standard. A "Hang Four" rating is recommended for aspiring "BC" pilots.

The latest version of the Sun IV is pictured in Fig. 2-18.
The aircraft specifications are as follows:

### Dimensions

| | |
|---|---|
| Wing Span | 31.5 ft |
| Wing Area | 185 sq ft |
| Aspect Ratio | 5.1 |
| Keel Length | 12 ft sail (3 ft stinger) |
| Leading Edge Length | 19 ft |
| Nose Angle | 105° |
| Billow | 2.5° or 3.0° |

### Weights and Loadings

| | |
|---|---|
| Empty Weight | 44 lbs |
| Max Flying Weight | 257 lbs |
| Useful load | 213 lbs |

### Performance ( at 220 lbs )

| | |
|---|---|
| Best L/D | 7.5-to-1 |
| Min Sink | 235 fpm |
| Stall Speed | 12 mph |
| Cruise Speed | 25 mph |
| Max Speed | 45 mph |

## KESTREL

The Kestrel is a high-aspect ratio Rogallo hybrid with a unique ram-air, flight-inflated, airfoil-shaped "bubble" over the center section leading edge. It is controlled solely by means of weight shifting.

The Kestrel illustrated in Fig. 2-19, is the latest in the Sky Sports product line and it represents a new technology for

Fig. 2-19. Tom Peghiny flies his Kestrel at the Grandfather Mountain, N.C., 1975, U.S. National Hang Gliding Championships.

Rogallo wing aerodynamics. The forward third of the wing is covered by a second sail which inflates in flight. This forms an airfoil which is claimed to improve efficiency and give mellow flight characteristics as well. Battens, located from the bubble leading edge back to the trailing edge, improve sail efficiency and stability. Like other high-aspect ratio kites with short keels, the quarter chord sweepback angle is greater than a standard's, which contributes to the Kestrel's pitch response and stability, too. The sail-roach pattern and battens eliminate the need for finite tip extensions as found on some other hybrid Rogallos. A double deflexer system is used on each leading edge to limit airframe deformation.

Takedown/setup times should be less than 10 minutes and the Kestrel may be transported like a standard. It can be flown either seated or prone. A "Hang Four" rating is necessary for aspiring Kestrel pilots.

The aircraft specifications (185 sq ft model) are:

### Dimensions

| | |
|---|---|
| Wing Span | 30.5 ft |
| Wing Area | 185 sq ft |
| Aspect Ratio | 5.0 |
| Keel Length | 11 ft |
| Leading Edge Length | 19.5 ft |
| Nose Angle | 102° |
| Billow | not given |

### Weights and Loadings

| | |
|---|---|
| Empty Weight | 40 lbs |
| Max Flying Weight | 225 lbs |
| Useful Load | 185 lbs |

### Performance (at 200 lbs)

| | |
|---|---|
| Best L/D | 7-to-1 |
| Min Sink | 250 fpm |
| Stall Speed | 15 mph |
| Cruise Speed | 25 mph |
| Max Speed | not given |

Fig. 2-20. The VJ-11 So-Lo, a 1941 design by Volmer Jensen.

## VJ-11 SO-LO

The VJ-11 So-Lo (see Fig. 2-20) is a fabric-covered, wooden-structured, Chanute-type biplane with a full, three-axis aerodynamic control system. It is probably the first hang glider in history to be so controlled.

The So-Lo was originally built during the 1940's while a wartime ban prohibited flying civil aircraft near the coast. It is a well engineered biplane with good stability and control. The glide ratio is better than 6-to-1. For those who like biplanes, this one is probably the best modern example of a Chanute type (Fig. 2-12).

Figure 2-22 is a three-view drawing of the VJ-11.

The following are the aircraft specifications:

### Dimensions

| | |
|---|---|
| Wing Span | 28 ft |
| Wing Area | 225 sq ft |
| Aspect Ratio | 6.97 |

| | |
|---|---|
| Length | 15 ft, 5 in |
| Height | 5 ft |
| Dihedral | 0° |
| Wing Airfoil | Single surfaced, undercambered |
| Tail Airfoil | Flat |

### Weights and Dimensions

| | |
|---|---|
| Empty Weight | 100 lbs |
| Max Flying Weight | 280 lbs |
| Useful Load | 180 lbs |

### Performance (at 235 lbs)

| | |
|---|---|
| Best L/D | 6-to-1 at 20 mph |
| Min Sink | 300 fpm |
| Stall Speed | 15 mph |
| Cruise Speed | 20 mph |
| Max Speed | not given |

Fig. 2-21. The VJ-11. It was built out of frustration caused by a ban on civil flying during WWII.

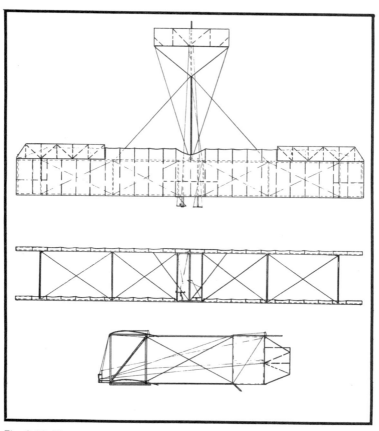

Fig. 2-22. Three-view drawing of the VJ-11. A modern version of Chanute's biplane.

## ICARUS II

The Icarus II, shown in Fig. 2-23, is a fabric-covered, metal-structured, double-surfaced, cable-braced, tailless, constant-chord, swept-back flying wing biplane. Wing tip rudders are used for directional and lateral control, while pitch is controlled by weight shifting.

The Icarus II will perform about the same as the hybrid Rogallo wings. Its cruise speed and wing loading are higher than a kite's giving it better penetration and a broader speed range. It requires a different operating technique due to the

Fig. 2-23. Larry Mauro soars gracefully out over the beach in the Icarus II, which he manufactures.

Fig. 2-24. Taras Kiceniuk, the designer, "butt" skimming in his Icarus II.

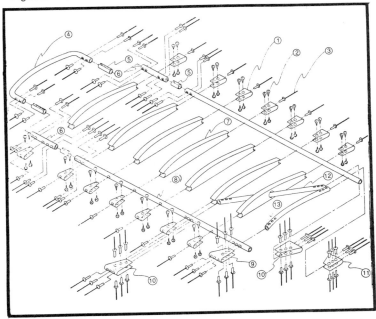

Fig. 2-25. Construction details of the Icarus II kit by Ultralight Flying Machines.

116

fact that it has a hang-tube, parallel-bar arrangement built into the lower wing. Each hang tube has a twist grip mounted on it and connected to the tip rudders via control lines. A swing seat is suspended from the upper wing and allows the pilot to alter pitch. Once flying, one must brace his feet on the front tube of the lower wing center section so that he is able to push back to pitch the nose up (see Fig. 2-24). Deflecting one rudder at a time produces a turn and bank about that rudder. Deflecting both rudders simultaneously, creates additional drag and steepens the angle of descent giving the pilot control over his glide ratio.

Takedown and assembly times are about 20 minutes, and the Icarus II must be carried in a special roof rack box to prevent transport damage. The Icarus II can be self-launched. It takes about 100 hours to build one from a kit. Both kits and factory-built units are available from Ultralight Flying Machines.

The construction details of the Icarus II are illustrated in Fig. 2-25, and Fig. 2-26 is a three-view drawing of this biplane.

The aircraft specifications are as follows:

### Dimensions

| | |
|---|---|
| Wing Span | 30 ft |
| Wing Area | 200 sq ft |
| Aspect Ratio | 9.0 |
| Length | 9 ft |
| Height | 6 ft |
| Dihedral | 7.5° |
| Wing Airfoil | double surface, reflex |
| Tail Airfoil | no tail |

### Weights and Loadings

| | |
|---|---|
| Empty Weight | 55 lbs |
| Max Flying Weight | 260 lbs |
| Useful Load | 210 lbs |

### Performance (at 215 lbs)

| | |
|---|---|
| Best L/D | 7-to-1 |
| Min Sink | 200 fpm |
| Stall Speed | 18 mph |
| Cruise Speed | 25 mph |
| Max Speed | 40 mph |

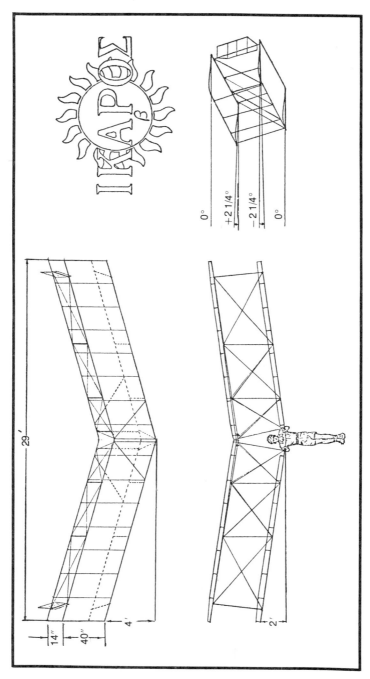

Fig. 2-26. Three-view drawing of the Icarus II flying wing biplane.

## VALKYRIE

The Valkyrie (Fig. 2-27) is a fabric-covered metal-structured, single-surfaced, cable-braced, tailless, flying wing of constant chord and straight leading edge. Wing tip rudders are used for directional and lateral control, while pitch control is achieved solely by means of weight shifting.

The Valkyrie will out perform the hybrid Rogallos with a glide ratio of 8 to 1. Its cruise speed is similar to a kite's, while its higher wing loading should provide for improved penetration. Kite pilots should be able to adapt to its form of control without too much difficulty, since it is basically a weight shift situation. Pitch is pure weight shift while the wing tip rudders (pictured in Fig. 2-28) may be deflected to induce drag for either turning or glide path control. Deflecting one rudder at a time produces a turn and bank about the deflected rudder, while deflecting both rudders simultaneously causes the glide angle to steepen.

Fig. 2-27. Bill Wolf's unique Valkyrie is a flying wing with no sweepback.

Fig. 2-28. The Valkyrie is readied for launch.

Takedown/setup times are about ten minutes without tools, and the Valkyrie should be carried on a special rack to minimize damage. The Valkyrie can be self-launched. Pilot suspension is via typical swing seat. It takes about 50 to 60 hours to build a kit.

Figure 2-29 is a three-view drawing of the Valkyrie.

The aircraft specifications are as follows:

### Dimensions

| | |
|---|---|
| Wing Span | 30 ft-9 in. |
| Wing Area | 138 sq ft |
| Aspect Ratio | 6.8 |
| Length | 6 ft, 3 in. |
| Height | 7 ft, 6 in. |
| Dihedral | 5° |
| Wing Airfoil | single surface, reflex |
| Tail Airfoil | no tail |

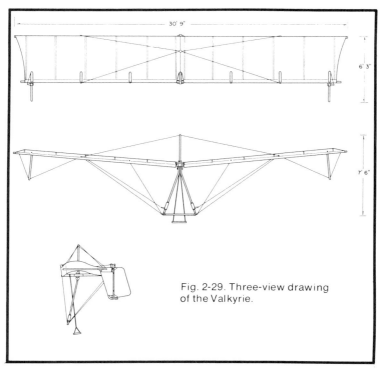

Fig. 2-29. Three-view drawing of the Valkyrie.

Fig. 2-30. Mountain Green's Fledgling is a swept-back, flying wing with drag rudders.

### Weights and Loadings

| | |
|---|---|
| Empty Weight | 50 lbs |
| Max Flying Weight | 250 lbs |
| Useful Load | 125 to 200 lbs |

### Performance (at 210 lbs)

| | |
|---|---|
| Best L/D | 8-to-1 |
| Min Sink | 180 fpm |
| Stall Speed | 15 mph |
| Cruise Speed | 20 mph |
| Max Speed | 45 mph |

## FLEDGLING

The Fledgling (Fig. 2-30) is a fabric-covered, metal-structured, single-surfaced, cable-braced, tailless, tapered-chord, swept-back flying wing monoplane. Wing tip rudders are used for directional and lateral control while pitch is controlled by weight shifting.

The Fledgling will outperform the hybrid Rogallo wings. Its cruise speed and wing loading are higher than a kite's which gives it improved penetration and a broad speed range. Its pilot suspension system is the typical kite swing seat and trapeze-bar arrangement. This setup ought to allow for easy transition from kites. Pitch control is done by weight shifting while the wing tip rudders are actuated by sideways body movements via cords connected to the harness. Only one rudder can be deflected at once.

Takedown/setup times are about 15 minutes without any tools required. The Fledgling folds to a package similar to that of a kite and can be carried on a typical kite carrying rack. The Fledgling can be self-launched.

Figure 2-31 is a three-view drawing of the Fledgling.

The aircraft specifications are:

### Dimensions

| | |
|---|---|
| Wing Span | 29 ft |
| Wing Area | 142 sq ft |
| Aspect Ratio | 5.92 |
| Length | 10 ft |
| Height | 8 ft |
| Dihedral | 5° |
| Wing Airfoil | single surface, reflex |
| Tail Airfoil | no tail |

### Weights and Loadings

| | |
|---|---|
| Empty Weight | 50 lbs |
| Max Flying Weight | 240 lbs |
| Useful Load | 190 lbs |

### Performance (at 210 lbs)

| | |
|---|---|
| Best L/D | 8-to-1 |
| Min Sink | 225 fpm |
| Stall Speed | 16 mph |
| Cruise Speed | 25 mph |
| Max Speed | 40 mph |

### ICARUS V

The Icarus V (see Fig. 2-32) is a fabric-covered, metal-structured, double-surfaced, cable-braced, tailless,

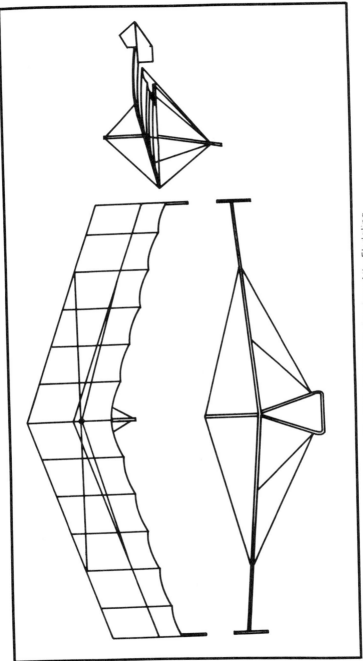

Fig. 2-31. Three-view drawing of the Fledgling.

constant-chord, swept-back flying wing monoplane. Wing tip rudders are used for directional and lateral control, while pitch is controlled by means of weight shifting.

The Icarus V will outperform most any hang glider in existence today. Its cruise speed and wing loading are higher than a kite's, which allows for improved penetration and a broader speed range. It is quite different from a kite and requires special training to operate. The typical trapeze arrangement is absent, and is replaced by a hang "cage" with parallel bars and a swing seat. Care must be taken to fly with one's feet braced against the front tube to aid   pushing-out (i.e.,pitching-up). The strength of leg muscles is required for most effective pitch control. Deflecting one rudder at a time produces a turn and bank about the deflected rudder. Deflecting both rudders simultaneously creates drag and steepens the angle of descent, much like spoilers on a conventional sailplane.

Takedown/setup times are about 30 minutes, and the Icarus V must be carried in a special roof rack box to prevent damage in transport. The Icarus V can be self-launched. It takes about 200 hours to build one from a kit.

A three-view drawing of the Icarus V is depicted in Fig. 2-33.

Fig. 2-32. The Icarus V by Free-Flight Systems.

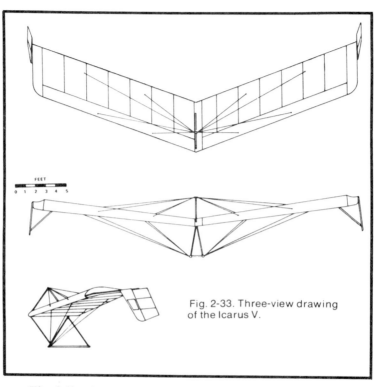

Fig. 2-33. Three-view drawing of the Icarus V.

The following are the aircraft specifications:

### Dimensions

| | |
|---|---|
| Wing Span | 32 ft |
| Wing Area | 160 sq ft |
| Aspect Ratio | 6.4 |
| Length | 12 ft, 10 in. |
| Height | 6 ft, 2 in. |
| Dihedral | 7° |
| Wing Airfoil | TK 7315 |
| Tail Airfoil | no tail |

### Weights and Loadings

| | |
|---|---|
| Empty Weight | 65 lbs |
| Max Flying Weight | 255 lbs |
| Useful Load | 190 lbs |

**Performance** (at 225 lbs)

| | |
|---|---|
| Best L/D | 10-t0-1 |
| Min Sink | 180 fpm |
| Stall Speed | 16 mph |
| Cruise Speed | 24 mph |
| Max Speed | 50 mph |

## SUNSEED

The Sunseed, as portrayed in Fig. 2-34, is a fabric-covered, metal-structured, partially double-surfaced, cable-braced, tailless, constant-chord, swept-back flying wing monoplane with tapered, anhedraled tips. Wing tip "draggons" (essentially, up only deflecting ailerons) are used for directional, lateral and glide-path control. Pitch is controlled by means of weight shifting.

The Sunseed will out-fly practically any hang glider available today. Its cruise speed and wing loading are higher than a kite's, giving it improved penetration. It uses a trapeze bar/swing seat arrangement similar to a kite's, but its higher

Fig. 2-34. Robert Trampenau and his unique Sunseed, a swept-back, flying wing with anhedralled tips and draggons.

127

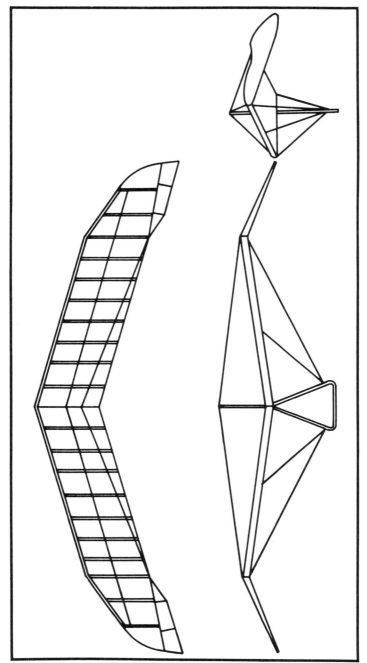

Fig. 2-35. Three-view drawing of the Sunseed.

performance will certainly require special training. The landing distance required is much greater than a kite's and more planning is necessary to set it down. The draggons can be deflected either singly, for a turn, or jointly, for a steeper descent. The unique drooped tip configuration aids the craft in actually turning toward a side gust, automatically.

Takedown/setup times are about 10 minutes, and the Sunseed folds into a package about the size of a Rogallo. The Sunseed can be self-launched.

Figure 2-35 is a three-view drawing of the Sunseed.

The aircraft specifications are:

### Dimensions

| | |
|---|---|
| Wing Span | 32 ft, 10 in. |
| Wing Area | 128.5 sq ft |
| Aspect Ratio | 8.37 |
| Length | 9 ft |
| Height | 7 ft |
| Dihedral | 8° |
| Wing Airfoil | 14% top, reflex |
| Tail Airfoil | no tail |

### Weights and Loadings

| | |
|---|---|
| Empty Weight | 50 lbs |
| Max Flying Weight | 250 lbs |
| Useful Load | 200 lbs |

### Performance (at 210 lbs)

| | |
|---|---|
| Best L/D | 11-t0-1 |
| Min Sink | 174 fpm |
| Stall Speed | 16 mph |
| Cruise Speed | 24 mph |
| Max Speed | 40 mph |

## QUICKSILVER "C"

The Quicksilver is a fabric-covered, metal-structured, cable-braced monoplane employing weight shift, coupled with rudder, for control (see Fig. 2-36).

In flight, it will generally outperform the hybrid Rogallos with a glide ratio of 7 to 1. Its cruise speed and wing loading

Fig. 2-36. Jack Schroeder likes to fly his Quicksilver supine for comfort and performance.

Fig. 2-37. The Quicksilver in a coordinated turn.

are higher than for most kites, thus, giving it improved penetration. Its response in roll is sluggish, while pitch and yaw seem to be adequate. Figure 2-37 reveals the Quicksilver in a coordinated turn. Most kite pilots should adapt to its form of control without too much difficulty, since it is basically a weight shift glider. The rudder is controlled by cords attached to the harness or swing seat suspension.

Takedown/setup times are about 15 minutes without tools, and the Quicksilver "C" should be carried on a special roof rack to minimize damage in handling. An assistant is required during assembly and launch to hold the tail up, off the ground, until it is flying. Pilot suspension is via typical swing seat.

Figure 2-38 depicts a design drawing of the Quicksilver, and Fig. 2-39 is a three-view drawing of this monoplane.

The following are the aircraft specifications:

### Dimensions

| | |
|---|---|
| Wing Span | 32 ft |
| Wing Area | 160 sq ft |
| Aspect Ratio | 6.4 |
| Length | 13 ft |
| Height | 9 ft, 6 in. |
| Dihedral | 5° |
| Wing Airfoil | Lovejoy 6.70 × 15 |
| Tail Airfoil | Flat |

### Weights and Loadings

| | |
|---|---|
| Empty Weight | 65 lbs |
| Max Flying Weight | 295 lbs |
| Useful Load | 150 to 230 lbs |

### Performance (at 225 lbs)

| | |
|---|---|
| Best L/D | 7-to-1 at cruise |
| Min Sink | 180 fpm |
| Stall Speed | 15 mph |
| Cruise Speed | 20 mph |
| Max Speed | 45 mph |

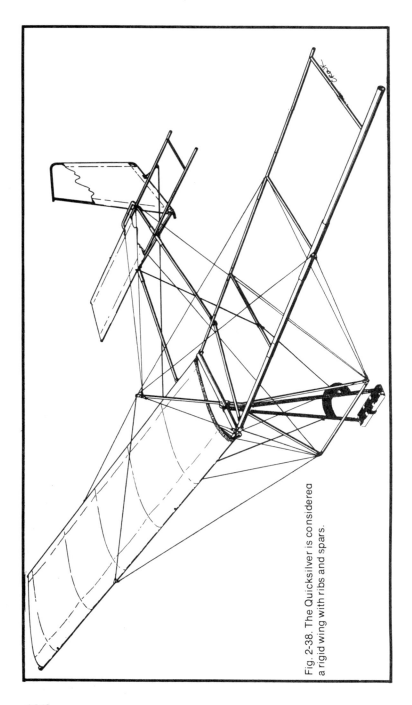

Fig. 2-38. The Quicksilver is considered a rigid wing with ribs and spars.

## VJ-23 SWINGWING

The VJ-23 Swingwing (see Figs. 2-40 and 2-41) is a fabric-covered, wooden-structured, cantilever monoplane with a joy stick, connected to a full, three-axis aerodynamic control system. The rudder and ailerons are coupled.

In flight, it will outperform almost any hang glider in existence. It is a masterpiece of engineering and its stability and control are superb. The glide ratio is 9 to 1 and it will fly when nothing else can. Its cruise speed and wing loading are higher than for most kites, giving it superior penetration. Its super thick, high-lift wing is quite efficient and allows for gentle, tip-toe landings.

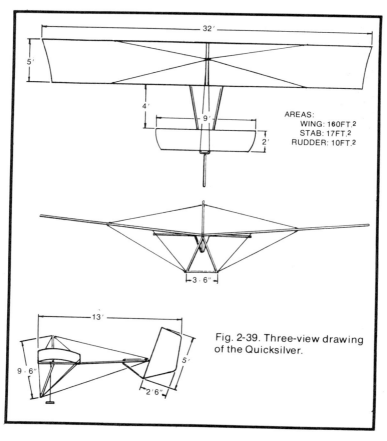

AREAS:
WING: 160 FT.2
STAB: 17 FT.2
RUDDER: 10 FT.2

Fig. 2-39. Three-view drawing of the Quicksilver.

Fig. 2-40. At 64, Volmer Jensen is the oldest active hang glider pilot and designer.

Unlike most other hang gliders, the VJ-23 (in fact, the entire VJ series) employs full, three-axis aerodynamic controls instead of weight shifting. An aircraft type joy stick is mounted forward on the right hang bar and connects to the control surfaces via 1/16 in. diameter aircraft cables. Control action is similar to a conventional aircraft's except the rudder pedals, as found in airplanes, are replaced by coupling and rudder and ailerons to the stick side motions. This control system provides for coordinated turns and gives excellent response in flight. The ailerons work differentially. That is to say, the one going up goes up more than the one going down, goes down. This equalizes the drag from each aileron, preventing "adverse aileron yaw."

The Swingwing weighs in at a good 100 pounds which makes self-launching difficult unless the wind is blowing at more than 10 mph, when the draft will lift its own weight. On-site assembly takes about 20 minutes with an assistant. A trailer is normally used for transportation to and from the flying site. Suspension is by the armpits and a special seat that is hung from the hang bars. The seat should be used, as a sudden up gust, or lift, could force one to fall out. It takes about 400 hours to build this airplane-like hang glider from scratch.

Fig. 2-41. Volmer soars when kites can't.

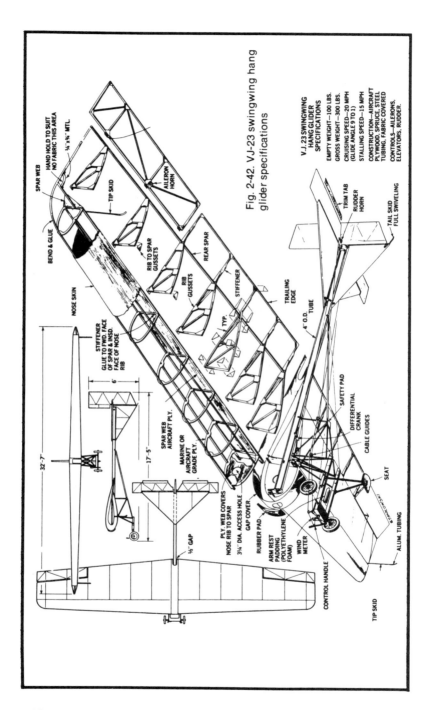

Fig. 2-42. VJ-23 swingwing hang glider specifications

V.J.23 SWINGWING HANG GLIDER SPECIFICATIONS

EMPTY WEIGHT—100 LBS.
GROSS WEIGHT—300 LBS.
CRUISING SPEED—20 MPH (GLIDE ANGLE 9 TO 1)
STALLING SPEED—15 MPH
CONSTRUCTION—AIRCRAFT PLYWOOD, SPRUCE, STEEL TUBING, FABRIC COVERED
CONTROLS—AILERONS, ELEVATORS, RUDDER.

HAND HOLD TO SUIT
NO FABRIC THIS AREA
¼ x ¾" MTL.

SPAR WEB

TIP SKID

AILERON HORN

BEND & GLUE

RIB TO SPAR GUSSETS

REAR SPAR

RIB GUSSETS

STIFFENER

NOSE SKIN

TYP.

TRAILING EDGE

STIFFENER
GLUE TO FWD. FACE OF SPAR & INSD. FACE OF NOSE RIB

4" O.D. TUBE

TRIM TAB
RUDDER HORN

TAIL SKID FULL SWIVELING

SAFETY PAD

DIFFERENTIAL CRANK

SPAR WEB AIRCRAFT PLY.

MARINE OR AIRCRAFT GRADE PLY.

CABLE GUIDES

6

32'-7"

17'-5"

SEAT

PLY. WEB COVERS
NOSE RIB TO SPAR
3¾" DIA. ACCESS HOLE
GAP COVER

½" GAP

RUBBER PAD

ARM REST PADDING (POLYETHYLENE FOAM)

WIND METER

ALUM. TUBING

CONTROL HANDLE

TIP SKID

136

The VJ-23 Swingwing specifications are depicted in Fig. 2-42.

The aircraft specifications are as follows:

### Dimensions

| | |
|---|---|
| Wing Span | 32 ft, 7 in. |
| Wing Area | 179 sq ft |
| Aspect Ratio | 5.93 |
| Length | 17 ft, 5 in. |
| Height | 6 ft |
| Dihedral | 0° |
| Wing Airfoil | culver |
| Tail Airfoil | flat |

### Weights and Loadings

| | |
|---|---|
| Empty Weight | 100 lbs |
| Max Flying Weight | 300 lbs |
| Useful Load | 200 lbs |

### Performance (at 235 lbs)

| | |
|---|---|
| Best L/D | 9-to-1 at cruise |
| Min Sink | 180 fpm |
| Stall Speed | 15 mph |
| Cruise Speed | 20 mph |
| Max Speed | not given |

## VJ-24 SUNFUN

The VJ-24 Sunfun, is a fabric-covered, metal-structured, strut-braced monoplane with a joy stick connected to a full, three-axis aerodynamic control system. The rudder and ailerons are coupled (see Figs. 2-43 and 2-44).

Basically, the Sunfun performs exactly like the Swingwing. The obvious changes are a rectangular wing with increased aspect ratio and lift struts bracing the wing. The increased aspect ratio makes up for the extra drag created by the struts. The wooden structure of the VJ-23 was also replaced by an aluminum tubing, sheet and pop rivet construction. This change has cut the total building time in half, or 200 hours.

Fig. 2-43. Volmer flies his metal structured VJ-24 Sunfun with ease.

Fig. 2-44. The VJ-24 requires only 200 hours to build. Half the time required for the "23."

The Sunfun has ten pounds on the Swingwing and requires the same setup time and help. Launching must be done into a wind. A trailer is used to transport it to and from the flying site. For those who prefer working with metal, the Sunfun could be one's ideal.

Figure 2-45 is a three view drawing of the VJ-24 Sunfun.

The aircraft specifications are:

### Dimensions

| | |
|---|---|
| Wing Span | 36 ft, 6 in. |
| Wing Area | 163 sq ft |
| Aspect Ratio | 8.17 |
| Length | 18 ft |
| Height | 6 ft |
| Dihedral | 1° |
| Wing Airfoil | culver |
| Tail Airfoil | flat |

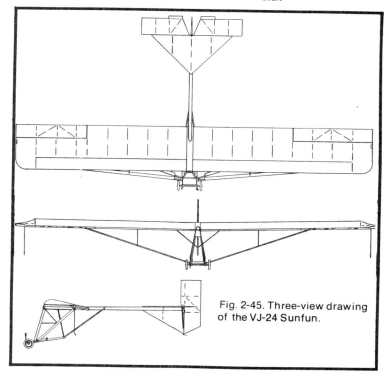

Fig. 2-45. Three-view drawing of the VJ-24 Sunfun.

## Weights and Loadings

| | |
|---|---|
| Empty Weight | 110 lbs |
| Max Flying Weight | 310 lbs |
| Useful Load | 200 lbs |

## Performance (at 245 lbs)

| | |
|---|---|
| Best L/D | 9-to-1 at cruise |
| Min Sink | 200 fpm |
| Stall Speed | 15 mph |
| Cruise Speed | 20 mph |
| Max Speed | not given |

### SUPER FLOATER

The Super Floater (see Figs. 2-46 and 2-47) is a fabric-covered, metal-structured, double-surfaced, strut-braced, tapered-chord monoplane. It has a two-axis (rudder and elevator) aerodynamic control system. It does not use weight shifting in any way.

Fig. 2-46. The Super Floater is foot launched but may be landed on its single wheel.

Fig. 2-47. Joy stick operated tail surfaces control the high performance Super Floater.

The Super Floater will outperform most any hang glider available today. In fact, it is not really a hang glider, as it is commonly defined but, instead, a foot-launched sailplane. It is foot-launched but may be landed on its single wheel or on the pilot's feet, as desired. The fuselage structure is fabric covered and makes for a good fairing, located behind the pilot. The nose framework is also designed to be faired in, if desired. The pilot flys on a seat in a semi-supine position, with his legs braced against the front tubes. A joy stick is operated by his right hand to control the rudder and elevator.

Takedown and setup times are about 30 minutes. The tail surfaces and wings are removable for transport which will probably require a trailer or special rack.

A three-view drawing of the Super Floater is depicted in Fig. 2-48.

The following are the aircraft specifications:

### Dimensions

| | |
|---|---|
| Wing Span | 32 ft |
| Wing Area | 132 sq ft |
| Aspect Ratio | 7.35 |

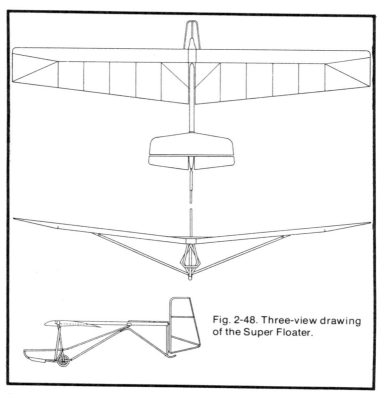

Fig. 2-48. Three-view drawing of the Super Floater.

| Length | 16 ft |
|---|---|
| Height | 5 ft, 6 in. |
| Dihedral | 6.5° |
| Wing Airfoil | 12% thick original |
| Tail Airfoil | flat |

### Weights and Loadings

| Empty Weight | 90 lbs |
|---|---|
| Max Flying Weight | 280 lbs |
| Useful Load | 190 lbs |

### Performance (at 270 lbs)

| Best L/D | 12-to-1 |
|---|---|
| Min Sink | 174 fpm |
| Stall Speed | 18 mph |
| Cruise Speed | 26 mph |
| Max Speed | 50 mph |

# Chapter 3
# Hang Gliding Technique

## HANG GLIDING TECHNIQUE

The beginner is confronted with a myriad of makes and types of hang gliders: rigid wing monoplanes, semi-rigid wing monoplanes, non-swept flying wings, swept back flying wings, biplanes of conventional and flying wing form, high aspect ratio kites and, of course, the so-called "standard" Rogallo wing (see Fig. 3-1). So how does one go about choosing the one which is right for him? This chapter should help one make the right decision.

## HANG GLIDER SELECTION

For a non-FAA type rated pilot with no knowledge of flight, the easiest craft to learn how to hang glide is probably a Rogallo kite. What's more, most hang gliding schools start the beginner out this way. It is an accepted and well-proven design for learning the basics of hang gliding.

Fig. 3-1. The beginning hang glider pilot has the most fantastic experiences of his life ahead of him. He'll actually be able to "fly like a bird."

Now, there are those who advocate the beginner get his first hang gliding experience in a standard Rogallo, the idea being that its basic simplicity of control and ease of handling will help the neophyte. It is suggested by many that weight shifting (which is how a Rogallo is controlled) is an instinctive motion, i.e., the body weight is shifted in the desired direction. This, in fact, may be true for the non-aeronautically educated person, but what about an FAA type rated pilot? Certainly, he is used to the motions of a control stick rather than his body! Well, experience in hang glider schools has proven that pilot's don't do any better than non-pilots when it comes to learning to fly a Rogallo; however, pilots relate quite readily to an aerodynamically controlled hang glider. Therefore, the decision as to which hang glider to choose is based on the individual.

Once the decision has been made to start hang gliding in a kite, the right size kite must be chosen according to one's particular body weight. Most standard kites flying today operate at a wing loading of one pound per square foot. This is to say that each square foot of projected sail area supports, or lifts, one pound of weight. Over the years, this has proven to be a good number for all around performance and control. For instance, a weight of the person (160 pounds), including clothing plus the weight of the kite (40 pounds) adds up to 200 pounds to be supported by 200 square feet, thus giving the proper wing loading of 1 pound per square foot! To carry this example one step further, a good choice is a 17′ keel, 90° nose angle kite or a 18′ keel, 80° nose angle kite. There is more sail area per keel length in a 90° nose angle kite.

If a kite is chosen that is too large for a person's particular weight it will be easier to launch from a shallower slope in a lighter wind, but will not be as controllable under normal conditions. On the other hand, if a kite is selected that is too small for a person, he'll have to run too fast to take-off and land though his control response will improve. For best all around performance under normal conditions, it is a good idea to fly at one pound per square foot wing loading. Also, check with the manufacturer, dealer or flight school for the proper size kite.

If one is an FAA type rated pilot with at least a glider license, then he'll probably learn hang gliding better in a control stick operated hang glider. He'll be much more at ease and be more familiar with the control stick situation. If he can find a school that offers this type of hang glider then he's in luck. Since aerodynamic controls are normally found on the higher performance hang gliders, they are usually more expensive and require a larger landing area than a kite. If control stick hang glider instruction is difficult to find in one's area, it might still be a good idea to check out a Rogallo-oriented school anyway. They know hang gliding and can advise one further.

At any rate, if one's heart is set on a higher performing, aerodynamically controlled hang glider then by all means look into what's available. Flying a kite and flying a higher performance craft are worlds apart. One may never even fly a kite or wish to. It's up to the individual. See the chapter on *Typical Hang Gliders* before making a decision.

## TRANSPORTING

Once the hang glider has been selected and purchased or constructed, it will have to be transported to a flying site, that is, unless a person is lucky enough to live on a suitable mountain or beach! At any rate, transporting a standard Rogallo is really a simple matter. All it normally requires is a good, sturdy ski rack for the car, a special bag for the kite, ropes and shock cords. The shock cords (or short ropes) can be used to tie the kite to the rack itself, while longer lengths of rope may be used to secure the front and rear of the kite to the bumpers. For the best results, regarding wear against the car bumpers, use nylon rope. Inside edges of bumpers can be quite sharp and eventually cut through the rope due to road vibrations, which may allow the kite to fall off the car.

While a kite bag is not an absolute necessity, it's certainly a good thing to have and use. Otherwise, the sail must be furled and securely tied with a long length of rope so that it doesn't flap in the breeze. Actually, cruising along at highway speeds, the wind is so violent that it will tear a loose piece of fabric to shreds! The wind may even pull a flapping sail kite off the car! Then too, a bag will protect a sail and prevent it from wearing and tearing at the areas at which it contacts the roof rack.

In addition to the normally available roof and ski racks, a specially designed Rogallo rack is being manufactured, complete with locks.

Transporting a monoplane or other high performance type hang glider, may be more difficult than a kite. Most rigid wings will not collapse, and need either a special transport box or even a trailer to haul around. Check with the manufacturer on this.

There is one type of high performance monoplane that is capable of being folded and car topped like a Rogallo. See the chapter on *Typical Hang Gliders* for more details.

An important point is that, since a car topped hang glider will most likely over hang the car's bumpers, it is wise to check on state laws regarding this. Many states require any over hang in excess of a certain amount to have a red flag or maybe even lights at the very aft end. If the glider must be trailered, it will most likely require a licensed trailer with lights. Be legal. Be safe when transporting your glider on the highways.

Another important item to keep in mind is the packing and carrying of a complete tool and spare parts kit. It's no fun to get to the flying site, which may be hours away from home, and find a wing nut or turnbuckle barrel missing. Always carry spares. Also, in disassembling the hang glider, make sure all hand tightened fasteners are tight before bagging. This should practically eliminate losing parts in transit.

## FLYING SITE SELECTION

A hang glider can be flown anywhere there is a suitably sloped, open land area facing the wind. A sand dune or grass covered hillside with a slope of about one foot of rise for every three feet of horizontal and a long flat area at the bottom is about right for a beginner with a standard Rogallo. (see Fig. 3-2). Since the glide ratio of kite is around 4 to 1, the 3 to 1 slope will allow for an easy launch while not letting a person gain too much height. The wind should be blowing directly up the hill at 10 mph or less. Be sure it is steady and

Fig. 3-2. A flyer sniffs the salty sea air of Cape Cod, waiting for the right moment to launch.

free of any gusts or turbulence that may dump one or cause other handling difficulties.

For more advanced gliders with a higher glide ratio, the slope requirements will be less. In general, a slope is needed that is about 75% of the glide ratio to make a good takeoff. Also, the higher the wind, the less slope is needed to take-off and vice versa. If the glider has a 10 to 1 glide ratio, then a 7.5 to 1 slope ought to be steep enough to take-off from. A landing area much larger than that for a Rogallo will be necessary.

If a person is lucky enough to live near a sand dune area, great! Sand is very forgiving of falls and, if located on a beach, will most likely have very smooth winds coming off the water. Be sure to find out ahead of time if the area is permissable to fly from. Many sand dunes are "protected" as erosion control area and one will be promptly asked to leave them. Fly only where it is permitted and considered safe. If there are sun bathers laying around on the beach below, it sould be very unwise to attempt launching and flying over those areas. Be thoughtful of others.

Sand areas away from the beach can be found in what are known as sand pits. These are sometimes used by state highway departments for winter road sanding operations or by sand and gravel companies. If they are exposed to the prevailing wind and have a large field or open area in front of them, then they are probably suitable for learning. If they are "dug out" of the ground, sheltered by trees or high walls, then don't try to fly there. Turbulence and "dead air" are likely to be prevalent. In any case, check with the owners first.

If sand areas are not nearby, don't despair. A nice, grass covered hill can be an excellent alternative. While not quite as soft and forgiving as sand, it will still be very useful for training purposes. In fact, many ski slopes are set up for hang gliding and more are following the example. The wide, shallower slope of a beginners ski area is quite often excellent for the hang gliding novice; the steeper, higher and narrower slopes being reserved for the experts and advanced flyers. A wide slope is essential for beginners to allow freedom of movement while learning to turn and also to minimize the turbulence of trees and buildings that may be on or near the slope.

Even if a ski slope or sand dune is not within easy reach, many areas have hills and treeless mountains that may be suitable. In any case, be sure the selected area is free of rocks, buildings, power lines and other obstructions which may make it unsafe for flight operations. Especially when learning, an impossible situation is to be avoided. The takeoff area, flight path and landing area should be completely open and free of all obstructions.

Incidentally, for a learning situation, all that is needed is a 50' vertical drop from take off to landing. At a 4 to 1 glide one

Fig. 3-3. After rigging the keel cables, a kite will stand without support.

can fly for 200 feet and 7 seconds. This should be adequate activity to keep the beginner busy. Of course, he'll start on the level anyway and gradually work his way to the top.

## ASSEMBLY FOR FLIGHT

First, the kite must be removed from the car. Be careful not to pick it up and swing it around or it may strike another car or person. Walk straight out from the car. Two people can remove it more easily: one taking the nose while the other handles the tail.

After the glider has been removed from the car top, take it to an area that's out of the way of actual flying or training operation. It wouldn't be wise in a landing area where one might cause an accident and injury to oneself or a flyer. At any rate, set the folded glider on the ground with the nose pointed directly into the wind and remove the transport bag. Next, rig the keel turnbuckle so that only three threads are engaged. The kite should stand alone as shown in Fig. 3-3. Now, attach the side turnbuckles to the three threads in the engaged position. Take one wing, swing it out and fasten it to the cross member (see Fig. 3-4). Then, swing the other wing out and connect it to the cross member. (A particular glider design may call for a different assembly procedure. Consult the manufacturer's suggested sequence.)

At this point, secure the bottom rigging to the control bar. All the while, the nose should be on the ground facing into the wind. Now, go around and tighten all the turnbuckles to the point that there is no slop or slack in the cables. This is important, for sloppy rigging will lead to sloppy control and may overstress bolts, cables or aluminum members by inducing sudden impact loads on the structure.

An important thing to keep in mind while rigging the glider is to check if any wire end thimbles are "hung-up" on a tang or turnbuckle. If something is going together with more difficulty than normal, check the cable ends. It's most likely a hung up thimble. If a rigging is forced, the thimble may be bent, necessitating a replacement of the entire cable! So don't force anything. It should all go together easily.

Gliders that employ aerodynamic control systems will have to be rigged as well. Be certain that right control gives

Fig. 3-4. Pull out one wing and then the other before completing assembly.

right rudder, spoiler or aileron, as the case may be, and up control gives up elevator and vice versa. As in the case of the structural rigging, be sure no thimbles are hung up or otherwise damaged. The control system should go together easily. Be sure all control cables are in excellent condition as well as their terminals and control sticks or twist grips. Check all pulleys and pulley guides for signs of wear and proper alignment. All cables should be tight with no slack. After all, one wants the control inputs to be transmitted, when given. The glider should now be completely assembled and ready to be pre-flight inspected.

One final item: See that the harness-to-kite hardware is in place and secure. Also, the harness, its associated items and safety helmet should be close by and ready for use.

## PRE-FLIGHT INSPECTION

The single most important thing one can and must do each time before flying his glider is to give it a thorough pre-flight inspection. This simply cannot be overemphasized for one's life is literally "hanging in the balance". Every single detail must be checked, and it's best to have a routine procedure for doing so.

After the glider is completely rigged, one may begin. Starting at the heart of the kite, inspect the harness pick up.

Be sure the fabric is in good shape as well as any associated hardware items. Also inspect the cross-member sleeve and see that its bolt is securely fastened. Look, also, at the control frame pivot bolt or pin for secureness of fastening. Next, look at the control bar. Check all the fittings, bolts and cable terminals that attach to it. Don't let a bent thimble or frayed cable go unnoticed. Repair or replace. Since a control bar is in contact with the ground, make sure all dirt is removed before inspection of it. Dirt could conceal a weak, loose, or missing part.

Next, follow the side bottom cables out to the cross member to leading edge intersection. Check all fittings, cable terminals, nuts, etc; look at the turnbuckle, its devices and cotter pin. Run your hand along the forward leading edge, feeling that it is in order and looking for any rips in the sail. Look at the top nose plate and see that all nuts are securely fastened. Check the keel turnbuckle and its associated hardware. Look over the front of the sail for any damage.

Pick up the nose of the glider (it should be facing into the wind) and check the front bottom rigging terminals and tangs. Set the nose down again and run a hand along the other forward leading edge. Check the sail and the cross member to leading-edge intersection, and inspect the hardware, as on the other wing. Run a hand along the aft leading edge, looking at the sail and checking the aft sail anchoring. If one side of the sail were to become loose in flight, it would slide forward and cause the glider to roll uncontrollably into the ground. Walk along the trailing edge, looking at the sail, until you reach the aft keel. Inspect all hardware and cable terminals. Also, see that the sail is anchored securely. If the aft keel portion of the sail were to slide forward it would cause the kite to enter a deep stall from which one may not be able to recover. One instance of this happening was published a while back. The aft-keel sail stays let go and the kite went into a deep stall. Luckily, the pilot was able to crawl out over the control bar and grab a hold of the front bottom cables and successfully land the glider. You might not be so lucky, so be sure the sail is secure. (By the way, the particular kite involved used only a single sheet metal screw to hold on the sail!) Now walk along the other wing trailing edge to inspect it and stop when arriving at the opposite wing tip (or aft leading edge) and see that the aft-sail stays are secure. Be certain the grommets are not pulling out from the fabric. Run a hand along this aft leading edge looking over the sail, and stop when coming to the cross member-to-leading edge intersection, the inspection starting point.

Now, look at the king post and its associated hardware. See that all is in order.

As a final step in this pre-flight inspection, step back, away from the glider and see that it looks good (and that everything is properly aligned and squared). All tubes should be straight, except for perhaps some aft-keel reflex. Hold the glider by its nose and sight down the leading edge and keel to check this out. The kite should now be ready for flight.

If flying a monoplane or other higher performing, aerodynamically controlled glider, give another check to the controls. See that they do exactly what they are supposed to do. Let's not take off only to discover that right and left are reversed and up and down are opposite what they should be. Also, see that any other particulars, such as control surfaces and hinges are properly aligned and working freely.

## HANG GLIDING FAMILIARIZATION

After the beginner "preflights," he is still not ready to fly. He must first become familiar with the glider and how to handle it on the ground. The first thing he must be able to do is pick the glider up and walk around with it. One method is to stoop in the control frame and wrap an arm around each upright (see Fig. 3-5). As he stands up, he should wedge his shoulders between the upper part of the control frame uprights and lift the glider up off the ground. To balance the craft, the shoulders should be used as pivot points and the kite should be rocked with hands and arms. Practice walking around with the kite, picking it up and setting it down, always into the wind. If a gust comes along, don't be afraid to "dump" the kite. Get that nose down, fast. It won't break. If a gust proves to be too much and the kite starts to get "blown over backwards," let it go. There will be less chance for damage. If one tries to resist its

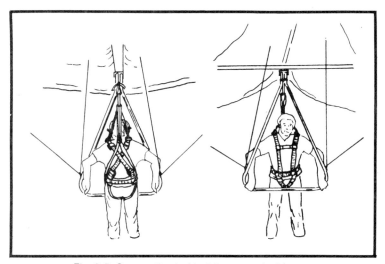

Fig. 3-5. One method of holding a control frame.

blowing over, the weight of the resistance is likely to break a wing tip or aft keel tube and probably rip the sail.

Once a kite has been blown over backwards, and its resting on its king post, the best way to right it is to use the wind that caused the upset to one's advantage. Pick up the nose and windward side of the glider, and rotate on the king post until the upwind leading edge is perpendicular to the wind. Lift this leading edge higher and allow it to catch some wind and be flipped over and right side up. A little practice and this procedure becomes very easy. Use the wind to an advantage whenever possible. Don't fight it when it can be a friend.

After becoming familiar with holding the kite and walking around with it on level ground, practice carrying it backwards, i.e., get into the control frame from the front. This is important, as one may wish to carry it uphill this way, so that he doesn't have to turn it around at the top and chance having it blown over. Since it will always be facing into the wind it will prevent one from strapping in backwards and trying to take off with the tail of the kite facing the wind. This may sound strange, but it has happened. Needless to say, it does not work very well.

Now, try several treks up a small hill. It's work, but it's worth it. Besides which, its good exercise. It will get the novice in good shape, fast. He'll probably discover muscles he never knew he had. Then, too, if one smokes, he'll probably want to quit, as smoking definitely hinders endurance, which is really needed for this sport. Many have given up cigarettes because of their desire to fly. All in all, it will improve health and general well-being.

It's important to know how to carry the kite down the hill as well. This may have to be done, someday, if the conditions deteriorate during preparation for take off. Never be unguarded by a feeling of cowardice. Use good judgment and don't be persuaded by peer or group pressure. If one doesn't feel the conditions are good enough, then by all means he should walk the kite down the hill. Live to fly another day, when it makes good sense to fly.

If the wind is blowing at around 10 mph, then it can be used to an advantage when climbing up the hill. Somewhere on the hill, perhaps at the bottom, with the kite resting on its control bar, pick up the nose and let the sail fill with air. Grab the front bottom cables, one in each hand, and nose the kite up until it starts lifting. At this point, one may be able to walk uphill, with the wind lifting the entire weight of the kite. One should maintain his balance by shifting his grip up and down the cables. For lower winds, move closer to the control frame, while higher winds will require a move toward the nose. If one wing goes higher than the other, because of a side gust, then pull that side down with appropriate cable. This process will soon become natural. It's much easier than carrying the kite uphill!

Back on the level, the next step is to practice holding the control frame in the take-off position. There are several methods; use the one that suits you best. One method involves a simple change from the ground handling grip as discussed above. Once the kite has been lifted off the ground and balanced, the beginner should unwrap his arms from around the uprights, all the while balancing the kite on his shoulders. Then he should grip them as close as possible to the control bar with his palms forward, thumbs on the inside of the control frame.

Facing the winds, with the kite angled so the sail is just barely inflated (it should be neutral, neither climbing nor diving) begin running forward into the wind. The beginner should run almost as fast as he can, leaning forward into the control frame. When he gets up to speed, he should gently push out (forward) on the control frame. The kite should rise into the air and "fly" itself as he provides the push. He should practice this over and over until he gets it perfect every time No stumbling, either.

Now for the harness, (the helmet should be worn at all times while handling the kite). The risers (straps connecting kite to harness) should be connected to the kite and the harness to oneself. It must be adjusted so that it is secure and one's legs are about 6 inches below the control bar when he is in the sitting position. To check this, lift the kite up by the uprights or else ask for assistance. Once harnessed and, of course, helmeted, repeat the above procedure of running to takeoff on level ground and into the wind. Grip the kite as mentioned, run forward as fast as possible without falling, leaning into the kite, and push out when up to speed. If done properly, fast enough and into a wind, one should feel the harness pulling up on him or he may even get light on his feet or even get off the ground briefly. Practice this until it can be done to perfection, consistently.

Throughout this hang glider familiarization discussion, having the nose pointed directly into the wind has been stressed quite heavily, and rightly so. Just as with any aircraft, birds and especially hang gliders, this is a cardinal rule. It minimizes the running length and speed necessary to get up to takeoff.What's more, if one tries to take off in a cross wind, the windward wing could be easily picked up so quickly that he could not bring it down. This might lead to a broken wing tip, leading edge, keel or body. One might even get blown back into the hill with disastrous results. The wind is nothing to fool with. Learn how to use it and it can be a friend. Disregard it and it can be disasterous. A hang glider, with its light wing loading and weight shift control, is really at the mercy of the wind more so than anything else that flies. So develop a deep respect for it and what it can do. It's the boss!

Anyway, a kite sail itself is a good indicator of wind direction, if one knows how to interpret it. Quite simply, if pointed directly into the wind, both cones of the sail will be equally inflated, i.e., if there is enough wind to inflate them (usually 3 to 5 mph, depending upon sail material weight and area.) If the kite is at an angle with respect to the wind line, the windward sail cone will be fully inflated while the leeward sail cone will be only partially inflated. To be aimed directly into the wind, simply turn the kite toward the direction of the fully inflated cone until both cones are equally inflated. Another method of determining the wind direction is to tie a length (about 12 inches) of light thread to one of the front-bottom cables. This little device is referred to as a "yaw string," and when it is lined up with the keel, the kite is facing into the wind. The yaw string can also be used as an indicator while flying, indicating whether one is slipping or skidding through a turn.

A word of caution must be stated. Before we go any further, it must be emphasized that the beginner be harnessed to the hang glider only when actually flying. He must hook on just before take-off and disconnect as soon as he lands and get the nose down into the wind. The wind pressure on top of the sail will prevent it and him from being blown away. Get into this and develop it as a good habit. It's just too easy to be picked up by an unexpected gust and be blown over backwards or actually lifted from the hill unprepared, and hurled through the air uncontrollably. It has happened too many times already and there is no need for it.

## TAKEOFF RUN DOWN SLOPE

The beginner has now arrived at the point where all his previous training and practice will be applied. Up until now, he's been running around on level ground and getting just a hint that flight is indeed possible with that conglomeration of aluminum and dacron.

Once he's carried the kite uphill a short distance to a point with a 10 to 15 foot vertical drop, it must be set nose down into the wind and the beginner should rest awhile to catch his breath. This is important. He'll need all his strength and calmness for his run to take off. After resting, put on the helmet and connect the harness and oneself to the kite. Now, pick up the kite, balancing and holding it as before. Angle the nose up so that the sail is "just barely inflated". If the nose is too low, the sail will not be full, and the kite will nose in after he begins running. If the nose is too high, the sail will be full, creating a lot of drag and hindering the beginner's run. So, just barely inflated is what is wanted.

The beginner should be sure that his grip is set for takeoff and that he is holding as low as possible to the control bar. His shoulders should be wedged lightly between the uprights. There are many ways to grip a kite for launch (see Fig. 3-6). Each instructor probably has a favored way for various reasons. Ask him about it. Now, with the sail barely inflated, kite pointed directly into the wind, begin running down hill. As one gains speed, all the while thrusting forward, leaning slightly forward, begin angling the nose up by pushing out on the control bar. This should occur almost automatically as one gently "pushed out," or pushes the control bar forward. This pitch up will "grab the air," generate lift and pick the kite off

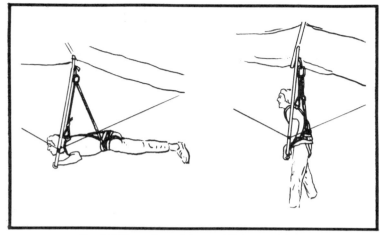
Fig. 3-6. Prone launching and flying positions.

the ground, if the correct combination of airspeed and nose angle has been achieved.

Since the beginner has started only from a vertical of 10 to 15 feet, he'll probably have just enough space to get light on his feet or be in the air for a second or two. Don't dismay. That's all that is possible. Assuming he has done everything correctly, and has managed to stay on his feet, neither stumbling or tripping, he should continue practicing until he can consistently perform his takeoff run.

If the beginner experiences difficulties, they are probably one of two things: 1. He started his run with the nose too high and couldn't build up enough speed to lift off, or 2. He started his run with the nose too low, built up too much speed, the wind got on top of the sail and unceremoniously dumped him into the ground. Thump! So, try again. Remember, the right combination of airspeed and pitch angle is the key. It's probably better to start out with the nose slightly high and gradually decrease it with each run until one becomes airborne or light. At least he won't be nosing in all the time.

One more thing, if the training slope is not of the right steepness, this could make learning very frustrating. Too shallow a slope will require a greater airspeed and/or nose up angle. If the wind is blowing at 10 mph, it will certainly help.

The higher running speed necessary on a shallow slope is also dangerous, and a fall at a higher speed will cause injury that much easier. Too steep a slope could make running and balancing difficult. Then too, the aft tip of the keel may actually be touching the slope making it almost impossible to nose-up the kite. Again, the best conditions are a slope of about 3 to 1 with a 10 mph wind blowing right up it. Then, practice, practice, practice.

## GROUND SKIMMING FLIGHT

After the beginner is confident about and consistent with his run to takeoff technique, he may begin advancing further up the slope, to a height of 20 to 25 feet vertical drop. Again, he should go through the same precedure as before, but being aware that he'll be able to truly get airborne for a few seconds of ground skimming flight (see Fig. 3-7). While not sounding like much time, it is all he'll be able to handle.

Once the beginner has actually gotten his first taste of flight, the first thing he'll have to contend with is maintaining his balance in pitch, (i.e. nose up, nose down position.) If he starts going up too rapidly, while his airspeed feels as though its dropping, he'll have to get the nose down by pulling the control bar in, toward his body. Don't jerk it. Be smooth. On the other hand, if he starts diving toward the ground while picking up airspeed, he had better push out or push the

Fig. 3-7. Ground skimming in a Seagull III.

163

control bar away, in order to bring the nose up and slow the kite.

Now, as one is flying, skimming over the ground, he will find himself very much involved with maintaining his balance in pitch. As one does this, he should keep in mind one very important fact: he is moving close to the ground at a rate of somewhere around 20 mph, which may be only a foot or so from his bottom. This could be extremely dangerous business. If the beginner bounces on his buttocks, he could easily injure or break his back and become paralyzed for life, never to walk, let alone fly again.

Ground skimming, and all hang gliding, is no game for kids or anyone else. It's quite serious business and must be approached conservatively, with that in mind. Sure, the feeling of one's first successful skims will be "unreal," as they say. Don't let the excitement of the feat ruin good judgement. One should keep a cool head and be very cautious in his approach to hang gliding. Remember, one wouldn't want to jump or fall from a vehicle traveling at 20 mph so don't do it in a hang glider either. He can get just as hurt, and more.

## LANDING FLARE (THE STALL)

As the beginner approaches the end of his flight at the bottom of the hill, he'll have to make a transitionary maneuver from flight to ground. This is commonly referred to as the landing flare which basically includes a push-out, nose-up action on the part of the pilot and his kite (see Fig. 3-8). It's a lowering of airspeed as the nose goes up. When properly executed, he may be able to make a stand-up tip-toe landing that is equivalent to stepping down from a curb. When done improperly, he can be seriously hurt and/or his kite broken.

When making his landing approach, it is important for the beginner to understand some basic aerodynamics. When flying along at 20 mph, the pilot and his glider possess momentum. His inertia wants to keep him moving at 20 mph. The way to slow his speed is by raising the nose of the glider by pushing out, until the glider "stalls." The stall is reached when the forward motion is almost halted and the kite begins to sink as the nose gently wants to drop. Aerodynamically, the nose is so high that it raises the drag to a point where it completely

Fig. 3-8. Push out to flare before touchdown.

counters the forward speed and the kite starts acting somewhat like a parachute. In fact, if a full stall is done at a height too great for a touch down, more than 5 feet up, one may be forced to actually "parachute in," i.e., float down without any forward motion at all! This can be done by some practice and involves pushing and pulling on the control bar (pumping) to keep one's balance in pitch. It is one feature of the Rogallo wing that lends itself well to the weight shift concept. Rigid wing type hang gliders tend to drop the nose more suddenly after stalling to regain flying speed, and they cannot be parachuted. This is fine if the pilot has enough altitude, but when ground skimming, he's not that high, hence the Rogallo appears to have somewhat of an advantage, at least from the standpoint of stalling.

A note of interest is that the "parachute" stall is quite often used in contest hang gliding as pilots aim for the center of a bull's eye, in a spot landing task.

As the beginner anticipates landing, say 3 to 4 feet above ground, he should push out on the control bar more and more as he slows, until he touches down. (Think of this action as trying to keep from touching ground.) This maneuver will certainly require diligent practice before it is perfected. If one pushes out too much, too soon and at too high an airspeed, the kite may "balloon," i.e., rise back up into the air, stall and descend to a crash. After a ballooning a parachute landing may be possible. If the pilot doesn't push out enough, or too little, too late, he may have to trot on touching down, or worse yet, be pushed into the ground causing him to trip and fall.

Ground skimming flight obviously implies flying close to the ground, within 5 to 10 feet. Even though this is low, it should provide enough height to practice flare to landing stall. The beginner should be absolutely sure of himself and his technique before launching from further on up the hill. Take it in easy, gradual stages. Learn how to walk before running.

### WINGS LEVEL

While still in the ground skimming stages of hang gliding, the beginner may experience an imbalance in the lateral or side-to-side direction. While gliding, a brief side gust of wind may cause him to be blown off his intended straight line course. For example, if a gust strikes him from the right, it will lift the right wing slightly, causing the glider to slip to the left. The proper method of counteracting this disturbance is to

Fig. 3-9. Joe Faust, editor of **Hang Glider Weekly**, shifts right to bring his wing level.

move his body to the high, right wing (see Fig. 3-9). This weight shift will then lower the high wing and correct his balance. Once he is headed in the desired direction, or toward the desired area, he should re-center himself on the control bar.

When preparing for takeoff, the pilot should be certain his wings are level with respect to the horizon as he begins his run with the sail just barely inflated.

## MORE FLYING

Once the beginner has learned the basics of beginner hang gliding, it will be necessary to practice them so that he can take off, skim and land with a high degree of regularity. Be sure. Be consistent, before advancing higher up the hill. As a beginner, as described here, he'll probably be able to fly from a hill with about a 100 foot vertical drop, provided it has a landing area large enough so that he won't have to turn. Also, he should reach a ground clearance of about 20 feet during the advanced stages of his beginning hang gliding.

Always seek a qualified instructor and hang gliding school to help you learn. Don't be fool enough to fly alone, only to repeat stupid mistakes that don't have to be made. You may be spared from many needless bumps, bruises and still worse, serious injury.

## BEGINNER HANG GLIDING (Hang 2)

Assuming the beginner continues to use a kite, the second stage of his beginning hang gliding will involve making deliberate turns, flying in winds up to a smooth 10 mph and clearing the ground by 40 feet (as shown in Fig. 3-10). He should be under the tutelage of a qualified instructor, as well as being at his original training site. To clear the ground by 40 feet in a kite, he'll need a hill of about 2 to 1 steepness and a 100 foot vertical drop.

If the beginner decides to discontinue kites and begin using a rigid wing type, he may or may not be able to do so at a reputable hang gliding school. If he has an FAA type rating, his prospects are probably good. If not, the school will probably require that he complete at least the "Hang 2" phase of the USHGA Hang Badge Program.

Fig. 3-10. The "Hang Two" achievement requires a ground clearance of 40 feet.

### The 45 Degree Turn

Now let's take a look at what the next kite flying experiences ought to be and how they might be performed. Before the beginner can get into a good 45 degree turn, he'll have to have some altitude, so let's work on that first. Continue flying, as before, but walk higher up on the hill; not all the way to the top but, gradually work toward it while continuing practicing. Feel completely confident about each step made toward the top before you fly from it. Don't be too anxious to be "king of the hill." Take time and exercise caution at all times.

Once the beginner has worked his way up to a height that will allow him to clear the ground by 40 feet, and he is completely adept at making consistent flights, with stand-up landings, he should set himself the task of landing on a predetermined spot in the landing area. Get a Hula-Hoop, or some such ring, and place it in the normal landing zone. Practice landing right in it. This will develop judgement in setting up the landing approach and also precision speed and pitch control. One thing to remember, especially if the landing area is approached with a little excess speed, is ground effect.

The pilot's proximity to the ground, as you may recall, may actually extend his glide ratio and cause him to overshoot the spot. So look for it and recognize what is happening and learn how to cope with it. A slight pitch up will normally slow one enough to degrade the glide ratio and land in the target. Too much pitch-up will, of course, cause one to "balloon" up into the air, most likely forcing him into a paracute situation, which could be dangerous.

As with any aircraft, a kite will lose altitude more rapidly in a turn as compared to flying in a straight line. Turning builds up drag and thus degrades the glide ratio which is already low. At any rate, this is an important fact to keep in mind. Indeed, the steeper a bank (tilt of the wing with respect to the horizon) the higher the sink rate and the higher the stalling speed of the aircraft. All turns should be entered with a little more speed than is used in straight flight.

Before the beginner launches for his flight, he should be sure to check the wind and see that he will be running directly into it. There is no sense in having a cross wind to contend with while learning. Also, before takeoff, one must plan exactly what he wants to do on the flight: left turn or right turn and where he hopes to land. By now, he should have a reasonably good idea, or feel, for estimating where he actually will touch down.

Once airborne and in a nice, trim glide, the pilot must focus his eyes on the desired landing spot. He should gently shift himself in the direction he wishes to turn. Be smooth about it. No jerky movement is necessary. If he chooses to turn right, he must shift right by moving the control bar to the left. This will not require any more thought than shifting his weight in the direction he wants to go. For the pilot's first turns, a shift off center about one foot, or less, should give him an easy, gentle turn. If, while turning, the nose goes up, pull in on the bar, i.e., he should pull his weight forward to bring the nose down, and vice-versa, being careful not to stall. When he has altered his flight path from the original straight line down the hill to a curved one and is in line with the desired landing spot, he must bring his weight back to the left to level the wings. This may require going to the left of center, depending on the situation. Winds and the amount of turn are important. Gliding straight and level, approach the landing spot and flare to touch down.

After the beginner has successfully completed his first turn, he should continue practicing in the same direction until he has it mastered. Then, he may try turning in the other direction and practice until he has it mastered, too. Now, these have been gentle, shallow turns, with banks of less than 10 degrees, having a small effect on the stall speed of the kite. As the beginner masters shallow turns, he'll want to get into steeper turns of 20 degrees which will increase the stall speed by 5%. A bank of 30 degrees increases the stall speed by 9%. Here, and more so in steeper turns, increasingly aggressive changes in pitch control will be required for coordinated turns and the prevention of stalls. Remember, about half of all flying accidents occur because of stalls in a turn.

The basic technique involved in turning is that of first shifting forward slightly to pick up a little excess speed, then shifting sideways while pushing-out to bring the nose into a "carved" turn situation. Dive slightly, roll and pitch-up to turn. The reasoning behind this maneuver is that in a banked condition, the glider does not have as much lift as when it is exactly level. In other words, it has a higher stalling speed. This can be thought of quite simply by considering the two extremes of roll. In level flight, the entire wing surface is providing lift in a vertical direction, which is equal to the weight of the pilot-glider system. In a banked situation the wing is, of course, tilted (as is the lift) toward the center of the turn. This counter-balances the centrifugal force that the pilot and the kite generate by turning. Thus, some of the vertical lift is lost in a bank. To get it back, speed up some. While actually in a bank, pitch-up the nose some as this acts somewhat like a rudder because of the horizontal component of the tilted lift force. This will cause a carved, coordinated turn, an important fact to remember, considering that a kite has no rudder to begin with.

In the extreme bank case, i.e., a 90 degree bank (which is practically impossible, and should not be tried) all the lift is now pointed level with the horizon, in towards the center of the turn. This leaves no vertical lift for flight. Theoretically, an infinite speed is needed to perform this maneuver. The point of being, of course, the steeper the banking angle, the faster on must fly to maintain lift and the higher the stall speed.

Now bear in mind that a kite may not be able to fly as fast as one may want it to, and as a result, it has what is called a limiting speed; a maximum speed at which the sail will luff and deflate and/or where structural damage may occur. Based on NASA test data, a standard Rogallo wing sail will luff and deflate in the low 30 mph range, which would seem to indicate that a maximum bank angle of 45 degrees may be possible, but that's pushing it. After all, one wouldn't want to stall during a bank. This is known universally to all types of aircraft, as a killer, and kites are certainly no exception. Several of the deaths recorded to date indicate that a stall, while attempting a 360 degree turn may have been or actually was, the fatal maneuver for the unfortunate pilot. 360s are definitely dangerous and should only be attempted under the best conditions and circumstances by the most advanced pilots at an altitude high enough to complete the turn. Kites have been known to lose 500 feet in a single turn! Don't be forced into doing a "360" by your peers or the group. Too many have already tried and died.

Once the beginner is able to take off, turn right and left and land standing up consistently, he is ready for the next task. Now, if he hasn't already done so, he should try turning with some wind blowing. The main thing to remember here, is to turn only into the wind as this will subtract from the ground speed, while turning with the wind will increase it. Don't ever attempt to turn with the wind, or downwind, as this will make it not only a faster landing, but will also tend to make one want to pitch-up, thereby stalling the kite even though he thinks he is going fast enough. Even though his ground speed may be high, his airspeed is what keeps him flying. Slowing downwind easily leads to a stall. The infamous "downwind turn" that everybody talks about should be avoided. It has been the cause far too many general aviation aircraft accidents as well. Adding a turn to a downwind makes for a vicious killer.

## The 90 Degree Turn

Once the beginner has mastered the 45 degree turns, he is ready for making right angle, or 90 degree turns as his next step. This will probably require a slightly higher hill, depending upon the steepness of the turn. If shallow, the turn will require more area to complete. If moderate, it will require less area. A steep bank of more than 20 degrees should not even be attempted near the ground. Turning 90 degrees will require more aggressive control than turning 45 degrees. Enter the turn with a little extra speed, shift off center of the control bar and, push-out while doing this. That's the technique which is basically an amplification of the 45 degree turn. Once the turn is accomplished you can do it in one direction, master it in the other. Again, keep in mind not to turn downwind.

### "S" Turns

The next maneuver the beginner must master is linking his 45 and 90 degree turns together in what are known as "S" turns. The wind should be blowing directly upslope and the slope should be at least 150 feet wide and just as high in vertical drop. Begin with a good takeoff, pick up a little extra speed, roll into a bank until the kite turns 45 degrees, then roll the opposite way and aggressively do a 90 degree turn for a short distance. Then roll into another 90 degree turn in the original turn direction, etc., until the kite has run out of hill and must land. The turns must be alternating right and left and should be smooth with little change in airspeed. One should never have to roll out of a turn because of too little or too much airspeed. Just the right amount of speed should make the turns smooth. Only diligent practice will enable one to do this. Only experience will make it happen.

Once the beginner has mastered the "S" turns, they should be made at preselected points on the hill, the idea being to force himself to be exact and precise in his control. Do this in no wind and with 10 mph up the slope. The two situations are quite different. While little difficulty may be encountered in the no wind case, wind drift effects will have to be contended with when it is blowing. Wind will require one to anticipate and lead his maneuvers even more than when there is no wind. If he can handle this part of his learning, he will be on his way to becoming a good pilot. Only through diligent practice, a lot of hard work and good judgement will it happen. Resign oneself to the task and proceed with it in all seriousness. It is no game.

## INTERMEDIATE HANG GLIDING (Hang 3)

Up until now, the beginner has been concerned mainly with learning the basics of hang gliding at a typical "class one" hill with a vertical drop of no more than 150 feet. His flights have been basically below the tree tops and in a relatively clear area. From now on, he will be involved with ridges and hills of greater than 150 feet in height. This stage is a very critical one and is where many pilots go astray. Don't become overconfident. Remember, one is still learning (for that matter a good pilot will always be learning throughout his flying career) and this is not the time to show off. Keep a cool head and train diligently and seriously.

By now, one should feel quite confident about flying from the beginners' hill. Before one begins intermediate flying though, it might be wise to fly other beginner hills to get more experience with slightly different situations, terrain and conditions. Then too, one should have some practice in cross winds. As long as the wind is about 15 degrees within being straight up the hill, he shouldn't have much of a problem. The main thing to remember is to take off into the wind, even if it means running diagonally across the hill. When flying straight down a hill with a slight cross wind, he'll experience wind drift. The wind will tend to blow him away from his intended course. The way to correct this, of course, is to lean slightly towards the wind, i.e., be off center of the control bar in the direction from which the wind is coming. Depending on the wind speed, the pilot will have to feel just how much off center he is to counteract the cross wind to stay on course. If, while doing this, he looks around, he'll notice that the kite nose is pointed, not in the direction he is going, but slightly into the cross wind. This is called "crabbing" which means that the kite is not going in the direction the nose is pointed. Crabbing is important later on, for soaring flight.

The next maneuver the beginner should learn is the 180 degree turn, i.e., a complete reversal in the direction of his flight path. To do this, he'll need a site that is at least 150 feet high and several times as wide. For his first attempt, he should chose a calm day and begin by running off the hill diagonally, or turn 90 degrees after launch to put himself parallel with the hill face or ridge line. Once he is flying across the hill, he should start a turn, like he has done previously. Begin by diving slightly to pick up some extra speed, shift sideways, to the side away from the hill, and push out some to pitch up and carve the turn. He must establish his normal turn rate and hold it until he has almost reversed his compass heading and is again parallel with the ridge but going in the opposite direction. Start your roll-out to level before the turn is complete (experience will tell one when) and by the time one is level he should, of course, be flying above the stall speed. Now, depending on the height, length and steepness of the site, the landing must be set up accordingly. Perhaps one will have to turn 90 degrees in the opposite direction of his 180, or maybe he'll be able to land straight ahead, which would be preferrable while learning. Remember to plan the flight path.

One should practice making 180 degree turns, first in one direction then the other. An extremely important thing to remember though, is to make all turns away from the hillside. If the pilot were to turn into the hill, the uphill wind would get behind him at some point and push him into the hill. More than one person has been killed in this manner, another example of a down wind turn. So, beware. Once the beginner has mastered 180s in both directions, he should try linking them together in a single flight. This maneuver is actually called a "figure 8" and will require a higher vertical drop for calm conditions, or else, near soaring winds for a class 1 ridge (i.e., 150 foot vertical). Depending on the particular hang glider, the wind, steepness of slope and direction, one's sink rate will vary. If the winds are high enough, actual soaring flight may be possible, but don't attempt it without expert instruction.

## ADVANCED HANG GLIDING (Hang 4)

By now, the beginner should have had many, many hang glider flights and have mastered all the items previously discussed. He should be completely confident in all that he should know. After being well experienced in gliding, turning, crabbing and landing, under varied conditions, he may want to try soaring (see Fig. 3-11). A few words of caution are in order. If hang gliding can be called a dangerous activity, then hang soaring can be called extremely dangerous. Air in motion is even less forgiving than calm air. It must be treated

Fig. 3-11. Taras Kiceniuk soars his Icarus II at Torrey Pines.

accordingly. One should not try soaring unless he really wants to, and then only under expert instruction.

If the wind is right and the beginner has practiced his 180s and "8s," then there's a good possibility he'll be able to soar instead of sink to the ground. He must, however, exercise extreme caution, for soaring is extremely dangerous. Maintain respect for the wind and let that respect grow. The wind is the boss. In considering soaring flight on a ridge, one must try to picture the airflow as it is approaching, striking and passing over the site (see Fig. 3-12). A typical beginner soaring area would be on a sand ridge facing the smooth, ocean air. First of all, the wind coming off the water is the smoothest to be found anywhere. It has nothing in its path to disturb it or make it turbulent. It has traveled miles and miles over the smooth surface of the water, and should be quite smooth, providing lift that is as smooth as silk.

As the wind strikes the rising beach ridge line, it deflects upward along the face of the slope. As it deflects, it accelerates

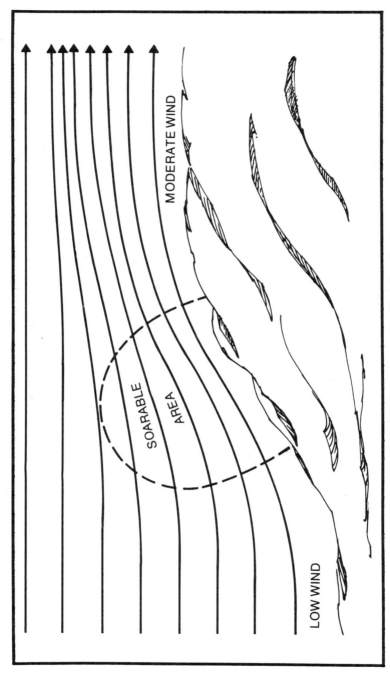

Fig. 3-12. A typical ridge soaring lift airflow situation.

in velocity until it is strongest at the top. In fact, the air at sea level may be only 5 mph, while on top of the ridge, it may be boiling at 20 mph, which is a very significant fact in flight planning. Anyway, as the air flows up and over the top and onto the level, it begins to slow down again, somewhere past the crest. This situation is much like the air flowing past a stalled or partially stalled wing, in that, a lot of turbulence and vortices are created which give rise to down drafts behind the crest. This turbulence is generally referred to as a "rotor" and is to be avoided at all times. If one were to fly in this, both he and his kite would be literally smashed into the ridge top and the pilot would be very seriously injured or maybe even killed. It has happened already, too many times. Be aware of the killer rotor.

The intensity of the rotor will depend on the wind velocity, steepness of the slope and sharpness of the ridge line. The higher any of these items are, the more intense the rotor at the top. Cliffs are certainly the worst cases. What is wanted is a smooth ridge with a slope angle of about 30 degrees; for instance, a sand ridge. This should provide the smoothest lift and minimize the rotor. In any case, stay forward of the top.

Cliffs have another bad characteristic, in the form of a bottom rotor as shown in Fig. 3-13. This is a vortex that creates a down draft near the cliff wall at some distance down from the top. The on coming air striking a sharp cliff is forced to separate. Some air flows over the top, some impacts directly into the wall, while some actually flows downward. At some distance down from the top of the cliff, the air is given a "top spin," and flows into and down the wall in a rotary motion (see Fig. 3-14). The up flow side of the bottom rotor would be located at some distance out from the base of the cliff and it is fed by the air blowing in the direction of the cliff bottom. This too, has already killed hang glider pilots. If one doesn't fly cliffs, he won't have this problem; the choice is his.

Assuming the beginner has located a good, gentle, soaring site, he may begin turning his 180s and figure "8s" into some soaring. Follow the example of seagull, and other hang soarers. First, one will probably want to take off and simply crab along the ridge in winds that are below soaring potential. As the ridge ends he can land at the bottom where the wind is

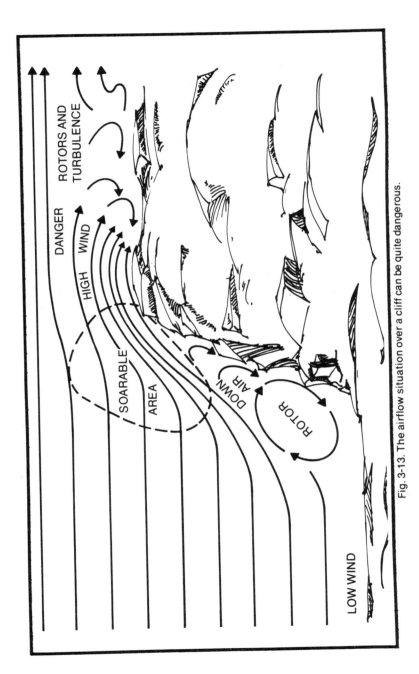

Fig. 3-13. The airflow situation over a cliff can be quite dangerous.

LOW WIND

DANGER

ROTORS AND TURBULENCE

HIGH WIND

SOARABLE AREA

DOWN AIR

ROTOR

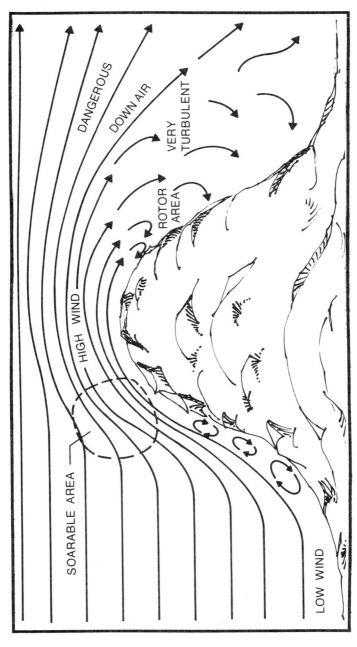

Fig. 3-14. The air behind a hill or mountain is very turbulent and full of downdrafts. Stay away from the lee side of all airflow obstructions.

179

low. Remember to keep up airspeed when landing, or you'll stall.

One very important thing to do during launching in soaring or near soaring conditions is to use the aid of an assistant. He should hold the bottom-front rigging cables to help aim the pilot into the wind and prevent his being blown over backwards. At this point, the kite should be pointed slightly nose down, into the lift, too. If not, when the pilot reaches the edge, the updraft will pitch up the nose of the kite and blow it up and over backwards, and probably into the top rotor. This too, has injured and killed many people. Be aware of it and launch properly with a helper. If one flies straight out, he may actually be able to hover, depending on the situation. A bowl shaped ridge would be conducive to this. It will, however, require great skill and balance and makes the pilot susceptible to being blown back.

Once the beginner has experienced the bouyancy of the ridge lift, he will probably be euphoric, but must remain cool. He should think, calculate and plan what he wants to do. When he puts it all together, the 180s, 8s, ridge lift and crabbing, he'll be soaring. To date, this soaring has been done for hours and miles at a time. It proves only one thing: the wind blows so hard for so long at a certain site. Don't try to set a world's record, just enjoy the newfound freedom, but don't get carried away with it. One must know what he is doing at all times.

It is very important to consider the physics of the soaring situation. The wind is blowing into the ridge, being deflected upward and the pilot is moving parallel to the ridge, while the kite is actually crabbing or pointing toward the wind, somewhat away from the ridge. The only time one wouldn't have to crab would be in a calm. If he didn't do so while in soaring conditions, his outside wing (the one closest to the wind) would be lifted up and he'd be blown into the ridge or its rotor. The higher the wind, the higher the crab angle required to soar it. Only experience will teach one how much and remember, one flies only by "the seat of his pants," and not much else.

Now it's up to the beginner to go out and practice soaring at an approved area under expert instruction. Do not try it alone. Once he's got the feel for it, he's on his way, but he must not rush it. Take time and do it well. Master a beginner soaring area first: a smooth, long ridge, preferably of sand, facing the beach and smooth winds. One must do his first landings at the bottom where there is no rotor to worry about. Just don't stall out in that slower moving air.

As long as one is soaring over a good ridge, without any gullies and bulges, he shouldn't have to do much more than is mentioned above. If he is soaring along a long ridge line however, chances are he will find breaks, gaps and budges in it. These will require much thought, before flight is attempted over them, as the airflow situation can be quite different than what he might expect. In fact, one might do well to avoid these areas and do a 180 back to where he came from.

If the beginner encounters a budge in his ridge line, it will most likely have a rotor and large area of sink on its top as shown in Fig. 3-15. To fly directly over it would be lunacy, unless one is quite high where the effects of the rotor were nonexistent. If this is the case, he might be able to "bore" over it and get back to the lift on the far side of the bulge. He'll have lift until he reaches the point at which the lift will diminish, perhaps necessitating a landing. In any case, if it looks uncertain, land at the bottom. At least the wind is lower there and is likely to be smoother.

If one encounters a gully in his ridge line, the airflow situation may look like the following. An area of sink will be found in line with the ridge, in front of the gully. One way to get across it may be to speed up after having gained altitude before reaching it, and then boring, or penetrating, through it. The other side of the gully is then actually like a bulge. It will have some sink and probably a rotor behind its point. The pilot must stay ahead of the point so he can be in the lift region. Remember, the far part of a gully leading to the point has the air moving practically parallel to it, generating little or no lift. If he can't make it across, he should land into the wind at the bottom of the ridge. Be safe, not sorry.

Of course, there is much, much more to be learned about ridge lift and soaring, but this should give the beginner some idea of what it's all about. In any case though, it is recommended that he obtain good flight instruction from a qualified instructor. Whatever he does, he should never fly

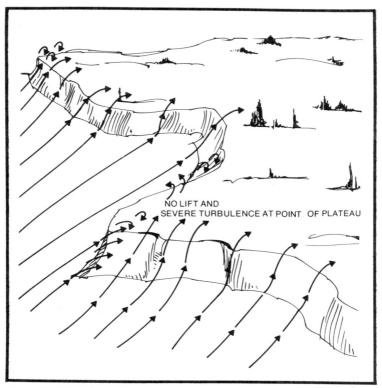

Fig. 3-15. What the airflow might look like along a ridge line with varying terrain.

alone. He must not try to learn on his own. There is no excuse whatever to make mistakes and get hurt. A good instructor can help immensely and start him off on the right track before he develops any bad habits. Always keep in mind that soaring is considered to be extremely dangerous business. Approach it conservatively and cautiously. Remember the old pilot's saying: "There are old pilots and there are bold pilots, but there are no old, bold pilots."

## SPECIAL, ADVANCED HANG GLIDING SKILLS (Hang 5)

After the beginner has been flying as a Hang 4 pilot for a year or more he may wish to qualify for a Hang 5 rating by having all the special skills witnessed by a qualified rater. By the time he's ready for this, he should possess maturity and use good judgement to act prudently so as not to be a hazard to himself or his flying sites. As of this writing, Hang 5 is considered to be the highest attainable skill level in hang gliding and can only be exceeded by many years of actual flying experience. The special skills called out are: turbulence flying, high altitude flying, cliff launching, cross country, and 360 degree turns.

**Turbulence Flying**

Under these conditions, the pilot is likely to be "bounced around" due to various local wind conditions and he must be able to respond accordingly. Turbulence will normally be associated with higher winds (above 15 mph) at inland flying sites that may be lined with trees or uneven terrain. It may also exhibit itself when thermals pass through an otherwise nonturbulent area. Thermals normally have clouds forming at their tops and can be thus identified. Expect turbulence when a cloud is approaching the area. The air feeding a thermal is approaching toward its core, radially from all directions and is felt as wind or a gust. A thermal passing behind a hill could cause an uphill gust, while one passing in front of a hill could cause a downhill gust near the surface and yet provide lift, of course, at a greater height.

Shoreline soaring normally provides the least turbulent conditions of all. The wind is usually quite smooth coming off the water. The same would also be true of the air coming from a large, extended plain area in front of a hill or ridge. Even so, turbulence can make its presence known by passing clouds (thermals) and passing weather fronts. Thunderclouds are especially capable of promoting turbulence as they are evidence of super developed thermal activity and its associated tremendous killer lift. A squall line will also produce gusts and very dangerous high winds that should not be flown in at all.

The pilot who chooses to fly in turbulent conditions must be able to handle possible sail inversions (extremely dangerous) and make instant, deliberate, aggressive, correct and substantial control inputs to his glider. Turbulence flying requires a lot of work and can quickly become fatiguing, unnerving and uncomfortable. It should be remembered that most hang gliding fatalities have occurred in high winds and/or turbulent conditions.

## Cliff Launching

A cliff is generally considered to be a sheer wall situation with an angle approaching 90 degrees with respect to the horizon. More specifically, according to the Hang Badge Program, it must be precipitous and over 100 feet high. Cliffs can be found that are less than 100 feet and perhaps one should practice at the lesser cliffs before tackling the bigger ones.

The main thing about a cliff launch is that it puts the pilot into the air at a great height, immediately. He has altitude as soon as he launches. Along with other factors, the psychological one of having the earth fall out from under him is quite dramatic. The biggest factor in cliff launching, however, is the wind flow situation in the vicinity of the cliff. In addition to forming a downdraft rotor on top of the cliff a small distance back from the edge and a downdraft rotor below the edge, in front of the face, a very powerful and concentrated updraft is formed at the edge of the cliff itself. This presents a definite problem for launching.

If one were to use his normal technique of launching down a slope, he would be in for nothing but trouble at a cliff site. As soon as the nose of the kite gets to the edge, with it tremendous updraft, it would pitch up violently and most likely be blown back into the top rotor. If he wants to fly in these conditions (which are quite dangerous) he should have an assistant holding the front-bottom cables while he is positioned near the edge. The assistant will prevent the pilot from being blown back by keeping the nose down. (A word of caution is in order for the launch assistant also. At least one person has been killed while holding nose cables and backing toward the cliff and falling off.) The assistant will, of course, let go only at the instant the pilot lunges forward and down, into the lifting airflow. This must be a very aggressive motion with positive control exhibited throughout. The nose must be able to penetrate the initial high lift to prevent being blown over backwards.

## The 360 Degree Turn

This is perhaps the single most controversial maneuver in the book. Many have died trying it in conventional aircraft as well as in hang gliders. It's really a problem of not being educated in the aerodynamics of the situation, and not following the correct procedures. For one thing, the pilot can easily lose a lot of altitude (as much as 500 feet) in a single 360, and he'll always lose some, except while thermalling. The big factor in making any turn is knowing that the stall speed increases with angle of bank. Know it well. The proper thing to do is to increase airspeed before entering the turn in order to assure oneself of being above the stall speed of the particular bank angle. One must know the stalling speeds of his hang glider at various bank angles and avoid them. Use an accurate airspeed indicator and mark various stall speeds on it. Be sure.

Where one makes a 360 is just as important as knowing how to make it. A 360 degree turn attempted near a ridge in any wind is extremely dangerous. Many have been killed on the downwind side of the turn as the wind blew them straight into the ridge or mountainside. They probably stalled out. No pilot in his right mind tries a 360 in a ridge lift situation. Even when the pilot is over flat ground and the wind is blowing, he will drift with the wind unless he knows how to handle it. His circles won't be circles. They will be elongated in the direction of the wind. In order to make perfect circles in a wind, or turn about a point in a wind, the basic technique involves banking shallow and flying slower on the upwind side of the circle and to bank steeper and be faster on the downwind side of the circle. The exact angles and speeds will vary with the wind and the size of the circle. Again, only practice will make one good at it.

The 360 degree turns require a great deal of skill and a good understanding of the aerodynamics involved. Banking and "cranking" is just not good enough. One must know, in detail, what is happening all the time as he flies, be it a turn or anything else.

The following are steps for making a good 360:

1. Before entering any turn, clear the area. First look in the desired direction of the turn to see that there is no

traffic in that airspace. This is done by picking up the wing that will be on the inside of the turn.

2. Immediately prior to beginning the turn, dive slightly to increase airspeed for good bank response and to put the glider well above its stall speed.

3. Shift the body weight sideways to get the desired angle of bank.

4. After the desired bank angle is established, push out, i.e., shift the body weight aft. Caution: If one does this prematurely he may cause the kite to stall while banked. Remember, stall speed increases with bank angle.

5. Move back toward the center of the control bar when proper pitch and airspeed is reached.

6. Be ready to trim as required while turning, and watch the horizon as a reference. It should remain at the same tilt all through the turn.

7. Complete the turn by re-positioning the body for a normal glide, weight forward and centered. One may have to shift to the opposite side of the control bar momentarily.

Note: If a stall or otherwise out of control condition feels like it's coming, reposition for a normal glide and react accordingly. Do not hesitate.

### High Altitude Hang Gliding

This type of flying will involve altitudes in excess of 1000 feet above the terrain and thus implies launching from mountains of still greater vertical drop (see Fig. 3-16). The big difference from low altitude flying is a loss of ground reference for speed. The psychological reality of being high above it all is also quite noticeable.

When flying close to the ground and local terrain, a mountainside, trees or whatever, the hang glider pilot experiences a great sense of flight. He sees the ground pass below and the trees or ridge line pass beside him. He is given a good reference for judging his relative speed. When he flies high, however, this sense of motion is reduced and perhaps gone altogether, depending on how high he is. Even while flying in a high speed jet airliner at 30,000 feet and 500 mph,

Fig. 3-16. Dick Eipper, hang glider pioneer, leaps from Cone Peak (elevation 5000 ft), Big Sur, Calif.

motion over the ground is barely perceptible. At any rate, this loss of relative motion with objects below may lead the neophyte into what is known as the "diving syndrome." As he flys higher and higher, it appears to him that he is moving slower and slower. This may tell him to lower the nose to increase his speed when it's not the thing to do. Unless he has an airspeed indicator mounted to his glider, he will not really be able to tell how fast he is flying. (A kite sail will begin to flap however, at some point over the cruise speed.) This can lead to quite serious trouble in any hang glider, but especially in a kite. If it is dived too fast, the sail will luff and deflate, and make the kite unstable in pitch. This could easily lead to a terminal dive to earth. Fully battened kite sails appear to improve stability.

In a rigid wing hang glider, depending on the design and its control system, a high speed dive may cause structural failure or perhaps instability and uncontrollability, making the glider incapable of being recovered. Check with the manufacturer's recommended top speed, never exceed ($V_{ne}$) and mount an airspeed indicator to better gauge oneself. With most kites, the top speed is in the low 30 mph range, based on NASA test data. It's a wise idea to adhere to this as a "red line" speed for kites with a wing loading of about 1 pound per square foot.

Note: The maneuver descriptions as presented in this book are given as they might be done and are not necessarily as they should be done. Consult a qualified instructor.

High altitude hang gliding may also involve other maneuvers that would be impossible to perform nearer to the ground. The 720 degree turn, i.e., two consecutive turns, can be done as well as figure 8s and opposite, linked, 360s. In rigid wing hang gliders, other, more exotic maneuvers may be possible, for instance, steeper banks. Check with the manufacturer first to see what the allowable limits of the glider are. In general, an all aerodynamically controlled hang glider should be more maneuverable and controllable than a weight shift glider, but may require more airspace in which to perform that maneuver.

The continuous 360 degree turns done at high altitudes are an example of the technique needed to gain altitude in a thermal. Since the thermal is a rising column of air, one must continually circle to stay in it and gain altitude. In order to maximize his rate of altitude gain, he'll have to fly at the speed for minimum sink, which is slightly above the stall speed. This then, requires great skill and information from the airspeed indicator and variometer, or sensitive rate of climb indicator. The variometer tells whether one is climbing or descending. It gives out an appropriate audio tone to indicate this. Higher tones mean he is going up and lower tones mean he is descending.

Besides launching from high mountains, it is possible to be towed aloft underneath a hot air balloon and dropped at some altitude. Only a well prepared expert should even consider this "stunt" as it requires special equipment and skills. To date, the world's altitude record in a hang glider is over 25,000 feet. It was done from a hot air balloon.

### Cross Country Hang Gliding

This is probably the utlimate thrill or goal as far as hang gliding is concerned. For this, the pilot must be very knowledgeable of and very skilled in the art of hang gliding. Cross country flying, to date, has been done by a mere handful and its accomplishment is quite something to be proud of. While most long distance flights have been made in standard kites, it makes good sense that the higher performance rigid wings will be the gliders to set the records of the future.

The cross country hang pilot must be able to recognize areas on the ground and relate their effect to his flight. He must know what potential sources for thermals are and use them if he has to gain altitude. He must be able to recognize areas of sink. He should fly with the attitude that he could be forced to land at any time if the lift or his glide runs out. He should know the weather and react accordingly. If forced to land, he must be able to establish a good approach and set down within a pre-selected area, allowing for possible surprises, such as a herd of cows. He should be able to select several probable landing sites, if possible. He must be able to determine the wind conditions at ground level by natural phenomena. He must know how to determine the possible location of ground obstructions such as fences, posts, wires, etc. He should fly at the proper airspeed for the task he is performing, whether it be climbing in lift or dashing for the next thermal or gliding in for a landing. In short, the cross country pilot must be an expert pilot, if he expects to live and fly another day. Cross country is a rating that takes time, practice and diligence to achieve. Since there are no established tests or requirements for this type of hang flying, one is entirely on his own.

## CONTEST HANG GLIDING

While the vast majority of hang glider pilots may never enter a contest, certainly some percentage will. Contests are what makes a sport a sport: each participant doing his best, pitting himself against his fellow flyers and the elements in an effort to determine who is the best. A typical contest will include spot landing, duration and various maneuvers for kites and maybe for rigid wings as well. Currently, the main events revolve around the so-called standard Rogallo class. Other classes include the "Self-Launch Open Class" and the "Open Class."

The Self-Launch Open Class includes any type of hang glider capable of being folded and carried to the launch site by the pilot only. It must be foot-launched without assistance. In reality, this is really a class for high aspect ratio or otherwise high performance hybrid Rogallo wings.

The Open Class includes any hang glider capable of being foot-launched with help from no more than one assistant, and landed using the pilot's legs. It may be taken to the launch site by any means. Realistically, this is the class for the so-called rigid wing hang gliders.

The spot landing event requires landing a bull's-eye composed of three concentric circles of increasingly smaller diameter and higher point value. It is often set in an area that requires a turn before the final approach, to make it more competitive. The flight before the final approach may also require slalom type "S" turns, depending on the contest site terrain.

The duration event is basically to see who can stay up the longest with a maximum time set for touch down. Points are subtracted for times over and under the set time.

A free style event may also be held in which pilots chose their own routine of maneuvers to perform in their best possible style. Perhaps music of the pilot's choice may even be played as a sort of "aerial ballet" similar to that found in ski meets.

A bomb dropping event is sometimes used as a test of skill and judgement. Water filled balloons are carried by the pilot's teeth and released over a designated target area.

A hang glider contest can be a lot of fun as there is much comradery among the participants. Others, like oneself, who are fascinated by their newfound aerial freedom, are eager to get together and share their experiences and good times. Once the beginner has been to several meets, his skill will improve at the particular events and perhaps he will want to travel to more distant meets. Many meets even hand out cash prizes or complete gliders to the winners.

The ultimate hang glider meet is probably the World Cup Competition, which is an elimination type contest to find the best pilots throughout the world. After winning in the various regionals, the 100 best pilots will meet at several pre-selected sites and pit their skills against each other to determine numero uno. Currently, this championship is set up for Rogallo wings only, and they must be designed and built to certain specifications. This then makes it a contest of pilots. Many other meets, including the SUHGA Nationals do, however, include self-launch open and open classes as well.

Other types of hang gliding, not already mentioned, are formation flying and several gliders using the same site and airspace at once. Formation flying is practiced by only a few dedicated professionals and is not normally done because of its difficulty and time-consuming nature. Many gliders in the air at once is fairly typical, so let's consider this situation.

In order to avoid utter disaster and chaos, some general "rules of the road" are necessary to conduct safe flying when many gliders are in the air at once. Each site will, no doubt, have a particular set of rules already established, based on their operating history. In general though, some things to keep in mind to make hang gliding safer for everyone involved are:

1. The lower glider has the right of way. It must land before a higher glider does, assuming it is the same performance glider.
2. When approaching another glider head-on, break right, i.e., turn to your right. If both of these gliders are in a ridge lift situation, the glider turning into the wind (his right) should give the other one more room, since he has to turn downwind which is very dangerous as discussed before. The glider closest to the ridge is in the most potential danger because of the infamous top rotor.
3. The slower glider has the right of way. Use caution when overtaking another glider and stay well clear of his wake. It is turbulent and may cause one to lose control.
4. The glider on the right of a side-by-side formation has the right of way.

# Chapter 4
# Physiological Factors

## PHYSIOLOGICAL FACTORS

Some people may tend to believe that hang gliding is, at last, everyman's aviation. With its low cost and lack of governmental regulations, almost anybody could get into it. While this may be true, the fact is hang gliding is physically a very demanding sport. Sure, one may hear of some older men (try 70) and see a young lady hang gliding, but these cases are few and far between. By far, the largest group of hang glider pilots is in the 20 to 35 year old age bracket.

Before one considers taking hang gliding lessons, he should be in excellent health, or else not bother. Perhaps, a physical is in order if you have any doubts or just to confirm your beliefs about yourself. That first lesson will certainly tell you how fit you are or aren't. Just toting a 40 pound kite around on level ground is enough, let alone carrying it up the hill! If you smoke, be advised to quit. Your lungs will need all the fresh air they can take in. In fact, many people have given up smoking when they took up hang gliding, which is certainly a plus for the sport.

One should definitely not be overweight when he takes up hang gliding. He'll only have to handle a bigger, heavier, more awkward kite anyway. Be advised to reduce. It will be beneficial. One might go on a diet and go jogging every day. After all, when he takes that first lesson he should be prepared to make the most of his investment in time and money. Be fit. Be alert. Whether one realizes it or not, hang gliding demands more fitness and alertness than almost any other human activity. Then too, lugging a kite around can actually keep one fit. Many people don't mind this part of the sport at all, for it gives them a chance to get fresh air and exercise that they may not normally get during the work week.

## AIRSICKNESS

Airsickness is not too common in hang gliding, but there is a possibility that it could occur, especially in the more advanced types of flying. Typically, it happens in rough air, or turbulence, and while circling continuously. The reason for this is disorientation due to various forces generated in the turn or by the turbulence. These cause an imbalance in the inner ear upsetting the pilot's equilibrium and may make him dizzy. One thing that should not be done is to look at some fixed point on the glider. Instead, focus on the horizon or the terrain. The pilot should try to get his mind off being sick, for just thinking about it can make it worse than it already is. Other causes of airsickness could also be extremes in temperature, an upset stomach, gas pains, or bad odors.

Airsickness can be relieved by motion sickness drugs, such as Dramamine, but one should not fly while under their influence. These drugs tend to relax the flyer and may prevent him from having good, positive control over the glider. Furthermore, no flying should ever be done after taking any drug or drinking any alcoholic beverages. The reason should be obvious!

## TEMPERATURE

Temperature is one of the biggest factors concerning the comfort of a hang glider pilot, especially on flights of duration longer than a few minutes. Typically, most northern pilots are used to some cold, and the normal winter weather as experienced in North America is no particular problem. The great body heat generated in carrying the glider around is usually enough to keep one warm, as long as he wears suitable clothing. When longer, higher flights are performed however, air temperature effects become more pronounced.

As altitude is gained from sea level, the average temperature of the surrounding air decreases at 3 1/2° F for every 1,000 feet of altitude. This is the temperature "lapse rate" to be discussed later. At any rate, it's easy to see that if one were to gain 5,000 feet on a flight, he would find himself in air that was 17 1/2 degrees cooler than from where he took off. This could be very uncomfortable and may be critical depending upon the initial take off temperature and altitude gained. Plan accordingly. If you takeoff hot and sweaty, the upper air may cool you too much and you'll become uncomfortable.

If hang flying in the cold is prolonged, it can lead to very dangerous consequences. First, the pilot will start shivering as his circulation begins to slow. Then, he may begin turning blue on parts of his body and perhaps develop frostbite at his extremities or exposed parts. Once cold sets in, his reflexes slow, making control difficult and flying more dangerous. Try moving around to get that circulation up. If the pilot is quite high when he first realizes the cold, he should plan to land as soon as he can. After all, it may take a while for the descent. If the sun is still shining, try to keep facing it if at all possible. Don't fly too fast either, because of the wind chill effects and the stability of the glider. Once a person experiences a cold flight, it's something he'll never try again. It's no fun and it could be hazardous to his health. If it's too cold to begin with, don't take off.

## PRESSURE CHANGES WITH ALTITUDE

As one climbs higher and higher in his quest for the "ultimate high," the pressure of the surrounding air decreases. Not only does this affect airspeed indicators and altimeters, but also his body, particularly the ears.

The eardrum is a thin membrane separating the outer and inner ears and is therefore sensitive to changes in air pressure. After all, sounds are nothing more than air pressure changes. Anyway, on climbing, the high pressure which exists inside one's head wants to push the eardrum outward while descents have the opposite effect. The problem is to equilize the air pressures inside and outside the head. During a climb, this is no particular problem, as the higher pressure inside the ear can flow down the eustachian tube and out of the mouth. Many people say their ears "popped." When making a descent however, the ear must be cleared many times, depending on the altitude lost, by swallowing, yawning or perhaps chewing gum. If this doesn't work, one might have to take more positive action. He can close his mouth, pinch his nose shut and blow air from his lungs to bring the inner ear pressure up to that of the outside air.

Any cavity inside the body that contains air will also be affected by changes in air pressure due to altitude. The sinuses are fairly large cavities in the head and, as such, contain a fair volume of air. If the nose or throat is blocked due to a common cold, great pain may be experienced in changing altitudes. The abdomen is also an area containing air and is a potential source of "gas" pains. Avoid eating anything that may cause gas as this will only make matters worse.

### EQUILIBRIUM

The equilibrium, or balance, of the human body is the job performed by the semi-circular canals, which are located in the inner ear. They are three, hair-covered, half-circular, perpendicularly oriented tubes filled with a liquid and they give the senses of roll, pitch and yaw.

When standing still, or moving at a constant velocity, one has a feeling that he is in balance. Up is up. Down is down. Left is left. And, right is right. This is due to gravity positioning the fluid in a particular place in each of the canals. Once gravity is interfered with, however, the fluid positions change. Accelerations, or changes in speed and direction, are the things that alter this fluid position. Since gravity is nothing more than a vertical acceleration, other directional accelerations can create a "false" gravity, or force, sufficient to re-orient the canal fluids.

As an example, when the pilot enters a turn, the acceleration of the turn, i.e., centrifugal force, tends to make him feel heavier. (A 60 degree bank produces a 2g load.) Also, one must not forget that even though his speed through a turn may be constant, he's still accelerating, for it's his velocity that's changing. (Velocity is composed of speed and direction. Changing one or the other results in acceleration.) In a turn, it's one's direction that's always changing. This acceleration due to turning will cause the inner ear fluids to re-orient and tell the pilot that he is turning. If, however, the turn is prolonged, the fluids will settle in another position and give one a false sense of orientation. He may actually think he is level when he really is not. His sense of balance says he is level while his eyes tell him he's not. This can be confusing and lead to dizziness. Then, when the pilot tries to level out, a new acceleration will be created giving him a sense of turning out of a balanced condition, even though his eyes tell him he's level again.

Other false senses of balance can be generated by a quick turning of the head with respect to the hang glider's acceleration. This can cause disorientation and confusion just as well as drugs or illness can.

It is for these reasons that flying blind in fog or clouds should be considered unwise and should never be attempted. It's too easy to develop a false sense of balance while one may actually be in a spiral dive, out of control. Since the pilot has no visual reference with the horizon, he'll soon go into a turn without even realizing it.

## OXYGEN AND BREATHING

Normally, oxygen will not be a worry to the hang glider pilot, since most people are okay up to about 10,000 feet. The only time it may be necessary to carry oxygen along is on an altitude record attempt, since that record now stands at about 25,000 feet. Somewhere around 25,000 feet, a pressure oxygen system will also be required in order to force enough oxygen into the bloodstream to prevent hypoxia, i.e. insufficient absorption of oxygen by the blood. If attempting a flight over 10,000 feet, which is entirely possible from some mountains, check with experts on the subject.

## "g" EFFECTS

One "g" is the acceleration due to gravity and it is measured as 32 feet per second per second. If you were to drop an object in a vacuum, it would fall at this ever increasing rate. A hang glider flying along in a straight and level glide in smooth air will experience a one g load i.e., its weight in the air is equal to its weight on the ground. If a gust of wind were to momentarily lift the glider up at the rate of 32 feet per second per second, the pilot would feel twice his weight in the harness. If a sudden downdraft equal to gravity were encountered, then the pilot would feel completely "weightless" and be in a very bad situation in a weight shifting glider. His weight would have no effect on the stability and control of the glider. If the downdraft were severe enough, the pilot's head may strike the keel and cause loss of orientation and control or consciousness.

In terms of g effects on the body, the average man can withstand about a positive 5 g load before blacking out. As g loads increase, vision becomes restricted, then gray, then totally black. If g loads go much higher, a person can actually become unconscious. Needless to say, high accelerations are to be avoided, but they are not normally encountered in typical hang gliding anyway.

The highest g loads that will probably be encountered in a hang glider are those produced by the rapid deceleration of a crash or bad landing.

## RAPID BREATHING

Rapid breathing, which is also called hyperventilation, can lead to an upset in the oxygen and carbon dioxide balance in the blood and cause fainting. It can be started quite easily in hang gliding by not resting awhile before takeoff, after having climbed a hill; the excitement of higher, longer or more ambitious flights; or by fear due to an uncontrollable situation. The best way to avoid it is to rest before takeoff. If one starts breathing fast while airborne, try to consciously slow it down. He must calm himself before it gets worse. Try to land as soon as possible.

## FATIGUE

As with any activity, fatigue can and does occur to people engaged in hang gliding. The point is to recognize it when it comes and then not attempt to fly. By the end of a long day, or even before, one may have managed to burn up much of the body's energy and as a result, he will be weaker and sluggish in his responses. He won't be able to run as fast for a good take-off and landing. His reaction time to gusts and his general ability to control the hang glider is reduced. Being fatigued can only lead to accidents. Don't fly when tired or hungry.

As with most other physiological factors, the pilot's susceptibility for fatigue will decrease the more physically fit he is, and the less drugs he takes, including alcohol and tobacco. The best situation to be in is excellent health, with no vices, and having complete knowledge of oneself, one's hang glider and the air he flies in.

# Chapter 5
# Hang Glider Design
# and Stability & Control

## HANG GLIDER DESIGN, STABILITY AND CONTROL

To begin with, this chapter is not intended to explain exactly *how* to design a hang glider. Instead, it will deal primarily with *what* one might look for in a given design that already exists. What features make one hang glider more desirable than another? What qualities are more nearly suited to the kind of flying one wants to do? Is he looking for a novice glider or a high performance glider?

This chapter is presented from the point of view of the pilot, or flyer, or would-be type, who is interested and concerned about building, or buying, and flying a good hang glider. This is not a "how-to-design" course. The design process involved in a hang glider or any aircraft is far from being a Simple Simon affair. Any flying machine is, or should be, a precisely balanced, stable and controllable device. After all, a human life is literally hanging in the balance.

At any rate, it is hoped that one will come to realize that, while overall performance is perhaps the most important consideration in hang glider design, it is not the only one. Suffice it to say, anything that flies is a compromise of umpteen zillion variables.

An aircraft designer is constantly trading off one thing for another. A small gain here for a small loss over there. Low landing speed or high cruising speed. Low rate of sink, or high lift to drag ratio. Low drag or low weight. Long span or short span. Weight shift or aerodynamic controls. And the list goes on...Finally, the designer settles on a basic set of critera based on how he wants to construct, transport, launch and fly the hang glider. Not only must the designer be a good engineer, but he must also be highly aware of how the glider will be used. Perhaps more than in any other form of aircraft design, the engineer must be fully aware of the human element. After all, the flyers legs are his landing gear, and he has little protection from the elements, save a good helmet. But then, that's what hang gliding is all about: being exposed to a maximum of elements of natural flight.

**REFERENCE AXES**

Before looking at hang glider design, it's a good idea to become familiar with some basic nomenclature to aid in communication. Unlike all other forms of travel (except for submarines) which can move only on a surface in essentially two dimensions, an aircraft has the freedom to move about in all three dimensions, the additional dimension being that of up and down, or the vertical dimension (see Fig. 5-1).

In describing the motion of a hang glider, two frames of reference are used. One is the hang glider itself with its reference center located at the balance point, or center of gravity. The other reference frame is the earth or some point on it. At any particular instant in time, the location and orientation of a hang glider can be described by using the reference axis. Motions forward, up and down, and from side to side are described by a set of Cartesian coordinates or just plain coordinates specified along the three reference axes. The orientation of the hang glider is described by its angular tilt along each of the three axes.

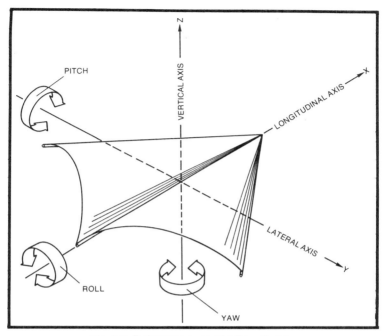

Fig. 5-1. Reference axes of a Rogallo kite.

The planes formed by the "X" and "Y" axes and "Z" and "Y" axes are called planes of symmetry that cut the hang glider into two equal halves. These planes of symmetry contain components of motion only along the "X" and "Z" axes and rotation about the "Y" axis.

The longitudinal motion of a hang glider is contained in the symmetric planes, while the lateral motions are made in the asymmetric planes.

The angle of tilt, or rotation, about the "Y" axis is called the angle of attack, which is denoted by the Greek letter $\alpha$. In a kite-type hang glider, this angle is readily noticed as the angle the keel (center spar) makes with respect to its direction of motion through the air.

The angle of tilt, or rotation, about the "X" axis is called the bank angle or roll angle. This is readily observed when a hang glider is making a turn: one wing is higher than the other. The "high" wing is on the outside of the turn.

The angle of tilt, or rotation, about the "Z" axis is called the yaw angle and it's denoted by the Greek letter $\beta$. This angle is evidenced when a hang glider flies in a crosswind. One can easily see this on a windy day by watching an airplane or bird as it seems to be pointed sideways to its direction of motion.

## EQUILIBRIUM, STABILITY AND CONTROL

In order for a hang glider to be "pleasant" to fly, it must possess certain qualities. The flyer should be able to fly hands off for a certain period of time before a correction is necessary.

Equilibrium is basically a condition of balance and a hang glider, or any body, is in equilibrium when it is at rest or moving at a constant velocity. The more commonly recognized forms of equilibrium are the cases when a body is at rest, having no movement with respect to the earth. Going one step further, there are three kinds of equilibrium: neutral, stable and unstable. Let's use a marble as an example for our study of equilibrium.

### Neutral Equilibrium

Neutral equilibrium is displayed when the marble is set on a flat surface, such as a level table top. It stays where it is put. If it is given a push, it rolls in the direction it was pushed until it stops, and once again, it stays where it stops. While this marble is at rest, it is said to be in a state of neutral equilibrium.

### Stable Equilibrium

This is demonstrated by placing the marble in the bottom center of a hemispherically shaped dish. If the marbel is pushed to one side, it tends to go back to the bottom center, its original location. It may, in fact, overshoot the bottom and go slightly up the other side and even oscillate (move back and forth) from side to side, before it finally stops. It will, however, always stop at the center. In this case, the marble at rest is in a state of stable equilibrium (see Fig. 5-2).

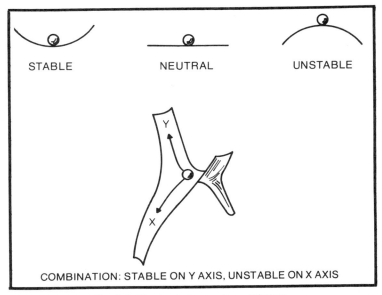

Fig. 5-2. The basic types of equilibrium.

### Unstable Equilibrium

This can be shown by turning the spherically shaped bowl upside down and placing the marble on top center. The marble will remain here but, if given a slight nudge it will roll away from top center, picking up speed. Here, the marble at rest on top center is said to be in a state of unstable equilibrium.

A combination of stable and unstable equilibrium can exist at the same time, if the marble is placed in a situation as represented.

Moving the marble off center in the "Y" axis direction and releasing it, it will tend to first oscillate and then finally stop on center. A slight move off center in the "X" axis direction however, results in the marble rolling off . This combination would be classed as unstable equilibrium, since one of the directions is unstable. This condition can possibly exist in a hang glider if it isn't properly designed.

### Stability

Stability refers to the hang glider's ability to return to its original flight condition after it is moved off center for some reason or another. There are two kinds of stability: static stability and dynamic stability.

The first of these, static stability, is exhibited when a hang glider, or marble, is disturbed but returns directly to its original position after the disturbance passes. Conversely, static instability is the situation that exists when the object is moved from its original position and does not return after the disturbance passes.

The second form of stability, dynamic stability, is more complicated than the static case, and involves an oscillation, or swinging back and forth, that gradually lessens or dampens out, until the object is back to its original position. If the marble were to be disturbed from its original position and it began to oscillate more and more, it is said to be dynamically unstable.

Ideally a hang glider should be both statically and dynamically stable!

Once a hang glider is stable, it must be able to be controlled. It should be able to be steered in the direction the pilot wants to go. The control of a hang glider has two functions. Number one is the ability to change from an initial condition of equilibrium to another condition of equilibrium. For example, in one case the pilot may want to fly slow, while in another, he may wish to speed up. The control available to the flyer must be such that the hang glider can be handled adequately in all the conditions it is to be used. The number two function of control is to provide the ability to maneuver the hang glider. A maneuver is essentially a condition where the hang glider is not in equilibrium, i.e., it is not still or not cruising at a constant speed. In other words, it is either accelerating or decelerating in or about at least one of its reference axes.

At this point, mention should be made of the time span, or period, of an oscillation associated with dynamic stability. If the marble is disturbed, and then let go, it will oscillate around bottom center of our dish at a certain rate until it stops. Now, if the dish were filled with water, the oscillation rate, or period, would be shorter. This second condition, with water in the dish, exhibits what we call dampening.

In other words, a certain period exists with a certain combination of marble size, mass, dish shape and liquid.

210

Molasses would make the oscillations stop in an extremely short period of time, and so it is with hang gliders. Certain design features will determine how well it can dampen itself from oscillating in dynamic stability.

In general, the basic problem of stability and control is that of designing a hang glider that not only flies, but is pleasant to operate. In other words, the hang glider designer and pilot is looking for nice flying qualities. This, however, is easier said than done and the experience factor is important to any designer.

Maneuverability and stability are almost at opposite ends of the stick, but are certainly interconnected. Too much stability would make maneuvering difficult and/or sluggish. Too little stability might quicken the maneuverability, but may make for a dangerous hang glider. A good example of maneuverability versus stability is the jet fighter and the airliner. The fighter is quick and agile and must be flown all the time. The airliner is stable and cruises along effortlessly, but mostly in a straight line.

## FLYING QUALITIES

Currently, there are no federal regulations governing the flying qualities of hang gliders.

Furthermore, hang gliding is such a new industry that little, if any, research has been done in this area. However, all is not lost. There are many manufacturers of hang gliders and many significant flights have been made by various people. In fact, the Hang Glider Manufacturers Association (HMA), which consists of most of the manufacturers across the country, is trying to develop certain specifications that a given make ought to meet to be considered airworthy. While the organization really has no power, it is a step in the right direction. Ultimately though, the Federal Aviation Administration might step in to publish and enforce various criteria. At present however, this remains to be seen. The following discussion will deal with the nature and not the details of what one might consider under the topic of flying qualities.

Longitudinal stability and control refers to the ability of the hang glider to fly and maneuver with respect to pitch, i.e.,

Fig. 5-3. The author's canard stabilized kite. A successful experiment of 1971. It made the stall more gentle and dive recovery automatic. More R&D is necessary.

nose up/nose down. Unlike all other aircraft, the greater percentage of the total flying weight of man plus hang glider lays with the man. This is very significant and important, especially with respect to Rogallo wings. Basically, the man is a kind of pendulum as he hangs down from the center of the kite. (To contribute to the kites' stability, the man must be holding the control frame.) It's easy to see that a pendulum is stable, hanging with all that weight.

If the pendulum is moved off center and released, it will swing down, past bottom center, and so forth until it stops. A pendulum is dynamically stable! However, the problem of stability is not at all that simple. It takes more than a mere pendulum to provide for stability. One must consider the "dish," or wing, also.

Of great importance is the contribution of the wing itself, or perhaps a horizontal stabilizer tail, as found on some high performance type hang gliders. The canard stabilized kite is shown in Fig. 5-3. As long as the sail on a good flying Rogallo wing is inflated, the stability and control appear to be adequate for flight in ideal conditions. Whenever the sail begins to luff (the front starts caving in) however, the Rogallo tends to dive in an unstable, or at best, neutrally stable condition. Then too, the pilot is no longer hanging straight down and perpendicular with respect to the keel, and his effect on the stability is significantly reduced. In fact, the new position of the man may aggravate the situation making a "recovery" of the dive extremely difficult, if not altogether impossible. Since the sail is luffed and flagging in the dive, there is nothing for the air to react against. It's sort of like a marble whose dish has been tilted such that the marble rolls out.

A possible solution to the dive instability in the conditions mentioned above, might come in the form of a tail surface that would force the sail to re-inflate automatically due to the various air pressures acting on it.

The pitch control of a Rogallo wing, and some other hang glider types as well, is accomplished by the pilot moving his body forward and backward, with respect to the control bar. This situation appears to be adequate under ideal flying conditions. On hang gliders with a moving horizontal tail, or elevator, connected to a control stick, the controllability appears to be good. These hang gliders don't use weight shifting for control and have certain advantages over it. Among these advantages is response, which is generally quicker than with weight shifting (which exhibits a definite lag from the time the body is moved until the time the hang glider responds). Also, properly designed hang gliders with movable elevators appear to be stable in a dive, the elevator being able to exert a strong enough downward force on the tail to lift the nose consistently and without fear of a luffed-sail induced dive.

## WEIGHT SHIFTING VERSUS AERODYNAMIC CONTROL

Today's most popular hang glider, the Rogallo wing, is controlled by weight shifting: the body is simply moved in the direction the pilot wants to go! This type of control seems natural and students can relate to it quite readily. Any one who has ridden a bike or skied knows basically how weight shift works. Furthermore, weight shifting allows the glider design to be simple, involving no mechanisms or moving parts.

The other primary method of hang glider control is aerodynamic i.e., movable control surfaces, located on the tail and/or wings, allowing the pilot to steer his craft where he wants to go. In its "purest" form, a control stick, which is common to conventional aircraft, is connected to the control surfaces and moved by the actions of the pilot's hand. Control sticking, too, is natural in that one moves the control stick in the direction he wants to go. However, it is perhaps not as "instinctive" as weight shifting. Aerodynamic controls also require mechanisms and moving parts which complicate the hang glider design.

A mixture of aerodynamic control and weight shifting is found on some hang glider types. Normally, pitch control is by weight shift, while lateral (turning) control is done by moving an aerodynamic control surface.

A modified control stick, or lines attached directly to the pilot, coordinate the movement of the aerodynamic controls with the weight shifting control.

One might ask, what's the difference in the three methods of control?

## Weight Shift

This is the common practice in hang glider control today, basically because most hang gliders (95%) are Rogallo wings. It maintains the simplicity of the concept, and it appears to be effective. Just how effective is it? One way to look at it is as follows. Consider the kite to be a kind of overhead seesaw. The pilot moves himself off center, and the wing with his weight under it drops, and the kite begins to turn in that direction (see Fig. 5-4). Fine, but how much control does he really have available? He can move his weight to the corner of the control bar, which is 2 feet off center. If he weighs 150 pounds, that means he has 2 feet times 150 pounds, or 300 foot-pounds of off center "moment" to bring down a wing. In other words he can balance a rolling moment which equals 300 foot-pounds and that's it! The most he can get is 300 foot-pounds.

Now, consider the pilot to be flying in a 10 mph wind with adequate control. What happens if he tried to fly in a 20 mph wind? First of all, remember he has only 300 foot-pounds of rolling moment, and it doesn't change, no matter what the wind. Secondly, when the wind goes from 10 mph to 20 mph, its force becomes four times as great! In other words, relative to

Fig. 5-4. A Rogallo pilot shifts left to control the lift coming off the ridge.

the wind, the pilot has only one-fourth the control power available at 20 mph that he had at 10 mph. Stated another way, to have the same control at 20 mph as he had at 10 mph, would require a rolling moment of $4 \times 300 = 1200$ foot-pounds! This, of course, could be had by his gaining weight to 600 pounds or being able to move off center 8 feet: clearly an impossible situation!

To sum it up then, one might say flying a kite in twice the wind is four times as dangerous! This kind of flying is done every day, so the choice is up to the pilot. Weight shifting does work, but it has limitations. Depending on the pilot's own body weight, plus manufacturers' recommendations, he can chose a kite size that is better suited to the conditions he expects to fly in. The larger the kite, the slower it flies and the less wind it can be controlled in. The smaller the kite, the faster it flies, and the higher the wind it can be controlled in.

**Pure Aerodynamic Control**

Not nearly so common as weight shift, aerodynamic control is used on only a few so-called high performance hang

Fig. 5-5. The VJ-23 Swingwing uses three-axis, aerodynamic controls.

glider designs, such as the one shown in Fig. 5-5. It is, more or less, expected to be used on these. Its added complexity goes along with the added complexity of the glider itself. How effective is this aerodynamic control, anyway? Since this is the "pure" form of aerodynamic control, there is no weight shifting involved. The pilot is centered in all attitudes of his flight, and he gets no aid from weight shift. Consider flight in a 10 mph wind with adequate control. What happens this time when one tries to fly in a 20 mph wind? First, the aerodynamic forces go up 4 times, as before, but since he is using controls that are aerodynamic, the control effectiveness also increases four times! The rolling moment goes up four times. In essence, he has the same relative control power at 20 mph as he did at 10 mph. What a bonanza! In fact, control response is maximized at some speed, and is generally better at faster speeds than at slower speeds.

Keep in mind that at the stall speed of the glider (the minimum speed at which it will fly) aerodynamic controls become sluggish and less effective than at normal cruising speed. Weight shift, on the other hand, remains somewhat effective below the stall speed.

### Aerodynamic Control Coupled to Weight Shift

As might be expected, this mixture does not necessarily combine the best of both worlds involved. It depends on the setup. Figures 5-6 and 5-7 show two versions of this type of glider.

In one type of hang glider, the pilot moves fore and aft for pitch control while he actuates tip rudders with twist grips. He remains centered in all turns because of the design, but can move to change pitch. The two functions are not connected and do not interact. The stability in turning is not effected.

In another type of hang glider, the pilot moves fore and aft for pitch control while a rudder is connected directly to his harness and is actuated as he shifts sideways for a turn. As the two functions are interconnected, they can interact. The stability in a turn can be affected and pilot induced oscillations can be generated between the freely swinging pilot and interconnected rudder.

In summary, then, no matter what type of control system a hang glider has, its particular limitations must be known and observed. Again, the choice is up to the individual.

Fig. 5-6. Kiceniuk's Icarus II uses weight shift for pitch and drag rudders for roll/yaw control.

Fig. 5-7. Dave Cronk turns Lovejoy's Quicksilver with a rudder connected to his harness via cords. Pitch is controlled by weight shift.

## LATERAL STABILITY AND CONTROL

Lateral stability and control refer to the ability of the hang glider to fly and maneuver with respect to roll, i.e., wings level or not. As in the longitudinal case, a part of the lateral stability in a hang glider arises from the so-called pendulum effect of the weight of the man hanging below the wing.

Another aerodynamic method of achieving lateral stability is to give the wings a dihedral angle (see Fig. 5-8). This is simply shown as a wide "V" angle between the wings, as seen in the front view. The dihedral angle itself lies between one wing and the horizon, as shown. As a matter of fact, most Rogallo wings have no noticeable dihedral, while higher performance gliders almost always do.

Dihedral produces stability in roll as explained. Suppose the hang glider is flying along, in straight and level flight, when it's suddenly struck by a gust of wind from the left side. The gust will lift the left wing and also push the hang glider to the right, off course. The sideways motion, called a sideslip, will cause the angle of attack of the right (low) wing to increase and thus produce greater lift. The result of this increased lift of the right wing will raise it back to the level, as it was before the gust arrived. All is not perfect however, because the hang glider will be flying in a slightly more right direction than before.

Thus we see, dihedral is an essential ingredient for restoring equilibrium in roll, and much like a pendulum, it tends to create an oscillation, or swinging back and forth before it finally settles on center.

In a well stabilized hang glider the oscillations in roll are adequately dampened even though dihedral may not be evident. Instead, it has at least an "apparent dihedral" or dihedral effect due to various elements of the design.

Another source of lateral stability is tied in closely with directional stability, and that is the angle of sweepback of the wings (see Fig. 5-9). In general, the "effective" dihedral due to sweepback is equal to about 1/10th the sweepback angle. In other words, 10° sweepback equals 1° of dihedral. A good example of this is a typical kite which, while not appearing to possess any obvious dihedral, does indeed have effective dihedral. The effective dihedral increases with angle of attack.

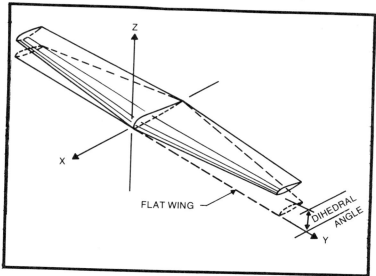

Fig. 5-8. A definition of the dihedral angle.

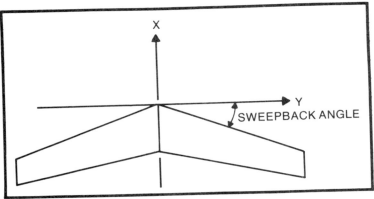

Fig. 5-9. A definition of the sweepback angle.

Basically, whenever a hang glider is banked to the left, for example, the angle of attack and therefore the lift of the left wing increases and tends to lift it back up toward the level position again. At the same time, the angle of attack of the right wing has been reduced, as has the lift, and it tends to drop down toward the level. These differences in lift, between the left and right wings, make up a dampening tendency in roll as well. This holds true in both cases, when the hang glider is rolling back to level or away from level. Thus, any oscillations in roll due to the stabilizing effect of dihedral are effectively damped out.

Besides dihedral, the good old effect of the pendulum can be used again for lateral stability. This is evidenced in the fact that the pilot is hanging below the wing. If a side gust of wind strikes the hang glider and raises a wing, the low slung weight of the man tends to level the wings. Note, however, the man must at least be holding fast to and centered at the control bar for his weight to add to the stability. If he is flying "hands off" and is free to swing independently of the hang glider's rolling tendency, his weight will add little to the lateral stability. Of course, if he shifts his weight toward the high wing, it will be lowered. All hang gliders today have the man hanging below the wing. The lower the man, the greater his contribution to lateral stability, and naturally, the less his maneuverability. If the pilot shifts too far toward the high wing he may actually overshoot and lower it below the horizon. This is called "over-controlling" and is eliminated only by experience. One might safely say, the more experience a pilot has, the better he is at dampening his glider's motions.

## DIRECTIONAL STABILITY AND CONTROL

Directional stability and control refers to the ability of the hang glider to fly and maneuver with respect to yaw (i.e., flying straight or not). Directional stability in a hang glider is due basically to vertical fin area located aft of the center of gravity. On monoplanes and other types so fitted, the vertical tail or fin is plainly evident. On a kite however, there is no vertical fin as such, but the vertical fin area still exists.

Vertical fin area as shown in Fig. 5-10, produces stability in yaw as follows. Suppose the hang glider is flying along in straight and level flight when it's suddenly struck by a gust of wind from the left side, as in the roll stability example.

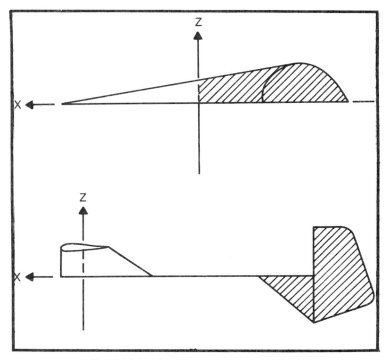

Fig. 5-10. Vertical fin area on a hang glider.

The gust will push the hang glider to the right, off course, but, because of the larger amount of vertical fin area aft of the c.g., the nose of the hang glider tries to point into the wind.

This rotation of the nose to the left is halted or dampened out because the direction of motion causes the wind to strike the right side of the fin, trying to straighten the flight path. This effect is sometimes referred to as "weathercock stability." There is always a lag in response, however, and the hang glider will be on a slightly different course than it was before the gust struck and the glider straightened out. The new course will be slightly to the right of the original. While in the transition, or lag period, the hand glider is said to be "skidding" as the yawing motion is dampened out.

The only way to get back on course is for the pilot to exert some control over the situation. Essentially, he must roll and yaw slightly to the left just enough to do the trick. In the case of a monoplane, or other types with a rudder, he can bring the hang glider back on course by deflecting the rudder appropriately. In the case of a pure weight shift situation, as in a kite, he must roll the hang glider slightly left, while pitching up slightly.

As mentioned previously, lateral and directional stability and control are inseparable. One does not exist without the other. Thus, it is often better to think in terms of "spiral stability."

All that has been said before about lateral and directional stability must be tempered by the following discussion.

A dihedral effect is required to roll a hang glider level whenever it is in a sideslip, i.e., whenever it has some side velocity, due to the fact that it is not pointed exactly in the direction it is going. This is referred to as a "yawed" condition, since it is concerned with rotation about the vertical, or yaw, axis of the hang glider. Generally speaking, the more dihedral the better, up to a point. One wants just enough to level the hang glider once it has sideslipped or started to spiral toward the ground.

At this point, consider the size of the vertical fin area, and what it does in sideslip. Think of the hang glider with no dihedral in a sideslip. What happens? It should be clear that the side wind, hitting the vertical fin, pushed it to the other side, causing a higher airspeed on the outer wing, which generated more lift! This outer wing then tilted up and the inner wing down. The pilot headed for a spiral dive and crash. If he had the correct amount of effective dihedral, this wouldn't have happened, because the inside (low) wing would have picked up!

Suppose now, the pilot has dihedral and no vertical fin areas, and is in a sideflip. What happens? This time, there is no way for a spiral dive to be induced, so the glider starts whipping back and forth, from side to side, in what is called a "Dutch Roll." This oscillation can build up and send the hang glider into a "barrel roll" which puts it upside down. A dangerous situation to say the least.

What is needed then, is a certain combination of dihedral and vertical fin area—vertical fin for weathercock stability, and the correct amount of dihedral to prevent the spiral dive. The larger the vertical, the more dihedral is needed. Unfortunately, there are no hard and fast formulas for determining the right amount of each, since there are so many variables. One, however, can come close by looking at what's been done and proven successful and trying to make a "guestimate." In the final analysis, the design must be test flown, and checked for its stability characteristics and altered appropriately if need be. Today, most wing type hang gliders have dihedral angles of around 6 to 8 degrees.

The following is a list of lateral and directional stability factors:

1. The greater the amount of "effective dihedral" (which includes geometric dihedral and sweepback angle) the larger vertical fin area will be required to prevent Dutch Roll.
2. The larger the man hanging from the glider the larger the vertical fin area required.
3. The more side area of the fuselage, the larger the vertical fin area required.
4. The faster the cruising speed, the larger the vertical fin area.
5. The farther away the vertical fin is from the center of gravity of the hang glider, the smaller it has to be.

6. The exact location or mounting point of the vertical fin will affect its optimum size. Such things as the wing, the man, and the horizontal tail affect it. In general, it's best to mount the vertical fin above or below the horizontal tail, to keep its required size the smallest.

7. No vertical area will be required if the properly designed horizontal tail, with either a dihedral or negative dihedral (cathedral) angle, is used on the hang glider. However, vertical area is normally very useful in practice. Birds don't have them, though.

8. Finally, the optimum size for the vertical fin and dihedral angle of the wings can only be determined from actual flight testing.

A list of items that increase spiral stability follows:

1. Geometric dihedral
2. Sweepback
3. Small vertical fin
4. Man hanging below wing
5. Lower aspect ratio
6. Fast cruise speed
7. Wingtip washout (negative tip angle)
8. Drag device—out on wing
9. Small tip chord (tapered wing)
10. Upswept wing tips

## ASSESSMENT OF FLYING AND OPERATING QUALITIES

It's difficult, at best, to assess the flying and operating qualities of a hang glider, especially if one is a beginner to the sport. First off, one might say "Just go to a local site and see how many of the various makes are there, the best will probably be the most numerous." Well, I would not especially agree with this philosophy. Quantity does not necessarily mean quality. Marketing sells gliders and not excellence. The best a beginner can do is to read as much of the literature as possible and try to look at it objectively. Then decide what he wants in a hang glider.

Essentially, a hang glider should be pleasant to fly, from takeoff to touchdown. The transition from running down hill to lift off, should be smooth. Trimming for best glide should be easy and natural. Ability to stall and parachute land (a kite) without sliding off to the side, is desirable. Figure 5-11 shows the center of gravity envelope for standard Rogallo wings. Higher performance hang gliders should stall straight ahead with no tendency to "fall off on a wing." Turns should be easily and naturally accomplished. The wider the control bar, the more turning power there is available.

Transporting, rigging and ground handling should be convenient. The lighter the hang glider, the easier it is to move around. However, structural integrity must not be sacrificed for weight. The hang glider must be able to not only withstand normal flight loads, but also normal ground loads due to nosing in or otherwise stopping abruptly. A lighter glider will also respond quicker to control inputs, be they either weight shift or aerodynamic, because it possesses less inertia.

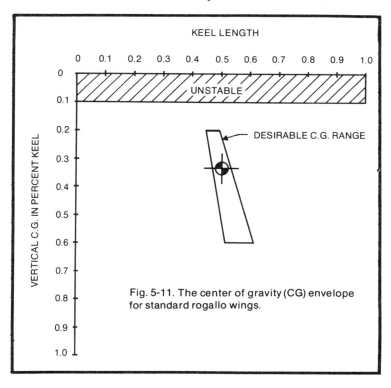

Fig. 5-11. The center of gravity (CG) envelope for standard rogallo wings.

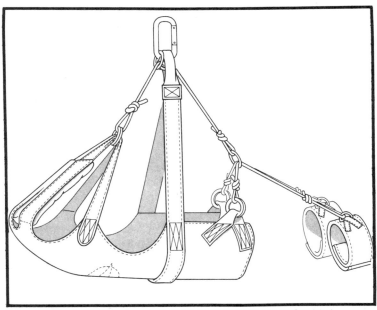

Fig. 5-12. An advanced design prone harness by Sunbird.

Rigging should be as convenient and fast as possible, with safety in mind. Normally, no tools should be required for just minutes assembly time. The rigging system should be "idiot proof." The assembly sequence should not allow an error or forgetfulness to enter the scene. Let's not have any midair failure or structural collapse.

The harness design should be safe and comfortable. It should have a "quality" look about it (see Fig. 5-12). There's no room for skimping here. High strength parachute-type hardware is a good sign. Also, some sort of quick release feature should be provided in the design. The harness should be comfortable and provide good support and balance. There's absolutely no excuse for falling or slipping out of a harness. Once one is in, he should stay in until he disconnects after the flight.

The longitudinal stability should be such that the pilot can fly "hands-off" for several seconds before a control correction is needed. In a weight shift hang glider, moving forward will cause the speed to increase, while moving back will cause it to decrease. In many hang gliders though (especially kites) the stability decreases as the speed increases: it becomes more difficult to "push-out" of a dive the steeper it becomes. To avoid this, don't dive the kite steeply and don't fly in conditions that might cause a steep dive or collapse of the sail.

The spiral stability should be such that the hang glider doesn't Dutch Roll or exhibit a roll-off or spiral dive tendency when sideslipping. The higher aspect ratio gliders are more susceptible to this instability. Directionally, the glider should tend to weathercock.

## STRUCTURAL CONSIDERATIONS

The hang glider should be strong enough to not only take the normal loads of flight, but, also tough enough to withstand the ground loads it will see during the beginner period. Many hang gliders today (of the kite variety) seem to be somewhat marginal, especially in their survival rate during the training period. (Weak king posts and/or control frames are always in need of replacement.) On the other hand, if the structure is too stiff it will not yield at all on impact, subjecting the pilot to a greater blow. There's a lot to be said for a partially deformable structure. It could save one from breaking a bone or more serious injury. Better to break or bend a tube rather than an arm.

A hang glider is so simple, one might ask, "What could go wrong?" No matter how simple it seems though, it is holding a person up in thin air. His life is literally hanging in the balance. Thus, it is important that only the best materials be used in the construction of a hang glider. One's life is certainly worth it! Either aircraft or high strength, heat treated industrial bolts must be used for fastening: no hardware store items. All cable should be either stainless steel or the galvanized aircraft type. All fittings should be stainless steel. All bottom or flying cables should be vinyl coated for one's protection. It will also allow them to last longer. All aluminum should be at least 6061-T6 or its equivalent. The sail material should be at least 3 oz stabilized Dacron sail cloth. Most hang gliders available today seem to use the good components. Any kite type hang glider should at least meet the HMA specifications.

Probably the biggest factor to consider when talking about safety is the hang glider pilot himself, the proverbial "nut behind the wheel." After all, it is he (or she) who decides to fly in the first place. Good judgment, common sense, conservatism and caution can not be overemphasized. If one uses his head and thinks before he leaps, he can minimize the risks involved in hang gliding. Don't be influenced by peer pressure. If it is too gusty, walk the glider down the hill. There will be another day when conditions are more favorable and enjoyable!

Flyers have been heard saying things like: "I lugged my kite all the way up this hill and I'll be darned if I'm gonna walk down with it," which has lead to disaster. Perhaps a broken hang glider, or worse yet, a broken bone has been the result of overly bold statements. Be intelligent enough to say no when conditions aren't good for flying. Even if one's buddies are egging him on, he should use good judgment. Remember, nobody but oneself will be suffering the results of his rash judgment and/or yielding to peer pressure.

Speaking of safety then, leads right in to the area of limitations and observing them. One should know what he and his particular hang glider can do. What kind of winds is the pilot and the hang glider good for? Is he a beginner, intermediate or advanced flyer? Is his hang glider a trainer, advanced design or high performance type? Does it use weight shift and/or aerodynamic controls? How stable is it? What kind of flying site is he using? Sand is a lot softer than rock! Slopes give gentler airflow than cliffs, as do coastal areas versus inland areas. What is the safest fast flying speed for his hang glider? Does he have an airspeed indicator mounted to his hang glider?

The pilot must always remember to think before he leaps. His life is hanging in the balance. When he's flying, there's no room for mistakes. It's not like a ground or water sport, where a fall is rarely fatal. Falling in a hang glider almost always means injury or death.

The air is a very non-forgiving medium. One must know all he can about it, about himself, and about his hang glider. Each flight is different, offering its own special challenges. The only way one can master it is to practice, practice, practice; and the only way he can continue to practice is to be conservative and observe limitations.

# Chapter 6
# The Atmosphere

## THE ATMOSPHERE

Before one gets into hang gliding, or any type of flight for that matter, it's a good idea to begin by looking at the medium that allows flight to take place. Herewith is an overview of the properties and phenomena of the space we call the atmosphere.

## EXTENT

The atmosphere has been called "the ocean of air that starts at your doorstep." Indeed, the earth is completely surrounded by it, the only continuous medium on the planet. It is the only continuous "highway" which allows uninterrupted travel from one point to the next. Weight wise however, the atmosphere makes up only one one-millionth of the entire mass of the planet!

The height of the atmosphere cannot actually be given, since its density decreases with altitude and it is capable of

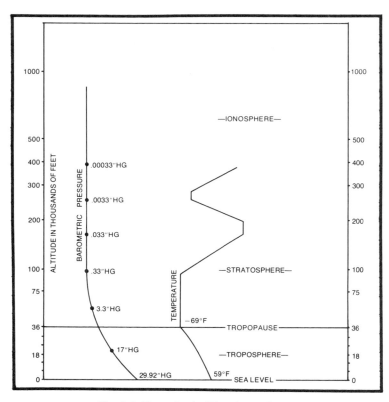

Fig. 6-1. The extent of the atmosphere.

indefinite expansion (see Fig. 6-1). However, one can get a better understanding of the concentration of the atmosphere from the barometric pressure at various altitudes. Looking at it this way, one finds that 50% of the atmosphere is below 26,000 feet while 90% of it is below 50,000 feet. Suffice to say, hand glider flight takes place in the lower 50% of the atmosphere!

## PROPERTIES AND CHARACTERISTICS

The atmosphere is a tasteless, odorless, colorless, mobile mixture of various gaseous elements. Furthermore, it has mass and thus weight and occupies the space of its container, having no definite shape.

## Weight

The weight of air is about .075 pounds to the cubic foot. Put another way, one pound of air occupies about 13 cubic feet! At any given height above sea level a given volume of air weighs less the higher up you go. More exactly, the weight of a chunk of air is in proportion to the barometric pressure at any particular altitude. For instance, at sea level, the common barometric pressure is around 29 inches of mercury or 14.7 pounds per square inch. If one were to go to the top of Mt. Everest, at 29,000 feet, he would find the barometer reading only 19 inches of mercury and our chunk of air would weigh only about .05 pounds per cubic foot—only 2/3 of its original sea level weight.

The weight, or density, of the air is an important factor in the design of all aircraft. The upward force of flight, called lift, depends on the density of air acted on, plus the surface area of the wing and its speed through the air. If all other factors remain the same, the lift developed by a wing will double if the air density is doubled.

## Composition

Air consists primarily of a mechanical, and not chemical, mixture of about 21% oxygen, 78% nitrogen and a 1% mixture of 10 other gases, by volume.

Their proportions remain essentially the same up to an altitude of about 60,000 ft. Air contains from 0 to .5% water vapor by volume which, under ordinary circumstances, can be considered to mix just like the other gases. The atmosphere also contains large amounts of impurities including dust. Under certain conditions, especially around large metropolitan areas, the impurities suspended in the air are so great that the horizon appears hazy; a condition often referred to and well known as smog.

## Color

While air is commonly thought of as transparent, it in fact offers some blockage to light and vision. This blockage, however, is greater horizontally than vertically, the entire amount of air above the earth being equivalent to only 26,000 feet of air at sea level density. In other words, its easier to see farther up than farther across the earth. Even so, scientists like to get as high as possible to observe such things as eclipses of the moon and other astronomical phenomena. Indeed, the clearest view is had aboard a spacecraft bound for outer space. This difference, however, should be of no concern to the hang glider pilot.

### Aerostatics: Air at Rest

Air at rest of any given pressure, temperature and composition is a relatively simple situation. However, one should understand the effects of these items to better know the air in which he will fly.

### Pressure

Air, along with all other gases, but unlike most liquids, can be compressed from a given volume to a smaller volume. This is to say that the volume of any given weight of air can be pressurized to a smaller volume with each increase in pressure. In hang gliding, as with most private aircraft, the compressibility of air is not at all noticeable. It isn't until the speed of sound is approached that the compressibility of air becomes evident. At this point, the so-called sonic boom is created as air is literally rammed up against the aircraft at such a rate that it cannot move out of the way without first being compressed and causing a loud boom.

Under normal circumstances, the space occupied by a certain volume of air is directly proportional to the pressure it is under, i.e., doubling the pressure halves the volume. This compression then leads to a temperature rise while conversely a decrease in pressure (volume expansion) results in a temperature drop.

### Liquid and Solid States

Every known form of matter, be it normally a solid, liquid or gas, can be changed to the other two states of matter by applying the proper amounts of temperature and pressure. Indeed, metals can be melted and even vaporized into gas, while liquids can be solidified, as is familiar when water solidifies, or freezes into ice. Gases are no different either. When put under the right amount of pressure and lowered to the correct temperature, they turn first to liquids and then solids. A good example is liquid oxygen (LOX) as used in space craft rocket boosters, its temperature being −220° Fahrenheit under a pressure of 574 pounds to the square inch! Cooling it still further would then result in solid oxygen!

**Aerodynamics: Air in Motion**

Aerodynamics is the study of air in motion, and more specifically how it relates to the flight of aircraft, which in this case are hang gliders. Air is an almost perfectly elastic fluid, as far as we are concerned, and its motion is so complex that it almost defies analysis. The wind tunnel, a large tube with a fan in one end drawing air through it, is commonly used by aeronautical engineers to test and refine their designs; mere calculations falling short of the task. At this point, we should look at the most important dynamic properties of the air, its inertia, elasticity and viscosity, to get a better insight into its actions and reactions.

**Inertia**. Air, as does all matter, has weight and possesses inertia which can be defined as: the tendency of a mass to remain either in a state of rest or motion, until acted upon by some disturbing or outside force. Since air is much lighter than either solids or liquids, it has much less inertia. However, it does exist. Natural phenomena such as bird flight and tornados prove its tremendous power and value in certain cases. One might think of it simply as "the air is hard enough if it is hit fast enough."

**Elasticity**. The property of elasticity is perhaps one of the most important when we consider the flight or movement of an object through the air. It is the ability of a substance to be deformed by some force and when the force is removed to return to its original condition. This property is very obvious in gases, such as air, and distinguishes it from liquids, which are essentially inelastic. In fact, air is one of the most perfectly elastic substances known to man. In other words, it can withstand tremendous amounts of pressure for unlimited periods of time and when the pressure is removed, it will instantly return to its original volume. This is a very important property for flight, for as a wing moves through the air, the air is slightly compressed. The air always returns to its original condition after the wing passes by.

**Viscosity.** This is a property of air and other fluids that can be defined as fluid friction or "stickiness." In other words, as air moves over a surface such as a wing or kite sail, it tends to stick to it, and slow its movement. As the speed of the wings increases through the air, the viscosity causes an increase in air resistance which is commonly referred to as "drag": a force tending to hold it back.

## METEOROLOGY

Meteorology is the study of weather phenomena occurring in that part of the atmosphere known as the troposphere. It is of primary importance to hang glider pilots. The basic factors in any given weather environment are: temperature, barometric pressure, humidity and how changes in these affect the local conditions.

These changes in turn result in the secondary effects of moisture condensation, precipitation, and the movement of air as winds.

### Temperature: The First Major Weather Determinant

Temperature is perhaps the single most important of the elements that make up the weather and its changes. Besides having seasonal variations with local and daily variations within a locality, there is also a worldwide average decrease in temperature of 3 1/2°F for every 1,000 feet of altitude gain. This effect is known as the "standard or temperature lapse rate" and is certainly important as one climbs higher and higher in the troposphere. It is evidenced by snowcapped mountains in even warmer climatic zones of the earth. The lapse rate, as shown in Fig. 6-2, continues with altitude until a temperature of about −69°F is reached at about 36,000 feet above sea level (28,000 feet at the poles and 54,000 feet at the equator). This is the ceiling of the troposphere, called the tropopause. Above this level, the temperature is a constant −69°F and the region, known as the stratosphere, is relatively free of all weather phenomena. It is always clear and the sun is always shining. Needless to say, hang glider pilots are concerned only with the troposphere and its fickle friend, the weather.

Air temperature is recorded on two basic scales: centigrade (C) and the more familiar Fahrenheit (F). The

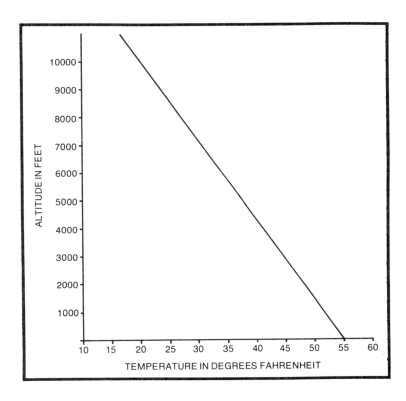

Fig. 6-2. The temperature "lapse rate". An important consideration in altitude gaining flights.

centigrade is used mostly in scientific applications and is part of the metric system. Conventional aircraft thermometers normally employ a centigrade scale. Fahrenheit is typically used on radio and TV broadcasts and is the scale most laymen are accustomed to. If one is known, conversion to the other is easily accomplished.

The centigrade scale is perhaps the more logical of the two for its zero is the point where water freezes and ice melts, while its boiling point is set at an even 100°C. The Fahrenheit scale on the other hand, has arbitrarily set 32°F as the freezing point and 212°F as the boiling point. Centigrade has 100 equal degrees between freezing and boiling, while Fahrenheit has 180 equal degrees between these two main points. In other words, a 5° change in C is equivalent to a 9° change in F. To convert one to the other, as illustrated in Fig. 6-3, is a simple matter of using the following relationships:

$$F = (9/5)°C + 32 \text{ and, } C = 5/9 (°F - 32)$$

The earth gets most of its heat from the sun, the contribution from stars and geothermal heat being negligible. It comes to us in the form of solar radiation which we can feel. Depending on the angle those rays strike the earth, the temperature will vary. The rays are more directly overhead during a summer midday, so the most possible heat gets in. At other times of the day and year, the earth gets less heat. During the night, the earth cools but it continues to radiate heat upward during the process.

Depending on local surface conditions, the rate of upward radiation will vary. Water, for instance, has a great capacity to retain its temperature for a long period of time, therefore it will radiate heat at night. Heated to a certain temperature, it tends to stay there. Sand, on the other hand, will heat and cool quite rapidly as it has a comparatively small capacity for heat.

**Barometric Pressure:**
**The Second Major Weather Determinant**

The weight of the atmosphere is generally shown as barometric pressure, which varies primarily with altitude but is also affected by temperature. At sea level and 59°F for instance, the barometer reads 29.92 inches of mercury or, stated another way, 14.7 pounds per square inch. One way to visualize barometric pressure is to consider a square, one inch on each side, laid on the ground. If one could put the square inch on a scale and weigh the column of air above it, all the way up to the top of the atmosphere, it would weigh 14.7 pounds. Barometric pressure is extremely important to flight. The heavier the air, the easier the flight attained. In other words, it's easier to fly at sea level, than in Denver, Colorado. But, more on this later. Air pressure is also important to instruments such as altimeters and airspeed indicators.

On a weather map, equal pressure lines are connected by isobars.

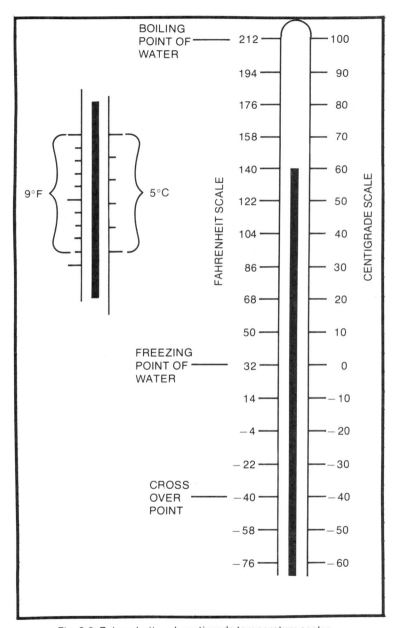

Fig. 6-3. Fahrenheit and centigrade temperature scales.

**Humidity: The Third Major Weather Determinant**

Humidity, or moisture, is the third major item that goes into determining weather conditions. It is commonly found in the atmosphere in one or more of the three states of matter: solid, liquid or gas. As a solid, it may take the form of snow, sleet, hail, and the ice crystals making up cloud and fog. As a liquid, it may take the form of rain, or as the tiny water droplets that form clouds and fog. As a gas, it appears in the form of water vapor.

Generally speaking, the common way of describing the amount of moisture in the air is to express it in terms of the "relative humidity." Given a mass of air at a certain temperature, it will be capable of holding a specific amount of water before it becomes totally saturated and falls out of the air, i.e., precipitates. Relative humidity refers to the amount of water in the air as compared to the amount the air could hold at a given temperature. For example, at 90°F, one cubic foot of air can hold about 1/31st of an ounce or about 1/18th cubic inch of water. If this same cubic foot of air were to be cooled, the water would fall out, or precipitate, in one of its forms, depending on how low the temperature dropped.

An easy way to demonstrate this is to cool a glass in the freezer for several minutes and then set it out in a normal temperatured room. Soon, it will "fog up." What has happened here is that the glass cooled the air around itself and caused the water in the air to precipitate out and condense on its surface.

Another method for knowing the relative moisture content of the air is the dew point. When the dew point and the air temperature are equal, the air is said to be saturated and the relative humidity is at 100%. This also says that the dew point can never exceed the temperature. When the air becomes saturated with water by cooling, the dew point has been reached. As a general rule of thumb, if the temperature is within 4° of dew point, fog or low flying clouds will probably be formed.

## CLOUDS

The moisture in the air originates from water areas and is visible in clouds, fog, rain and other forms of precipitation.

When warm moisture laden air rises and cools, or is surrounded by cooler air, it condenses and forms clouds. Obviously, not all condensation produces precipitation. Clouds are made up of ice crystals and water droplets, suspended in free air, and there are four main types: high clouds, middle clouds, low clouds and, clouds with vertical development.

High clouds are located between 20,000 and 40,000 feet and they range from cirrus, cirrocumulus and cirrostratus.

Middle clouds are located between 6,500 and 20,000 feet and they range from altostratus to altocumulus.

Low clouds are located from the surface to 6,500 feet and they range from stratus, nimbostratus and stratocumulus.

Clouds from vertical development start at 1,500 feet and on up. They range from cumulus to cumulonimbus.

Cirrus type clouds are high and generally streaky. Cumulus clouds are billowy. Stratus clouds are low and spread out. Clouds with the root word nimbus usually produce precipitation. A thundercloud is a cumulus that has developed vertically into a cumulonimbus with an "anvil" shape on top due to horizontal winds aloft. Storm clouds are usually dark and threatening looking.

Nice, puffy cumulus clouds with vertical development and a grey bottom are the kind favored by soaring pilots. These indicate the top of a thermal, or column of rising warm air, that has reached its dew point and condensed. The grey bottom is merely a concave area that the thermal updraft has pushed up and its rim is blocking the sun. A cloud "street" is formed when puffy "cums" with vertical development are seen lined up, sometimes for miles, providing a street of rising air.

Altocumulus lenticularis, or just plain lenticular clouds, indicate the presence of waves, which may form some distance from the lee side of a mountain. These particular clouds often look like "flying saucers" and indicate extremely high lift which may possibly be soared.

## WINDS

Wind is the movement of air and is the single most important aspect of hang gliding flight (see Fig. 6-4). One must develop a deep, abiding respect for it right from the beginning of his flying experiences. It can be friend or foe. It can kill a

Fig. 6-4. Use a wind meter to aid your judgement of wind conditions.

person or lift him to his highest of heights. He is entirely at its mercy when he hang glides for he literally becomes part of it! The wind chill factor is shown in Fig. 6-5.

Basically, wind can be horizontal, vertical or both and affects hang gliders very much. Winds also bring changes in the weather as they affect temperature, pressure and moisture. If air were always perfectly still everywhere, the weather would remain practically constant.

Winds are due primarily to temperature changes. For instance, air heated by a 50° F change, expands to about 10% more than its original volume. If expansion is not allowed, pressure is increased. Anyway, the heated, expanded air goes up. Hot air rises. Its rate of rise depends on both the temperature change and the total volume of air so heated. As this air rises, it causes an upward compression with a radial inflow from the surrounding air to fill the space the heated air just rose from. As the heated air travels upward (this is called a thermal, see Fig. 6-6) into the cooler regions of the atmosphere, it loses its head and changes its direction from up to horizontal (and finally starts going down somewhere else from where it originally ascended).

As air is heated and therefore expands, its weight is reduced which allows it to rise. The lessened weight also means that the barometric pressure in that location drops. This is an important event, because a falling barometer is generally interpreted as an indication to upcoming foul weather. In other words, the warm air that rose nicely into the blue and changed to a horizontal flow at the top (winds aloft) is replaced by cooler air which often contains condensed water vapor or clouds! If the clouds are sufficiently laden and the temperature correct, they will precipitate. By the way, the cooler air that rushes in to replace the rising, warm thermal air is commonly called wind, at ground level.

Basically, there are two modes of heating the atmosphere. The first is due to the daily appearance and disappearance of

**WIND SPEED**
**M.P.H.**

|  | 5 | 10 | 15 | 20 | 25 | 30 | 35 | 40 |
|---|---|---|---|---|---|---|---|---|
| 35 | 33 | 21 | 16 | 12 | 7 | 5 | 3 | 1 |
| 30 | 27 | 16 | 11 | 3 | 0 | -2 | -4 | -6 |
| 25 | 21 | 9 | 1 | -4 | -7 | -11 | -13 | -17 |
| 20 | 16 | 2 | -6 | -9 | -15 | -18 | -20 | -22 |
| 15 | 12 | -2 | -11 | -17 | -22 | -26 | -27 | -29 |
| 10 | 7 | -9 | -18 | -24 | -29 | -33 | -35 | -36 |
| 5 | 1 | -15 | -25 | -32 | -37 | -41 | -43 | -45 |
| 0 | -6 | -22 | -33 | -40 | -45 | -49 | -52 | -54 |
| -5 | -11 | -27 | -40 | -46 | -52 | -56 | -60 | -62 |
| -10 | -15 | -31 | -45 | -52 | -58 | -63 | -67 | -69 |
| -15 | -20 | -38 | -51 | -60 | -67 | -70 | -72 | -76 |
| -20 | -25 | -45 | -60 | -68 | -75 | -78 | -83 | -87 |

TEMPERATURE - DEGREES F

**WIND CHILL TEMPERATURE**

Fig. 6-5. Knowing the wind chill factor can help you dress.

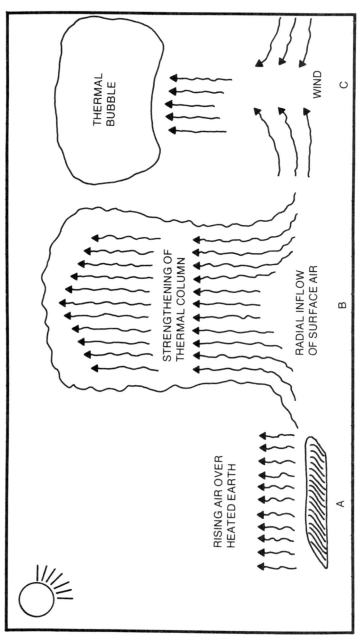

THERMAL BUBBLE

STRENGTHENING OF THERMAL COLUMN

RADIAL INFLOW OF SURFACE AIR

WIND

RISING AIR OVER HEATED EARTH

A    B    C

Fig. 6-6. Formation of a typical thermal.

the sun. The air is progressively heated and cooled as the sun moves across the sky. This can be pictured as a sort of general wave motion in the atmosphere. The second basic atmospheric heating mode is due to local areas on the earth and their ability to retain heat. For instance, deserts reflect heat and get hotter than the surrounding earth during the day. This great heating gives rise to the strongest thermal currents in the sky. At night, the desert cools rapidly, and becomes a kind of "sink hole" or down flow area.

Coastal winds are commonly found along most seashores and larger lake shorelines. Here, one can see just how effective temperature changes really are in creating wind. A day at the seashore normally begins with a light breeze off the water and rising to a moderate wind by noontime, only to subside to a calm by evening. Then, as it gets darker, the breeze changes direction and blows out to sea with its highest velocity at some time during the night, calming down before morning. This type of localized, off and on shore breeze situation is seldom felt more than 25 to 30 miles inland, and is usually accompanied by an opposite wind at about 500 to 1,000 feet above sea level. This is a good demonstration that shows the wind travels in a complete circle: up, across the sky, down and across the land.

Going in to more detail, consider the heat holding abilities of land and water. Water is by far the most stable, or shall we say, water has a huge capacity for maintaining a given temperature. Land, on the other hand, gives up and also takes on heat faster than does water. This simple fact explains why coastal areas are warmer in the winter and cooler in the summer: the winter water being warmer than the winter land and the summer water being cooler than the summer land. Generally speaking, air rises over land during the day and the breeze is on shore. During the night, air rises over the water and then flows off shore to replace the gap left by the rising sea air.

A few paragraphs ago, we spoke about the two modes of atmospheric heating: daily and local. The previous was one of local, now lets talk about the daily mode: prevailing winds. Across the North American continent and probably the rest of the northern hemisphere as well, the wind prevails, or blows primarily from west to east, but with seasonal variations in each particular area. These changes are due basically to the cold polar air which flows to replace the heated, rising equatorial air. You would think that those winds should flow most often north and south, but due to the earth's rotation and the shape of the land areas and water in the northern hemisphere, they don't. Instead, as the polar air goes toward the equator, it is caused to blow westerly. The seasonal variations we mentioned seem to follow the sun. For instance, in the northern U.S. prevailing is northwest.

The winds aloft or those over the prevailing ground winds are, at some altitude, going in the opposite direction of the ground winds. In the higher latitudes of the earth, these often come down to the surfaces and produce an easterly flow.

Whirlwinds, tornados and dustdevils are extremely localized winds of tremendous violence of a rotary nature. They are caused by intense local heating of the air and its rapid rising. This, or course, leads to a super quick inflow of the surrounding air and forms a vortex, or rotor, very similar to that formed when water flows down the drain in a bath tub. Luckily, these rotary type winds are short lived, and small in size. However, if one is present, don't dare fly. A simple dustdevil can cause a hang glider to go completely out of control. It is easily spotted though, as a swirling funnel of dust and debris. Stay away from it!

The velocity of the wind varies continuously, and is due to many factors. The highest winds ever recorded have been in excess of 300 mph inside a tornado, while the highest horizontal wind was recorded at the top of Mt. Washington, in New Hampshire, at 213 mph!

Heated air and its intensity of heat change is the main factor in creating wind. Once the wind is started and is flowing horizontally, one must look at the local topography to get a better understanding of the situation. In general, if a wind hits an object or obstruction, it is deflected away from it, after first ramming into it and being slightly "pressurized."

If the obstruction is a bluff body, the wind will tend to flow over and around it (see Fig. 6-7), being deflected in all directions, essentially following the path of least resistance. If the obstruction is a long ridge line of sand, hills, or mountains,

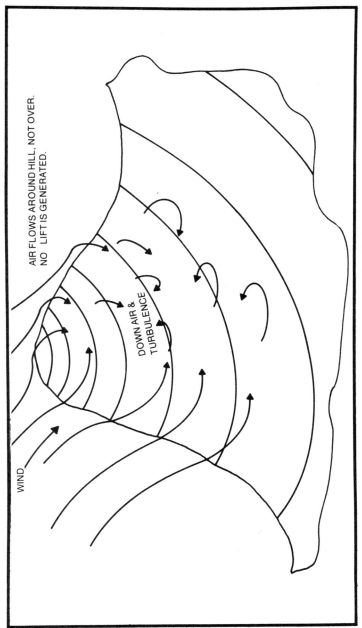

AIR FLOWS AROUND HILL, NOT OVER.
NO LIFT IS GENERATED.

DOWN AIR &
TURBULENCE

WIND

Fig. 6-7. Wind flowing over, around and behind a hill.

the wind is deflected upward in front of it. Somewhere over and in front of the top of this ridge, is a line of maximum vertical velocity. This situation is what pilots call "ridge lift" and is the primary means of soaring, or staying up, in a hang glider.

Another way to stay up in a hang glider, is to use the rising heated air of a thermal, as discussed previously.

In general, as air flows across a flat surface, such as a plain, the velocity at any given height above the surface is different. Right at the surface itself, believe it or not, there is no wind velocity at all! This is due to the "viscocity" talked about earlier. A good example of this strange phenomenon can be seen quite easily on a dusty automobile. No matter how fast one may drive, it just won't blow off! As soon as one moves up from the earth's surface, the velocity picks up until he gets up to about 150 feet where it is fairly uniform up to some greater altitude. This is called the "boundary layer" of the earth.

Another general characteristic of wind and the most important to a hang glider is that due to surface irregularities, like trees, small hills, buildings, etc., the wind near the ground can be highly irregular and turbulent (see Fig. 6-8), rising in front of obstructions, flowing around and down on the backside, like water over a dam.

This last characteristic is very dangerous and is often referred to as "down air" or down drafts! Down air is found on the leeward side of mountains, ridges, trees, and other wind blocking objects.

## FORECASTING THE WEATHER

Hang gliding, as with any outdoor activity, requires suitable weather in which to operate. Thus, it would be nice if one had the ability to predict what the weather is going to be, with a fair degree of accuracy. Well, of course, it can be done. By being observant and really aware of the environment, the weather and its various elements, one should be able to decide if he ought to make that outing to go hang gliding.

### Signs of Good Weather

An old sailors' expression, "red sky at night, sailor's delight," holds true in many instances. What this means is that

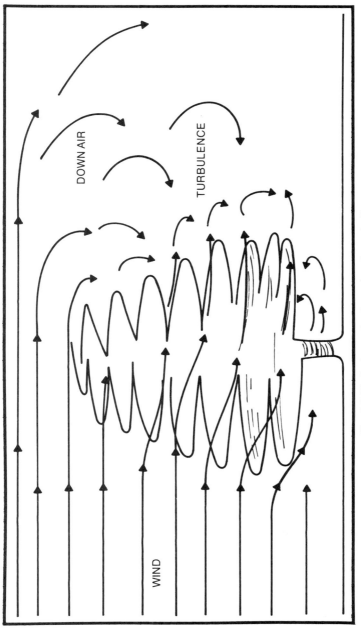

Fig. 6-8. Turbulence due to surface irregularities.

249

the clouds of sunset are reflecting the last of the sunlight because the skies are clear to the west, from where most of our weather comes. Tomorrow should dawn bright and clear.

If the stars are out, there's a good chance it'll be cool at night and clear in the morning.

High flying birds are a sign of a high pressure area and good weather. These birds are probably chasing insects that have been picked up by thermals and the high pressure region which aids flight. These same factors make smoke rise easily as well.

If dew or frost is present in the morning, it'll probably be a good day, since there were no clouds out the night before to absorb the moisture left on cooled surface objects.

**Signs of Bad Weather**

Another old sailors expression, "Red sky in morning, sailors take warning," is also fairly reliable. If clouds are present to the west, the rising sun will reflect off them with a red color. Rain or at least clouds will soon be overhead.

If the stars are not out at night, it is cloudy and may rain.

If the air is extremely still, birds are not flying and smoke is sinking, then a low pressure, moisture laden air mass has entered the area. The moisture has been absorbed by the smoke ashes and weighted them down. The birds just sense it.

Other ways of getting information on the weather are the local radio, TV stations and newspapers. The National Weather Service, also, has a recording, updated every 6 hours, that one can call in most metropolitan areas. Conventional aircraft pilots also use Flight Service Stations (FSS) for the latest weather when planning a flight. Many airports have FSSs and all one has to do is call the one for his area of concern. Here, he can find out the winds aloft, temperature, etc.

**Weather Fronts**

An approaching cold front is a good sign for hang glider pilots. As this wedge-shaped air mass moves in, it displaces warmer air by pushing it up, and out of the way.

After a cold front passes, strong winds and convection follow, along with a 90 degree shift in wind direction. Only advanced soaring pilots should attempt to use this phenomenon though. It is dangerous!

# Chapter 7
# Hang Glider Performance

## HANG GLIDER PERFORMANCE

Basically, a hang glider is designed to fly, giving some particular level of performance. That is to say, the hang glider makes the "best" use of the atmospheric energy that is available. More specifically, the hang glider designer is striving for first, the lowest possible rate of sink, or descending speed, and second, the highest glide ratio, both consistent with adequate structural integrity, stability and control. It is useful to study hang glider performance (see Fig. 7-1), not only to gain a know how of what to look for in a good design, but also to equip oneself with the knowledge necessary to get the most out of his hang glider whenever he flies it.

Before actually trying out the techniques outlined in part one, one must study the theory of flight. Why does the hang glider fly in the first place? So, lets find out how such a device as simple as a hang glider flies.

Fig. 7-1. Any hang glider will offer its maximum performance when flown prone.

## THEORY OF FLIGHT

Why does a hang glider fly? It has no engine. How can it apparently defy the law of gravity? How can it glide forward after giving a running start down an incline? Indeed, how can it be made to sustain for a given period of time and even to gain altitude under certain circumstances?

To begin with, all aircraft (i.e., any heavier than air, man-made device that derives its ability to fly by moving forward through the air in stable equilibrium) are subject to four basic forces: lift, drag, thrust and weight. Lift is the upward force that holds the hang glider in the air. Drag is the retarding force, or "air resistance," that tries to keep the hang glider from moving forward. Thrust is the driving force that overcomes the drag and makes the hang glider move forward, and weight is, of course, the force of gravity pulling the mass of the hang glider toward the earth.

The conditions for stable equilibrium flight are that the lift, L, be equal to the weight, W, and that the drag, D, be equal to the thrust, T. And so it is. This seemingly simple situation is easy enough to understand except it's not exactly true as relates to a hang glider. It is exactly true in the case of a powered aircraft.

254

Since a hang glider does not have an engine and thus produces no thrust, it must derive its forward velocity at the expense of losing altitude. A hang glider is always descending with respect to the surrounding air.

The only way it can rise from a given position, with respect to the earth, is to be in wind that is rising (e.g., slope lift or thermal lift) faster than the hang glider drops, or sinks, in still air. Obviously, the lower the value of the sink rate of the glider in still air, the lighter the vertical wind has to be to enable the hang glider to be suspended or to gain altitude with respect to the earth (see Fig. 7-2). This requirement, that the hang glider

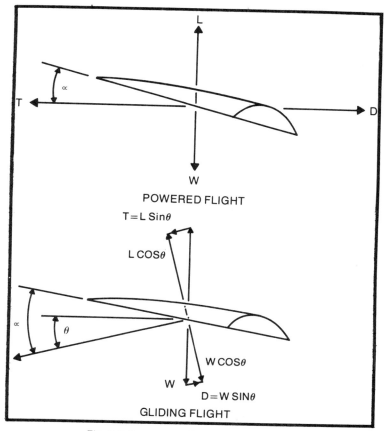

Fig. 7-2. Forces on a hang glider in flight.

be always descending with respect to our air, modifies the diagram of forces.

Now one should learn what gliding flight is all about. The most obvious thing about the diagram is that the glide path is at some angle, $\theta$, below the horizon. This is merely in accordance with the law of gravity which attracts all objects within its influence. This glide angle, with steepness dependent on the particular glider design, gives a force diagram that is slightly more complicated than in the first case. As can be seen, the weight, W, as before, pulls down perpendicular to the horizon. However, due to the particular glide angle, the lift force, L, is tilted forward at an angle equal to the glide angle. From this, it should be easily seen that the forward leaning lift force has a component of itself projecting forward with respect to the horizon. This is where the thrust comes from! A hang glider gives up some lift in order to move forward. Depending on how much lift it gives up, or put another way, how much drag it has, will determine the best, or shallowest gliding angle for that particular design.

The conditions for stable equilibrium gliding flight are that the lift, L, be equal to Wcos $\theta$ (which is slightly less than the total weight of the flight system) and that the drag, D, be equal to Wsin $\theta$ (which is actually the component of the lift force which is tilted forward.) So, once again, the four basic forces of flight are balanced in the hang gliding situation.

Going one step further, one can find where the two basic performance figures (i.e., sink rate and glide ratio) come from. Looking again, one sees that while the hang glider moves, or flies, along its glide path, both a horizontal and a vertical speed are established. The vertical speed, $V_{r\,s}$, or rate of sink, is simply the speed at which the hang glider descends through still air. As an example, if a hang glider took off from the top of a 100 foot hill and the flight lasted 20 seconds, the sink rate would be 100 feet divided by 20 seconds, or 5 feet per second as shown in Fig. 7-3. (If the glider was in a slope or thermal lift of 5 feet/sec it would not sink toward the ground but remain at the same height.) The horizontal speed, $V_H$, is in most cases, so close to the glide speed, V, that they are taken as one in the same. However, it can be clearly seen that this is not exactly true for glide angles, $\theta$, that are greater than 10°

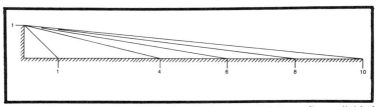

Fig. 7-3. The glide ratio is defined as the horizontal distance flown divided by the vertical drop. It is numerically equal to the L/D ratio of the glider.

below the horizon. If the hang glider were to again launch from the top of the 100 foot hill and flew for 20 seconds, and went forward 500 feet, its forward speed would be 500 feet divided by 20 seconds or 25 feet per second, i.e., about 17 mph.

Taking the forward speed and dividing it by the sinking speed, one can calculate the glide ratio of his hang glider. As in the example above, take the forward speed of 25 feet/sec, divide it by the sinking speed of 5 feet per second, and calculate the number 5. In other words, this says that the glider will go 5 feet forward for every foot dropped. The glide ratio would be found by simply dividing the horizontal distance traveled, 500 feet, by the vertical distance dropped, 100 feet, yielding again the number 5.

The above discussion on the two basic performance figures, sink rate and glide ratio, assumes that the air is calm and the hang glider is at least one wing span, in altitude, above the ground. The air must be still or else incorrect performance data will result. If the hang glider is less than a wing span above the ground the air between it and the ground is slightly pressurized and tends to make the hang glider fly further than in free air. Free air exists essentially above one wing span above the ground. The pressurization resulting in flight below one wing span in altitude is known as "ground effect." It is especially noticeable when the level ground is skimmed prior to landing. The glide seems to be stretched out. More on this later.

Using the above relationships, one can calculate the performance of his hang glider and therefore know all the better how to get the most out of it. Before one gets into that, he should take a look at how the force of lift is generated in the first place.

## LIFT: WHAT IS IT?

Basically, lift is the force that holds a hang glider in the air. It is low pressure on top of a wing and high pressure on the bottom. It is due to the angle of attack. It is due to air being deflected downward. It can be explained by Bernoulli's principle. It is because the wing or airfoil is curved. It's all of the above!

According to the dictionary, a theory is: 1. a coherent group of general propositions used as principles of explanation for a class of phenomena, and 2. a proposed explanation whose status is still conjectural; in contrast to well-established propositions that are regarded as reporting matters of actual fact. And so it is with the so-called "theory-of-flight;" many are still arguing about it. This is, however, no great problem for, indeed, the gross effect of flight is realized every day. Like so many other complicated phenomenon, lift can be described in many different ways, all correct and useable for problem solving.

The classical explanation of lift is called the Bernoulli Principle of lift. It deals with the basic fact that high speed air offers a lower pressure while low speed air, a higher pressure. Some people will say this is not so, lift being merely the downward deflection of air behind and under a wing. The following examines the various theories, or ways of thinking about how lift is generated.

## BERNOULLI'S PRINCIPLE

Daniel Bernoulli was a Swiss scientist who, in 1738, discovered the fundamental relationship between air pressure and velocity. Briefly, Bernoulli's Principle states that whenever the velocity of a fluid, which is air in the case of a hang glider, is increased, there is a corresponding decrease in the pressure of that fluid. Conversely, whenever the velocity of a fluid is decreased, there is a corresponding increase in the pressure of that fluid. These statements can be proven very easily at home. Simply hold a sheet of paper and blow across the top. One can then be witness to Bernoulli. Try it. It really works!

Another example of Bernoulli's Principle is to take an ordinary spool of thread, a 3 × 5 card and a straight pin. Insert the pin through the center of the card, and then into the spool hole. Hold the card facing the floor, blow, and let go of the card. It will stay attached to the spool, no matter how hard one blows! In fact, the harder one blows, the more the card wants to cling to the spool! This example is illustrated in Fig. 7-4.

Another way of viewing Bernoulli's Principle can be found in the venturi tube. In this case the tube is necked down at its center, with air blowing through it. If a certain amount of air is entering the tube, that same amount must come out the other end. Since the air cannot be compressed (at least under low speed hang glider flight conditions), it must speed up as the restriction is approached and is maximum at the narrowest point. This makes a lot of sense. Furthermore, if one takes a pressure reading at the restriction he finds it to be lower, while the velocity is higher than in the rest of the tube.

Using the venturi effect above leads directly to the wing of a hang glider. Take away the top of the necked down area and an airfoil becomes apparent, as shown in Fig. 7-5. The same thing happens, only this time the reduced pressure is free to give rise to a lift force and thus allows flight.

As in the case of the venturi, one has a situation where the curvature of the airfoil causes a "restriction" in the local airflow which results in higher velocity and hence lower pressure on top and, therefore, lifts. At this point, it would be good to know that curvature is not entirely necessary to cause

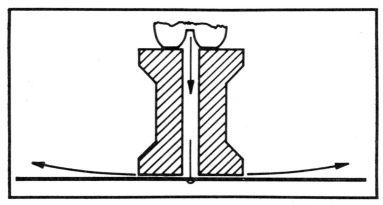

Fig. 7-4. A demonstration of Bernoulli's Principle.

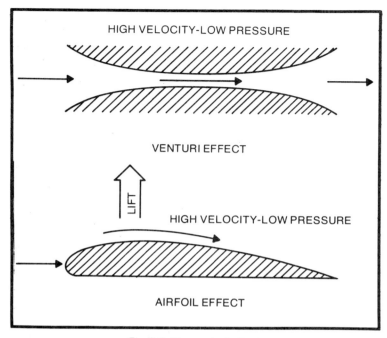

Fig. 7-5. The venturi effect.

the above phenomenon. An inclined flat plate will lift, though not nearly as well as a curved one. The air flow tends to curve around the inclined plate, not being able to turn the leading edge corner very sharply. A flat plate, however, lifts only about half as much as a curved airfoil in addition to having other detrimental characteristics.

Delving further into Bernoulli's Principle, look at an actual airfoil section in flight, with its various air pressures shown (see Fig. 7-6). The line (A) around the airfoil represents the atmospheric pressure surrounding the airfoil when it is standing still, hence, this is known as the static pressure, which at sea level equals 14.7 pounds per square inch. The line (B) represents the change in pressure on the airfoil as it moves through the air, or the air moves past it, both giving the same result (see Fig. 7-6). If one were to consider just line (B), the top portion would indicate a vacuum, while the bottom indicates a positive pressure. In fact, a vacuum can't really exist in nature. What is really the case is shown by line (C), the total pressure around the airfoil. It is derived simply by adding lines (A) and (B). The pressure on top of the wing is still positive, but it is "less positive" than the pressure below the wing. The net effect is, of course, an upward force called lift. Now, if one cleans up by subtracting pressures on both sides, he comes up with a "net pressure distribution" and a resulting total net force R. This resultant is then resolved into its two basic components: the one perpendicular to the direction of airflow being called lift, while the one parallel to the general air flow is called drag.

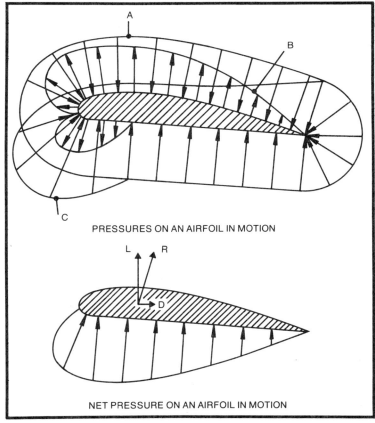

PRESSURES ON AN AIRFOIL IN MOTION

NET PRESSURE ON AN AIRFOIL IN MOTION

Fig. 7-6. The various pressures acting on a airfoil in flight.

## DOWNWARD DEFLECTION OF AIR

Another way to look at the generation of lift is to consider the air being deflected downward at the tail of the airfoil. This is simply an application of Newton's 3rd law which states: For every action there is an equal but opposite reaction. In other words, the airfoil deflects the air downward and is in turn pushed upward. This seems so simple, but its true. When the airflow leaves the trailing edge of the airfoil, it is curved downward. The "action-reaction" bit is merely saying that a force acting for a given time will move an object at a certain speed. Now, mass times velocity is momentum, so, for an airfoil, the lift is equal to the downward momentum given to the air that it is in relative motion with. One should now have a good idea of how the generation of lift is explained: Bernoulli's Principle and the momentum theory. But which one is correct? Well, they both are! You simply can't have one without the other. As the air flows over a wing, a pressure difference does exist between top and bottom, and the airflow is deflected downward. The difference in pressure gives rise to the downward deflection of the airflow and a downward deflection of the airflow generates a pressure difference! So, it can be seen that both explanations are correct.

## PRACTICAL APPLICATIONS

Now that one has an understanding of the theory of lift or how it happens, he should take a look at the practical side of things. After all, this is what one concerns himself with when discussing a real hang glider.

To begin with, the amount of lift that is generated by a given wing section is determined by five basic variables: 1. the density of the air it is in, 2. the relative velocity of that air, 3. the area of the wing, 4. the angle of attack, and 5. the shape of the airfoil.

### The Density of the Air

Recalling the discussion earlier in Chapter Six about meteorology, it was stated that "the heavier the air, the easier flight is attained." This "heaviness" is, of course, the density or weight per unit volume (a cubic foot of sea level air weighs about .075 pounds at 59° F). The denser the air, the more lift can be generated. The less dense the air, as happens with increases in altitude, the faster one must glide, all other things begin held constant. For example, it is easier to launch a hang glider near sea level than it is at Denver, Colorado, which is one mile above sea level. A higher air density also means higher viscosity and higher drag. One just can't get increased lift for nothing. By the way, colder air is denser than warmer air, hence less velocity is needed for the same lift.

**The Velocity of the Air**

The second major factor in the generation of lift is the velocity at which the air is flowing past the wing, or the velocity of the wing moving through the air. It makes no difference. The only thing that matters is the "relative" velocity between wing and air. Accepting this fact, all one needs to know is that the forces on a wing in flight vary with the square of the relative airspeed. In other words, doubling the airspeed quadruples the lift and drag, all other factors being held constant! From this, it is easy to see that a person weighing four times as much as another, would have to run twice as fast as the other to take off with a hang glider. If he could do it, that is. On the other hand, if one lost a few pounds, his take off speed would be lower. This discussion, of course, applies to actual flying speed as well as to takeoff speed.

**The Area of the Wing**

The third major factor in determining the amount of lift generated is the surface area of the wing. How many square feet does it cover? The larger the wing area, the lower the flying speed. In fact, the airspeed is inversely proportional to the square root of the wing area. Double the wing area and one flies $1/\sqrt{2}$ times as fast, all other factors held constant. While the drag is increased with increasing wing area, it is not necessarily proportional, but more on that later.

**The Angle of Attack**

The fourth major factor in determining the amount of lift generated by a given wing is the angle of attack. How much is the wing tilted relative to the air flow? The greater the angle of attack, the greater the lift. Like in the wing area case, the lift

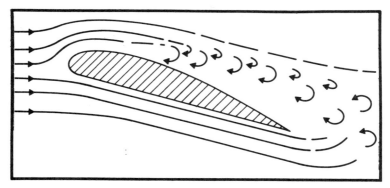

Fig. 7-7. A stalled airfoil has high drag and a breakdown in lift.

is proportional to the angle of attack, but only up to a certain angle called the "stall." At this point, the lift peaks out and, depending on the exact shape of the airfoil, starts to drop off while the drag goes up very sharply (see Fig. 7-7). At the stall angle (around 16° for the average airfoil and 40° for a kite) the airflow separates from the top surface creating a gigantic, turbulent wake and its attendant high drag. The lift force is breaking down.

When the stall does occur, the nose of a hang glider will tend to drop and lose altitude to pick up flying speed again. The particular airfoil, hang glider stability and control, and pilot skill, will determine exactly how much altitude is lost in the stall.

### The Shape of the Airfoil

The fifth major factor in determining the lifting force of a wing is the shape of the airfoil (see Fig. 7-8). Typically, a rigid wing airfoil is a smoothly flowing curve. It is rounded at the nose and pointed at the tail. The maximum depth of the curve is known as its percentage camber. In general, the fatter the nose, the gentler the stalls; the deeper and further aft the maximum camber, the greater the lift. The conventional airfoil needs a tail to stabilize it or else it will dive and "tuck under."

The type of airfoil used on tailless, flying-wing hang gliders has a turned up tail which eliminates the tendency to tuck under. The airfoil on a kite is cambered but, due to the

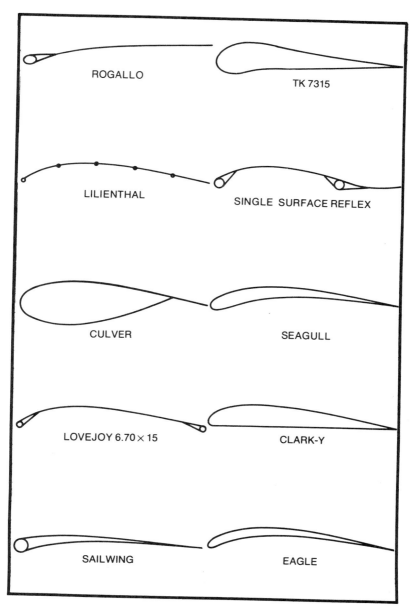

Fig. 7-8. Examples of various types of airfoils.

geometry of the wing and the sail's billow, it can fly stably as long as the sail is inflated.

## LANDING

When landing, the angle of attack of a hang glider wing is normally increased to the stall, lowering the airspeed to a point where a walking or tip-toe landing can be made. In many cases, depending upon pilot skill, a so-called "dynamic stall" is made with a kite by pushing the nose up very abruptly and steeply making the kite act like a drouge chute, allowing a landing to be made on a dime.

### The Parachute Mode

In a maneuver peculiar to kites, kites can be made to "parachute" to the ground if not high enough to make a diving recovery from a stall. This parachute mode is accomplished by precise movements, primarily in pitch (i.e., pushing and pulling on the control bar), balancing the kite while descending. In general though, the stall of the kite is very gentle. That is to say, when the stall is approached, the nose will drop slowly without drastic losses in altitude. The stall in a high performance hang glider is not usually as gentle, however, it being of more sudden nature, depending on the airfoil.

### The Mush

Another sort of semi-stall is called "mushing." This is a high angle of attack condition with a large increase in drag, but the lift seems to hang on; it doesn't break down, the nose doesn't drop. In this case, which is exhibited by some hang glider designs, the lift and stable flight is maintained while allowing the drag to increase, leading to a steeper glide angle. It can be useful landing in a small field surrounded by trees. It shortens the runway required for landing.

## THE COEFFICIENT OF LIFT

By now one must be wondering how in the world all these aerodynamic variables can be arranged to arrive at a workable combination. How can one compare apples and oranges? Is there some common ground for a basis of comparison? Well, luckily there is! In a word, its called

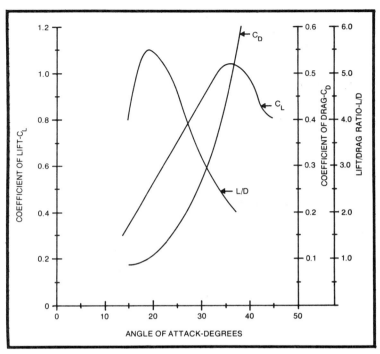

Fig. 7-9. Typical standard Rogallo wing lift and drag characteristics according to NASA wind tunnel tests for a 5° billow, 80° nose angle kite.

coefficient (see Fig. 7-9), which is a non-dimensional number, a number arrived at by dividing an aerodynamic force or moment by some given number which is the product of the basic variables involved.

In the case of lift, we know that it is dependent upon the five basic variables: 1. air density, 2. air velocity, 3. wing area, 4. the angle of attack, and 5. the airfoil shape.

As it turns out, the coefficient of lift, $C_L$, is ultimately a function of the angle of attack of the wing. It is a non-dimensional number that one must include to calculate the lift of a wing given the other factors of density, velocity, wing area and angle of attack.

Now, one might ask how the coefficient of lift is arrived at? Well, this is where wind tunnel testing comes into play. First of all, a wind tunnel can be described as being basically a tube with a fan at one end drawing air through it. Somewhere inside the tube is a mount on which to fasten a model wing or complete model and subject it to the wind created by the fan. The model mount is connected to sensitive scales and instruments which tell the aerodynamicist how much lift and drag there is at any given angle of attack. By taking a series of lift readings at various angles of attack, a graph can be plotted to show how the wing acts.

The product, $1/2 \rho V^2 S$, is typical for all wings; therefore, by dividing the actual lift by it, one arrives at the coefficient of lift. In this way, one can talk about different wing sections and compare their characteristics on an "even ground" which is of course $1/2 \rho V^2 S$. The $1/2 \rho V^2$ part is often called the dynamic pressure or impact pressure and its dimensions are $16/ft^2$. It is commonly referred to as "q" ($q = 1/2 \rho V^2$). For example, a "q" would equal 1 lb/sq ft at 20.5 fps at sea level. Aerodynamics has often been called the "science of coefficients" and indeed it is. How else can one compare so many different factors without some common ground?

## DRAG

As mentioned previously, drag is air resistance, or the force tending to hold back anything that moves through the atmosphere. It requires thrust to be overcome in the form of either an engine, or gravity, as in the case of a hang glider. Drag too, can be expressed as a coefficient in a manner similar to lift as shown in Fig. 7-10. First of all, drag depends on exactly the same factors as lift: density, velocity, wing area, angle of attack and airfoil shape. This time, though, one uses a coefficient of drag, $C_D$, to compare various airfoils.

Unlike lift, which comes solely from the wing, drag is produced by all parts of a hang glider: the wing, pilot, cables, control frame, king post, and any other objects that may be exposed to the airflow. The total drag curve for a standard Rogallo is shown in Fig. 7-11. Thus, it seems logical that there are various kinds of drag, which are as follows.

Induced Drag; this is a drag due to lift and is dependent upon $C_L$, aspect ratio, AR, and wing efficiency, e. The induced drag coefficient can be expressed as:

$$C_{Di} = C_L^2 / \pi ARe.$$

Where: $C_{Di}$ = coefficient of induced drag
$C_L{}^2$ = coefficient of lift squared
$\pi$ = 3.14
AR = Aspect ratio = $b^2/S = \dfrac{b \times b}{b \times c}$
e = wing efficiency factor

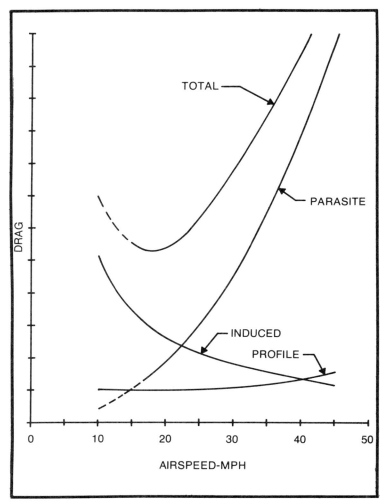

Fig. 7-10. The main drag characteristics of a typical standard Rogallo wing hang glider.

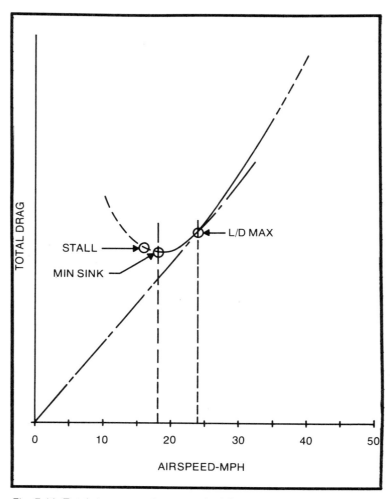

Fig. 7-11. Total drag curve for a standard Rogallo showing its significant points.

Note: Aspect ratio is defined as the wing span (b) divided by the average wing chord (c) or generally, the wing span squared $(b)^2$, divided by the wing area (S). AR is a measure of the wing's slenderness. The higher the aspect ratio, the longer and narrower the wing and the more "efficient" it is.

Examining the equation, we see that the coefficient of induced drag varies with the square of the coefficient of lift. For example, doubling the $C_L$, makes the $C_{Di}$ four times as large. Also, $C_{Di}$ varies inversely with AR. Doubling AR makes $C_{Di}$ half its original value. The span efficiency factor "e" depends largely on the taper ratio of the wing, i.e., the tip chord, $C_t$, divided by the root chord, $C_r$. From Fig. 7-12, it is easy to see one reason why standard Rogallo wings, with $C_t/C_r = 0$, are not very efficient. The best value of e seems to occur at around a $C_t/C_r = 0.4$. Theoretically, for maximum wing efficiency, a wing should be shaped, in plan form, like an ellipse. Figure 7-13 illustrates efficiency and performance of basic hang glider wing types.

The explanation for this lies in the flow across the wing, as a three dimensional body. If one could see the airflow over a lifting wing (Fig. 7-14) flying through the air, it would look something like this. The more positively pressurized air on the bottom of the wing tends to be "sucked" around the wing tip into the less positively pressurized air on the upper surface of the wing. This outflow on the bottom, inflow on the top, then gives rise to what is known as a "wing tip vortex." It can

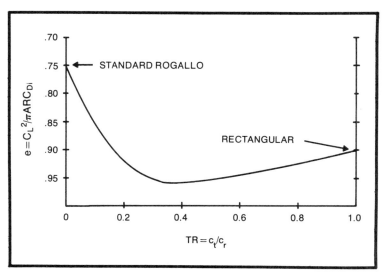

Fig. 7-12. How wing efficiency "e" varies with wing taper ratio.

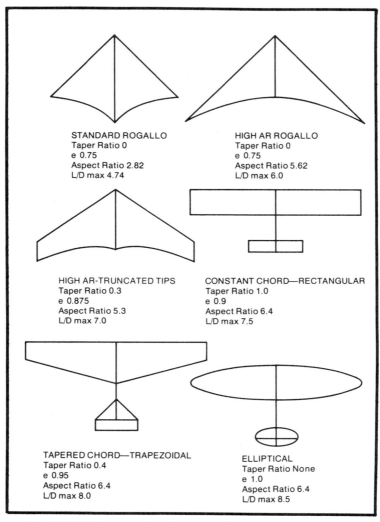

STANDARD ROGALLO
Taper Ratio 0
e 0.75
Aspect Ratio 2.82
L/D max 4.74

HIGH AR ROGALLO
Taper Ratio 0
e 0.75
Aspect Ratio 5.62
L/D max 6.0

HIGH AR-TRUNCATED TIPS
Taper Ratio 0.3
e 0.875
Aspect Ratio 5.3
L/D max 7.0

CONSTANT CHORD—RECTANGULAR
Taper Ratio 1.0
e 0.9
Aspect Ratio 6.4
L/D max 7.5

TAPERED CHORD—TRAPEZOIDAL
Taper Ratio 0.4
e 0.95
Aspect Ratio 6.4
L/D max 8.0

ELLIPTICAL
Taper Ratio None
e 1.0
Aspect Ratio 6.4
L/D max 8.5

Fig. 7-13. Efficiency and performance of basic hang glider wing types.

sometimes be seen as a vapor trail on a humid day. Large jet aircraft, like the 747 have such a large wing tip vortex at takeoff, that a small plane caught in one can be turned upside down and caused to crash. This has necessitated large spacings between takeoffs. Another example of wing tip vortex can be seen by flying a hang glider, especially a Rogallo, low, over a leaf covered slope. The leaves on either side of the wing tips will kick up into a whirling motion as the glider goes by.

Rogallos with pointed tips have a particularly large wing tip vortex and, therefore, a high induced drag. This can be helped by adding tip extensions, as some manufacturers are now offering.

### Induced Drag and Ground Effect

When flying near the ground within about one wing span in height, the pilot notices that the glide of his hang glider seems to "stretch out" or improve. This is shown in Fig. 7-15. The

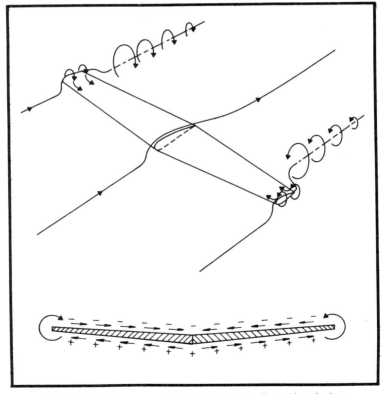

Fig. 7-14. Airflow over and around a three-dimensional wing.

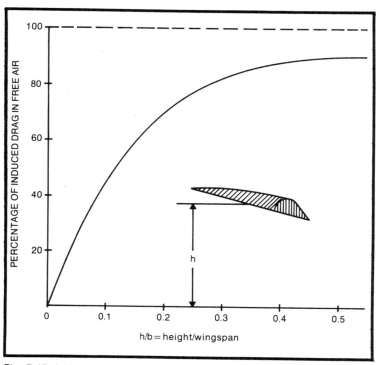

Fig. 7-15. Induced drag decreases in "ground effect" when flying a half span or less above the ground.

reason for this is a reduction in induced drag. As mentioned previously, the airflow behind a wing has a downward trend and is called downwash. Well, as it turns out, near the ground, the downwash is partly bounced back up (one might say the air is pressurized more beneath the wing) and tends to reduce the size of the wing tip vortices. When this is the case, the pilot is said to be flying in "ground effect."

### Induced Drag and Tip Plates

One method of reducing the formation of wing tip vortices and hence induce drag, is by adding vertical plates to the wing tips (see Fig. 7-16). This can be thought of as a wall or barrier blocking the buildup of the tip vortex. Happily, this tip plate effect can be realized by placing the plates either on top, bottom, front or rear within reasonable limits of the tip. Drag rudders, as found on some flying wing type hang gliders, can serve as tip plates.

One must be careful in the use of tip plates regarding their overall drag reduction. While they decrease the induced drag, they will increase the parasite drag.

**Induced Drag and Biplanes**

There have been a few biplanes designed and marketed in the hang glider industry. They have not, however, seen widespread use. While offering an extremely tough structural arrangement, biplanes suffer from "interference" drag between the two wings. The monoplane is superior to the biplane concerning induced drag as is illustrated in Fig. 7-17. The airflow over one effects the airflow over the other. The prime factor in keeping the interference to a minimum is to

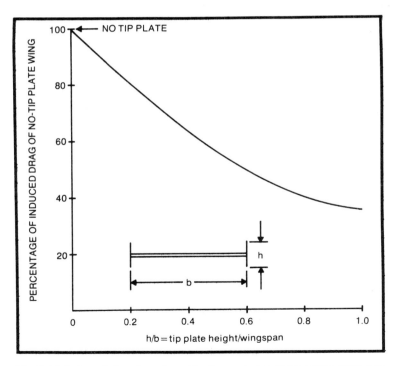

Fig. 7-16. Induced drag is reduced by the presence of tip plates. Drag rudders can serve this useful function.

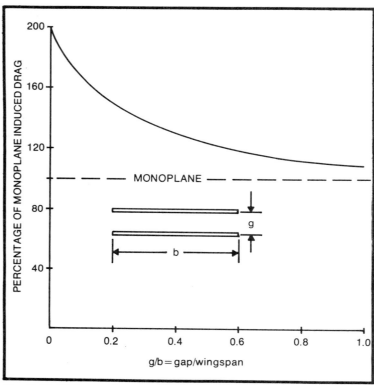

Fig. 7-17. Biplanes always have more induced drag than monoplanes, making them inferior in performance.

place the two wings far enough apart. This spacing is called the "gap" which is compared to the wing chord. A typical gap value would equal the chord of the wings. Obviously, if the wings are far enough apart, they will have a diminished effect on each other.

## Profile Drag

Profile drag is generated by the wing section itself and depends on its particular shape, and not on the lift. More specifically, it is the airfoil drag at zero lift, and is added to whatever the induced drag is to arrive at the total wing drag. The profile drag can be broken down into two components: form drag and skin friction drag.

276

**Form Drag.** Form drag is the sum of all the forces on an airfoil acting to retard its motion and is due primarily to the wake formed by the airfoil's passage through air. When a wing, or any object for that matter, moves through the air, it causes the air to separate at the nose and flow over the top and bottom surfaces. When the two flows reach the trailing edge of the wing they join back together in the wake, which is turbulent and consists of "eddies" or small vortices. The more streamlined the wing or object, the smaller the wake and thus, the smaller the profile form drag.

**Skin Friction Drag.** Skin friction develops because of the air flowing over the skin or surface of a wing. Its value depends on the total surface area and the smoothness of that surface. Recalling our discussion of airflow over the earth, we again find that a boundary layer exists near the surface of a wing (see Fig. 7-18). The air immediately in contact with the surface actually has no velocity. Due to the viscosity (or stickiness) of the air, it tends to stick to the wing. As one moves away from the surface, however, the local air velocity

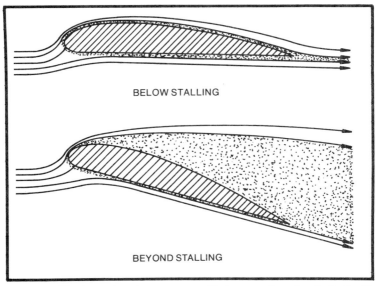

BELOW STALLING

BEYOND STALLING

Fig. 7-18. The boundary layer grows with increased angle of attack. It's huge at the stall.

increases until its full value (the flying speed) is reached at some small distance from the wing surface.

## Drag Induced by Turbulent or Laminar Flow

The depth of the boundary layer depends on the viscosity and whether the flow is turbulent or laminar. Turbulent flow is typified by eddies and is a mixing of the flying velocity (free stream) air particles and the slower velocities found in the boundary layer, with the result that the skin friction is higher. Laminar flow occurs when there is no turbulence. The various air particles stay in their respective positions or streamlines, not intermixing.

While laminar flow at first appears to be what we want (and indeed it is, provided certain conditions exist), this may not be necessarily so. For example, assuming that the airflow starts laminar on a typical hang glider wing, it stays so only until the highest point of the airfoil is reached. From there on, it leaves the surface and forms a larger wake than if the flow were turbulent. This then, leads to more wake or form drag, while perhaps having less skin friction than the laminar case.

In the turbulent case, the wake is smaller and even though the skin friction drag is up, the total profile drag is down. You see, the mixing, turbulent air takes energy from the higher velocity air outside the boundary layer and mixes it with the dead air in the boundary layers. This causes it to follow the airfoil shape more closely, and, thus, minimizing the size of the wake, form drag and the total profile drag. A good example of the better performance of wings with turbulent flow is exhibited in model planes that have poor, or rough finishes.

Today, there are certain airfoils known as laminar flow sections. Those have a somewhat different shape than the conventional airfoil, the main difference being that the high point is more rearward than the normal 1/4 to 1/3 chord position.

By placing the high point more aft than normal, the laminar flow region of the airfoil is increased and thus the skin friction drag is lower. These advanced airfoils, however, require extreme care in use to maintain their effectiveness. For instance, a smashed insect on the wing surface can ruin the clean laminar flow. To date no laminar flow sections have been employed in a hang glider.

**Parasite Drag**

Aside from the wing which produces both induced drag and profile drag, the other parts that make up a hang glider produce drag as well. In their case, however, it is due purely because of the fact they are on the glider experiencing the effects of airflow, but not contributing to the lift. They are simply going along for the ride. Hence, we call their drag parasite drag.

The various parts of a hang glider that produce parasite drag are:

1. fuselage (usually none, or a tube)
2. control frame
3. king post
4. bracing cables
5. the man (his body position is important)
6. horizontal tail
7. vertical tail
8. cross member

To give one an idea of the relative importance of the various parts of a hang glider, in regards to the amount of drag they produce, the following table of drag values for a typical Rogallo wing is presented. (Case is for best glide ratio or an L/D of 4 to 1.)

$$\text{Induced drag} = 50\%$$
$$\text{Profile drag} = 33\%$$
$$\text{Parasite drag} = 17\%$$

Now, the parasite drag can be broken down even further for each particular component.

| Component | % of Parasite | % of Total |
|---|---|---|
| Man (seated) | 40.0 | 6.80 |
| Cables | 2.0 | 0.34 |
| Control Frame | 20.0 | 3.40 |
| King Post | 8.0 | 1.36 |
| Cross Member | 30.0 | 5.10 |

As one can see, the largest part of the drag is induced and this is as it should be. According to theory, the induced drag will be equal to 50% of the total drag at the best glide angle of any aircraft. The way to reduce induced drag is to increase the aspect ratio (AR), reduce billow and add tip extensions to a point tipped wing, such as a Rogallo.

In the area of parasite drag, the man is the largest contributor. This figure can be reduced by flying prone or supine for about a 3% reduction in drag. Not very much! Another big parasite drag source is the cross-member. This could be reduced significantly, by about 4% of the total drag, if one "faired" the cross-member into an airfoil shape. The control frame and king post also represent a good part of the parasite drag. If these, too, were properly faired, one might gain another 3% in performance. In total then, if the pilot assumed the prone position, faired the cross member, control frame and king post to an airfoil shape, he could gain about a 10% reduction in total drag. In other words, his 4 to 1 glide ratio would go up to about 4.4 to 1, which is a definite improvement in performance. Instead of flying 400 feet out from a 100 foot vertical drop, he'd be able to fly out 440 feet and perhaps clear the next ridge.

A typical monoplane hang glider will also have half its total drag of the induced variety, while the $C_{Di}$ (coefficient of induced drag) might be on the order of 1/3 that of a Rogallo.

The $C_{Dpro}$ (coefficient of profile drag) might also be about 1/3 of a Rogallo's. In essence, all this tells one that the total drag coefficient for a monoplane might be on the order of 1/2 that of a standard Rogallo. Or in other words, the L/D, which is numerically equivalent to $C_L/C_D$, will be about twice as great and the glide angle half as great.

## THE HANG GLIDER POLAR CURVE

The hang glider polar curve, (see Fig. 7-19), or simply "polar," is a graphical representation of the performance of a particular design and body position. With it, one can see and better understand what performance really is and the variables that effect it.

The polar may be interpreted as follows, by its four main points:

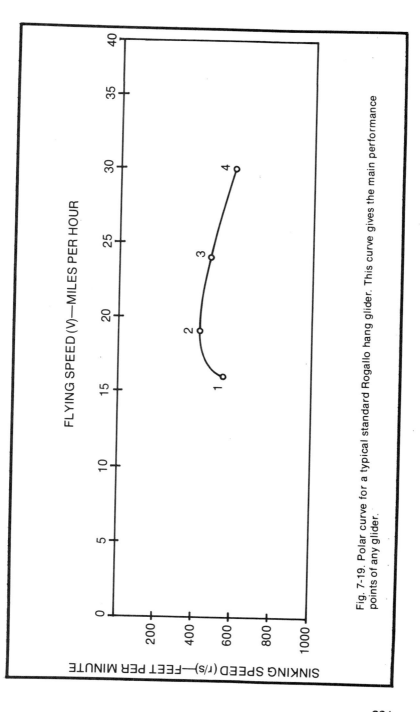

Fig. 7-19. Polar curve for a typical standard Rogallo hang glider. This curve gives the main performance points of any glider.

**The Stall Speed, $V_s$**

This is the slowest speed at which flight is possible.

$$V = V_s = \sqrt{2/\rho C_{Lmax}} \sqrt{W/S}.$$

It's L/D is a line drawn from the origin to itself or $(L/D) = V/R_s$ .

**The Speed for Minimum Sink, $V_{R/Smin}$**

This is the speed to fly for the least amount of vertical speed. It is where one will be able to gain the most altitude for a given lift. It will allow him to remain airborne for a maximum period of time. It's value is:

$$V_{R/Smin} = \sqrt[4]{4/3\pi ARe C_{Do} \rho_0{}^2} \sqrt{W/S}$$

The lowest speed for minimum sink can not be below the stall speed of the aircraft. The formula for $V_{R\,Smin}$ assumes a coefficient of lift equal to or less than $C_{Lmax}$ , the highest lift possible.

**The Best Glide Speed, $V_{L/Dmax}$**

This is the speed to fly for maximum distance. Its value is given by:

$$V_{L/Dmax} = \sqrt[4]{4/\pi ARe C_{Do} \rho_0{}^2} \sqrt{W/S}$$

A line drawn from the origin will touch tangent to the polar at the maximum L/D point. Its value is:

$$L/D \max = 1/2 \sqrt{\pi ARe/C_{Do}}$$

**The Maximum Flying Speed Never To Be Exceeded, $V_{ne}$**

For kites and other Rogallo type flexible wing hang gliders, this is the point where the sail begins to luff and collapse, after which the kite goes into an unstable dive. For fixed wing designs, $V_{ne}$ is traditionally a design limitation which, if exceeded, could lead to structural failure. Its value is:

$$V_{ne} = \sqrt{2/\rho C_{LVne}} \sqrt{W/S}$$

A word of caution. Anyone flying at or near the $V_{ne}$ is asking for trouble. Don't do it. Besides which, the L/D is low and the sink rate is high. There is no good reason to fly at this dangerous speed. Incidentally, the sail trailing edge on kites will start to flap, which is audible somewhere above the best gliding speed and before luffing (caving in) of the leading edge occurs. Trailing edge flapping should be warning enough to get that nose up.

## ANALYZING THE HANG GLIDER POLAR

In analyzing the hang glider polar, we notice several interesting things about it. These are described in the following paragraphs.

### The Wing Loading

The wing loading, W/S, affects everything on the curve except the L/D ratio, which is completely independent of wing loading. The higher the wing loading of a given design, the higher the appropriate speeds, and sink rates. They grow and diminish by the square root of the wing loading. Halving the wing loading will decrease speeds $V_2$ and $V_3$ by a factor of $\sqrt{2}/2$, or, .707.

### The Aspect Ratio

The aspect ratio, AR, directly affects speeds $V_2$ and $V_3$ . In fact, the two points are related by:

$$V_{R/Smin} = .758 \times V L/D \max.$$

In other words, the speed for minimum sink is about 3/4 the best gliding speed. Holding all other variables constant and doubling the AR will decrease speeds $V_1$ and $V_2$ by a factor of .84 and increase L/D max by a factor of $\sqrt{2}$, i.e., 1.414. Increasing the AR also increases the lift curve slope according to the relationship, lift curve slope, $\alpha, = 1/(1 + 2/AR)$.

By this, one can easily see the overwhelming effects of the aspect ratio (see Fig. 7-20.)

### The Wing Efficiency Factor

The wing efficiency factor, e, directly affects the speed for minimum sink and the best glide speed. Increasing it will lower speeds $V_2$ and $V_3$ and increase the glide ratio. It depends primarily on wing taper ratio and has a maximum value of 1.0 for elliptical planform wings. Standard kites may have an e equal to about 0.75 while monoplanes may reach a

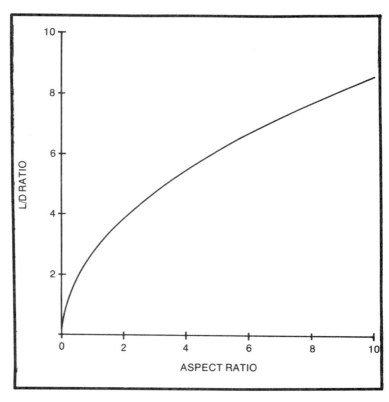

Fig. 7-20. How L/D ratio varies with aspect ratio for conical Rogallo wing hang gliders.

value in excess of 0.90. The e tells how efficient the wing is as a lifting surface. Stated another way, a standard kite wing is only about 75% effective as a lifting surface.

### The Coefficient of Drag at Zero Lift

The coefficient of drag at zero lift, $C_{Do}$, directly affects the speed for minimum sink and the best glide speed. Reduce $C_{Do}$ by 50% and one increases speeds $V_3$ and $V_2$ by a factor of 1.19. Zero lift implies no induced drag and so, $C_D$ is composed of wing profile drag $C_{Dpro}$, and the gliders non-lifting parasite drag, $C_{Dpar}$.

## PERFORMANCE FACTORS PERTINENT TO THE ROGALLO

Sail billow is probably the single most important factor affecting the overall performance of the Rogallo wing. This is basically because billow actually determines the amount of camber and twist possessed by the wing. Billow is normally defined as the difference in angles between the sail flat pattern and frame nose angle, with most hang gliders having between three and four degrees.

### Sail Billow

Reducing the billow of a sail reduces both the camber and twist of the wing airfoil sections, and improves the performance. All, however, is for a price. For while the performance goes up, reduced billow means reduced directional stability and a tendency for the kite to sideslip. Sails with as little as one degree billow have been flown, but they are extremely dangerous.

Another way of describing billow might be to express it in terms of a percentage. This method would involve dividing the difference in angles between the sail flat pattern and frame nose angle, by the frame nose angle. In so doing, we find that wider nose angle kites with the same billow in degrees as a lesser nose angle kite, actually have less billow and should therefore perform better. For example, assume there are two kites with four degrees of billow: an 80 degree nose and a 90 degree nose. Simple division yields the result that the 80 degree kite has 5% billow, while the 90 degree kite has only 4.4% billow. The 90 degree nose kite's sail is flatter. Reducing billow by one degree reduces the flat plate area of the kite by approximately one square foot, which leads to about a 10% improvement in performance. Instead of gliding 4 to 1, one will glide somewhere around 4.5 to 1, when changing from five to four degrees of billow.

Looking at billow another way, one sees how it effects the wing efficiency factor, e, as mentioned previously. The flatter a sail is, the higher the value of e. For instance, e for a typical four degree billow sail, is on the order of .75, while a three degree billow, high performance sail may possess an e value of 0.8 or so. NASA tests of five degree billow sails produced disgustingly low e values of around 0.7. It is, therefore, very easy to see just how important billow really is.

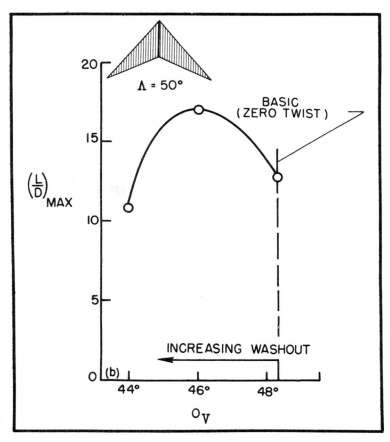

Fig. 7-21. Optimum billow for a NASA high aspect ratio cylindrical Rogallo wing.

Generally speaking, the minimum sinking speed of a glider varies as $1/e^4$. In other words, increasing e from 0.7 (five degrees billow) to 0.8 (three degrees billow) can reduce the sinking speed to 58% of its original value. The L/D is also improved by about 14%. Overall, this is quite an improvement in performance. (L/D varies directly with e.)

**Wing-Tip Modifications**

Another way to improve Rogallo wing performance is to get rid of the pointed tip. As discussed previously, this little item also affects the wing efficiency factor, e. By changing the wing taper ratio from zero (a pointed tip) to some finite value, one can reduce the spanwise variation of airfoil section lift coefficients and thus improve the wing's efficiency as a lifter. NASA conducted some studies in this area and found that by increasing the wing taper ratio from zero to 0.08 on a short keeled Rogallo, the L/D max went up from 13.6 to a phenomenal 16.2.

Other advantages of the finite tips were a delay in the occurrence of an unstable break in the pitching moment and a slight increase in the maximum lift coefficient. Many manufacturers are currently experimenting with and offering conical Rogallos with tip extensions (sometimes called truncated tips) in the form of tubing or sail battens.

### Optimum Billow

In an effort to pinpoint the effects of billow (camber and twist), NASA ran a series of tests with a short keeled, cylindrical Rogallo (see Fig. 7-21). Starting with the basic zero twist sail (1.77 degrees billow) the L/D max increased from 13.6 to an amazing 17.0. The frame nose angle was 80 degrees. Just imagine what tip extensions would do for an optimally billowed, short keeled, cylindrical kite.

### Leading Edge Shape

Another method of controlling wing camber and twist is to alter the shape of the leading edges and keel. Today, most kites have straight leading edges and keels causing their sails to form two cone shaped halves, thus the name conical Rogallo. This is a basic form of the Rogallo, the other being the cylindrical (see Fig. 7-22). The cylindrical Rogallo has its leading edges formed into the arc of a circle. Modifications and combinations of the two basic forms have led to hybrids that attempt to combine the advantages of both types.

In order to get a feel for what a change in leading edge shape does, one can look at some more NASA data, which should prove the superiority of the cylindrical Rogallo as shown in Fig. 7-23. In fact, the experimental data gave an L/D max of 6.2 for the conical and 10.0 for the cylindrical (both had equal leading edge and keel lengths, 80 degree noses). The

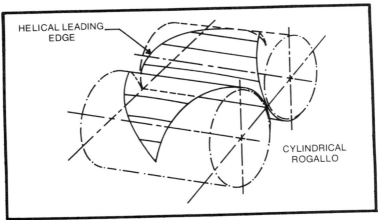

Fig. 7-22A. Defining drawing for the cylindrical Rogallo wing.

data are, of course, for kites without the drag of a man, but they do serve as a good basis for comparison. On the short keeled, long wing Rogallos, NASA got L/D max values of 7.8 for the conical form and 13.6 for the cylindrical version.

One might ask why no one manufactures a high aspect ratio cylindrical kite. Well, unfortunately, the improved performance leaves something to be desired in the area of stability. The conical kites possess a good deal of camber and

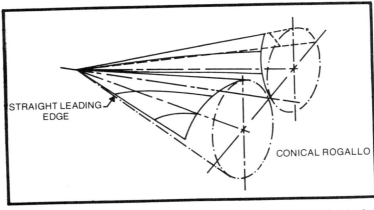

Fig. 7-22B. Defining drawing for the conical Rogallo wing, the typical hang glider type.

twist, which, while keeping their performance down, provide for a good degree of stability (see Fig. 7-24). The pure cylindrical kites, on the other hand, have little or no twist and camber—high performance, but lower stability. The pure cylindricals have a nasty tendency to tip stall and drop a wing when it's least desired—suddenly. The cylindricals however, certainly deserve more research and development time. Only one manufacturer actually produces a conical with a slight curve in the forward leading edge. It demonstrates a slight performance gain but is reputed to be more difficult to parachute land than a straight conical. Figure 7-25 compares several aspects of the conical and cylindrical wings.

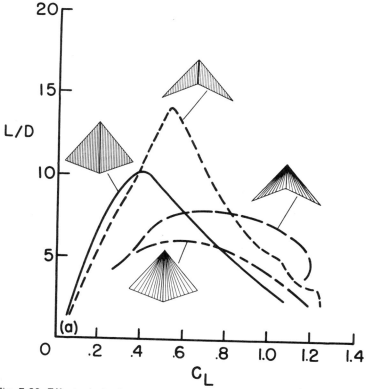

Fig. 7-23. Effect of planform and canopy shape on Rogallo wing L/D according to NASA wind tunnel data. Radial lines indicate conical while parallel lines indicate cylindrical.

Fig. 7-24. Dave Kilbourne's cylindrical Rogallo with cable bowed leading edges.

Another interesting fact to consider is that at lower air speeds ($C_L$ s above 0.8), where soaring might be done, the conicals have a slight edge on the cylindricals. At higher airspeeds ($C_L$ s below 0.8), however, the cylindricals have it all over the conicals. L/D max figures are as much as 73% higher for the cylindricals. The cylindricals can also fly faster than the conicals before the onset of sail luffing and collapse.

## LOOKING FOR PERFORMANCE

So, what does one look for in the performance of a hang glider? The task seems enormous. With all those variables, how can one possibly choose?

To begin with, one must first decide what type of hang gliding he wants to do. Is he a beginner, novice, intermediate or expert? What is the local terrain like where he'll be flying? The winds? Is there a club in the area to assist him? Don't be a lone wolf. There's a lot of knowledge and expertise available. Find it and take advantage of it. Don't repeat mistakes that have already been made.

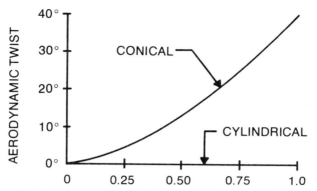

Fig. 7-25A. Aerodynamic twist of conical and cylindrical Rogallo wings.

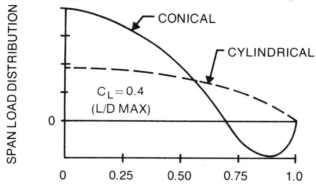

Fig. 7-25B. Spanwise lift distribution for conical and cylindrical Rogallo wings at cruise (L/Dmax) speed.

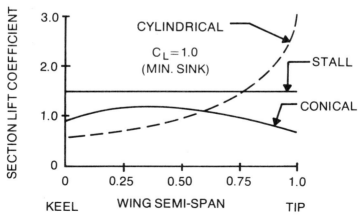

Fig. 7-26. Airfoil section lift coefficients during a minimum sink condition for conical and cylindrical Rogallo wings.

One major factor in choosing a hang glider can be the pilot's weight. The pilot's weight versus wing loading is illustrated in Fig. 7-26.

Currently, at least at most hang gliding schools, one's first hang gliding experience will come via the standard kite. A lot is known about its characteristics and if one observes its various limitations, a kite can give him his first taste of hang gliding. This is not to say one must fly a kite, but most instructors will probably advise that one do so before getting into a higher performance glider. This might seem incorrect but, since weight shift control is so natural, it makes learning to hang glide that much easier, versus learning in an aerodynamically controlled hang glider. On the other hand, if one has had conventional airplane flying experience, he should adapt easier to an aerodynamically controlled hang glider.

Speaking more specifically about performance, the two main areas of concern are sink rate and glide ratio. They are not inseparable however. A low sink rate can be achieved by lowering the wing loading, for example, by flying a larger kite. This may work, but it has been proven that wing loadings below one pound per square foot while being "floaters," are hard to control in any sort of wind. Lower wing loadings lower the flying speed and make the hang glider more susceptible to gusts and less controllable in higher winds. Lower wing loadings yield poor penetration characteristics. The glider simply cannot bore through the air very well. One way around this is to go to a higher wing loading and a better glide ratio. The higher wing loading will increase one's flying speed and hence penetration, while the improved glide ratio will lower the rate of sink! Remember: $L/D$ = flying speed divided by sinking speed.

It seems rather ironic that the simple Rogallo wing, with its low performance, currently holds all the records for duration flying—this, however, merely proves one thing: the wind blows so hard for so long into a given slope providing the updraft necessary for such a feat. It's all done by magic as they say. The magic being, of course, the brute force of the wind: a force that makes such flying extremely hazardous. One wrong movement in strong ridge lift can mean being blown into the face of the cliff or over the top and down the leeward side. It is dangerous business, to put it mildly.

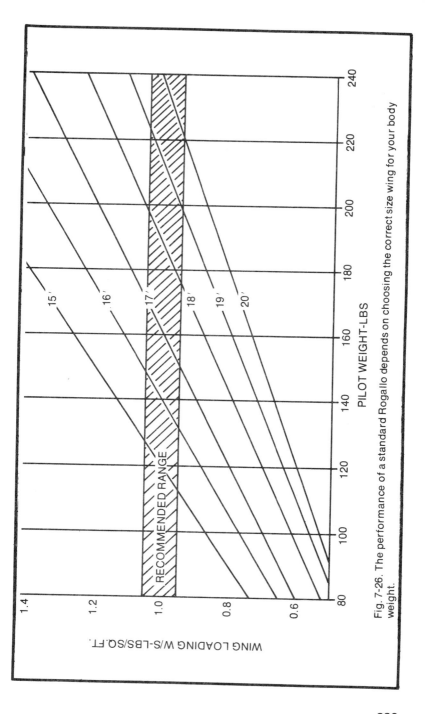

Fig. 7-26. The performance of a standard Rogallo depends on choosing the correct size wing for your body weight.

293

While a hang glider, such as a kite, having a low glide ratio coupled with a low wing loading will indeed soar, it is risky business. This combination, along with weight shift control, has severe limitations and should be treated accordingly. If that's the kind of performance one wants, it's up to him. On the other end of the spectrum we have the higher glide ratio and higher wing loading. This combination buys us improved

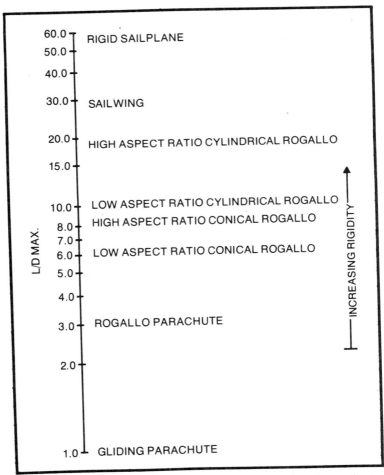

Fig. 7-27. The complete performance spectrum for various types of man-made wings.

penetration and, most commonly, improved control, for mere weight shifting is not enough. Aerodynamic controls must be used. Also, the sink rate is lower and allows one to fly in lighter winds and hence, more safely. He has more time to think, and to react to various conditions.

In summary then, as a beginner one might start his hang gliding experience choosing a glider with a low glide ratio (4 to 1) and a higher rate of sink (7 fps) and fly it in light winds from slopes of about 3 to 1 steepness. Figure 7-27 shows the complete performance spectrum for various types of man-made wings. If his local area, however, has only relatively shallow slopes, he'll be forced to go to a hang glider with a higher glide ratio, greater than the slope of the terrain.

As one advances his hang gliding skills, or his desires are such, he can go to the higher performance hang glider. It will offer more penetration, a lower sink rate, higher glide ratio and improved stability and control. It can open up such areas as thermal soaring and cross country flying—areas that a low performance glider can't touch. It should be an all-around more rewarding hang gliding experience.

# Chapter 8
# Materials and Hardware

## MATERIALS AND HARDWARE

It is simply impossible to overemphasize the importance of the use of proper materials in a hang glider, as one's life is literally hanging in the balance. The glider must be designed and built to withstand a certain amount of stress from the loads seen in flight and on the ground. Although light weight is important in a hang glider, as it is in any aircraft, structural integrity should not be sacrificed for it (see Fig. 8-1). After all, a hang glider that's light and won't stay together is of little use. It's job is to safely support the pilot in the air as he performs various maneuvers.

The two categories of materials used for hang gliders are: one, those making up the airframe (framework), and two, those used for covering the airframe. A particular material is chosen for its strength, stiffness and weight characteristics. It must be strong enough for safety in flight, stiff enough that it holds the shape desired and yet light enough to be easy to

Fig. 8-1. Proper materials and hardware are necessary for an airworthy hang glider. VJ-23 details shown here.

handle in the air as well as on the ground. In addition to these, the hang glider should be durable. It shouldn't break every time one uses it.

## ALUMINUM

Just as in the aircraft industry, aluminum has proven to be the most useful material for the construction of hang glider airframes. It's light in weight, easy to handle and work with, strong, durable, and resistant to corrosion.

### Properties

Pure aluminum, the elemental metal, is soft and pliable, without any alloys added. It wasn't until the 1920's when strong aluminum alloys became available that aluminum saw any great use in the aircraft industry. In fact, aluminum was discovered only within the last century, and a method of separating it from its ores was not developed until 1886. Even though it is a relatively new metal and is found in abundance all over the world in common clay.

Pure aluminum is corrosion resistant, light in weight, white and shiny in appearance. To improve its strength, forming and welding characteristics, certain percentages of various other metals are alloyed with aluminum and heat treated (see Table 8-1). These alloys are still mostly aluminum, around 95%. The light weight is still retained, while the strength may be increased two or three times.

### Alloy Identification

In order to identify the various alloys, a four digit numbering system is used by industry and designers to designate the alloy and heat treatment. The first digit of the number is used to indicate the alloy type (major alloy element added to the aluminum):

| | |
|---|---|
| 1 Aluminum-99% minimum ("pure" aluminum) | 5 Magnesium |
| | 6 Magnesium and silicon |
| 2 Copper | 7 Zinc |
| 3 Manganese | 8 Other element |
| 4 Silicon | 9 Unused series |

## Table 8-1. Mechanical Property Limits of Commonly Used Aluminum Alloys

### Mechanical property limits of commonly used alloys

| ALLOY AND TEMPER | THICKNESS ① in. | TENSILE STRENGTH—ksi (m lbs. per sq. in.) ULTIMATE min | YIELD min | ELONGA-TION percent min in 2 in. or 4D |
|---|---|---|---|---|
| **2014** | | | | |
| 2014-0 ③ | All | . . . | . . . | 12 |
| 2014-T4, -T4510 and -T4511 ⑤ | All | 50.0 | 35.0 | 12 |
| 2014-T42 ② | All | 50.0 | 29.0 | 12 |
| 2014-T6, -T6510 and -T6511 ⑤ | Up thru 0.499 / 0.750 and over | 60.0 / 68.0 | 53.0 / 58.0 | 7 / 6 |
| 2014-T62 ② | Up thru 0.749 / 0.750 and over | 60.0 / 60.0 | 53.0 / 53.0 | 7 / 6-7 |
| **2024** | | | | |
| 2024-0 ③ | All | . . . | . . . | 12 |
| 2024-T4, -T3510 and -T3511 ⑤ | Up thru 0.249 / 1.500 and over | 57.0 / 70.0 | 42.0 / 52.0 | 12 ⑥ / 8-10 |
| 2024-T42 ② | Up thru 0.749 / 1.500 and over | 57.0 / 57.0 | 38.0 / 38.0 | 12 / 8-10 |
| 2024-T81, -T8510 and -T8511 ⑤ | 0.050-0.249 / 1.500 and over | 64.0 / 66.0 | 56.0 / 58.0 | 4 / 5 |
| **6061** | | | | |
| 6061-0 ③ ④ | All | . . . | . . . | 16 |
| 6061-T4, -T4510 and -T4511 ⑤ | All | 26.0 | 16.0 | 16 |
| 6061-T42 ② | All | 26.0 | 12.0 | 16 |
| 6061-T6, -T62 ②, -T6510 and -T6511 ⑤ | Up thru 0.249 / 0.250 and over | 38.0 / 38.0 | 35.0 / 35.0 | 8 / 10 |
| **6063** | | | | |
| 6063-0 ③ ④ | All | . . . | . . . | 18 |
| 6063-T1 † | Up thru 0.500 / 0.501-1.000 | 17.0 / 16.0 | 9.0 / 8.0 | 12 / 12 |
| 6063-T4 and -T42 ② | Up thru 0.500 / 0.501-1.000 | 19.0 / 18.0 | 10.0 / 9.0 | 14 / 14 |
| 6063-T5 | Up thru 0.500 / 0.501-1.000 | 22.0 / 21.0 | 16.0 / 15.0 | 8 / 8 |
| 6063-T52 | Up thru 1.000 | 22.0 | 16.0 | 8 |
| 6063-T6 and -T62 ② | Up thru 0.124 / 0.125-1.000 | 30.0 / 30.0 | 25.0 / 25.0 | 8 / 10 |
| **7075** | | | | |
| 7075-0 ④ | All | . . . | . . . | 10 |
| 7075-T6, -T62 ②, -T6510 and -T6511 ⑤ | Up thru 0.249 / 4.500-5.000 | 78.0 / 78.0 | 70.0 / 68.0 | 7 / 6 |
| 7075-T73 | 0.062-0.249 / 0.500-1.499 | 66.0 / 70.0 | 58.0 / 61.0 | 7 / 7 |

① The thickness of the cross section from which the tension test specimen is taken determines the applicable mechanical properties.

② Material heat-treated from any temper by the user should attain the mechanical properties applicable to this temper.

③ Annealed (-0 temper) material shall upon heat treatment be capable of developing the mechanical properties applicable to -T42 temper material. Also applicable to material heat-treated from -0 temper by the producer.

④ Annealed (-0 temper) material shall upon heat treatment and aging, be capable of developing the mechanical properties applicable to -T62 temper material.

⑤ For stress-relieved tempers characteristics and properties other than those specified may differ somewhat from the corresponding characteristics and properties of material in the basic temper.

⑥ Minimum elongation for tube, 10 percent.

† Formerly designated T42.

## Heat Treat and Temper Identificaton

In most alloys, a heat treatment process will be performed to improve the strength characteristics of the aluminum even

302

more. The four digit numbering system mentioned is modified by a dash, a capital letter and a number.

Temper designations and sub-divisions for aluminum alloys are as follows:

-T1  Naturally aged at room temperature
-T2  Annealed (casting only)
-T3  Solution heat treated then cold worked
-T4  Solution heat treated
-T5  Artificially aged only
-T6  Solution heat treated then artificially aged
-T7  Solution heat treated then stabilized
-T8  Solution heat treated, cold worked, then artificially aged
-T9  Solution heat treated, artificially aged, then cold worked

**Shapes of Aluminum**

Aluminum comes in a variety of stock shapes and sizes: bar, sheet, plate, tube, pipe, channel, angle, "I" section and other miscellaneous forms. For hang gliders, sheet, tubing and channel stock seem to be the most popular.

There are two basic methods for forming the various shapes: drawing and extruding. Aluminum can also be stamped, formed or spun. Drawing involves forming by a distorting or stretching process and gives more accurate parts. Extruding involves shaping a part by forcing the hot metal in a plastic state through a die under pressure. It is less expensive than drawing but gives less accurate shapes, resulting in less uniform wall thickness and hence strengths. Drawn tubing is most popular on hang gliders today.

**Aluminum Finishes**

While Alclad surfaces offer superlative corrosion resistance properties, they can only be applied to sheet stock. The most common method of finishing aluminum is referred to as anodizing. The aluminum is made ready by removing all dirt and grease, with carbon tetrachloride if necessary. The part is then suspended in a chromic acid or sulfuric acid solution in which it becomes the anode or positive terminal. The steel container of the batch is the cathode. By passing

| ALLOY | CHARACTERISTICS [1] | | | | | TYPICAL APPLICATIONS |
|---|---|---|---|---|---|---|
| | Corrosion Resistance | Machinability | Weldability [2] | Maximum Strength [3] | Annealed Strength [4] | |
| 2014 | C-C | B-B | B-C | 70 | 27 | Truck frames; aircraft structures |
| 2024 | C-C | B-B | B-B | 75 | 27 | Truck wheels; screw machine products; aircraft structures |
| 6061 | A-A | B-C | A-A | 45 | 18 | Heavy-duty structures where corrosion resistance needed; truck and marine; railroad cars, furniture, pipelines |
| 6063 | A-A | D-C | A-A | 42 | 13 | Pipe railing; furniture, architectural extrusions |
| 7075 | C | B | D | 83 | 33 | Aircraft and other structures; keys |

[1] Relative ratings in decreasing order of merit—A, B, C, D. Where applicable, ratings for both annealed and hardest tempers are given (for example, A-C).

[2] Weldability: A—generally weldable; B—weldable with special techniques for specific applications; C—limited weldability; D—not weldable. Ratings are given for arc welding. Gas welding and brazeability ratings are the same or differ by only one;

exceptions are most of the 2000 and 7000 series alloys.

[3] Typical maximum tensile strength in kips per square inch, for fully work-hardened condition or heat-treated to highest strength level. (Multiply by 0.703 to convert to kilograms per square millimeter.)

[4] Typical annealed tensile strength in kips per square inch. (Multiply by 0.703 to convert to kilograms per square millimeter.)

electricity through this setup (electrolysis), oxygen is deposited on the parts' surface forming aluminum hydroxide. Color can be added by another process called alumiliting.

A surface which has been anodized, while nice to look at, is soft and easily scratched. A Sanford Hardcoat is often applied which can be extremely scratch resistant although not as bright in color as regular color anodizing.

Anodizing will also show cracks in the aluminum and is valuable for this as well as for its corrosion resistance and beautifying properties. It is very common on hang gliders. Anodizing lowers the fatigue strength of aluminum by about 60%, in some cases.

Aluminum parts can be fabricated by forming, machining and welding (see Table 8-2).

## STEEL

Steel is also used in hang glider construction, although to a much lesser extent than aluminum. Typically, a stainless or plated variety of steel is used on tangs, some nose plates, bolts, cable and miscellaneous fittings requiring high strength in a small size.

## Table 8-3. Uses and Properties of Nickel Stainless Steel

NOMINAL COMPOSITIONS AND USES OF NICKEL STAINLESS STEELS

| AISI Type | Cr | Ni | C max | Mn max | Si max | Other | Purpose |
|---|---|---|---|---|---|---|---|
| 301 | 16-18 | 6-8 | 0.15 | 2 | 1 | — | High work hardening rate; applications requiring high strength and ductility |
| 302 | 17-19 | 8-10 | 0.15 | 2 | 1 | — | General purpose austenitic type |
| 303 | 17-19 | 8-10 | 0.15 | 2 | 1 | — | Free machining modification of Type 302 |
| 304 | 18-20 | 8-12 | 0.08 | 2 | 1 | — | Lower carbon modification of Type 302 |
| 305 | 17-19 | 10-13 | 0.12 | 2 | 1 | — | Low work hardening rate; spin forming and severe deep drawing operation |
| 309 | 22-24 | 12-15 | 0.20 | 2 | 1 | — | High strength and resistance to high temperatures |
| 310 | 24-26 | 19-22 | 0.25 | 2 | 1.5 | — | Higher alloy content improves basic characteristics of Type 309 |
| 316 | 16-18 | 10-14 | 0.08 | 2 | 1 | 2-3 Mo | Mo added to improve corrosion and pitting resistance |

## Properties

Steel is really iron that has been purified by having its carbon content lowered. Iron has been around for thousands of years and it is obtained from ore. It is then refined by a smelting process which oxidizes the carbon and various other impurities. Steel, as it is known, is iron that has no more than 2% carbon content.

To alter the properties of steel for various uses, it, like aluminum, can be alloyed with other elements. Some these alloys and tensile properties are shown in Tables 8-3 and 8-4.

## Table 8-4. Uses and Properties of Nickel Stainless Steel

TENSILE PROPERTIES OF ANNEALED NICKEL STAINLESS STEEL IN VARIOUS FORMS

| AISI Type | Form | Tensile Strength, psi | Yield Strength (0.2% offset) psi | Elongation (in 2 in.) % | Reduction of Area, % | Hardness Brinell | Hardness Rockwell B |
|---|---|---|---|---|---|---|---|
| 301 | Sheet & Strip | 110,000 | 40,000 | 60 | — | — | 85 |
| | Plate | 105,000 | 40,000 | 55 | 70 | 165 | — |
| 302 | Sheet & Strip | 90,000 | 40,000 | 50 | — | — | 85 |
| | Plate | 90,000 | 35,000 | 60 | 70 | — | 80 |
| | Bars | 85,000 | 35,000 | 60 | 70 | 150 | — |
| 303 | Bars | 90,000 | 35,000 | 50 | 55 | 160 | — |
| 304 | Sheet & Strip | 85,000 | 35,000 | 50 | — | — | 80 |
| | Plate | 85,000 | 30,000 | 60 | 70 | 150 | — |
| | Bars | 85,000 | 30,000 | 60 | 70 | 150 | — |
| 305 | Sheet & Strip | 85,000 | 38,000 | 50 | — | — | 80 |
| | Plate | 85,000 | 35,000 | 55 | — | — | — |
| 309 | Sheet & Strip | 90,000 | 45,000 | 45 | — | — | 85 |
| | Plate | 95,000 | 40,000 | 45 | — | 170 | — |
| | Bars | 95,000 | 40,000 | 45 | 65 | 160 | 83 |
| 310 | Sheet & Strip | 95,000 | 45,000 | 45 | — | — | 85 |
| | Plate | 95,000 | 45,000 | 50 | 65 | 170 | — |
| | Bars | 95,000 | 45,000 | 50 | 65 | 185 | 89 |
| 316 | Sheet & Strip | 90,000 | 40,000 | 50 | — | — | 85 |
| | Plate | 85,000 | 35,000 | 55 | — | 150 | — |
| | Bars | 80,000 | 30,000 | 60 | 70 | 150 | 78 |

## Alloy Identification

In order to identify the various alloys of steel a numbering system has been devised by the SAE (Society of Automotive Engineers). Basic numbers classify the principal alloys as follows:

1 Carbon steels
2 Nickel steels
3 Nickel-chromium steels
4 Molybdenum steels
5 Chromium steels
6 Chromium-vanadium steels
7 Tungsten steels
8 Silicomagnanese steels

Stainless steel is the type commonly used in hang glider applications. Generally, they are alloys of iron and chromium that contain no less than 10.5% chromium. This combination offers tremendous corrosion resistance and high strength, which is important in the case of a hang glider.

Of all the stainless steel alloys available, the most common for hang glider fittings is the 300 series (i.e., alloys of iron-chromium and nickel). In this case, the carbon content is usually low (less than .15%) while there is at least 16% chromium as well. Stainless steels containing 18% chromium and 8% nickel are commonly referred to as 18-8 steels.

Normally, type 304 stainless is used for tangs and cable, and it is available in various degrees of hardness. It can also be had in the annealed condition. It has excellent atmospheric corrosion resistance. Type 303 alloy is more machinable than 302 but, at a sacrifice of some atmospheric resistance. It can be used for tangs. Type 302 alloy does not have quite the atmospheric resistance as does 304. It can be used for sheet and tangs, but is best for cable. Other interesting properties of these stainless steels are that they are not hardenable by heat treating and are nonmagnetic.

## Working Steel

Some of the various methods of working steel are: forming, cutting, machining and welding.

Steel can be formed by the same methods and machines as can aluminum except that harder dies and heavier, more powerful machines must be used. After all, steel is stronger and heavier (3 times so) than aluminum and appropriate measures must be taken to deal with it.

When making bends, be sure to bend across or perpendicular to the grain of the steel to prevent cracking.

Unlike aluminum, steel will not oxidize during the welding process, and therefore, it is not necessary to do it in an inert atmosphere. The common, acetelyene gas flame welding techniques are applicable to the carbon steels. Stainless steel can be joined by all the shielded fusion welding and resistance welding processes.

### Protection of Steel Surfaces

**Plating.** All areas of a hang glider are subject to the effects of corrosion, therefore, some sort of plating is required on all steels that are not stainless. Normally, "AN" type bolts and hardware will be cadmium plated by an electrolytic process which deposits the material on the surface of the part. Commercial bolts and hardware are usually plated with a zinc-chromate solution which offers good wear resistance and good appearance.

Galvanizing is plating done in a lead-zinc bath. It provides good corrosion resistance and is often referred to as "galvy." Cables are commonly galvanized.

**Lubrication.** Any part that sees continual wear, such as bushings, bearings, hinges and control stick bearings should be lubricated with an anti-friction grease or oil. Not only does this make the parts free-moving but also helps protect them from corrosion in the event of a surface plating wear through.

### Forms of Steel

Steel comes in a variety of stock shapes and sizes: sheet, bar, tube, pipe, channel, angle, "I" beams and other miscellaneous forms. For hang gliders, sheet, bar, channel, wire and rod are the most popular.

### FABRICS AND FABRICATION AIDS

Today, virtually all hang gliders use some type of fabric for their wing coverings, harnesses and transport bags. In general, stabilized Dacron sailcloth is used for the flexible surfaced gliders while unfinished aircraft type Dacron is normally used on rigid-wing designs. Harnesses can employ a variety of fabrics, but the most common material (at least for straps) is nylon webbing. Most any type of tough, durable fabric is used for transportation bags, as long as it's water proof. Heavy nylon and cotton duck are typical.

To better understand what fabric is all about, some terms must be defined. To begin with, the thread of the fabric is woven at right angles, with the warp being parallel to the length of the cloth while the woof (or fill) is perpendicular to the warp. This fill binds the selvage edge of the material and will not allow it to unravel. The selvage edge indicates the warp direction and can be used as a reference line. On most Rogallo type hang gliders, the selvage and warp are located at an angle halfway between the leading edge and keel. A rigid wing would most likely use the fabric with the selvage parallel to the keel or fuselage.

A fold, cut or seam that is made on a diagonal line between the warp and the fill is called a bias. While not commonly used on hang gliders, it could be used where stretching and fitting of the fabric is necessary.

To determine how closely woven a fabric is, one must know the number of threads per inch. This will indicate its fineness. The closer the weave, the more threads per inch and the finer the material.

As material is woven, a nap (or fuzzy surface) remains, caused by the millions of individual fiber ends. To eliminate this, the fabric is put through a process known as calendering, which irons the material as it passes between a series of wet, hot and cold rollers. This produces a smooth finish which again promotes aerodynamic efficiency and also wear qualities. After being calendered, the fabric is given some body by application of a textile glue known as sizing. This serves to both stiffen and protect the individual threads and overall fabric material.

When all is said and done, the fabric will have a particular weight, and to keep things straight, one always refers to the square yard weight of a fabric. For instance, most Rogallo wings use between three oz. and four oz. Dacron (i.e., it weighs between three and four oz. per square yard).

## Dacron

Dacron is a synthetic, woven fabric which was developed by the DuPont Company (see Fig. 8-2). It comes in a variety of brilliant colors and weights, on a roll which is approximately 38 inches wide. Generally speaking, the heavier the cloth, the longer it will last. Weights between 2.2 to 4.5 oz. are available.

Stabilized Dacron sailcloth is the fabric found on most flexible wing hang gliders. Stabilized means that the material is sent through rollers that are heated to approximately 220° F. This is really the calendering process mentioned and it determines the porosity or permeability of the finished cloth. The weight of the cloth doesn't really affect its permeability either. It's the calendering which is important to low porosity and hence aerodynamic efficiency. It's just not good to have air leaking through to fabric, as this causes drag which will lower the possible glide angle.

By definition, the permeability (porosity) of a fabric is measured by the amount of air, in cubic feet, that will flow through one square foot of the fabric as it is placed under a pressure differential of 1/2 inches of water, during a time period of sixty seconds.

Dacron is a good, all around choice for a hang glider sail, especially in comparison to nylon. Dacron is highly resistant to sunlight (ultraviolet rays) and has a low stretch ratio. On the other hand, nylon deteriorates with exposure to the sun (ultraviolet rays) and also stretches a great deal with use.

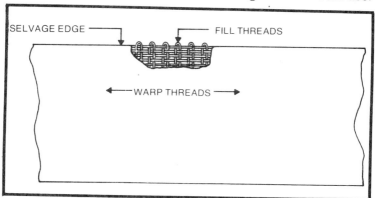

Fig. 8-2. Detail of a typical piece of Dacron.

Stretch may be allowed on a spinnaker sail or parachute, but not on a hang glider sail. The form of a hang glider sail is critical and a material with low stretch must be used.

A nylon coated Dacron is currently seeing some experimental use, its advantage being strictly zero porosity. Perhaps there will be more widespread use of it as time goes on. As of this writing, no other fabric, except for Dacron, can be recommended for hang glider usage.

When unfinished Dacron is used for covering rigid wing designs, it is normally shrunk in place by doping. This is a painting procedure that seals the fabric, makes it taut it and gives it zero porosity. The weight of unfinished Dacron is less than the calendered fabric mentioned. Glider weight cotton fabric may be used.

## Harnesses

Harnesses typically use nylon webbing for at least the straps, if not the entire assembly. It is tough and long lasting. Most widths are 1-3/4″ and good for anywhere from 2500 to 6000 pound test; certainly adequate to suspend a man. Other materials used in harness construction may be lambs wool for lining and foam rubber for padding.

## Threads and Cords

Thread is a thin, continuous length of fabric composed of many smaller strands which are normally wound in what is known as a left-hand or machine twist. It is used to sew together different pieces of fabric cloth to form a desired shape, such as a hang glider sail. Cords are made by weaving a number of strands of thread together to form either a solid or hollow core in the center. Cord is used for lacing and tying, such as for hang glider transport bags.

Machine thread is quite simply thread with a left-hand twist as used on a sewing machine. The left twist (also called Z-twist) is necessary because many sewing machines have a tendency to unravel a right-hand twist thread. For most hang glider applications, it is generally accepted that all seams are of double zigzag stitch with eight stitches per inch being typical. The double stitching provides more than adequate strength for the seam while adding a degree of redundancy and safety.

A popular thread size is #69 Dacron (size E) which has a tensile strength of 9.5 pounds. A thread made of the same material as the sail should be used. Also, unlike straight stitch, a zigzag stitch does not takeup the fabric and gives when the fabric is loaded.

Hand sewing can be done for repairs in sails and bags. A sewing awl with specially designed needles and a bobbin container will allow one to sew a lock stitch similar to a machine's. Care must be taken so as not to disturb the original sail form, size, and shape.

**Tape**

Fabric tape is made of material similar to that of the sail (e.g., Dacron) and has a warp thread which is larger than its fill thread. It is used primarily for leading edge and keel pockets and serves to prevent wear and wrinkling of the sail itself. Tape is typically available in white Dacron in widths from 3/4 up to 6″ and in weights from 3 oz. to 10.5 oz.

The leading edges and keel areas see rubbing with the airframe and often contain many cutouts and grommets. Thus, a separate, heavier fabric is a good idea for greater durability. Since the sail itself only rubs with the air, it won't see quite the abrasion as those areas that come into contact with the airframe.

Any good hang glider sail will employ a separate tape for its airframe member pockets for another good reason. If a sail pocket is formed by simply folding over and stitching, it will cause wrinkling and bunching due to the bias of the fabric with respect to the fold line. The only way to avoid this happening is to use a separate tape material in those areas that contact the airframe.

## MACHINE SEWN SEAMS AND SAILS

There are four basic types of machine sewn seams suitable for hang glider sail making: plain overlap, folded fell, French fell and modified French fell. The plain overlap seam is the simplest and most common in use today.

A sail is made to the proper size, shape and cut, and includes tape "pockets" in which the appropriate airframe members are placed and fastened. The fabric is prepared by cutting the yardage to the correct dimensions and sewing together with the plain overlap seam. Reinforcing patches and tapes are also sewn in and grommets installed. Trailing edges may be a simple fold-over and stitch, or perhaps a small width tape may be used, depending on the design.

The design and fabrication of a hang glider sail is not something to be taken very lightly. Sailmaking is an art and the sail is certainly the most important element with regard to performance, stability and control of any hang glider. A sail that has been developed over a period of time, inflates free of wrinkles and does not flutter at cruising speed, is what we are looking for. It must be perfectly symmetrical about the longitudinal axis with a cut, shape and billow that will give a good glide ratio with good stability. Too flat a cut and the sail flaps. Too little billow and the kite is squirrelly, i.e., touchy and unstable. Too much billow, and the glide angle suffers. A good hang glider sail is a well balanced compromise. Make sure it has been made by a professional who knows all about sail making.

## SAILS AND AEROELASTICITY

The particular shape and cut of a sail depends not only on aerodynamics, but also on aeroelasticity. In other words, as the sail inflates and is loaded in flight it, of course, loads the airframe, causing it to deflect. For instance, the aft leading edges (or tips) will bend in and up while the forward leading edge (between the cross member and nose) will also bend in and up, though not as much. The fore and aft keel will also bend upward in their centers due to airloads. If these bends or deflections are not considered in the design of the sail, then it will not perform properly or optimally. The sail must be cut and shaped to allow for airframe deflections. Another good idea is to have the trailing edge cut in a large scallop to distribute the end loads more evenly and to help minimize flutter.

## FASTENING AND JOINING

There are many ways to fasten one part of a hang glider to another. They run the gamut from nuts, bolts, screws and rivets to nico-press swaging, gluing and welding. The following paragraphs examine the various methods and where and why one method is used instead of another.

**Bolts**

Bolts are, by far, the simplest, most common and efficient way to put together the various parts that go into the structure of a hang glider. They lend themselves well to the tubular aluminum members used in most of today's hang gliders. They also allow for the easy removal and replacement of bent, broken or otherwise damaged parts. This same convenience is also evidenced in safety inspection and cleaning as well.

Most bolts used in hang glider construction have a hexagon head and are often referred to as "hex head cap screws" or just plain "cap screws." Their manufacture involves a forged head and shaft which is then threaded as desired. As a commercial bolt comes off the assembly line, it has a certain strength, or allowable stress rating, which is designated by the head being plain on top. The various grades of bolts are shown in Table 8-5. This is the so-called "grade 2" bolt and is typical of the kind found in hardware stores. It is very weak! Don't ever use one on a hang glider. To make a bolt stronger, it is put through a heat treatment process which raises its allowable stress level. Next, it is normally zinc electroplated and baked to relieve hydrogen brittleness caused by the plating process. The grade 5 bolt is made by heat treating a grade 2 to an allowable stress level of 120,000 psi. (This is the lowest grade bolt recommended by the HMA.) A grade 8 bolt is made by heat treating a grade 5 still further, until it reaches an allowable of 150,000 psi. Grade 9s are also available and they are good for 180,000 psi. The cost of the bolt increases with each successive operation performed on it. The percentage of the total cost of the hang glider in bolts is so low (on the order of 1%) that it's certainly well worth it to use top grade bolts!

The most common type of bolt used on a hang glider is the military of AN, type. These are hexheaded and heat treated to at best 150,000 PSI, and plated. The AN system is a standardization of all hardware including pulleys, turnbuckles, etc., as well as bolts. (see Fig. 8-3). Table 8-6 shows the AN bolt dash numbers and lengths. Other governmental

# Table 8-5. ASTM and SAE Grade Markings for Steel Bolts and Screws

| Grade Marking | Specification | Material | Bolt and Screw Size, in | Proof Load, psi | Tensile Strength min, psi |
|---|---|---|---|---|---|
| NO MARK | SAE---Grade 1 | | 1/4 thru 1 1/2 | 33,000 | 60,000 |
| | ASTM--A 307 | Low Carbon Steel | 1/4 thru 1 1/2 | 33,000 | 60,000 |
| | | | Over 1 1/2 thru 4 | . . . . . | 55,000 |
| | SAE---Grade 2 | Low Carbon Steel | 1/4 thru 3/4 | 55,000 | 74,000 |
| | | | Over 3/4 thru 1 1/2 | 33,000 | 60,000 |
| | SAE---Grade 3 | Medium Carbon Steel, Cold Worked | 1/4 thru 1/2 | 85,000 | 110,000 |
| | | | Over 1/2 thru 5/8 | 80,000 | 100,000 |
| | SAE---Grade 5 | Medium Carbon Steel, Quenched and Tempered | 1/4 thru 1 | 85,000 | 120,000 |
| | | | Over 1 thru 1 1/2 | 74,000 | 105,000 |
| | ASTM--A 449 | | 1/4 thru 1 | 85,000 | 120,000 |
| | | | Over 1 thru 1 1/2 | 74,000 | 105,000 |
| | | | Over 1 1/2 thru 3 | 55,000 | 90,000 |
| A325 | ASTM--A 325 | Medium Carbon Steel, Quenched and Tempered | 1/2, 5/8, 3/4 | 85,000 | 120,000 |
| | | | 7/8, 1 | 78,000 | 115,000 |
| | | | 1 1/8 thru 1 1/2 | 74,000 | 105,000 |
| BB | ASTM--A 354 Grade BB | Low Alloy Steel, Quenched and Tempered | 1/4 thru 2 1/2 | 80,000 | 105,000 |
| | | | Over 2 1/2 thru 4 | 75,000 | 100,000 |
| BC | ASTM--A 354 Grade BC | Low Alloy Steel, Quenched and Tempered | 1/4 thru 2 1/2 | 105,000 | 125,000 |
| | | | Over 2 1/2 thru 4 | 95,000 | 115,000 |
| | SAE---Grade 5.1 | Low or Medium Carbon Steel, Quenched and Tempered with Assembled Lock Washer | Up to 3/8 incl. | 85,000 | 120,000 |
| | SAE---Grade 7 | Medium Carbon Alloy Steel, Quenched and Tempered, Roll Threaded after heat treatment | 1/4 thru 1 1/2 | 105,000 | 133,000 |
| | SAE---Grade 8 | Medium Carbon Alloy Steel, Quenched and Tempered | 1/4 thru 1 1/2 | 120,000 | 150,000 |
| | ASTM--A 354 Grade BD | Alloy Steel, Quenched and Tempered | | | |
| A490 | ASTM--A 490 | Alloy Steel, Quenched and Tempered | 1/2 thru 2 1/2 | 120,000 | 150,000 |
| | | | Over 2 1/2 thru 4 | 105,000 | 140,000 |

**ASTM Specifications**
A 307 -- Low Carbon Steel Externally and Internally Threaded Standard Fasteners.
A 325 -- High Strength Bolts for Structural Steel Joints, Including Suitable Nuts and Plain Hardened Washers.
A 449 -- Quenched and Tempered Steel Bolts and Studs.
A 354 -- Quenched and Tempered Alloy Steel Bolts and Studs with Suitable Nuts.
A 490 -- High Strength Alloy Steel Bolts for Structural Steel Joints, Including Suitable Nuts and Plain Hardened Washers

**SAE Specification**
J 429c -- Mechanical and Quality Requirements for Threaded Fasteners.

agencies who are interested in parts standardization also have a numbering system as follows:

| AC Numbers | Air Force |
|---|---|
| NAS | National Aircraft Standards |
| NAF | Naval Aircraft Factory |
| MX | Military Aeronautical Standards |

Most hang glider manufacturers try to use the standard parts whenever practicable. One can be sure of their quality and strength, as these "standard parts" meet various military specifications (MIL SPECS) (see Fig. 8-4).

In addition to the above standardization of parts, hexhead bolts come under two general thread classifications: coarse and fine. The coarse thread is referred to as Unified Thread Form Coarse (UNC) and the fine thread is referred to as Unified Thread Form Fine (UNF). The difference is that the fine threads are closer together, i.e., there are more threads per inch. Fine threads are commonly used in hang gliders and in general this series has greater tensile stress area than comparable sizes of coarse series. They are also used where

**Table 8-6. AN Bolt Dash Numbers and Lengths**

| DASH NO. | AN3 GRIP 1/64 | AN3 LENGTH 1/32 1/64 | AN4 GRIP 1/64 | AN4 LENGTH 1/32 1/64 | AN5 GRIP 1/64 | AN5 LENGTH 1/32 1/64 |
|---|---|---|---|---|---|---|
| 3 | 1/16 | 15/32 | 1/16 | 15/32 | ---- | ---- |
| 4 | 1/8 | 17/32 | 1/16 | 17/32 | 1/16 | 19/32 |
| 5 | 1/4 | 21/32 | 3/16 | 21/32 | 3/16 | 23/32 |
| 6 | 3/8 | 25/32 | 5/16 | 25/32 | 5/16 | 27/32 |
| 7 | 1/2 | 29/32 | 7/16 | 29/32 | 7/16 | 31/32 |
| 10 | 5/8 | 1-1/32 | 9/16 | 1-1/32 | 9/16 | 1-1/32 |
| 11 | 3/4 | 1-5/32 | 11/16 | 1-5/32 | 11/16 | 1-7/32 |
| 12 | 7/8 | 1-9/32 | 13/16 | 1-9/32 | 13/16 | 1-11/32 |
| 13 | 1 | 1-13/32 | 15/16 | 1-13/32 | 15/16 | 1-15/32 |
| 14 | 1-1/8 | 1-17/32 | 1-1/16 | 1-17/32 | 1-1/16 | 1-19/32 |
| 15 | 1-1/4 | 1-21/32 | 1-3/16 | 1-21/32 | 1-3/16 | 1-23/32 |
| 16 | 1-3/8 | 1-25/32 | 1-5/16 | 1-25/32 | 1-5/16 | 1-27/32 |
| 17 | 1-1/2 | 1-29/32 | 1-7/16 | 1-29/32 | 1-7/16 | 1-31/32 |
| 20 | 1-5/8 | 2-1/32 | 1-9/16 | 2-1/32 | 1-9/16 | 2-3/32 |
| 21 | 1-3/4 | 2-5/32 | 1-11/16 | 2-5/32 | 1-11/16 | 2-7/32 |
| 22 | 1-7/8 | 2-9/32 | 1-13/16 | 2-9/32 | 1-13/16 | 2-11/32 |
| 23 | 2 | 2-13/32 | 1-15/16 | 2-13/32 | 1-15/16 | 2-15/32 |
| 24 | 2-1/8 | 2-17/32 | 2-1/16 | 2-17/32 | 2-1/16 | 2-19/32 |
| 25 | 2-1/4 | 2-21/32 | 2-3/16 | 2-21/32 | 2-3/16 | 2-23/32 |
| 26 | 2-3/8 | 2-25/32 | 2-5/16 | 2-25/32 | 2-5/16 | 2-27/32 |
| 27 | 2-1/2 | 2-29/32 | 2-7/16 | 2-29/32 | 2-7/16 | 2-31/32 |
| 30 | 2-5/8 | 3-1/32 | 2-9/16 | 3-1/32 | 2-9/16 | 3-3/2 |
| 31 | 2-3/4 | 3-5/32 | 2-11/16 | 3-5/32 | 2-11/16 | 3-7/32 |
| 32 | 2-7/8 | 3-9/32 | 2-13/16 | 3-9/32 | 2-13/16 | 3-11/32 |
| 33 | 3 | 3-13/32 | 2-15/16 | 3-13/32 | 2-15/16 | 3-15/32 |
| 34 | 3-1/8 | 3-17/32 | 3-1/16 | 3-27/32 | 3-1/16 | 3-19/32 |
| 35 | 3-1/4 | 3-21/32 | 3-3/16 | 3-21/32 | 3-3/16 | 3-23/32 |
| 36 | 3-3/8 | 3-25/32 | 3-5/16 | 3-25/32 | 3-5/16 | 3-27/32 |
| 37 | 3-1/2 | 3-29/32 | 3-7/16 | 3-29/32 | 3-7/16 | 3-31 |
| 40 | 3-5/8 | 4-1/32 | 3-9/16 | 4-1/32 | 3-9/16 | 4-3/32 |
| 41 | 3-3/4 | 4-5/32 | 3-11/16 | 4-5/32 | 3-11/16 | 4-7/32 |
| 42 | 3-7/8 | 4-9/32 | 3-13/16 | 4-9/32 | 3-13/16 | 4-11/32 |
| 43 | 4 | 4-13/32 | 3-15/16 | 4-13/32 | 3-15/16 | 4-15/32 |
| 44 | 4-1/8 | 4-17/32 | 4-1/16 | 4-17/32 | 4-1/16 | 4-19/32 |
| 45 | 4-1/4 | 4-21/32 | 4-3/16 | 4-21/32 | 4-3/16 | 4-23/32 |
| 46 | 4-3/8 | 4-25/32 | 4-5/16 | 4-25/32 | 4-5/16 | 4-27/32 |
| 47 | 4-1/2 | 4-29/32 | 4-7/16 | 4-29/32 | 4-7/16 | 4-31/32 |
| 50 | 4-5/8 | 5-1/32 | 4-9/16 | 5-1/32 | 4-9/16 | 5-3/32 |
| 51 | 4-3/4 | 5-5/32 | 4-11/16 | 5-5/32 | 4-11/16 | 5-7/32 |
| 52 | 4-7/8 | 5-9/32 | 4-13/16 | 5-9/32 | 4-13/16 | 5-11/32 |
| 53 | 5 | 5-13/32 | 4-15/16 | 5-13/32 | 4-15/16 | 5-15/32 |
| 54 | 5-1/8 | 5-17/32 | 5-1/16 | 5-17/32 | 5-1/16 | 5-19/32 |

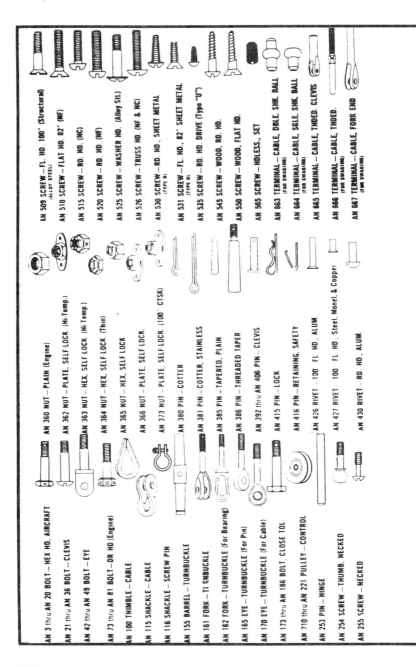

AN 3 thru AN 20 BOLT — HEX HD. AIRCRAFT

AN 21 thru AN 36 BOLT — CLEVIS

AN 42 thru AN 49 BOLT — EYE

AN 73 thru AN 81 BOLT — DR HD (Engine)

AN 100 THIMBLE — CABLE

AN 115 SHACKLE — CABLE

AN 116 SHACKLE — SCREW PIN

AN 155 BARREL — TURNBUCKLE

AN 161 FORK — TURNBUCKLE

AN 162 FORK — TURNBUCKLE (For Bearing)

AN 165 EYE — TURNBUCKLE (For Pin)

AN 170 EYE — TURNBUCKLE (For Cable)

AN 173 thru AN 186 BOLT, CLOSE TOL.

AN 210 thru AN 221 PULLEY — CONTROL

AN 253 PIN — HINGE

AN 254 SCREW — THUMB, NECKED

AN 255 SCREW — NECKED

AN 360 NUT — PLAIN (Engine)

AN 362 NUT — PLATE, SELF LOCK (Hi-Temp.)

AN 363 NUT — HEX, SELF LOCK (Hi-Temp.)

AN 364 NUT — HEX, SELF LOCK (Thin)

AN 365 NUT — HEX, SELF LOCK

AN 366 NUT — PLATE, SELF LOCK.

AN 373 NUT — PLATE, SELF LOCK (100˚ CTSK)

AN 380 PIN — COTTER

AN 381 PIN — COTTER, STAINLESS

AN 385 PIN — TAPERED, PLAIN

AN 386 PIN — THREADED TAPER

AN 392 thru AN 406 PIN — CLEVIS

AN 415 PIN — LOCK

AN 416 PIN — RETAINING, SAFETY

AN 426 RIVET - 100  FL  HD.  ALUM

AN 427 RIVET  100  FL  HD . Steel, Monel, & Copper

AN 430 RIVET — RD  HD.  ALUM

AN 509 SCREW — FL. HD. 100˚ (Structural)
(ALLOY STEEL)

AN 510 SCREW — FLAT HD. 82˚ (NF)

AN 515 SCREW — RD. HD. (NC)

AN 520 SCREW — RD. HD (NF)

AN 525 SCREW — WASHER HD. (Alloy Stl.)

AN 526 SCREW — TRUSS HD. (NF & NC)

AN 530 SCREW — RD. HD. SHEET METAL
(TYPE B)

AN 531 SCREW — FL. HD., 82˚ SHEET METAL
(TYPE B)

AN 535 SCREW — RD. HD. DRIVE (Type "U")

AN 545 SCREW — WOOD, RD. HD.

AN 550 SCREW — WOOD, FLAT HD.

AN 565 SCREW — NDLESS., SET

AN 663 TERMINAL — CABLE, DBLE SHK. BALL
(FOR SWAGING)

AN 664 TERMINAL — CABLE, SGLE SHK. BALL
(FOR SWAGING)

AN 665 TERMINAL — CABLE, THDED CLEVIS

AN 666 TERMINAL — CABLE, THDED.
(FOR SWAGING)

AN 667 TERMINAL — CABLE, FORK END
(FOR SWAGING)

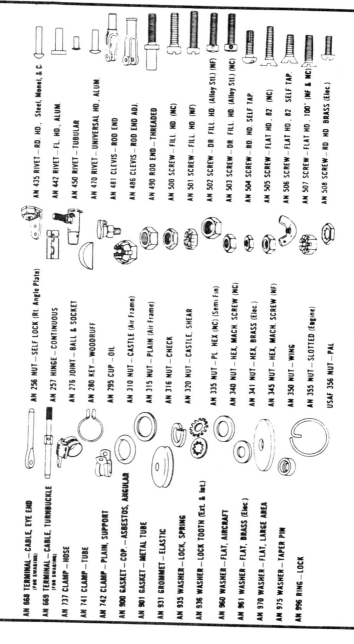

AN 668 TERMINAL—CABLE, EYE END (FOR SWAGING)

AN 669 TERMINAL—CABLE, TURNBUCKLE (FOR SWAGING)

AN 737 CLAMP—HOSE

AN 741 CLAMP—TUBE

AN 742 CLAMP—PLAIN, SUPPORT

AN 900 GASKET—COP.—ASBESTOS, ANGULAR

AN 901 GASKET—METAL TUBE

AN 931 GROMMET—ELASTIC

AN 935 WASHER—LOCK, SPRING

AN 936 WASHER—LOCK TOOTH (Ext. & Int.)

AN 960 WASHER—FLAT, AIRCRAFT

AN 961 WASHER—FLAT, BRASS (Elec.)

AN 970 WASHER—FLAT, LARGE AREA

AN 975 WASHER—TAPER PIN

AN 996 RING—LOCK

AN 256 NUT—SELF LOCK (Rt. Angle Plate)

AN 257 HINGE—CONTINUOUS

AN 276 JOINT—BALL & SOCKET

AN 280 KEY—WOODRUFF

AN 295 CUP—OIL

AN 310 NUT—CASTLE (Air Frame)

AN 315 NUT—PLAIN (Air Frame)

AN 316 NUT—CHECK

AN 320 NUT—CASTLE, SHEAR

AN 335 NUT—PL HEX (NC) (Semi Fin)

AN 340 NUT—HEX, MACH. SCREW (NC)

AN 341 NUT—HEX, BRASS (Elec.)

AN 345 NUT—HEX, MACH. SCREW (NF)

AN 350 NUT—WING

AN 355 NUT—SLOTTED (Engine)

USAF 356 NUT—PAL

AN 435 RIVET—RD. HD.  Steel, Monel, & C

AN 442 RIVET—FL. HD. ALUM.

AN 450 RIVET—TUBULAR

AN 470 RIVET—UNIVERSAL HD. ALUM.

AN 481 CLEVIS—ROD END

AN 486 CLEVIS—ROD END ADJ.

AN 490 ROD END—THREADED

AN 500 SCREW—FILL HD (NC)

AN 501 SCREW—FILL HD (NF)

AN 502 SCREW—DR FILL HD (Alloy Stl.) (NF)

AN 503 SCREW—DR FILL. HD. (Alloy Stl.) (NC)

AN 504 SCREW—RD. HD. SELF TAP.

AN 505 SCREW—FLAT HD. 82 (NC)

AN 506 SCREW—FLAT HD. 82  SELF TAP.

AN 507 SCREW—FLAT HD. 100° (NF & NC)

AN 508 SCREW—RD HD BRASS (Elec.)

Fig. 8-3. Basic AN hardware.

317

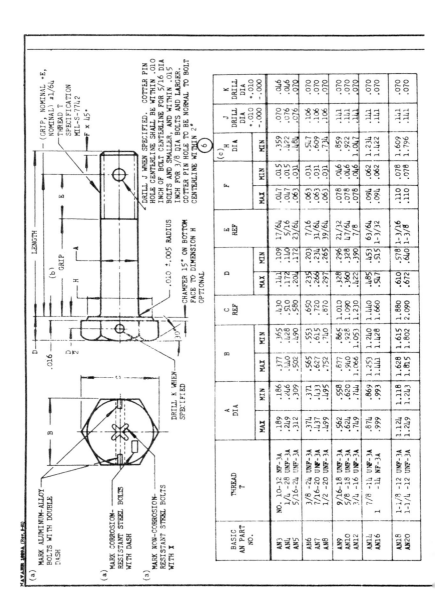

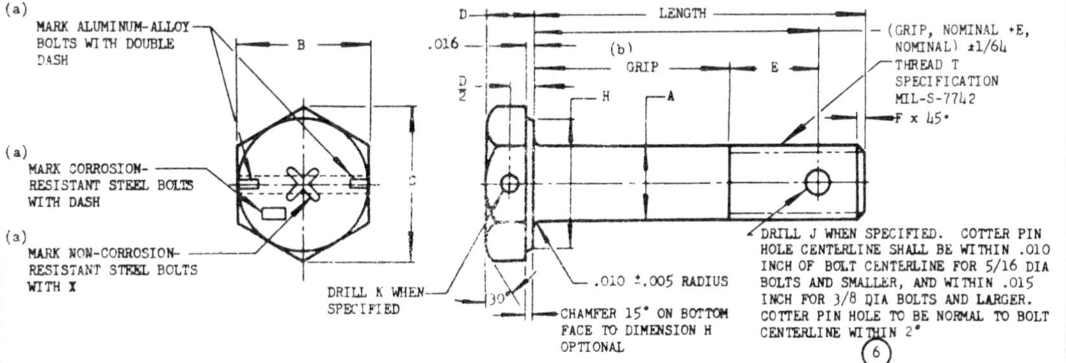
(a) MARK ALUMINUM-ALLOY BOLTS WITH DOUBLE DASH
(a) MARK CORROSION-RESISTANT STEEL BOLTS WITH DASH
(a) MARK NON-CORROSION-RESISTANT STEEL BOLTS WITH X
B
C
DRILL K WHEN SPECIFIED
D
.016
D/2
30°
LENGTH
(b) GRIP
H
A
E
(GRIP, NOMINAL +E, NOMINAL) ±1/64
THREAD T SPECIFICATION MIL-S-7742
F x 45°
.010 ±.005 RADIUS
CHAMFER 15° ON BOTTOM FACE TO DIMENSION H OPTIONAL
DRILL J WHEN SPECIFIED. COTTER PIN HOLE CENTERLINE SHALL BE WITHIN .010 INCH OF BOLT CENTERLINE FOR 5/16 DIA BOLTS AND SMALLER, AND WITHIN .015 INCH FOR 3/8 DIA BOLTS AND LARGER. COTTER PIN HOLE TO BE NORMAL TO BOLT CENTERLINE WITHIN 2°
6

| BASIC AN PART NO. | THREAD T | A DIA | | B | | C REF | D | | E REF | F | | (c) H DIA | J DRILL DIA +.010 -.000 | K DRILL DIA +.010 -.000 |
|---|---|---|---|---|---|---|---|---|---|---|---|---|---|---|
| | | MAX | MIN | MAX | MIN | | MAX | MIN | | MAX | MIN | MIN | | |
| AN3 | NO. 10-32 NF-3A | .189 | .186 | .377 | .365 | .430 | .141 | .109 | 17/64 | .047 | .015 | .359 | .070 | .046 |
| AN4 | 1/4 -28 UNF-3A | .249 | .246 | .440 | .428 | .510 | .172 | .140 | 5/16 | .047 | .015 | .422 | .076 | .046 |
| AN5 | 5/16-24 UNF-3A | .312 | .309 | .502 | .490 | .580 | .204 | .172 | 23/64 | .063 | .031 | .484 | .076 | .070 |
| AN6 | 3/8 -24 UNF-3A | .374 | .371 | .565 | .553 | .650 | .235 | .203 | 7/16 | .063 | .031 | .547 | .106 | .070 |
| AN7 | 7/16-20 UNF-3A | .437 | .433 | .627 | .615 | .720 | .266 | .234 | 31/64 | .063 | .031 | .609 | .106 | .070 |
| AN8 | 1/2 -20 UNF-3A | .499 | .495 | .752 | .740 | .870 | .297 | .265 | 39/64 | .063 | .031 | .734 | .106 | .070 |
| AN9 | 9/16-18 UNF-3A | .562 | .558 | .877 | .865 | 1.010 | .328 | .296 | 21/32 | .078 | .046 | .859 | .141 | .070 |
| AN10 | 5/8 -18 UNF-3A | .624 | .620 | .940 | .928 | 1.090 | .360 | .328 | 47/64 | .078 | .046 | .922 | .141 | .070 |
| AN12 | 3/4 -16 UNF-3A | .749 | .744 | 1.066 | 1.053 | 1.230 | .422 | .390 | 7/8 | .078 | .046 | 1.047 | .141 | .070 |
| AN14 | 7/8 -14 UNF-3A | .874 | .869 | 1.253 | 1.240 | 1.440 | .485 | .453 | 63/64 | .094 | .062 | 1.234 | .141 | .070 |
| AN16 | 1 -14 NF-3A | .999 | .993 | 1.441 | 1.428 | 1.660 | .547 | .515 | 1-3/32 | .094 | .062 | 1.422 | .141 | .070 |
| AN18 | 1-1/8 -12 UNF-3A | 1.124 | 1.118 | 1.628 | 1.615 | 1.880 | .610 | .578 | 1-3/16 | .110 | .078 | 1.609 | .141 | .070 |
| AN20 | 1-1/4 -12 UNF-3A | 1.249 | 1.243 | 1.815 | 1.802 | 2.090 | .672 | .640 | 1-3/8 | .110 | .078 | 1.796 | .141 | .070 |

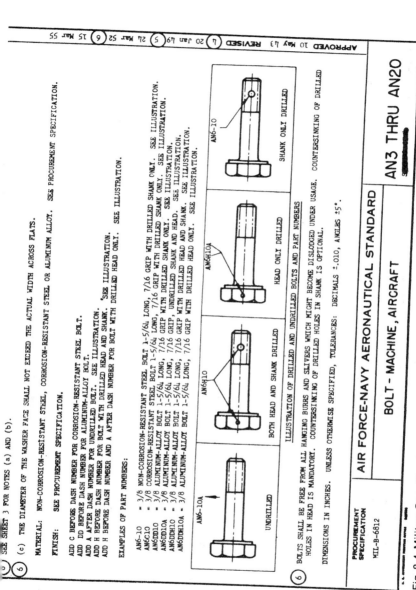

SEE SHEET 3 FOR NOTES (a) AND (b).

(c) THE DIAMETER OF THE WASHER FACE SHALL NOT EXCEED THE ACTUAL WIDTH ACROSS FLATS.

MATERIAL: NON-CORROSION-RESISTANT STEEL, CORROSION-RESISTANT STEEL OR ALUMINUM ALLOY. SEE PROCUREMENT SPECIFICATION.

FINISH: SEE PROCUREMENT SPECIFICATION.

ADD C BEFORE DASH NUMBER FOR CORROSION-RESISTANT STEEL BOLT.
ADD DD BEFORE DASH NUMBER FOR ALUMINUM-ALLOY BOLT.
ADD A AFTER DASH NUMBER FOR UNDRILLED BOLT. SEE ILLUSTRATION.
ADD H BEFORE DASH NUMBER FOR BOLT WITH DRILLED HEAD AND SHANK. SEE ILLUSTRATION.
ADD H BEFORE DASH NUMBER AND A AFTER DASH NUMBER FOR BOLT WITH DRILLED HEAD ONLY. SEE ILLUSTRATION.

EXAMPLES OF PART NUMBERS:

AN6-10    = 3/8 NON-CORROSION-RESISTANT STEEL BOLT 1-5/64 LONG, 7/16 GRIP WITH DRILLED SHANK ONLY. SEE ILLUSTRATION.
AN6C10    = 3/8 CORROSION-RESISTANT STEEL BOLT 1-5/64 LONG, 7/16 GRIP WITH DRILLED SHANK ONLY. SEE ILLUSTRATION.
AN6DD10   = 3/8 ALUMINUM-ALLOY BOLT 1-5/64 LONG, 7/16 GRIP WITH DRILLED SHANK ONLY. SEE ILLUSTRATION.
AN6DD10A  = 3/8 ALUMINUM-ALLOY BOLT 1-5/64 LONG, 7/16 GRIP, UNDRILLED SHANK ONLY. SEE ILLUSTRATION.
AN6DH10   = 3/8 ALUMINUM-ALLOY BOLT 1-5/64 LONG, 7/16 GRIP WITH DRILLED SHANK AND HEAD. SEE ILLUSTRATION.
AN6DH10A  = 3/8 ALUMINUM-ALLOY BOLT 1-5/64 LONG, 7/16 GRIP WITH DRILLED HEAD AND SHANK. SEE ILLUSTRATION.

ILLUSTRATION OF DRILLED AND UNDRILLED BOLTS AND PART NUMBERS

| UNDRILLED | BOTH HEAD AND SHANK DRILLED | HEAD ONLY DRILLED | SHANK ONLY DRILLED |

AN6-10A    AN6H10    AN6H10A    AN6-10

BOLTS SHALL BE FREE FROM ALL HANGING BURRS AND SLIVERS WHICH MIGHT BECOME DISLODGED UNDER USAGE. COUNTERSINKING OF DRILLED HOLES IN HEAD IS MANDATORY. COUNTERSINKING OF DRILLED HOLES IN SHANK IS OPTIONAL.

DIMENSIONS IN INCHES. UNLESS OTHERWISE SPECIFIED, TOLERANCES: DECIMALS ±.010, ANGLES ±5°.

| PROCUREMENT SPECIFICATION | AIR FORCE-NAVY AERONAUTICAL STANDARD | |
| MIL-B-6812 | BOLT - MACHINE, AIRCRAFT | AN3 THRU AN20 |
| | | SUPERSEDES FORMER ANA STANDARD AND AIR FORCE AND NAVY STANDARD ISSUES OF AN3 THROUGH AN20. |

APPROVED 10 May 43 REVISED (4) 20 Jan 49 (5) 24 Mar 52 (6) 15 Mar 55

Fig. 8-4. Military Specifications of standard parts.

319

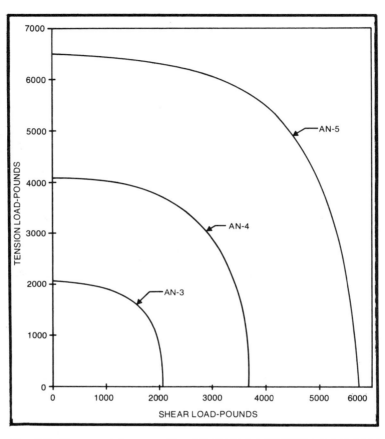

Fig. 8-5. Shear and tension allowable loads on AN bolts used in hang gliders.

engagement length is short or where wall thickness demands finer pitch. Coarse threaded bolts, however, give more flank engagement and thus have a slightly greater tensile proof load (e.g., grade 5 UNF = 120,00 psi, grade 5 UNF = 109,000 psi according to latest SAE specs). In general, the volume of the thread of which coarse threads have more, and not the stress area of which fine threads have more, determines the ultimate stripping strength of the bolt.

Figure 8-5 and Table 8-7 show shear and tensile strength of AN bolts.

**Table 8-7. Shear and Tensile Strength Maximums of AN Bolts Used in Hang Gliders**

SHEAR AND TENSILE STRENGTHS OF AN BOLTS

| AN SIZE | DIA. | SHEAR | TENSILE |
|---------|------|-------|---------|
| AN-3 | 3/16 | 2,070 | 2,070 |
| AN-4 | 1/4 | 3,680 | 4,080 |
| AN-5 | 5/16 | 5,750 | 6,500 |

Note:
Shear and Tensile strengths are given in pounds, based on a heat treated condition of: 125,000 psi tensile and 75,000 psi shear.

In certain cases, the head and/or the end of the threaded portion of an aircraft bolt will have a hole drilled through. While uncommon to hang glider applications, these holes allow insertion of a cotter pin or wire to prevent rotation of either the bolt or its attached nut.

### Eyebolts

Besides the standard hex head bolts, an often used type is the eyebolt (see Fig. 8-6). This is available in the AN series. Eyebolts have been used as a dual purpose fastener serving as a structural as well as cable anchoring device. Be sure to consult strength values before using. Under no circumstances should one use "hardware store" eyebolts. They have a split eye which will open under hang glider loads. Then too, they are mild steel as are most other hardware store fasteners.

### Nuts

A nut is used to secure a bolt. In hang glider applications, either the so-called ESNA nut or AN castle nut (see Figs. 8-7 through 8-9) are the favorites. ESNA nuts have a fibrous or nylon unthreaded insert inbedded in the end threads. When turned on to the bolt, the insert is "threaded" and grips the bolt sufficiently to prevent rotation. This type of nut should be used only once since the gripping power of the insert is diminished each time it is threaded onto a bolt.

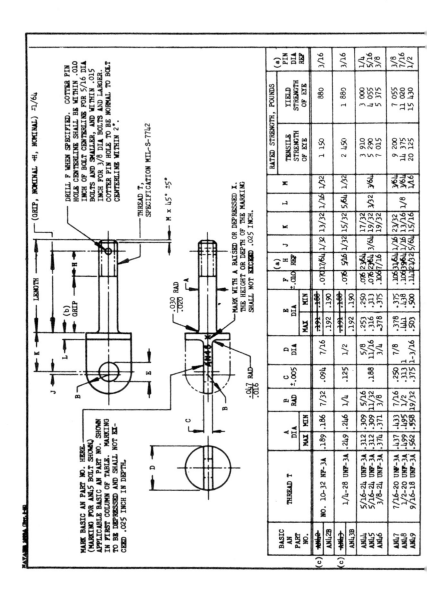

MARK BASIC AN PART NO. HERE. (MARKING FOR AN45 BOLT SHOWN). APPLICABLE BASIC AN PART NO. SHOWN IN FIRST COLUMN OF TABLE. MARKING TO BE DEPRESSED AND SHALL NOT EXCEED .025 INCH IN DEPTH.

DRILL F WHEN SPECIFIED. COTTER PIN HOLE CENTERLINE SHALL BE WITHIN .010 INCH OF BOLT CENTERLINE FOR 5/16 DIA BOLTS AND SMALLER, AND WITHIN .015 INCH FOR 3/8 DIA BOLTS AND LARGER. COTTER PIN HOLE TO BE NORMAL TO BOLT CENTERLINE WITHIN 2°.

THREAD T, SPECIFICATION MIL-S-7742

M x 45° ±5°

MARK WITH A RAISED OR DEPRESSED X. THE HEIGHT OR DEPTH OF THE MARKING SHALL NOT EXCEED .025 INCH.

(GRIP, NOMINAL +H, NOMINAL) 51/64

| BASIC AN PART NO. | THREAD T | A DIA MAX | A DIA MIN | B RAD | C ±.005 | D DIA | E DIA MAX | E DIA MIN | F ±.COLOR | H REF | J | K | L | M | TENSILE STRENGTH OF EYE | YIELD STRENGTH OF EYE | (a) PIN DIA REF |
|---|---|---|---|---|---|---|---|---|---|---|---|---|---|---|---|---|---|
| AN4 | NO. 10-32 NF-3A | .189 | .186 | 7/32 | .094 | 7/16 | .193 | .190 | .070 | 17/64 | 1/32 | 13/32 | 1/16 | 1/32 | 1 150 | 880 | 3/16 |
| AN42B | | | | | | | .192 | .190 | | | | | | | | | |
| AN4 | 1/4-28 UNF-3A | .249 | .246 | 1/4 | .125 | 1/2 | .193 | .190 | .076 | 5/16 | 1/32 | 15/32 | 5/64 | 1/32 | 2 450 | 1 880 | 3/16 |
| AN43B | | | | | | | .192 | .190 | | | | | | | | | |
| AN44 | 5/16-24 UNF-3A | .312 | .309 | 5/16 | .188 | 5/8 | .253 | .250 | .076 | 23/64 | 3/64 | 17/32 | 3/32 | 3/64 | 3 910 | 3 000 | 1/4 |
| AN45 | 5/16-24 UNF-3A | .312 | .309 | 11/32 | .188 | 11/16 | .316 | .313 | .076 | 23/64 | 3/64 | 19/32 | 3/32 | 3/64 | 5 290 | 4 055 | 5/16 |
| AN46 | 3/8-24 UNF-3A | .374 | .371 | 3/8 | .188 | 3/4 | .378 | .375 | .106 | 7/16 | 3/64 | 19/32 | | 3/64 | 7 015 | 5 375 | 3/8 |
| AN47 | 7/16-20 UNF-3A | .437 | .433 | 7/16 | .250 | 7/8 | .378 | .375 | .106 | 7/16 | 1/16 | 23/32 | 1/8 | 3/64 | 9 200 | 7 055 | 3/8 |
| AN48 | 1/2-20 UNF-3A | .499 | .495 | 1/2 | .313 | 1 | .441 | .438 | .106 | 9/16 | 1/16 | 13/16 | 1/8 | 3/64 | 14 375 | 11 020 | 7/16 |
| AN49 | 9/16-18 UNF-3A | .562 | .558 | 19/32 | .375 | 1-3/16 | .503 | .500 | .112 | 5/8 | 5/64 | 15/16 | 1/8 | 1/16 | 20 125 | 15 430 | 1/2 |

(b) GRIP LENGTH OF BOLTS SHALL BE MEASURED FROM THE UNDERSIDE OF THE HEAD TO THE END OF THE FULL CYLINDRICAL PORTION OF THE SHANK. COMPLETE THREADS SHALL BEGIN WITHIN TWO THREAD PITCH MAXIMUM. TWO THREAD PITCH MAXIMUM MAY CONSIST OF INCOMPLETE THREAD OR EXTRUSION ANGLE.

(c) BOLTS WITH BASIC PART NUMBERS AN42 AND AN43 INACTIVE FOR DESIGN AFTER 4 APRIL 1955.   IN LIEU THEREOF, USE BOLTS WITH BASIC PART NUMBERS AN42B AND AN43B.

FOR DEFINITION AND APPLICATION OF DRAWING STATUS NOTES, SEE ANA BULLETIN NO. 337.

MATERIAL: NON-CORROSION-RESISTANT STEEL OR CORROSION-RESISTANT STEEL.   SEE PROCUREMENT SPECIFICATION.

FINISH: SEE PROCUREMENT SPECIFICATION.

ADD A AFTER DASH NUMBER FOR BOLT WITHOUT DRILLED HOLE IN SHANK.

ADD C BEFORE DASH NUMBER FOR CORROSION-RESISTANT STEEL BOLT.

EXAMPLES OF PART NUMBERS: AN46-10 - 3/8-24 NON-CORROSION-RESISTANT STEEL EYE BOLT, 1-5/64 LONG HAVING 7/16 GRIP AND WITH
                                          DRILLED HOLE IN SHANK.
                          AN46-10A - 3/8-24 NON-CORROSION-RESISTANT STEEL EYE BOLT, 1-5/64 LONG HAVING 7/16 GRIP AND WITHOUT
                                          DRILLED HOLE IN SHANK.
                          AN46-C10 - 3/8-24 CORROSION-RESISTANT STEEL EYE BOLT, 1-5/64 LONG HAVING 7/16 GRIP AND WITH DRILLED
                                          HOLE IN SHANK.
                          AN46-C10A - 3/8-24 CORROSION-RESISTANT STEEL EYE BOLT, 1-5/64 LONG HAVING 7/16 GRIP AND WITHOUT
                                          DRILLED HOLE IN SHANK.
                          AN43B-C10A - 1/4-28 CORROSION-RESISTANT STEEL EYE BOLT,1+/32 LONG HAVING 9/16 GRIP AND WITHOUT
                                          DRILLED HOLE IN SHANK.

BOLTS SHALL BE FREE FROM ALL HANGING BURRS AND SLIVERS WHICH MIGHT BECOME DISLODGED UNDER USAGE.

COUNTERSINKING OF DRILLED HOLE IN SHANK IS OPTIONAL.  PIN HOLE E SHALL NOT BE COUNTERSUNK.

DIMENSIONS IN INCHES. UNLESS OTHERWISE SPECIFIED, TOLERANCES: FRACTIONS ±1/64.

(3) ENTIRE DRAWING REVISED.

| PROCUREMENT SPECIFICATION | AIR FORCE-NAVY AERONAUTICAL STANDARD | AN42 THRU AN49 |
|---|---|---|
| MIL-B-6812 | BOLT, EYE | (3) |

SUPERSEDES FORMER AIR FORCE AND NAVY
STANDARD ISSUES OF AN42 THROUGH AN49.

Fig. 8-6. Military specs pertaining to eye bolts.

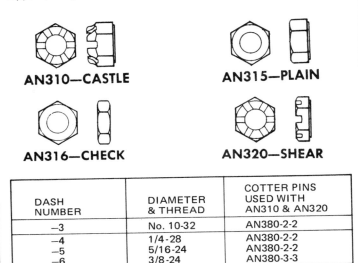

All nuts on this page are manufactured to the latest revision of Specification MIL-N-6034. Steel nuts are cadmium plated and dichromate dipped per Specification QQ-P-416, Type 2, Class 3.

**AN310—CASTLE**     **AN315—PLAIN**

**AN316—CHECK**     **AN320—SHEAR**

| DASH NUMBER | DIAMETER & THREAD | COTTER PINS USED WITH AN310 & AN320 |
|---|---|---|
| —3 | No. 10-32 | AN380-2-2 |
| —4 | 1/4-28 | AN380-2-2 |
| —5 | 5/16-24 | AN380-2-2 |
| —6 | 3/8-24 | AN380-3-3 |
| —7 | 7/16-20 | AN380-3-3 |
| —8 | 1/2-20 | AN380-3-3 |
| —9 | 9/16-18 | AN380-4-4 |
| —10 | 5/8-18 | AN380-4-4 |
| —12 | 3/4-16 | AN380-4-5 |

Fig. 8-7. Typical AN nuts.

Castle nuts have six grooves cut into their tops. These allow for a cotter pin to be inserted through two of the grooves and the drilled bolt tip. This makes a nut-bolt fastening that will not rotate loose. Cotter pins should be used only once!

In general, nuts are softer than the bolts they engage. To understand why this is so, one must look at what is really happening to a nut-bolt combination under high tension load. As the nut is rotated onto the bolt, it puts the bolt in tension and itself into compression. If it is softer than the bolt, it will deform and adjust itself to the load and actually "distribute" the load more evenly over the engaged threads than will a hard nut. So a soft nut, with a little give, in conjunction

## AN363 REGULAR HEX (to 550° F)

| MILITARY NUMBER | THREAD SIZE |
|---|---|
| AN363-632 | 6-32 |
| AN363-832 | 8-32 |
| AN363-1032 | 10-32 |
| AN363-428 | 1/4-28 |
| AN363-524 | 5/16-24 |
| AN363-624 | 3/8-24 |

Fig. 8-8. High temperature AN locking nuts are used by some manufacturers.

## AN365 (MS20365)
## NM, NE REGULAR HEX, LIGHT

NM          NE

| MILITARY NUMBER | ESNA NUMBER | THREAD SIZE |
|---|---|---|
| CADMIUM PLATED STEEL: | | |
| MS20365-440 | 22NM-40 | 4-40 |
| MS20365-632 | -62 | 6-32 |
| MS20365-640 | -60 | 6-40 |
| MS20365-832 | -82 | 8-32 |
| MS20365-1032 | -02 | 10-32 |
| MS20365-420 | 42NE-040 | 1/4-20 |
| MS20365-428 | -048 | 1/4-28 |
| MS20365-518 | -058 | 5/16-18 |
| MS20365-524 | -054 | 5/16-24 |
| MS20365-616 | 52NE-066 | 3/8-16 |
| MS20365-624 | -064 | 3/8-24 |
| MS20365-720 | -070 | 7/16-20 |
| MS20365-820 | -080 | 1/2-20 |
| MS20365-918 | -098 | 9/16-18 |
| MS20365-1018 | -108 | 5/8-18 |
| MS20365-1216 | -126 | 3/4-16 |
| BRASS: | | |
| MS20365B-1032 | 99NM-82 | 8-32 |
| ALUMINUM ALLOY: | | |
| MS20365D-832 | 68NM-82 | 8-32 |
| MS20365D-1032 | -02 | 10-32 |

Fig 8-9. ESNA type, nylon insert locking nuts are used by many manufacturers.

**AN350 WING NUT**
These are plain wing nuts available in commercial steel, cadmium plated per Spec. QQ-P-416 and in commercial brass. Hole is drilled in one wing for lockwire.

Fig. 8-10. AN wing nut with safety wire hole.

| PART NUMBER | SIZE AND THREAD |
|---|---|
| AN350-632 | #6-32 |
| AN350-832 | #8-32 |
| AN350-1032 | #10-32 |
| AN350-4 | 1/4-28 |
| AN350-5 | 5/16-24 |
| AN350-6 | 3/8-24 |

with a hard bolt will give the best all-around nut-bolt combination. So, for bolts, never use hardware store variety nuts; only high commercial grade or aircraft quality.

**Wing Nuts**

A more specialized nut type is the wing nut. This is a threaded, conical body with two "wings" protruding. It is used for no-tool assembly and its associated convenience. Commercial wing nuts are plain while AN series wing nuts come with a hole drilled through one wing for the attachment of a safety wire (see Fig. 8-10). All wing nut installations must be safetied with a safety wire.

**Rivets**

A rivet is basically an unthreaded bolt or headed pin used for pinning metal. In hang gliders, the rivet is seeing more and more use in the so-called "pop-rivet" form. Its use involves the drilling of appropriate holes in each piece to be joined, inserting the rivet through both holes and forming the unheaded inside end so as to make the outer head tight against the surface of the metal.

Pop rivets are good for shear and tension loads. Consult a manufacturer's chart for actual values. Normally, they are considered primarily as shear loaded only.

Rivets come in various diameters, lengths and shear strengths (see Figs. 8-11 and 8-12). Depending on the particular application, the size and number or rivets used to fasten metal together will vary. The hang glider designer using rivets will be aware of this and consider it in the design process.

Rivets are light and inexpensive and can do a good job of fastening metal parts that are not intended to be separated, as shown in Fig. 8-13. Once a rivet is in, it can only be removed by drilling it out.

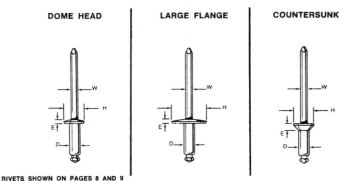

RIVETS SHOWN ON PAGES 8 AND 9

| | | | DOME HEAD | | LARGE FLANGE | | 100° COUNTERSUNK | |
|---|---|---|---|---|---|---|---|---|
| | D | W | H | E | H | E | H | E |
| Nominal Rivet Diameter | Nominal Body Diameter | Nominal Mandrel Diameter | Nominal Head Diameter | Maximum Head Height | Nominal Head Diameter | Maximum Head Height | Nominal Head Diameter | Ref Head Height |
| 3/32 | .094 | .057 | .188 | .032 | — | — | — | — |
| 1/8 | .125 | .076 | .250 | .040 | .375 | .045 | .220 | .045 |
| 5/32 | .156 | .095 | .312 | .047 | .468 | .056 | — | — |
| 3/16 | .187 | .114 | .375 | .055* | .625 | .083 | — | — |
| 1/4 | .250 | .151 | .500 | .073 | — | — | — | — |

*May be .068 on SD 68 BS

RIVETS SHOWN ON PAGES 10 AND 11

| | | | MONEL DOME HEAD | | STEEL and MONEL 120° COUNTERSUNK | | ALUMINUM 120° COUNTERSUNK | |
|---|---|---|---|---|---|---|---|---|
| | D | W | H | E | H | E | H | E |
| Nominal Rivet Diameter | Nominal Body Diameter | Nominal Mandrel Diameter | Nominal Head Diameter | Nominal Head Height | Nominal Head Diameter | Ref Head Height | Nominal Head Diameter | Ref Head Height |
| 3/64 | .109 | .072 | .192 | .020 | .192 | .028 | — | — |
| 1/8 | .125 | .076 | .236 | .025 | .236 | .036 | .236 | .036 |
| 5/32 | .156 | .090 | .263 | .028 | .263 | .039 | .263 | .039 |
| 3/16 | .187 | .114 | .320 | .040 | .320 | .045 | .375 | .064 |
| 1/4 | .253 | .152 | .427 | .053 | — | — | — | — |

NOTE: Maximum Length of Rivet Under Head (L) Dimensions are found on Pages 8 through 13.

Fig. 8-11 Various pop rivet types.

| Plated Carbon Steel Body with Coated Carbon Steel Mandrel IFI Grade 30 | | | Type 305 Stainless Steel Body with Coated Carbon Steel Mandrel IFI Grade 50 | | | Type 305 Stainless Steel Body with Stainless Steel Mandrel IFI Grade 51 | | |
|---|---|---|---|---|---|---|---|---|
| Part Number | Typical Ultimate Strength (Lbs.) | | Part Number | Typical Ultimate Strength (Lbs.) | | Part Number | Typical Ultimate Strength (Lbs.) | |
| | Shear | Tensile | | Shear | Tensile | | Shear | Tensile |
| **DOME HEAD RIVETS** | | | | | | | | |
| SD32BS SD34BS | 150 | 205 | | | | | | |
| SD41BS SD42BS SD43BS SD44BS SD45BS SD46BS SD48BS | 295 | 425 | SSD42BS SSD43BS SSD44BS | 550 | 700 | SSD42SSBS SSD43SSBS SSD44SSBS | 550 | 700 |
| SD52BS — SD54BS SD56BS — | 410 | 570 | SSD52BS SSD54BS SSD56BS | 900 | 1130 | | | |
| SD62BS SD64BS SD66BS SD68BS SD610BS SD612BS — | 590 | 815 | SSD62BS SSD64BS SSD66BS SSD68BS — — | 1000 | 1375 | SSD64SSBS SSD66SSBS — — | 1000 | 1375 |
| SD84BS SD86BS SD88BS — SD812BS SD816BS | 1245 | 1505 | | | | | | |
| **LARGE FLANGE "POP" RIVETS** | | | | | | | | |
| SD42BSLF SD44BSLF | 295 | 425 | SSD42BSLF | 550 | 700 | SSD42SSBSLF | 550 | 700 |
| SD54BSLF | 410 | 570 | | | | | | |
| SD64BSLF SD66BSLF SD68BSLF SD610BSLF SD612BSLF | 590 | 815 | | | | | | |

#110 Copper Body with Coated Steel Mandrel IFI Grade 20

| Rivet Diameter | Hole Drill Number | Maximum Length Under Head | Grip Range Inches | Part Number | Typical Ultimate Strength (Lbs.) | |
|---|---|---|---|---|---|---|
| | | | | | Shear | Tensile |
| ⅛" | .129-.133 #30 | .265 .390 | .032-.125 .126-.250 | CD42BS CD44BS | 215 | 300 |

Fig. 8-12. Pop rivet sizing chart for various loads.

## Turnbuckles

A turnbuckle is a barreled device with two steel shank ends of opposite thread (see Fig. 8-14). It is used to tension landing (upper) cables and control system cables. The most typical type found on hang gliders has a fork end and a cable eye end. Another type of end would be the pin eye. Never use hardware store variety or any type with a split eye end or hook end. Also, never lubricate a turnbuckle. In practice, most hang glider turnbuckles are not safetied from rotation and are, therefore, free to turn. Since only the landing cables have turnbuckles installed, their loosening in flight would still allow for a safe landing. However, to be as safe as possible, one should safety wire a turnbuckle, especially on long duration flights. A loosening of the bracing can lead to sloppy control response and abnormal impact loads on the airframe. Control system turnbuckles and any that see movement should most definitely be safetied in place. The older style AN turnbuckles used a zinc coated steel wire of slightly less than 1/16 inch in diameter which was discarded after one use. The newer MS style turnbuckles use a special locking clip, hence, the two types are incompatible. No more than three threads may be shown for a properly engaged turnbuckle.

### Pulleys

Pulleys used for hang glider aerodynamic control systems should be of the AN or MS variety (see Fig. 8-15). Never use hardware store pulleys for they are not designed for in-flight use. Aircraft pulleys are either of phenolic or aluminum construction and are available in a variety of sizes. Most hang glider control systems employ pulleys for 1/16″ (7 × 7) cable.

### Clevis Pins

A clevis pin as shown in Fig. 8-16, is a cadmium plated steel rod with a flat head at one end and a hole drilled through

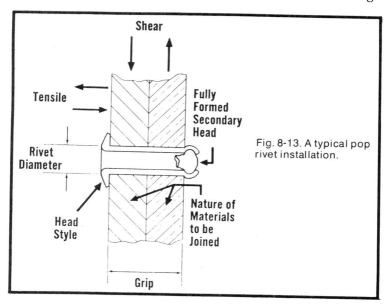

Fig. 8-13. A typical pop rivet installation.

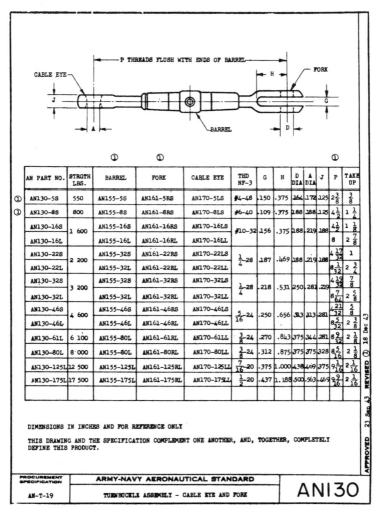

| AN PART NO. | STRGTH LBS. | BARREL | FORK | CABLE EYE | THD NF-3 | G | H | D DIA | A DIA | J | P | TAKE UP |
|---|---|---|---|---|---|---|---|---|---|---|---|---|
| ① AN130-5S | 550 | AN155-5S | AN161-5RS | AN170-5LS | #4-48 | .150 | .375 | .164 | .172 | .125 | 2 3/8 | 3/8 |
| ① AN130-8S | 800 | AN155-8S | AN161-8RS | AN170-8LS | #6-40 | .109 | .375 | .188 | .188 | .125 | 4 1/2 | 1 1/4 |
| AN130-16S | 1 600 | AN155-16S | AN161-16RS | AN170-16LS | #10-32 | .156 | .375 | .188 | .219 | .188 | 4 1/2 | 1 1/8 |
| AN130-16L | | AN155-16L | AN161-16RL | AN170-16LL | | | | | | | 8 | 2 7/8 |
| AN130-22S | 2 200 | AN155-32S | AN161-22RS | AN170-22LS | 1/4-28 | .187 | .469 | .188 | .219 | .188 | 4 17/32 | 1 |
| AN130-22L | | AN155-32L | AN161-22RL | AN170-22LL | | | | | | | 8 1/32 | 2 3/4 |
| AN130-32S | 3 200 | AN155-32S | AN161-32RS | AN170-32LS | 1/4-28 | .218 | .531 | .250 | .281 | .219 | 4 19/32 | 7/8 |
| AN130-32L | | AN155-32L | AN161-32RL | AN170-32LL | | | | | | | 8 7/64 | 2 5/8 |
| AN130-46S | 4 600 | AN155-46S | AN161-46RS | AN170-46LS | 5/16-24 | .250 | .656 | .313 | .313 | .281 | 4 21/32 | 5/8 |
| AN130-46L | | AN155-46L | AN161-46RL | AN170-46LL | | | | | | | 8 5/32 | 2 3/8 |
| AN130-61L | 6 100 | AN155-80L | AN161-61RL | AN170-61LL | 3/8-24 | .270 | .843 | .375 | .344 | .281 | 8 9/32 | 2 1/8 |
| AN130-80L | 8 000 | AN155-80L | AN161-80RL | AN170-80LL | 3/8-24 | .312 | .875 | .375 | .375 | .328 | 8 5/16 | 2 1/8 |
| AN130-125L | 12 500 | AN155-125L | AN161-125RL | AN170-125LL | 7/16-20 | .375 | 1.000 | .438 | .469 | .375 | 9 1/16 | 2 1/16 |
| AN130-175L | 17 500 | AN155-175L | AN161-175RL | AN170-175LL | 1/2-20 | .437 | 1.188 | .500 | .563 | .469 | 9 9/16 | 2 1/16 |

DIMENSIONS IN INCHES AND FOR REFERENCE ONLY

THIS DRAWING AND THE SPECIFICATION COMPLEMENT ONE ANOTHER, AND, TOGETHER, COMPLETELY DEFINE THIS PRODUCT.

| PROCUREMENT SPECIFICATION | ARMY-NAVY AERONAUTICAL STANDARD | AN130 |
|---|---|---|
| AN-T-19 | TURNBUCKLE ASSEMBLY - CABLE EYE AND FORK | |

REVISED ① 18 Dec 43 · 23 Jan 43 · APPROVED ①

Fig. 8-14. Military standards for turnbuckles.

the other. They are used in shear applications only where there is no axial load. Typically, they secure turnbuckle forks to tangs, control system shackles and can be used for pulley cable guards. A cotter pin is inserted in the hole and bent over to prevent the clevis pin from falling out of place.

## Cotter Pins

Cotter pins are made of half-rounded cadmium plate steel wire and are normally used to secure clevis pins and castle nut-bolt combinations in place (see Fig. 8-17). They might also be used for control system cable guards.

## Washers

Plain, flat washers, of the AN960 variety are the most common to hang glider applications as shown in Fig. 8-18. They are used on a nut-bolt combination where there is a need to spread out the load and increase the bearing area. Typical places would be between leading edges and hinge plates. Washers are not necessary where a bolt/nut combination employs a tang. (The tang serves as the washer.)

## Cowling Lock Pins

These pins are made from corrosion-resistant steel wire and are commonly used to tighten and loosen turnbuckles on a rigged hang glider (see Fig. 8-19). They normally stay with the turnbuckle throughout flight and transportation. One can be used for one hang glider; it being switched from one turnbuckle to another.

## Cowling Safety Pins

Cowling safety pins as shown in Fig. 8-20, look similar to regular household safety pins, but of course, they are stronger. They, too, can be used for turnbuckle tightening and loosening.

## Rapid Links

These French made, screw together steel ovals can be used to connect various rigging systems in a hang glider as illustrated in Fig. 8-21. The turn screw should be completely tight to prevent loosening. An open rapid link will pull apart under relatively light loads.

Two sizes can be used for hang glider applications:

1. 3/4 × 1-3/8 of 1/8″ rod (good for approximately 1000 lb breaking strength).
2. 1 × 2 of 3/16″ rod (good for approximately 2900 lb breaking strength).

Fig. 8-15. Aerodynamic control system pulleys.

PHENOLIC PULLEYS are machined from fabric-reinforced, high impact phenolic sheets exceeding specification requirements. Bearing ring bonds bearing to pulley. Bearing lubricated with MIL-G-3278 grease (a grease retainer shield also protects the bearing. Sheave material will not corrode tin or zinc coated carbon steel cable. Fungus resistant sheave per MIL-P-7034.

ALUMINUM PULLEYS are machined to exacting tolerances; lighter in weight than specific phenolic sheets exceeding specification requirements and superior in strength. Sheave material conforms to QQ-268-T4 and QQ-A-355-T4 anodized to specification AN-QQ-A-696.

NOTE: 1. All "MS" Pulleys conform to Procurement Spec. MIL-P-7034.

2. AN and MS pulleys of like dash numbers are universally, functionally, and dimensionally interchangeable.

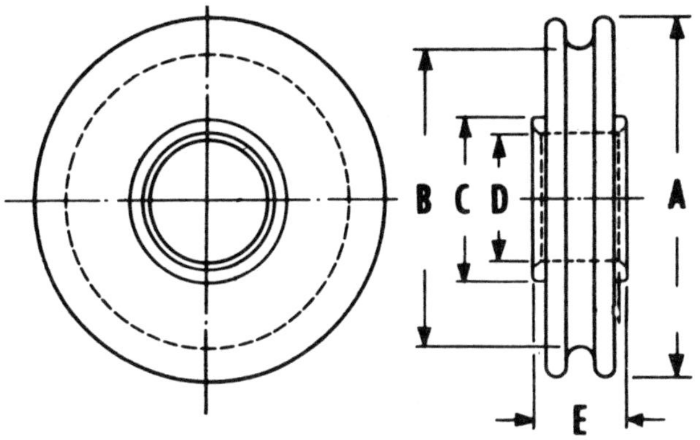

# MS 20219

SECONDARY CONTROL PULLEY. MS 20219A1 and MS20219A3 available in aluminum only. MS20219-2, -4 and -5 available in phenolic or aluminum. Examples of part numbers:

MS20219-2  Pulley with phenolic sheave.

MS20219A2  Pulley with aluminum sheave.

| MS PART NUMBER | OLD AN PART NUMBER | BEARING NO. | CABLE SIZE | A diam. ±.005 | B diam. ±.005 | C diam. Ref. | D diam. -.0005 | E -.005 | ALLOWABLE LIMIT LOAD ON PULLEY |
|---|---|---|---|---|---|---|---|---|---|
| MS20219A1 | AN219A1 | P4K | 1/16 | 1.312 | 1.000 | .423 | .2500 | .438 | 480 |
| MS20219-2 | AN219-2 | P4K | and | 1.750 | 1.438 | .423 | .2500 | .438 | 480 |
| MS20219A3 | AN219A3 | P10K | | 1.750 | 1.438 | .769 | .6250 | .438 | 480 |
| MS20219-4 | AN219-4 | P4K | 3/32 | 2.625 | 2.312 | .423 | .2500 | .438 | 920 |
| MS20219-5 | AN219-5 | P10K | | 2.625 | 2.312 | .769 | .6250 | .438 | 920 |

332

# MS20220

FLIGHT CONTROL PULLEY.
All parts listed available in either phenolic or aluminum. Examples of part numbers:

MS20220-2 Pulley with phenolic sheave
MS20220A2 Pulley with aluminum sheave

NOTE: "D" diameter on all MS20220 pulleys is .3145 inches.

| MS PART NUMBER | OLD AN PART NO. | BEARING NO. | CABLE SIZE | A Dia. -.010 | B Dia. -.010 | C .030 Dia. | E .005 | ALLOWABLE LIMIT LOAD ON PULLEY |
|---|---|---|---|---|---|---|---|---|
| MS20220-1 | AN220-1 | P5K | 1/8, | 1.755 | 1.255 | .465 | .625 | 500 |
| MS20220-2 | AN220-2 | PD5K | 5/32, | 3.005 | 2.505 | .515 | .625 | 1680 |
| MS20220-3 | AN220-3 | PD5K | AND | 4.255 | 3.755 | .515 | .625 | 2500 |
| MS20220-4 | AN220-4 | PD5K | 3/16 | 5.505 | 5.005 | .515 | .625 | 2500 |

# MS20221

HEAVY DUTY CONTROL PULLEY. MS20221A1 available in aluminum only. MS20221-2 and -3 furnished in phenolic or aluminum. Examples of part numbers:

MS20221-2 Pulley with phenolic sheave
MS20221A2 Pulley with aluminum sheave

| MS PART NUMBER | OLD AN PART NO. | BEARING NO. | CABLE SIZE | A DIA. -.010 | B DIA. -.010 | C DIA. | D DIA. | E -.005 | ALLOWABLE LIMIT LOAD ON PULLEY |
|---|---|---|---|---|---|---|---|---|---|
| MS20221A1 | AN221A1 | PD5K | 3/16, | 2.630 | 2.005 | .515—.030 | .3145—.0025 | .625 | 2800 |
| MS20221-2 | AN221-2 | P8 | 7/32, AND | 4.130 | 3.505 | .800—.050 | .505—.005 | .625 | 4900 |
| MS20221-3 | AN221-3 | P8 | 1/4 | 5.630 | 5.005 | .800—.050 | .505—.005 | .750 | 7000 |

# MS24566

ANTI-FRICTION BEARING PULLEY. Note: AN210-1A, -2A, -3A and -4A pulleys to Spec. AN-P-60 are available, subject to availability of bearings. AN 210-A pulleys are dimensionally the same as the "B" pulleys, but have metal shielded bearings rather than removable composition seal type bearings. All MS24566 pulleys available in phenolic or aluminum. Examples of part numbers:

MS24566-1B Pulley with phenolic sheave
MS24566A1B Pulley with aluminum sheave

| MS PART NUMBER | OLD AN PART NUMBER | CABLE SIZE | B DIA. +.000 -.010 | A DIA. +.000 -.010 | D +.0000 -.0005 DIA. | E +.000 -.005 | MAXIMUM ALLOWABLE DESIGN LOAD LB. | BEARING NO. |
|---|---|---|---|---|---|---|---|---|
| MS24566-1B | AN210-1B | 1/16, 5/64, 3/32 | .972 | 1.250 | .1900 | .297 | 185 | KP3AK |
| MS24566-2B | AN210-2B | 1/16, 5/64, 3/32 | 2.222 | 2.500 | .1900 | .297 | 500 | KP3K |
| MS24566-3B | AN210-3B | 1/8, 5/32, 3/16 | 1.510 | 2.000 | .2500 | .484 | 450 (a) | KP4K |
| MS24566-4B | AN210-4B | 1/8, 5/32, 3/16 | 3.010 | 3.500 | .2500 | .484 | 1200 | KP4K |
| MS24566-5B | AN210-5B | 3/16, 7/32, 1/4 | 4.374 | 5.000 | .3750 | .620 | 2000 | KP6 |
| MS24566-6B | AN210-6B | 3/16, 7/32, 1/4 | 5.374 | 6.000 | .3750 | .620 | 2500 | KP6 |

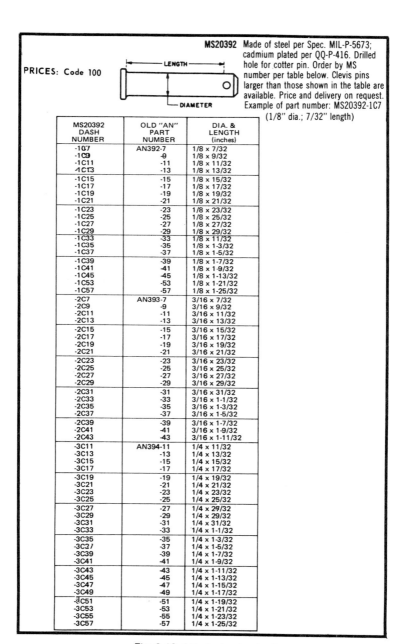

**MS20392** Made of steel per Spec. MIL-P-5673; cadmium plated per QQ-P-416. Drilled hole for cotter pin. Order by MS number per table below. Clevis pins larger than those shown in the table are available. Price and delivery on request. Example of part number: MS20392-1C7 (1/8" dia.; 7/32" length)

PRICES: Code 100

| MS20392 DASH NUMBER | OLD "AN" PART NUMBER | DIA. & LENGTH (inches) |
|---|---|---|
| -1C7 | AN392-7 | 1/8 x 7/32 |
| -1C9 | -9 | 1/8 x 9/32 |
| -1C11 | -11 | 1/8 x 11/32 |
| -1C13 | -13 | 1/8 x 13/32 |
| -1C15 | -15 | 1/8 x 15/32 |
| -1C17 | -17 | 1/8 x 17/32 |
| -1C19 | -19 | 1/8 x 19/32 |
| -1C21 | -21 | 1/8 x 21/32 |
| -1C23 | -23 | 1/8 x 23/32 |
| -1C25 | -25 | 1/8 x 25/32 |
| -1C27 | -27 | 1/8 x 27/32 |
| -1C29 | -29 | 1/8 x 29/32 |
| -1C33 | -33 | 1/8 x 11/32 |
| -1C35 | -35 | 1/8 x 1-3/32 |
| -1C37 | -37 | 1/8 x 1-5/32 |
| -1C39 | -39 | 1/8 x 1-7/32 |
| -1C41 | -41 | 1/8 x 1-9/32 |
| -1C45 | -45 | 1/8 x 1-13/32 |
| -1C53 | -53 | 1/8 x 1-21/32 |
| -1C57 | -57 | 1/8 x 1-25/32 |
| -2C7 | AN393-7 | 3/16 x 7/32 |
| -2C9 | -9 | 3/16 x 9/32 |
| -2C11 | -11 | 3/16 x 11/32 |
| -2C13 | -13 | 3/16 x 13/32 |
| -2C15 | -15 | 3/16 x 15/32 |
| -2C17 | -17 | 3/16 x 17/32 |
| -2C19 | -19 | 3/16 x 19/32 |
| -2C21 | -21 | 3/16 x 21/32 |
| -2C23 | -23 | 3/16 x 23/32 |
| -2C25 | -25 | 3/16 x 25/32 |
| -2C27 | -27 | 3/16 x 27/32 |
| -2C29 | -29 | 3/16 x 29/32 |
| -2C31 | -31 | 3/16 x 31/32 |
| -2C33 | -33 | 3/16 x 1-1/32 |
| -2C35 | -35 | 3/16 x 1-3/32 |
| -2C37 | -37 | 3/16 x 1-5/32 |
| -2C39 | -39 | 3/16 x 1-7/32 |
| -2C41 | -41 | 3/16 x 1-9/32 |
| -2C43 | -43 | 3/16 x 1-11/32 |
| -3C11 | AN394-11 | 1/4 x 11/32 |
| -3C13 | -13 | 1/4 x 13/32 |
| -3C15 | -15 | 1/4 x 15/32 |
| -3C17 | -17 | 1/4 x 17/32 |
| -3C19 | -19 | 1/4 x 19/32 |
| -3C21 | -21 | 1/4 x 21/32 |
| -3C23 | -23 | 1/4 x 23/32 |
| -3C25 | -25 | 1/4 x 25/32 |
| -3C27 | -27 | 1/4 x 27/32 |
| -3C29 | -29 | 1/4 x 29/32 |
| -3C31 | -31 | 1/4 x 31/32 |
| -3C33 | -33 | 1/4 x 1-1/32 |
| -3C35 | -35 | 1/4 x 1-3/32 |
| -3C37 | -37 | 1/4 x 1-5/32 |
| -3C39 | -39 | 1/4 x 1-7/32 |
| -3C41 | -41 | 1/4 x 1-9/32 |
| -3C43 | -43 | 1/4 x 1-11/32 |
| -3C45 | -45 | 1/4 x 1-13/32 |
| -3C47 | -47 | 1/4 x 1-15/32 |
| -3C49 | -49 | 1/4 x 1-17/32 |
| -3C51 | -51 | 1/4 x 1-19/32 |
| -3C53 | -53 | 1/4 x 1-21/32 |
| -3C55 | -55 | 1/4 x 1-23/32 |
| -3C57 | -57 | 1/4 x 1-25/32 |

Fig. 8-16. AN clevis pin chart.

## MS24665

Available in cadmium plated carbon steel, passivated corrosion resisting steel, brass and nickel copper alloy. The ordering table only list the more popular cadmium plated and corrosion resisting steel sizes. Cotter pins not shown are available on request. Order by MS number. Example: MS24665-7 (Cadmium plated steel; 1/32" dia.; 3/4" length). AN380 and MS24665 carbon steel pins of the same dia. and length are interchangeable, as are the AN381 and MS24665 corrosion resistant pins.

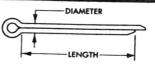

| DIAMETER and LENGTH (inches) | CARB MS24665 DASH NO. | CORR MS24665 DASH NO. |
|---|---|---|
| 1/32 x 3/8 | -3 | -20 |
| 1/32 x 1/2 | -5 | -22 |
| 1/32 x 3/4 | -7 | -24 |
| 1/32 x 1 | -9 | -26 |
| 1/16 x 5/16 | --- | -148 |
| 1/16 x 3/8 | -130 | -149 |
| 1/16 x 7/16 | --- | -150 |
| 1/16 x 1/2 | -132 | -151 |
| 1/16 x 5/8 | --- | -152 |
| 1/16 x 3/4 | -134 | -153 |
| 1/16 x 7/8 | --- | -154 |
| 1/16 x 1 | -136 | -155 |
| 1/16 x 1-1/4 | -138 | -157 |
| 1/16 x 1-1/2 | -140 | -159 |
| 1/16 x 1-3/4 | -142 | -161 |
| 1/16 x 2 | -143 | -162 |
| 1/16 x 2-1/2 | -144 | -163 |
| 1/16 x 3 | -145 | -164 |
| 5/64 x 1/2 | -208 | -227 |
| 5/64 x 5/8 | --- | -228 |
| 5/64 x 3/4 | -210 | -229 |
| 5/64 x 1 | -212 | -231 |
| 3/32 x 1/2 | -281 | -298 |
| 3/32 x 5/8 | --- | -299 |
| 3/32 x 3/4 | -283 | -300 |
| 3/32 x 7/8 | --- | -301 |
| 3/32 x 1 | -285 | -302 |
| 3/32 x 1-1/8 | -285 | -302 |
| 3/32 x 1-1/4 | -287 | -304 |
| 3/32 x 1-1/2 | -289 | -306 |
| 3/32 x 1-3/4 | -291 | -308 |
| 3/32 x 2 | -292 | -309 |
| 3/32 x 2-1/2 | -294 | -311 |
| 3/32 x 3 | -295 | -312 |
| 1/8 x 1/2 | -349 | -366 |
| 1/8 x 3/4 | -351 | -368 |
| 1/8 x 1 | -353 | -370 |
| 1/8 x 1-1/8 | --- | -371 |
| 1/8 x 1-1/4 | -355 | -372 |
| 1/8 x 1-1/2 | -357 | -374 |
| 1/8 x 1-3/4 | -359 | -376 |
| 1/8 x 2 | -360 | -377 |
| 1/8 x 2-1/4 | -361 | -378 |
| 1/8 x 2-1/2 | -362 | -379 |
| 5/32 x 1 | -419 | -437 |
| 5/32 x 1-1/2 | -423 | -441 |
| 5/32 x 2-1/2 | -428 | -446 |

Fig. 8-17. AN cotter pin chart.

## AN960 FLAT WASHERS

AN960—Cadmium plated steel, AN960B—
Commercial brass, AN960C—Corrosion
resisting steel, AN960D—
Aluminum alloy anodized. Ordering
note: Specify material by AN number;
use AN dash number for size; and add
"L" if light series is desired.

Examples
AN960 C 3 (Corrosion resisting steel)
AN960 C3L (Corrosion resisting steel, light)

| REGULAR | | I.D. | I.D. | SCREW OR BOLT SIZE | LIGHT | |
|---------|---|------|------|------|-------|---|
| DASH NO. | T (inches) | (inches) | (inches) | | DASH NO. | T (inches) |
| -2 | .032 | .099 | .250 | #2 | -2L | .016 |
| -3 | .032 | .109 | .250 | #3 | -3L | .016 |
| -4 | .032 | .125 | .312 | #4 | -4L | .016 |
| -6 | .032 | .149 | .375 | #6 | -6L | .016 |
| -8 | .032 | .174 | .375 | #8 | -8L | .016 |
| -10 | .064 | .203 | .438 | #10 | -10L | .032 |
| -416 | .064 | .265 | .500 | 1/4" | -416L | .032 |
| -516 | .064 | .326 | .562 | 5/16" | -516L | .032 |
| -616 | .064 | .390 | .625 | 3/8" | -616L | .032 |
| -716 | .064 | .453 | .750 | 7/16" | -716L | .032 |
| -816 | .064 | .515 | .875 | 1/2" | -816L | .032 |
| -916 | .064 | .578 | 1.062 | 9/16" | -916L | .032 |
| -1016 | .091 | .640 | 1.188 | 5/8" | -1016L | .032 |

Fig 8-18. AN flat washer chart.

Made of spring steel and cadmium plated.
Easily inserted and removed from cowling
studs without the use of tools. In two
diameters.

| | DIAM. OF WIRE "A" | LENGTH "L" | PRICE |
|---|------|------|------|
| 200 | .062 | 1-1/4 | .10 |
| 201 | .080 | 1-1/4 | .10 |

Fig. 8-19. Cowl lock pin chart.

336

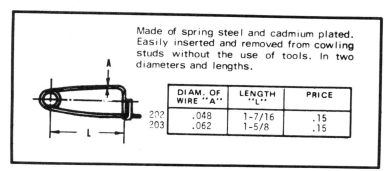

Made of spring steel and cadmium plated. Easily inserted and removed from cowling studs without the use of tools. In two diameters and lengths.

| | DIAM. OF WIRE "A" | LENGTH "L" | PRICE |
|---|---|---|---|
| 202 | .048 | 1-7/16 | .15 |
| 203 | .062 | 1-5/8 | .15 |

Fig. 8-20. Cowl safety pin chart.

## Cable (Wire Rope)

Most hang gliders today are cable braced, with few exceptions. Generally speaking, it is possible to make a cable braced structure for 1/2 to 2/3 the weight of an equivalent cantilever (no external bracing whatsoever) structure, thus, the predominance of cable bracing in hang gliders.

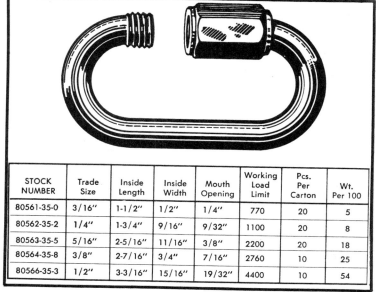

| STOCK NUMBER | Trade Size | Inside Length | Inside Width | Mouth Opening | Working Load Limit | Pcs. Per Carton | Wt. Per 100 |
|---|---|---|---|---|---|---|---|
| 80561-35-0 | 3/16" | 1-1/2" | 1/2" | 1/4" | 770 | 20 | 5 |
| 80562-35-2 | 1/4" | 1-3/4" | 9/16" | 9/32" | 1100 | 20 | 8 |
| 80563-35-5 | 5/16" | 2-5/16" | 11/16" | 3/8" | 2200 | 20 | 18 |
| 80564-35-8 | 3/8" | 2-7/16" | 3/4" | 7/16" | 2760 | 10 | 25 |
| 80566-35-3 | 1/2" | 3-3/16" | 15/16" | 19/32" | 4400 | 10 | 54 |

Fig. 8-21. Rapid links are used by some manufacturers to facilitate assembly. They are made by the Peerless Chain Company.

| Diameter in Inches | Construction | Breaking Strength in Lbs. Galvanized | Stainless | Weight in Lbs. Per M/Ft. |
|---|---|---|---|---|
| 3/64 | 1x19 | 375 | 335 | 5.5 |
| 3/64 | 7x7 | 270 | 270 | 4.2 |
| 1/16 | 1x7 | 500 | 500 | 8.5 |
| 1/16 | 1x19 | 500 | 500 | 8.5 |
| 1/16 | 7x7 | 480 | 480 | 7.5 |
| 3/32 | 1x19 | 1,200 | 1,200 | 20 |
| 3/32 | 7x7 | 920 | 920 | 16 |
| 3/32 | 7x19 | 1,050 | 1,050 | 16 |
| 1/8 | 1x19 | 2,100 | 2,100 | 35 |
| 1/8 | 7x7 | 1,700 | 1,700 | 28.5 |
| 1/8 | 7x19 | 2,000 | 1,760 | 29 |
| 5/32 | 1x19 | 3,300 | 3,300 | 55 |
| 5/32 | 7x7 | 2,600 | 2,400 | 43 |
| 5/32 | 7x19 | 2,800 | 2,400 | 45 |
| 3/16 | 1x19 | 4,700 | 4,700 | 77 |
| 3/16 | 7x7 | 3,700 | 3,700 | 62 |
| 3/16 | 7x19 | 4,200 | 3,700 | 65 |
| 7/32 | 1x19 | 6,300 | 6,300 | 102 |
| 7/32 | 7x7 | 4,800 | 4,800 | 83 |
| 7/32 | 7x19 | 5,600 | 5,000 | 86 |
| 1/4 | 1x19 | 8,200 | 8,200 | 135 |
| 1/4 | 7x7 | 6,100 | 6,100 | 106 |
| 1/4 | 7x19 | 7,000 | 6,100 | 110 |
| 9/32 | 1x19 | 9,900 | 9,900 | 170 |
| 9/32 | 7x7 | 7,400 | 7,400 | 134 |
| 9/32 | 7x19 | 8,000 | 7,800 | 139 |
| 5/16 | 1x19 | 12,500 | 12,500 | 210 |
| 5/16 | 7x7 | 9,200 | 9,100 | 167 |
| 5/16 | 7x19 | 9,800 | 9,000 | 173 |
| 3/8 | 1x19 | 18,000 | 17,500 | 300 |
| 3/8 | 7x7 | 13,300 | 12,600 | 236 |
| 3/8 | 7x19 | 14,400 | 12,000 | 243 |
| 7/16 | 6x19 IWRC | 17,600 | 16,300 | 356 |
| 1/2 | 6x19 IWRC | 22,800 | 21,000 | 458 |

1x7 SEMI-FLEXIBLE

1x19 SEMI-FLEXIBLE

7x7 FLEXIBLE

7x19 and 6x19 IWRC
EXTRA FLEXIBLE

Fig. 8-22. Aircraft cable properties and construction.

The cable used in hang gliders is made from either stainless steel or galvanized aircraft cable (see Fig. 8-22). Both have the exact same breaking strength while "galvy," as it is called, is slightly less expensive. The galvanized will rust if the galvanization plating is scratched off. This, however, does not normally occur in hang glider usage. The stainless can also corrode eventually. At any rate, both are used and both are good.

The cable is built in what is known as a 7 × 7 flexible construction. That is, seven main strands are each made up of seven smaller wires which are "preformed." Preforming means that the individual wires are formed into the helical shape they will assume in the final cable before they are laid into the cable. This increases flexibility, relieves internal stress, makes swaging easier, minimizes the tendency to kink, and prevents the cable from unraveling when it is cut. Other types of construction include 1 × 7, 1 × 19 semi-flexible, and 7 × 19 and 6 × 19 wire rope cord, extra flexible.

The non-flexibles see no use in hang gliding while the extra flexible may be used for control systems. In general though, the 7 × 7 construction cable is used almost exclusively for hang gliders for all applications. As for diameters, most hang gliders employ 3/32″ for rigging, and 1/16″ for control systems.

All bottom rigging, or "flying wires," should be vinyl coated for safety. A bare cable can cut and abrade skin easily if struck with any speed. What's more, they are almost invisible to a non-hang glider pilot or even a pilot, and can be walked into quite readily. The coating should also be clear so the condition of the cable can be observed easily.

Cable should always be removed by drawing it straight off the reel, to eliminate the possibility of kinking. Drawn off the end of a reel, cable will wrap around itself and may kink easily. If a kink should occur, discard that portion of the cable that includes the kink, as it weakens the cable.

Cable can be cut most effectively with wire rope cutters (see section on tools). These have special, triangular cutting jaws and make a square clean cut that never leaves a frayed end. Also, a good cold chisel and hammer might possibly be used although this is time-consuming and not as neat as the wire rope cutters.

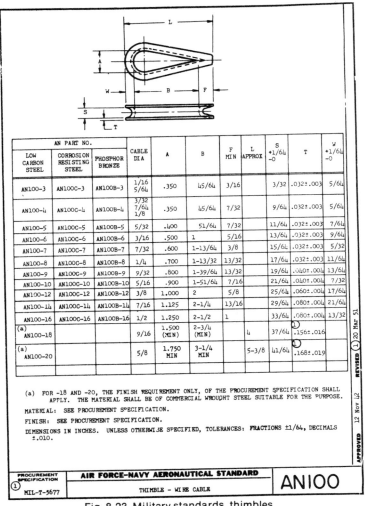

| AN PART NO. | | | CABLE DIA | A | B | F MIN | L APPROX | S +1/64 -0 | T | W +1/64 -0 |
|---|---|---|---|---|---|---|---|---|---|---|
| LOW CARBON STEEL | CORROSION RESISTING STEEL | PHOSPHOR BRONZE | | | | | | | | |
| AN100-3 | AN100C-3 | AN100B-3 | 1/16 5/64 | .350 | 45/64 | 3/16 | | 3/32 | .032±.003 | 5/64 |
| AN100-4 | AN100C-4 | AN100B-4 | 3/32 7/64 1/8 | .350 | 45/64 | 7/32 | | 9/64 | .032±.003 | 5/64 |
| AN100-5 | AN100C-5 | AN100B-5 | 5/32 | .400 | 51/64 | 7/32 | | 11/64 | .032±.003 | 7/64 |
| AN100-6 | AN100C-6 | AN100B-6 | 3/16 | .500 | 1 | 5/16 | | 13/64 | .032±.003 | 9/64 |
| AN100-7 | AN100C-7 | AN100B-7 | 7/32 | .600 | 1-13/64 | 3/8 | | 15/64 | .032±.003 | 5/32 |
| AN100-8 | AN100C-8 | AN100B-8 | 1/4 | .700 | 1-13/32 | 13/32 | | 17/64 | .032±.003 | 11/64 |
| AN100-9 | AN100C-9 | AN100B-9 | 9/32 | .800 | 1-39/64 | 13/32 | | 19/64 | .040±.004 | 13/64 |
| AN100-10 | AN100C-10 | AN100B-10 | 5/16 | .900 | 1-51/64 | 7/16 | | 21/64 | .040±.004 | 7/32 |
| AN100-12 | AN100C-12 | AN100B-12 | 3/8 | 1.000 | 2 | 7/16 | | 25/64 | .060±.004 | 17/64 |
| AN100-14 | AN100C-14 | AN100B-14 | 7/16 | 1.125 | 2-1/4 | 13/16 | | 29/64 | .080±.004 | 21/64 |
| AN100-16 | AN100C-16 | AN100B-16 | 1/2 | 1.250 | 2-1/2 | 1 | | 33/64 | .080±.004 | 13/32 |
| (a) AN100-18 | | | 9/16 | 1.500 (MIN) | 2-3/4 (MIN) | | 4 | 37/64 | .156±.016 | |
| (a) AN100-20 | | | 5/8 | 1.750 MIN | 3-1/4 MIN | | 5-3/8 | 41/64 | .168±.019 | |

(a) FOR -18 AND -20, THE FINISH REQUIREMENT ONLY, OF THE PROCUREMENT SPECIFICATION SHALL APPLY. THE MATERIAL SHALL BE OF COMMERCIAL WROUGHT STEEL SUITABLE FOR THE PURPOSE.

MATERIAL: SEE PROCUREMENT SPECIFICATION.

FINISH: SEE PROCUREMENT SPECIFICATION.

DIMENSIONS IN INCHES. UNLESS OTHERWISE SPECIFIED, TOLERANCES: FRACTIONS ±1/64, DECIMALS ±.010.

| PROCUREMENT SPECIFICATION | AIR FORCE-NAVY AERONAUTICAL STANDARD | AN100 |
|---|---|---|
| ① MIL-T-5677 | THIMBLE - WIRE CABLE | |

REVISED ① 20 Mar 51    12 Nov 42    APPROVED

Fig. 8-23. Military standards, thimbles.

After some period of time involving normal use, hang glider cables will stretch because of either abuse or repeated flying. They may also show signs of cracking or splitting, especially where they bend around a thimble. If this is evidenced, replace the cables immediately. They have seen their better days. Also, be on the lookout for rust and corrosion as they both weaken the cable.

## Cable Terminals and Swaging

Cable terminals are just that, the hardware that goes into a cable end. More specifically, they are: thimbles, swageable terminals, nico stops and nico sleeves.

Thimbles are, as shown in Fig. 8-23, by far, the most popular form of cable terminal used in the hang glider industry today. They are most commonly of stainless steel with the most popular size being that for 3/32″ diameter cable, or AN100-C4 control systems of 1/16″ diameter cable will use the AN100-C3 type.

Nico stops are a very simple form of cable terminal in that they are applied by mechanical hand tools. (see Fig. 8-24). They are sometimes used where a cable attaches to a king

| TO FIT CABLE DIA. | | ALUMINUM OVAL | COPPER* OVAL | ALUMINUM STOP | COPPER STOP |
|---|---|---|---|---|---|
| 3/64″ | Use Tool No. | 00 or 1 | 00 or 1 | 00 or 1 | 00 or 1 |
| | Wgt. in lbs. M/pcs. | 1 | 2 | 1 | 1.5 |
| 1/16″ | Use Tool No. | 00 or 1 | 00 or 1 | 00 or 1 | 00 or 1 |
| | Wgt. in lbs. M/pcs. | 1.5 | 3 | 1.5 | 2 |
| 3/32″ | Use Tool No. | 0-3/32 or 1 | 0-3/32 or 1 | 0-3/32 or 1 | 0-3/32 or 1 |
| | Wgt. in lbs. M/pcs. | 3 | 6 | 3 | 8 |
| 1/8″ | Use Tool No. | 0-1/8 or 1 | 0-1/8 or 1 | 0-3/32 or 1 | 0-3/32 or 1 |
| | Wgt. in lbs. M/pcs. | 6 | 16 | 3 | 8 |
| 5/32″ | Use Tool No. | 0-5/32 or 1 | 0-5/32 or 1 | 0-1/8 or 1 | 0-1/8 or 1 |
| | Wgt. in lbs. M/pcs. | 8 | 23 | 4 | 13 |
| 3/16″ | Use Tool No. | 0-3/16 or 1 | 0-3/16 or 1 | 0-1/8 or 1 | 0-1/8 or 1 |
| | Wgt. in lbs. M/pcs. | 15 | 51 | 4 | 12 |
| 7/32″ | Use Tool No. | F2 | F2 | 0-1/8 or 1 | 0-1/8 or 1 |
| | Wgt. in lbs. M/pcs. | 14 | 46 | 5 | 20 |
| 1/4″ | Use Tool No. | F6 | F6 | F6 | F6 |
| | Wgt. in lbs. M/pcs. | 24 | 80 | 18 | 60 |
| 9/32″ | Use Tool No. | F6 | Not Avail. | F6 | Not Avail. |
| | Wgt. in lbs. M/pcs. | 30 | | 8 | |
| 5/16″ | Use Tool No. | G9 | G9 | F6 | F6 |
| | Wgt. in lbs. M/pcs. | 44 | 131 | 18 | 60 |
| 3/8″ | 3/8″ Sleeves and Larger Must be Swaged Either by | 61 | 284 | Not Avail. | Not Avail. |
| 7/16″ | Power Press or Hydraulic Press. We will Supply Die | 109 | 290 | Not Avail. | Not Avail. |
| 1/2″ | Dimensions or will Do Swaging for You. | 234 | 384 | Not Avail. | Not Avail. |

Fig. 8-24. Nico press sleeves and stops come in a variety of sizes.

post. They come in plain copper, sinc plated copper, and aluminum. The most common for hang glider applications are the zinc plated stops as they can be used on steel cables and resist corrosion. Copper tends to corrode, especially near salty atmospheres. Aluminum stops are about one third the weight of copper stops and have about the same holding power (i.e., about equal to 64% of the cable breaking strength, or 920 lb. for 3/32″ cable).

Nico oval sleeves are the most common items used to form a cable terminal around a thimble, as they are installed with a simple, mechanical hand tool. Like the nico stops, they are available in copper, zinc plated copper and aluminum. Properly installed, that is with the right amount of compression, they develop the full rated strength of the cable. Theoretically, one nico sleeve per cable thimble terminal is enough; however, many hang glider manufacturers use two. The second is used for safety sake and to seal off the cable end so it doesn't fray and cut sails and skin.

### Velcro

Velcro is a very versatile nylon tape fastener that can be used almost anywhere a snap, button or zipper is used. It is composed of two separate mating tapes. One contains thousands of finely woven nylon monofilaments formed into permanent hooks (called hook type), the other is covered with soft nylon loops (called pile type). When the two tapes are pressed together, they interlock and hold extremely well. Velcro can be installed by a sewing machine and is available in a few widths: 5/8″, 1″ and 2″. It is noncorrosive.

### Zippers

Delrin zippers can be used quite effectively on accessory items such as transportation bags, making for quick and easy opening and closing. The jacket type chain with double slider is most common and is available in various lengths from 24″ to 120″ in 12″ increments. It is noncorrosive.

### Repair Tape

If one's sail should get torn, he may give it an emergency, temporary repair with RiPair tape. It is made of ripstop nylon and, comes with a sticky back in a number of colors. Be sure the affected area is clean and free of any dirt before applying the tape.

## Grommets

Grommets are used wherever it is necessary to reinforce holes in sails, bags and harnesses (see Fig. 8-25). On sails, they

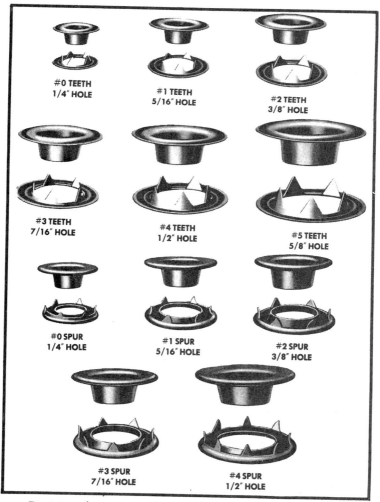

**#0 TEETH**
**1/4″ HOLE**

**#1 TEETH**
**5/16″ HOLE**

**#2 TEETH**
**3/8″ HOLE**

**#3 TEETH**
**7/16″ HOLE**

**#4 TEETH**
**1/2″ HOLE**

**#5 TEETH**
**5/8″ HOLE**

**#0 SPUR**
**1/4″ HOLE**

**#1 SPUR**
**5/16″ HOLE**

**#2 SPUR**
**3/8″ HOLE**

**#3 SPUR**
**7/16″ HOLE**

**#4 SPUR**
**1/2″ HOLE**

Fig. 8-25. Grommets are used on sails and other fabric products.

are normally installed on the fore and aft parts of the keel and on the aft parts of the leading edge. A bolt is then passed through them and the airframe to make for a secure hold. Most transportation and storage bags have grommets installed with lacing passing through them to tighten and close the ends. Harnesses may employ grommets in various places depending on the particular design. A typical location may be where the spreader bar is installed.

A metal grommet is a two piece affair made of either aluminum or brass, but typically brass. The male part looks like a flat washer that has had its center raised while the female part is almost flat. The female can be plain or spurred. They are installed by first cutting a hole in the fabric with a special cutting die for that particular size grommet and then actually inserting the grommet with a special forming die. As the die is struck with a hammer, it causes the grommet to flatten and form to grip the fabric very tightly. Grommets are always installed in reinforced areas and never on a single surface or else they'll be prone to easily tearing out. They come in a number of sizes: #00 = 5/32″ hole, #0 = 1/4″ hole, #1 - 5/6″ hole, #2 = 3/8″ hole, #3 = 7/16″ hole and #4 = 1/2″ hole.

**Rod Ends**

Before ending the discussion on materials and hardware, one more item must be added to the list: rod ends (see Figs. 8-26 and 8-27). Since more and more aerodynamically controlled hang gliders are being developed and marketed, the existence of these standard pieces of hardware should be known. Typically, rod ends can be used as control surface bearings and on pushrod ends.

**NEW MATERIALS AND HARDWARE**

As of this writing, all the materials and hardware mentioned thus far are in common use in the hang glider industry and represent the current state of the art. This however, should not be interpreted as the last word. New and better materials, hardware, practices and techniques are being developed all the time. A word of caution is in order to

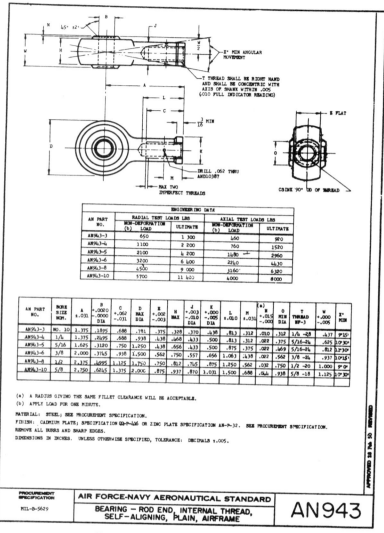

| ENGINEER DWG DATA | | | | |
|---|---|---|---|---|
| AN PART NO. | RADIAL TEST LOADS LBS | | AXIAL TEST LOADS LBS | |
| | NON-DEFORMATION (b) LOAD | ULTIMATE | NON-DEFORMATION (b) LOAD | ULTIMATE |
| AN943-3 | 650 | 1 300 | 460 | 920 |
| AN943-4 | 1100 | 2 200 | 760 | 1520 |
| AN943-5 | 2100 | 4 200 | 1480 | 2960 |
| AN943-6 | 3200 | 6 400 | 2240 | 4430 |
| AN943-8 | 4500 | 9 000 | 3160 | 6320 |
| AN943-10 | 5700 | 11 400 | 4000 | 8000 |

| AN PART NO. | BORE SIZE NOM. | A ±.031 | B +.0020/-.0000 DIA | C +.062/-.031 | D MAX DIA | E +.002/-.003 | H MAX | J +.003/-.010 DIA | K +.000/-.005 DIA | L ±.010 | M ±.031 | (a) N +.015/-.000 | O MIN DIA | T THREAD NF-3 | W +.000/-.005 | X° MIN |
|---|---|---|---|---|---|---|---|---|---|---|---|---|---|---|---|---|
| AN943-3 | NO. 10 | 1.375 | .1895 | .688 | .781 | .375 | .328 | .370 | .438 | .813 | .312 | .010 | .312 | 1/4 -28 | .437 | 9°15' |
| AN943-4 | 1/4 | 1.375 | .2495 | .688 | .938 | .438 | .468 | .433 | .500 | .813 | .312 | .022 | .375 | 5/16-24 | .625 | 10°30' |
| AN943-5 | 5/16 | 1.625 | .3120 | .750 | 1.250 | .438 | .656 | .433 | .500 | .875 | .375 | .022 | .469 | 5/16-24 | .812 | 11°30' |
| AN943-6 | 3/8 | 2.000 | .3745 | .938 | 1.500 | .562 | .750 | .557 | .656 | 1.063 | .438 | .022 | .562 | 3/8 -24 | .937 | 10°15' |
| AN943-8 | 1/2 | 2.375 | .4995 | 1.125 | 1.750 | .750 | .812 | .745 | .875 | 1.250 | .562 | .032 | .750 | 1/2 -20 | 1.000 | 9°0' |
| AN943-10 | 5/8 | 2.750 | .6245 | 1.375 | 2.000 | .875 | .937 | .870 | 1.031 | 1.500 | .688 | .044 | .938 | 5/8 -18 | 1.125 | 10°30' |

(a) A RADIUS GIVING THE SAME FILLET CLEARANCE WILL BE ACCEPTABLE.

(b) APPLY LOAD FOR ONE MINUTE.

MATERIAL: STEEL; SEE PROCUREMENT SPECIFICATION.

FINISH: CADMIUM PLATE; SPECIFICATION QQ-P-416 OR ZINC PLATE SPECIFICATION AN-P-32. SEE PROCUREMENT SPECIFICATION.

REMOVE ALL BURRS AND SHARP EDGES.

DIMENSIONS IN INCHES. UNLESS OTHERWISE SPECIFIED, TOLERANCE: DECIMALS ±.005.

| PROCUREMENT SPECIFICATION | AIR FORCE-NAVY AERONAUTICAL STANDARD | AN943 |
|---|---|---|
| MIL-B-5629 | BEARING — ROD END, INTERNAL THREAD, SELF-ALIGNING, PLAIN, AIRFRAME | |

APPROVED 18 Feb. 50 REVISED

Fig. 8-26. Standards for rod ends.

the would-be user of a new item. Be certain it was properly designed and tested by a competent engineer before buying it. Since there is no real enforcing agency at this time, one cannot be too careful in making a good choice.

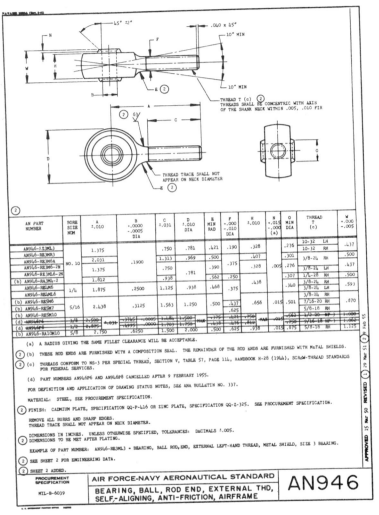

Fig. 8-27. Military standards for rod ends.

At any rate, someday we may have a super fantastic hang glider with high performance, stability and control and easily transported with an empty weight of only 20 pounds! It may be made possible by the advances in the materials industry and

| Inch Frac | Inch Decimal | Millimeter | Inch Frac | Inch Decimal | Millimeter | Inch Frac | Inch Decimal | Millimeter |
|---|---|---|---|---|---|---|---|---|
| --- | .003937 | 0.1 | 9/32 | .28125 | 7.1438 | 21/32 | .65625 | 16.668 |
| --- | .007474 | 0.2 | 19/64 | .29685 | 7.5406 | --- | .669291 | 17. |
| --- | .011811 | 0.3 | 5/16 | .3125 | 7.9375 | 43/64 | .671871 | 17.0656 |
| 1/64 | .015625 | 0.3969 | --- | .314961 | 8. | 11/16 | .6875 | 17.4625 |
| --- | .015748 | 0.4 | 21/64 | .328125 | 8.3344 | 45/64 | .703125 | 17.8594 |
| --- | .019685 | 0.5 | 11/32 | .34375 | 8.7313 | --- | .708661 | 18. |
| --- | .023622 | 0.6 | --- | .354331 | 9. | 23/32 | .718175 | 18.2563 |
| --- | .027559 | 0.7 | 23/64 | .359375 | 9.1281 | 47/64 | .734375 | 18.6531 |
| 1/32 | .03125 | 0.7938 | 3/8 | .375 | 9.525 | --- | .748031 | 19. |
| --- | .031496 | 0.8 | 25/64 | .390625 | 9.9219 | 3/4 | .750 | 19.050 |
| --- | .03543 | 0.9 | --- | .393701 | 10. | 49/64 | .765625 | 19.4469 |
| --- | .03937 | 1.0 | 13/32 | .40625 | 10.3188 | 25/32 | .78125 | 19.8438 |
| 3/64 | .046875 | 1.1906 | 27/64 | .421875 | 10.7156 | --- | .787402 | 20. |
| 1/16 | .0625 | 1.5875 | --- | .433871 | 11. | 51/64 | .796875 | 20.2406 |
| 5/64 | .078125 | 1.9844 | 7/16 | .4375 | 11.1125 | 13/16 | .8125 | 20.6375 |
| --- | .07874 | 2. | 29/64 | .453125 | 11.5094 | --- | .826772 | 21. |
| 3/32 | .09375 | 2.3813 | 15/32 | .46875 | 11.9063 | 53/64 | .828125 | 21.0344 |
| 7/64 | .109375 | 2.7781 | --- | .472441 | 12. | 27/32 | .84375 | 21.4314 |
| --- | .11811 | 3. | 31/64 | .484375 | 12.3031 | 55/64 | .859375 | 21.8281 |
| 1/8 | .125 | 3.175 | 1/2 | .500 | 12.700 | --- | .866142 | 22. |
| 9/64 | .140625 | 3.5719 | --- | .511811 | 13. | 7/8 | .875 | 22.225 |
| 5/32 | .15625 | 3.9688 | 33/64 | .515825 | 13.0969 | 57/64 | .890625 | 22.6219 |
| --- | .15748 | 4. | 17/32 | .53125 | 13.4938 | --- | .905512 | 23. |
| 11/64 | .171875 | 4.3656 | 35/64 | .546875 | 13.8906 | 29/32 | .90625 | 23.0188 |
| 3/16 | .1875 | 4.7625 | --- | .5511811 | 14. | 59/64 | .921875 | 23.4156 |
| --- | .19685 | 5. | 9/16 | .5625 | 14.2875 | 15/16 | .9375 | 23.8125 |
| 13/64 | .203125 | 5.1594 | 37/64 | .578125 | 14.6844 | --- | .944882 | 24. |
| 7/32 | .21875 | 5.5563 | --- | .590511 | 15. | 61/64 | .953125 | 24.2094 |
| 15/64 | .234375 | 5.9531 | 19/32 | .59375 | 15.0813 | 31/32 | .96875 | 24.6063 |
| --- | .23622 | 6. | 39/64 | .609375 | 15.4781 | --- | .984252 | 25. |
| 1/4 | .250 | 6.7469 | 5/8 | .625 | 15.4781 | 63/64 | .984375 | 25.0031 |

347

Table 8-9. A Handy English-Metric Conversion Table

| | | | |
|------|-------|-------|-------|
| 1/64 | .0156 | 33/64 | .5156 |
| 1/32 | .0312 | 17/32 | .5312 |
| 3/64 | .0469 | 35/64 | .5469 |
| 1/16 | .0625 | 9/16 | .5625 |
| 5/64 | .0781 | 37/64 | .5781 |
| 3/32 | .0938 | 19/32 | .5938 |
| 7/64 | .1094 | 39/64 | .6094 |
| 1/8 | .125 | 5/8 | .625 |
| 9/64 | .1406 | 41/64 | .6406 |
| 5/32 | .1562 | 21/32 | .6562 |
| 11/64 | .1719 | 43/64 | .6719 |
| 3/16 | .1875 | 11/64 | .6875 |
| 13/64 | .2031 | 45/64 | .7031 |
| 7/32 | .2188 | 23/32 | .7188 |
| 15/64 | .2344 | 47/64 | .7344 |
| 1/4 | .25 | 3/4 | .75 |
| 17/64 | .2656 | 49/64 | .7656 |
| 9/32 | .2812 | 25/32 | .7812 |
| 19/64 | .2969 | 51/64 | .7969 |
| 5/16 | .3125 | 13/16 | .8125 |
| 21/64 | .3281 | 53/64 | .8281 |
| 11/32 | .3438 | 27/32 | .8438 |
| 23/64 | .3594 | 55/64 | .8594 |
| 3/8 | .375 | 7/8 | .875 |
| 25/64 | .3906 | 57/64 | .8906 |
| 13/32 | .4062 | 29/32 | .9062 |
| 27/64 | .4219 | 59/64 | .9219 |
| 7/16 | .4375 | 15/16 | .9375 |
| 29/64 | .4531 | 61/64 | .9531 |
| 15/32 | .4688 | 31/32 | .9688 |
| 31/64 | .4844 | 63/64 | .9844 |
| 1/2 | .50 | 1/1 | 1.00 |

especially the offshoots from the U.S. space program. After all, look what the Rogallo wing has done to flight.

Table 8-8 shows decimal conversions and Table 8-9 shows metric conversions.

# Chapter 9
## Construction and Components

## CONSTRUCTION AND COMPONENTS

Next to using the proper materials for the job, the importance of sound construction techniques and components is paramount. The glider must use the available materials in the most effective and efficient manner in order to maximize strength and minimize weight. Figures 9-1 and 9-2 show construction and airframe of a standard Rogallo. Since a hang glider is an aircraft, it is considered good practice to use aircraft techniques and construction. A good design will be constructed with well known machine shop procedures to insure accurate duplication of the designer's drawings.

## HANG GLIDER BODY COMPONENTS

The components of a hang glider are varied and unique. For proper construction as well as safe flying, one must be aware of these items. The following paragraphs describe briefly the various components of a hang glider.

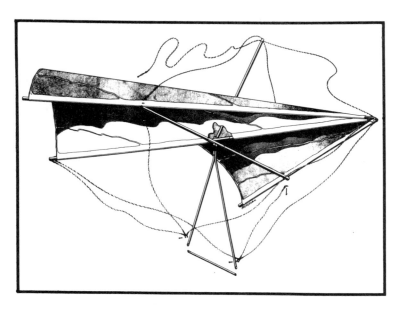

Fig. 9-1. Typical Rogallo wing kite construction by Eipper-Formance.

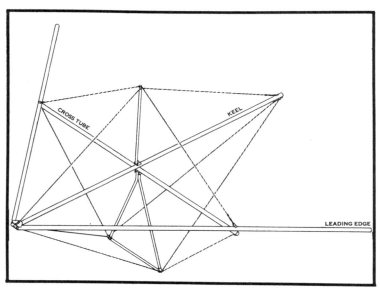

Fig. 9-2. The unsailed airframe of a standard Rogallo.

## Nose Hinges

Nose hinges are located at the apex of a Rogallo wing and they are used to join the keel and leading edges (see Fig. 9-3). Normally, they are rounded or angled up to help prevent dig-ins and the resulting abrupt stop in the event of a nose in. Aluminum alloy or stainless steel is used in their manufacture.

## Sleeves

A sleeve is a length of tubing that is used to both join and reinforce another tube. On most Rogallo hang gliders, an external sleeve is used at all main pivot bolt areas. Most tubing comes from the mill in stock lengths of twelve feet. This is an industry standard based primarily on shipping convenience. Sleeves may also be used internally in some other designs.

## Dowels

Hang gliders use hardwood dowel plugs to reinforce tubing locally for compression loads (see Fig. 9-4). Then too, the "heart bolt" used on all kites necessitates a wood plug at least in the central keel area or else the compressive loads coming from the king post would crush the keel and lead to local buckling. With wood dowels, one must contend with rotting, expansion in wet weather and splitting in dry weather, which may cause problems.

## Bushings

Anywhere there is relative motion between mating parts, a bushing installation is normally required. A bushing is nothing more than a small tube which has been inserted into the holes of a larger tube, and peened over to set tight as shown in Fig. 9-5. A good example is a leading edge hinge. Typically, a 3/8" hole is drilled through and a 3/8" OD × .028"W tube is installed. This allows for the contact area between the hinge bolt and tube to be vastly increased and the wear decreased. If no bushing was installed, the two holes in the leading edge would wear and elongate, making the hinge sloppy.

## Tangs

A tang is a flat rectangular piece of stainless steel (see Fig. 9-6), measuring about 1" × 2" by 1/8" thick, rounded on

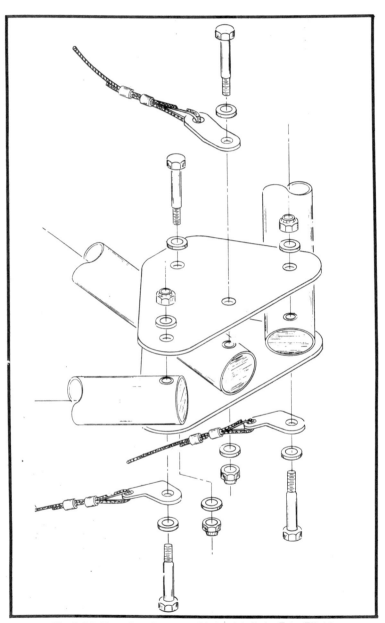

Fig. 9-3A. Rogallo wing nose hinge details by Free-Flight.

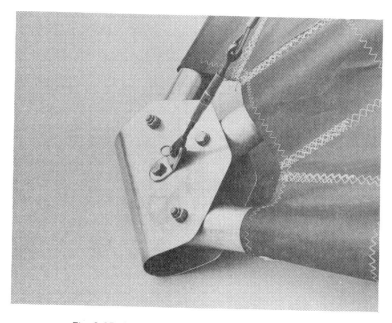

Fig. 9-3B. A one piece, aerodynamic nose plate.

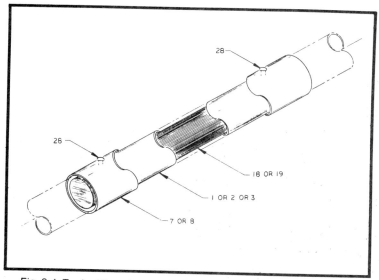

Fig. 9-4. Typical Rogallo spar sleeve and dowel installation method.

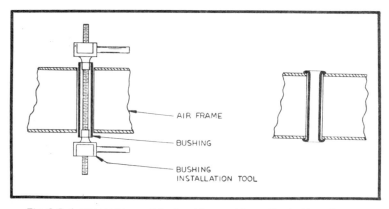

Fig. 9-5. A typical hang glider bushing and its method of installation.

the ends, bent up about 30°, with 2 holes, one in each end. Hole size depends upon application but are normally 1/4″ or 5/16″ in diameter.

### Elbow Fittings

As mentioned previously, speed-rail fittings have been largely replaced by specially designed aluminum fittings that

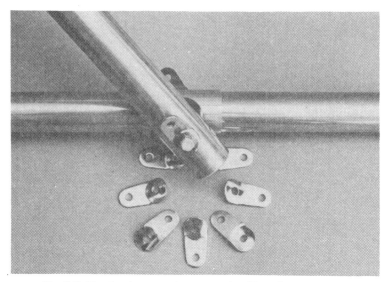

Fig. 9-6. Rigging tangs and an example of how they are used.

fit inside the tubing. These are "elbow fittings" and they are used on the bottom corners of the control frame (illustrated in Fig. 9-7). Some manufacturers have their own particular design while others just buy from a competitor. At any rate, they are designed to join the control bar and uprights. Generally, one half is bolted to the upright, while the other is bolted to the control bar. A pivot bolt joins the two fitting halves together. Round bottom control frames do not use elbow fittings.

### Shackles

A shackle is a "U" shaped steel fitting used as an anchoring point where one or more cables terminate (see Fig. 9-8). It is commonly found fastened to the control frame elbow fitting pivot bolt and secures the three cables most kites use

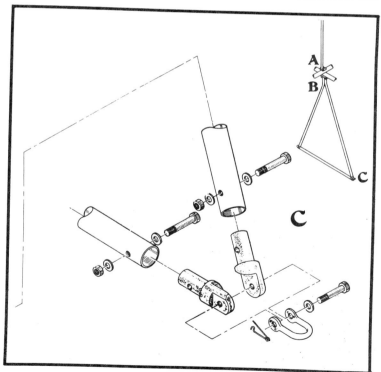

Fig. 9-7. Typical elbow fitting on triangle control bar.

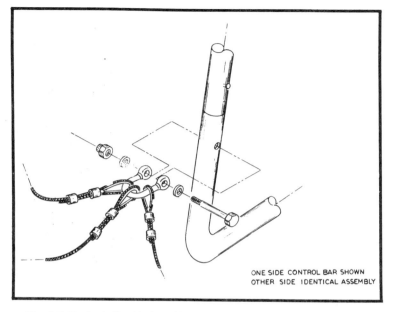

Fig. 9-8. Typical shackle installation on a rounded type control frame.

for half of their bottom rigging. (There is one at each elbow.) Shackles of the MS20115 (Military Standard) variety are often used on cable ends as they connect to turnbuckles and control horns in hang gliders equipped with aerodynamic controls.

### Keel/Cross Member Intersection

This is the central structure of a Rogallo wing hang glider and it is where the center of gravity is located. It is also the point from which the pilot is suspended, thus its importance cannot be overemphasized. It must be strong! Typically, a single bolt holds it all together as illustrated in Fig. 9-9.

### King Posts

A king post is the tube jutting up, perpendicularly from the keel/cross member intersection (see Fig. 9-10). It typically has a cable going to the nose, tail and both wings. In a straight glide it sees no real loads however, as the sail is unloaded and deflates in landing, the weight and inertia of the glider pulls on the top cables (landing wires) and puts the king post in

358

compression. Also, in maneuvering flight, as the load distribution changes across the wing, the upper cables see a varying load situation which also loads the king post and helps transfer pilot control inputs more rapidly and with less slop. If there were no king post, the wing would droop while on the ground and most likely break in a normal landing.

## Uprights

Uprights, or downtubes, are the two vertical tubes of a typical control frame that connect the control bar to the keel as shown in Fig. 9-11. They are normally under compression loads.

## Keels

The keel is the main, longitudinal center tube on a Rogallo and the fuselage tube on many rigid wing gliders. It is

Fig. 9-9. Rogallo keel cross member intersection detail showing sleeves and saddles.

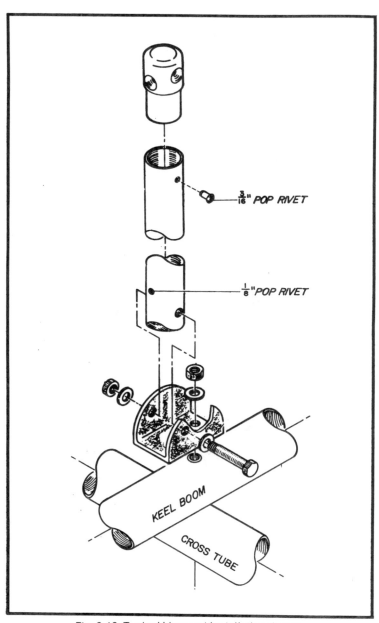

$\frac{3}{16}$" *POP RIVET*

$\frac{1}{8}$" *POP RIVET*

KEEL BOOM

CROSS TUBE

Fig. 9-10. Typical kingpost installation details.

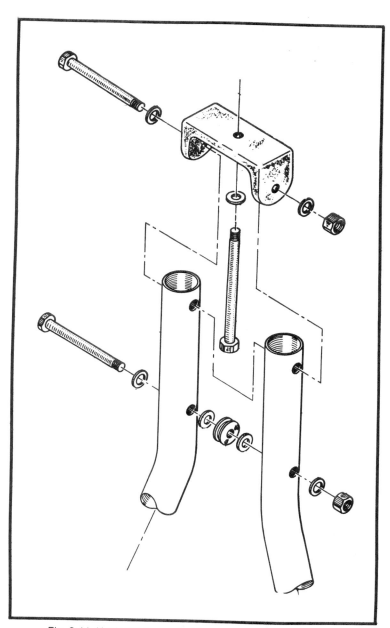

Fig. 9-11. Uprights-to-control frame mount bracket details.

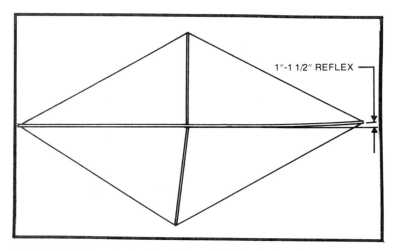

1"-1 1/2" REFLEX

Fig. 9-12. Positive keel reflex is important for longitudinal stability and trim.

normally under compression and is considered to be a beam-column, i.e., it is a beam, because of the distributed load from the sail which tends to give it negative reflex between the nose and cross member, cross member and keel. It is a column because the cables pull in on it and compress it.

**Keel Reflex**

Keel reflex (see Fig. 9-12) is an attempt at compensating for the deflection at the aft portion of the keel and to add stability. Here, the tail is rigged up from a straight line down the center of the keel. Reflex is opposite to the beam load and thus, under load, the aft keel tends to straighten out. Keel reflex alters the trim of the kite, making it tend to climb if all else remains the same. A kite must never have negative reflex (rigged down). Every kite has a particular manufacturer's recommended reflex.

**Leading Edges**

A leading edge is that member of a wing which is located along the front of a wing. On standard Rogallos it is swept back at an angle from between 45° to 50°. Put another way, a 45° swept leading-edge Rogallo has a 90° included angle, while a 50° swept leading-edge Rogallo has an 80° included angle, and so on. A monoplane with tail surfaces typically has a non-swept, or straight leading edge (180° included angle). However, most flying wings without tail surfaces have some degree of sweepback for stability reasons (less than 180° included angle).

Since a leading edge is the first part of a wing to see any airflow, its shape and condition is extremely important. Air must meet a smooth surface to minimize drag and turbulence. No dents, holes, bends or tears in sails and wing covering should be along the leading edge, or anywhere else, for that matter. This is important not only from an aerodynamic standpoint, but also for structural reasons. Of particular concern are leading edge tips (wing tips) since they are essentially cantilever tubes and may be prone to bending. They can be bent quite easily by abusive ground handling or rough landings. Check for straightness. It is important in trim to have straight and level glides.

As far as loads go, Rogallo leading edges are primarily under bending, while rigid wing leading edges see both bending and compression.

### Plugs and Caps

In order to prevent the filling of open tube ends with gravel, etc., many hang glider manufacturers install either a cap or plug to close the tube end. They are normally made of a plastic material. This is a good idea, for any buildup of foreign material in a tube could lead to corrosion or an unbalanced flight condition, which might cause a crash. A drain hole should be provided to vent a tube of moisture whenever plugs are used.

### Cross Member

A cross member is the tube that joins the leading edges and keel near the center of gravity of a kite. The cross member is typically a single piece unit that rotates around the so-called "heart bolt." Cross members are loaded in compression only!

### Control Bars

A control bar is the bottom horizontal tube that connects the two uprights of a control frame as shown in Fig. 9-13. It is normally gripped during flight and used to shift weight and

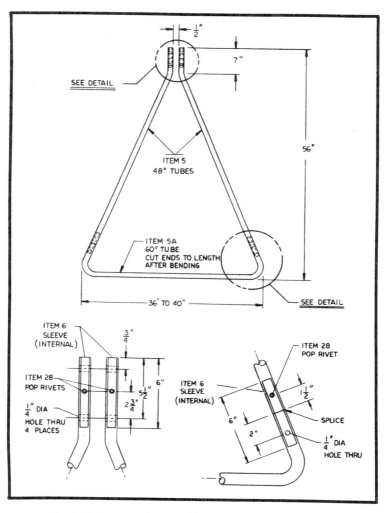

Fig. 9-13. A rounded control bar-control frame assembly.

control the flight path of a kite. Push the bar right to go left (it is easier to think of it as shifting the body in the direction one wants to go) and vice versa. Control bars are normally under tension loading.

In addition to being straight, which most are, some control bars may be had with a belly bulge that will allow more forward motion of the body while the pilot is sitting. This is primarily done for nose down capability in a particular design.

## TOOLS

The typical home workshop or garage should contain most of the tools necessary to fabricate and assemble a hang glider. More specifically, the tools normally required are as follows: hand-held power drill, drill bits, hacksaw, ballpeen hammer, adjustable wrench, pliers, socket wrench, file and emery cloth, center punch, wire strippers or razor knife, wire rope cutters and nico press swaging tool. Of this list, the last two probably won't be found in one's home. They will either have to be bought or rented from an airport, marina or hang glider dealer.

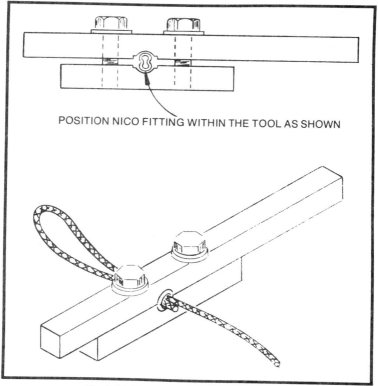

POSITION NICO FITTING WITHIN THE TOOL AS SHOWN

Fig. 9-14. How to use the "swage-it" tool.

Fig. 9-15. Control system pulley installation on a VJ-24.

The wire rope cutters are a plier sized tool with triangular shaped cutting jaws. The only possible substitute for these would be a good cold chisel and hammer, which will cut cable. As for the nico press tool, two kinds are available: the standard National Telephone type or the less expensive "swage-it" tool type (see Fig. 9-14). The former works like a pair of oversized pliers while the later requires the tightening of two bolts with each swage. A nico-swage should be checked with a proper gauge.

For the scratch builder, a few additional tools will be required: a pipe bender, soldering iron or hot knife, and sewing awl. The bender will be necessary for bending control frames and any other bent tube forms. The soldering iron (hot knife) will come in handy when finishing a sail, to seal its edges, burn grommet holes, etc. A sewing awl can be useful for sail repair.

## HANG GLIDER CONTROL SYSTEMS

There are many hang glider control systems. The two most common systems are weight shifting and aerodynamic.

The following paragraphs describe some of these control systems.

**Aerodynamic**

Hang glider control mechanisms are used where aerodynamic control surfaces are employed, as is commonly found on higher performing monoplanes. They serve to transmit motion from the pilot's controls at the control frame or hang cage to the appropriate control surface; generally by a cable-pulley arrangement.

Control cables are typically 7 × 7 construction, 1/16th diameter stainless steel or galvanized aircraft cable, depending on application. They are generally strung over AN210 (MS24566-1B) pulleys and, if the span is long, fairleads are also used (see Fig. 9-15). Cable guards which could be MS24665 cotter pins, are installed on the pulley brackets to prevent the cable from jumping out of the groove when slack.

Fig. 9-16. Rogallo wings rely solely on weight shifting for control.

Cable thimbles (AN100-3) are generally used to splice cable ends to a turnbuckle-eye (AN-130) end. Nico press sleeves are used most often for the splice.

It cannot be overemphasized to properly string a control system. All cables must go to the proper control and for the proper movement. Up elevator must be with back stick, right rudder must be with right stick, etc. All cable guards must also be properly installed to keep the cable on the pulley at all times.

Proper and true alignment of the pulley with the cable is also a must. If a cable does not pull true with a pulley, i.e., if it is not centered in the groove, then pulloff might occur. Even if pulloff doesn't occur, a misalignment where the cable is chafing the pulley sides is also bad and can lead to pulley failure and control system friction and binding. A good way to check cable/pulley alignment is to slip a piece of paper between the cable and pulley side. If properly aligned, no pulloff will occur. A simple sighting of the particular cable/pulley system should also reveal any misalignment problems.

Finally, after the system is properly adjusted and tensioned, it should be checked to see that all loose parts are safetied. Turnbuckles must also be safetied before flight so that no rotation, and its conseqent slackening of the cables, can occur; a condition that could lead to sloppy control at best and an out-of-control crash at worst!

**Weight Shift-Trapeze Bar**

This is the simplest, most common control system used today in hang gliders and most exclusively on kites. It consists of a triangular control frame and a harness suspended pilot. The pilot steers the hang glider merely by shifting his weight in the desired direction of movement (see Fig. 9-16). To go right, he shifts right and shifts left for a left turn. To dive, he pulls the control bar in while he does the opposite to stall. The system is direct and reliable as long as its limitations are observed. (i.e., stay away from high winds, cross winds and turbulence.)

**Weight Shift-Aerodynamic**

This control system combines both aerodynamic and weight shifting techniques in one hang glider. The common setup is to employ weight shift for pitch control and rudders for yaw/roll control. By shifting his weight fore and aft while suspended in a harness, the pilot can change the longitudinal balance much as in a standard kite. This system is better than pure weight shift, but not as good as an all aerodynamic control system. Then, too, a monoplane design definitely needs aerodynamic augmentation for control about the directional and lateral axis. Although standard kites are of low aspect ratio, a monoplane with its longer span and higher aspect ratio would be impossible to turn with weight shift alone.

The Icarus II and V are prime examples of this mongrel type control system (see Fig. 9-17). They both employ weight shift for pitch control and wing tip rudders for yaw/roll

Fig. 9-17. The Icarus V uses weight shift for pitch control and drag rudders for turning.

Fig. 9-18. The Quicksilver uses weight shift for pitch and rudder for turns.

control. Outward deflection of one rudder will slow that particular wing causing it to lose lift, gain drag, and set up a coordinated turn and bank. Outward deflection of both rudders also aids in descent control. They act to increase drag and thus steepen the glide angle which may help when in tight spots.

The Quicksilver design, as shown in Fig. 9-18, also uses a combination of weight shifting and aerodynamic controls. A control frame and trapeze harness system, similar to a standard kite's, controls pitch. A rudder is connected directly to the harness and deflects with sideways body movements, via lines connected directly to the rudder.

### Bell Cranks

A bellcrank (see Fig. 9-19) is a small lever used to alter the motion or geometry of a control system. Normally, they use a special bearing in the center and have cables and pushrods connected. They are typically used in the aileron or lateral control system of a hang glider.

### Control Horns

Control horns are the small arms that jut perpendicularly from an aerodynamic control surface, near its hinge line as

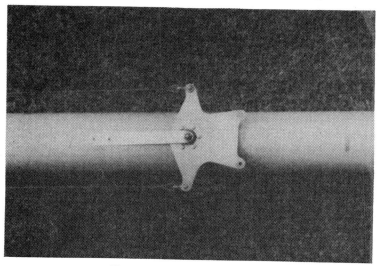

Fig. 9-19. Bellcrank on a VJ-24.

371

Fig. 9-20. Control horn on a VJ-24 aileron.

Fig. 9-21. Control stick on a VJ-23.

illustrated in Fig. 9-20. Control cables run from their ends to a control stick or twist grip. They commonly have two sets of holes: the outer set for less sensitivity, or control surface deflection per given stick deflection, and an inner set for more sensitivity. Their particular shape depends upon control system geometry.

**Control Stick**

A control stick (Fig 9-21), also called a joy stick, is a hand held, vertically neutral lever, located within easy and

Fig. 9-22. The Icarus II has twist grips connected to drag rudders which are used singly to turn the craft and simultaneously to steepen the glide path.

Fig. 9-23. The Electra Flyer uses deflexers to limit wing tip deflection under load.

convenient reach of the pilot's hand. It is mounted on a gimbal or universal joint to allow free movement in all directions: left, right, up, down, and combinations. Cables are attached to the stick at various locations to transmit control inputs to the control surfaces.

### Twist Grips

Another method of pilot input to aerodynamic controls are twist grips. These are normally mounted around a portion of the parallel bars at a location convenient to the pilot's hands (see Fig. 9-22). They are commonly used for deflecting wing tip rudders.

### DEFLEXERS AND SAILS

One method of preventing the deflection of the aft leading edges or wing tips is to install what are known as deflexers (see Fig. 9-23). These are simply small outriggers which jut downward and outward from the cross member to the leading edge intersection and are anchored by cable to the nose and wing tip. This setup makes for a small truss which takes the deflection out of the tip, i.e., prevents it from bending as the sail loads up in flight. Deflexers are not supposed to be used to generate a cylindrical type leading edge.

Today, deflexers are considered to be a high performance item. They improve glide ratio and control response while minimizing structural deformation. A beginning flyer should not bother deflexers, as his main concern is learning the basics of hang gliding. If he is still in the ground skimming stages of flying, he should just forget about improving the performance of his glider. His biggest performance gains will be realized by plain practice. Besides, the extra cable and fittings involved are an added hassle in setup and ground handling, and one needs all he can possibly have going for him as a beginner.

## Shaping the Sail

When Rogallo type hang gliders were first made, their sails had what is known as a straight, flat, cut. This is to say that if a sail were laid on a flat surface, each half would form a perfect, straight sided triangle. The angle of the sail at the nose was typically five degrees greater than the angle formed between the keel and leading edge. This formed a cone when inflated, hence the name conical Rogallo. All, however, was not quite so simple. While under normal flight loads, the airframe would deflect due to the pull from the sail since it is made from an elastic material, namely aluminum. This deflection would cause the sail to "kick up" in the area behind the cross member making it loose and allowing it to flutter and flap as it flew. After much thought and experimentation, someone came up with the brillant idea of cutting the sail differently from a straight sided triangle. Since the aft leading edge (behind the cross member) saw the most deflection, this was where the first modifications occurred. Observe a kite in flight, photograph it, measure the change in angle of the aft leading edge and cut the sail to suit!

Starting at the leading-edge/cross-member intersection, cut off a triangular, pie shaped piece of sail that is equal to the deflection angle of the aft leading edge (in sailmaker's lingo, this is called cutting a pie). This should do it. Well, it certainly did help. The sail was quieter and had less wrinkles, but there was still some flapping. More thought was necessary.

Looking at the now pie-cut modified leading edge, and also the keel, one notices that the trailing edge is unsupported; free to move about as it pleases. That's what the Rogallo flexible wing is all about, isn't it? At this point, apply some engineering sense and look at the straight trailing edge. It is a well known engineering fact that a curve will put chordwise tension in a sail, or line, so why not employ this principle. Thus, an arc was cut in the trailing edge and presto, a quiet, wrinkle free sail.

This solution is fine for steady, straight gliding, but not for turning and advanced maneuvers. While in a normal glide, the glider is essentially under a one g load. The tips are deflected in and up equally and at a given angle. Now, as soon as one turns, the lift distribution across the wing changes. One wing now sees more load than before, and the other may be less. Now the tip deflections are no longer the same. The more heavily loaded side has a tip that deflects more and hence causes the sail to loosen, wrinkle and flutter. The performance goes down.

Since the sail can be cut only for one particular flight condition, something else must be done to the glider to improve the situation. The goal is, of course, to minimize the bending of the tips under varying flight loads by stiffening the tips. There are two ways of doing this: one is to increase the diameter and wall thickness of the tubing, and the other is to make a cable braced truss out of it. The first method will work to a certain extent, but it still doesn't offer infinite rigidity. Besides, it increases the weight of the glider and, what's worse, it increases the weight at the tips, which is bad for inertial response reasons as well. It's harder to start and stop a mass from moving, the heavier and farther away it is from the center of rotation. (This is Newton's first law of motion). The lighter the better, especially at the extremities.

### Adding Deflexers

The second method involves the deflexer, which is really a cable braced, end loaded, truss. As we learned previously, in the chapter on design, if we end load a member we can make it equally as strong as a heavier cantilever member. This is really great, for we keep the weight down, the inertia down and add to the tip's rigidity. (The entire deflexer unit can weigh almost as little as a half pound!) There is a slight drag penalty for the cables, fittings and deflexer strut, but it is most certainly outweighed by the improvements it makes to the sail.

If one is an advanced pilot looking for that last ounce of performance, then perhaps he ought to look into deflexers. They are simple to mount. The strut should be mounted at an angle directly opposing the tip deflection angle. A small turnbuckle should also be a part of each deflexer truss so that one can adjust and fine tune his sail. This must be approached cautiously and under controlled conditions.

First of all, all testing should be done over a hill where the slope is very close to the glide ratio of the glider. Your first flight should be flown with the deflexer loose. Here the tip is as free as it was prior to installing the deflexer. Note the glide. Next, begin closing the turnbuckles, being sure to do both wings equally. This first adjustment ought to remove any slack in the cables. Now, fly the hill again and note the glide. It should start improving. A word of caution. As one closes the turnbuckles and tightens each deflexer unit, he will be actually flattening the sail behind the center of gravity. This will have a "down elevator" effect and begin changing the trim of his glider, perhaps making it necessary to push out a little more during the glide. This can be trimmed out by moving the sail relative to the frame. For instance, sliding the sail forward on the keel, an inch or so, will make the glider tend to climb. More reflex will also add "up" trim. At any rate, one will have to feel it out as he goes.

The third closing of the turnbuckles should be about 1/8 in., then fly again. Continue this procedure until the tip is straight under flight loads and trim the glider as required. By the end of the session one should notice an improvement in glide. He should be landing out further from the same vertical drop. Also, his sail should be wrinkle-free and quiet. Don't overdo it though. Too tight an aft sail will make the glider squirrelly and unstable.

In addition to improving an already good sail, the deflexer setup may also help an old flat cut sail or worn stretched sail, but don't expect miracles.

After the deflexers are adjusted and the glider trimmed out, one should be ready for some super flying. The sail will have less wrinkles and be quieter. The glider will respond more quickly to one's movements and just seem to cut through the air better.

## HANG GLIDER STRENGTH

How strong should a hang glider be, anyway? As strong as possible, of course, but there are other things to consider. Naturally, it would be great if the glider were strong enough to withstand a wing tip digging into the ground or crashing into a tree. It would also be nice if the control frame didn't bend so easily, or would it? Certainly a hang glider can be made so strong that it would be almost indestructable, but it would also be too heavy to even move about with. Then too, wouldn't it be better to have some part of the airframe bend or break, absorbing the shock, rather than the pilot getting seriously hurt or breaking a bone? Of course, it would! Therefore, the structural design, as well as other areas of hang glider design, involves a compromise on the part of the designer. The strength of the hang glider, along with its performance stability, control and portability, is determined largely by how the hang glider is going to be used. Typically, higher performing hang gliders require more strength for the atmospheric conditions they'll encounter and the maneuvers they'll perform. Trainer types too, require good strength characteristics in order to survive the abnormal, neophyte landings and general abuse they'll see in service.

To get an understanding of what hang glider strength is all about, we must learn how loads effect the various members (load carrying parts) of a hang glider. Basically, there are five types of stress that can be developed from applying loads to the hang glider. They are: tension, compression, bending, torsion and shear. Each particular member may see one, or a combination of two or more, of these stresses at any given time.

### Tension

Tension is developed in a member when there is a load tending to pull it apart. A tug of war, consisting of a rope held by two opposing men, is a good example of tension. The rope is said to be under tension. The stress it sees depends upon two things: it's cross-sectional area and the amount of

378

pull between the two men. For instance, suppose the men are pulling with a force of 100 pounds on a rope that measures 1/4 of a square in. in cross section. To determine the tensile stress in this rope, merely divide the force by the area, thus the tensile stress is 400 pounds per square in. (psi) is the standard way of denoting stress.

On a hang glider, the cables are a good example of tension members. Furthermore, cables can withstand only tension and no other kind of stress.

## Compression

Compression is the opposite of tension. It tends to shorten or push a member together. A good example of compression exists in ordinary household furniture: a person's weight on a chair puts the four legs in compression. Once again, the compressive stress is measured in pounds per square inch (psi). For instance, suppose a person weighed 160 lbs and he sat on a chair whose four legs each had one square in. of cross-sectional area. We can calculate the compression stress fc, as follows: divide the total load (the person's weight) by the total area (four square in.).

In other words, the compressive stress in each leg is equal to 40 psi.

On a hang glider, the uprights of the control frame are in compression. They are compressed by the pilot's weight pushing down on them while the lift, from the tension in the cables, is pushing up on them. Ideally, uprights see only compression.

## Bending

Bending is developed in a member when it is subjected to a load perpendicular to its length. A good example of bending is exhibited when a person stands on a diving board: the board bends downward. In this case, calculating the bending stress is a little more complicated than the two previous cases of tension and compression. One needs to know not only the weight of the person on the board, but also the distance he is from the point where the board is mounted and the "area moment of inertia" of the board as well. This "area moment of inertia" is derived from the shape of the cross section.

## Torsion

Torsion is exhibited whenever a member is twisted or is caused to rotate about its axis. A good example of torsion can be seen in steering a bicycle. Torsion must be applied to the shaft to turn the wheel. The torsional stress depends on three things: the actual torsional moment (or torque), the radius of the shaft, and the "polar moment of inertia."

On a hang glider, the wings of a monoplane can be subjected to torsional stress. They are being twisted by the air loads on them.

## Shear

Shear occurs whenever a member is subjected to a force perpendicular to itself. An example of shear is found in cutting a metal sheet with a pair of shears. In fact, that's how the tool got its name. It shears the sheet apart. Another example of shear would be to take two sheets of metal and bolt them together. Again a tug-of-war situation, trying to pull two sheets apart puts a shear stress on the bolt and the plates.

On a hang glider, shear stress occurs in wings and keels. Note also, that wherever there is bending stress, there is shearing stress as well.

Therefore, there are five basic types of stress. As mentioned previously, these may act singly or as a combination on a particular member of a hang glider. Also, depending on the load situation, a given member may see one type of stress one time, while it sees another type of stress at another time! For example, while flying, the wing tips are mostly in bending. If a tip strikes the ground perpendicularly however, it will be subjected to a large amount of compression and bending. This will often break it. Similarly, other members may be subject to changing states of stress. One can see for himself by examining the hang glider airframe and imagining different loads and the stresses they generate.

One thing to remember is that a member can not carry tension and compression at the same time. These are "opposite stresses." Members can, however, see tension one time and compresson at another.

An example of tension only members are cables. They can not possibly carry any other kind of load. They can only be pulled, or tensed.

Torsion can be found in the wing structural members of a rigid wing hang glider as the airloads try to twist the wing. There is very little evidence of torsional stress in a Rogallo wing, however, except those with tip extensions.

Shear stress is found all over a hang glider airframe. In fact, most bolts are in shear and certainly all rivets see shear. Bolts may carry tension on some occasions, but are normally designed to carry shear alone for maximum strength.

## BEST STRUCTURAL DESIGN

For the highest strength, lightest weight hang glider design, it is best to have the various members carry end loads rather than side loads. In other words, members should be designed to carry tension, compression, or shear, and to avoid bending and torsion. In general, an end loaded structure will weigh from 1/2 to 2/3 the weight of a non-end cantilever loaded design as shown in Fig. 9-24.

To prove that members are stronger in tension and compression than in bending, one can try a little experiment. Take a small length of wood, say a wooden yardstick, and try to pull it apart: nothing happens. Similarly, compress it (make sure a friend holds the center from bowing out). Again, nothing happens. Now, try bending it. It breaks fairly easily.

In hang gliders, the common cable, or strut bracing technique effectively loads members at their ends. The Rogallo kite is a good example of an end loaded design. For instance, the bracing between and with the control frame and cross member together, form what is known as a truss.

### The Pratt Truss

A truss can be defined as a structure which is composed entirely of end-loaded members. In most hang gliders, the members have a single bolt or pin connection at each end, and the loads are applied only at the bolt or pin, usually by a cable. The type of truss used in a typical cable braced hang glider is known as a Pratt Truss (see Fig. 9-25), named after Mr. Pratt, or course. Here, the longitudinal member (such as a cross

Fig. 9-24. The VJ-23 Swingwing is the only production cantilever wing design available.

member) and the vertical members, such as a control frame upright, are tubes. The cables are the diagonal members. For general discussion purposes, vertical and diagonal members

Fig. 9-25. The Fledgling is a good example of a Pratt truss.

Fig. 9-26. The VJ-24 SunFun struts form a Warren truss with the wing.

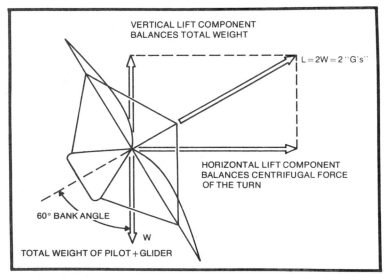

VERTICAL LIFT COMPONENT
BALANCES TOTAL WEIGHT

L = 2W = 2 "G's"

HORIZONTAL LIFT COMPONENT
BALANCES CENTRIFUGAL FORCE
OF THE TURN

60° BANK ANGLE

W

TOTAL WEIGHT OF PILOT + GLIDER

Fig. 9-27. A hang glider in a 60° bank is subjected to a 2 g load situation.

are called "web members" while horizontal members are called "chord members".

One must examine the truss and see what kind of stress each member sees. Now, the load going into the truss is the weight of the pilot due to gravity. The pilot's weight goes directly into the diagonals and puts them into compression, a situation called column loading. The cable is then put into tension. It sees tension stress. The cable pulling on the cross member puts it into compression; it is another column. The weight of the pilot and the hang glider as well is, of course, held in the air by the lift generated as the glider moves forward. All the while, in flight, the king post and anti-lift cables see no loads.

Upon landing, the weight of the glider is transferred to the anti-lift cables and puts them into tension. The cable tension then puts the kingpost into compression. The lift cable is essentially unloaded while the hang glider sits on the ground.

### The Warren Truss

Another basic type of truss is known as the Warren Truss (see Fig. 9-26), named after Mr. Warren! In this case, any member can carry any of the loads of tension and compression. A strut-braced monoplane is a good example of this type of truss. Notice the lack of king post and anti-lift cables.

One can look at the loads and stresses in each member. In flight, the pilot's weight is again split up, half going into each upright. The lift from each wing (half the total lift) is pulling upward, putting the diagonal member (called a strut) into tension. This then puts the wing spar into compression.

On landing, the weight of the glider's wings rests on the struts and puts them into compression. The spar sees tension.

The Warren truss is a good example of the changing states of stress a given member can see during normal, everyday use.

### The Ultimate Load Factor

A hang glider designer can, of course, calculate and analyze the various stresses of the particular members in a given design. He can determine the loads created by different flight situations and design, or size each member to suit the stresses involved. The airframe must not only be strong enough to carry the pilot's weight, but also strong enough to withstand the not-so-gentle landings of the beginner as well as the extra g loads imposed by flight maneuvers and gusts. For instance, in a 60° bank, the g load is two, as illustrated in Fig. 9-27. The pilot and the hang glider weigh twice as much as normal.

It should be easy to see that in order for the vertical force, the lift, to be equal to the pilot plus glider weight, the actual load on the airframe must equal twice the normal. The component is of the 2L being equal to L, through the 60° angle. Now, of course, the g load varies with the angle of bank, varying between 1 and 2 for angles of bank between 0° and 60° (see Fig. 9-28).

Most banks made in a hang glider are at less than 60°. In fact, more like 10° to 20°, where the increase in g load is hardly noticeable. Nevertheless, g load can be created by other factors as well. Sharp gusts, for instance, can load a hang glider suddenly and make it see a 2 g load quite readily even while in level flight. A sharp gust, coupled with a

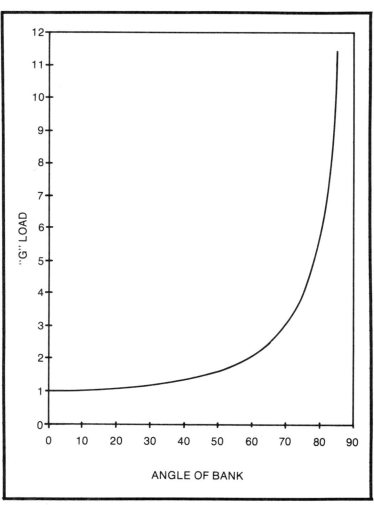

Fig. 9-28. g loads increase as the tangent of the bank angle.

steep bank or other maneuver, could load the hang glider to almost 4 g's. Consequently, a hang glider must be designed to withstand such loads to insure the draft doesn't bend or breakup in mid air. Then too, to be absolutely certain of structural integrity, a safety factor of 1 1/2 is multiplied into the design. To be strong enough for normal use, one must multiply 4 g's times 1.5 to come up with what is known as the ultimate load factor, equal to 6. This says that every single member in the airframe will be able to withstand at least 6 times the gross weight of the pilot plus hang glider weight.

A hang glider is designed to be strong enough to withstand any load it might see in normal use. This, of course, assumes proper maintenance of the various members. If corrosion sets in, it will weaken a member and lead to a dangerous situation. If a certain part were to become corroded, cracked, dented, bent or nicked, it could make the member, and hence the airframe, unfit for flight. Remember, the airframe is only as strong as its weakest member. It's up to the pilot to see to it that he properly maintains his hang glider and all its various components.

# Appendices

## THE WORLD CUP IN HANG GLIDING

The World Cup in Hang Gliding is a series of competitions between hang glider pilots from around the world. They demonstrate their skills in a 5-week round robin of events. Each will be notably different, but will retain a format easy to judge and safe to perfrom. The overall winner will be the most consistent flyer in various tests of pilot judgement, accuracy, soarability, and skill at aerial maneuvers.

Because of the length of the World Cup tour, and the distance between events, the contestants are limited to 100 of the world's finest flyers from eighteen areas.

Qualifications: Five man teams from 18 world areas.
Start Numbers:

1-5 International
6-10 Canada
11-15 USA No. 1 East of the Mississippi

16-20 USA No. 2 West of the Mississippi
21-25 USA No. 3 So. California
26-30 USA No. 4 Hawaii-No. California
31-35 Japan
36-40 Australia
41-45 South America
46-50 South Africa
51-55 Scandinavia
56-60 Great Britain
61-65 New Zealand
66-70 France
71-75 Switzerland
76-80 West Germany
81-85 Austria
86-90 Italy
91-95 Open to 5 extra International
95-100 Open to 5 from host nation

The International class will be composed of flyers from all other nations not listed. For example, Egypt, Poland, Spain, etc.

**QUALIFICATIONS**

1. To be under the control of the Hang Glider Association of each country.
2. Flyers must use hang gliders not exceeding World Cup standards.
3. The events must be varied and numerous.
4. Qualification events must be held before the given deadline.
5. The list of qualifiers must arrive at World Cup Headquarters not later than the given deadline.
6. Residence requirements—six months regional for USA—passport required for all contestants.
7. Team order and numbers will be kept throughout the tour.
8. Starting lists will be changed for each event.
   Example: 1st round  1-100          1st round 2-100
            2nd round 51-100          99-1 odd
                      1-50            2nd round 1-99, 100-2

9. Open qualifications—There are ten places left open before each event. Five places for the winners of an International qualification round held before each event, and five places for the host country. The ten must requalify for each new area.
10. The contestants are expected to complete the entire tour. If for some reason the contestant cannot make the tour, it is up to the team captain to choose the next qualified alternate. If a contestant leaves the team because of illness, injury, or emergency, the team leader may compete in his place.
11. Insurance—Available in Europe—All contestants must have proof of 3 types of international insurance policies before competing in the World Cup.
   A. Third party risk with a minimum of 500,000 Swiss francs for competition.
   B. A personal accident policy to include the sport of hang gliding in competition.
   C. Travel insurance to cover all baggage and glider material for the tour.

## EVENTS

1. Because there should be an equal opportunity for all flyers to win the Cup, each competition will have 2 rounds, making a total of 8 events before the 3 finals.
2. Points will be awarded for each round with a maximum of 500 per round, with the exception of the parallel event.
3. Each of the 4 preliminary events will have a maximum of 1000.
4. The finals will consist of 3 events of 1 round each. Each round will have double points for a maximum of 1000.
5. The finals will then have a possible maximum of 3000 points toward the World Cup.
6. The World Cup will have a possible maximum of 7000 points.
7. The flyer who has amassed the most points throughout the World Cup tour will be declared the winner.
8. Time schedule:
   Monday—Travel-International team qualifications.

Tuesday—Team leaders meeting—Training site familiarization.

Wednesday—Training

Thursday—Training or bad weather day

Friday—1st round contest

Saturday—2nd round contest-Flyers dance

Sunday—Open class competition and show flights

9. Bad weather. On Tuesday's meeting, the weather will be discussed and alternate days chosen for competition if needed. If only one round can be held, that round will be awarded double points.

10. Each event will be a test of pilot skill and judgement. There are many possibilities for judging, and the best will be adopted for the contest where suitable to the location.

11. Examples: The first event at Lake Como, Italy, will be a test of soarability (maximum air time = maximum points), judgement of distance (more distance markers passed = bonus points), and the quality of the landing (final approach, standup, dead stop landing).

A. Spectator appeal: The beautiful location of Lake Como chosen for the 1976 World Cup, and the high steep mountains surrounding the lake, will make the 1st event of the World Cup exciting for spectators and flyers alike. The landing area will be 30 meters in diameter with a bonus bull's-eye of 2 meters. Because of the mountains and the lack of adequate spectator viewing, landings will be made on a floating platform 50 meters from shore. Flyers landing on the platform receive all distance and soaring points. Those landing in the water, obviously, get wet. Two of the three distance markers are along the shore. The third is around a small island. Good judgement will be required.

B. Safety: All tube ends must be capped. All pilots will mount a safety float at the cross tube-control bar junction. A safety vest will be provided. Lifeguard boats will be in place.

12. Final Events (3): Dolomite Mountains of Italy for 1976.

A. Spot Landings: In Corvara-Alta Badia, this is solely a landing contest where contestants are judged on form and skill of the final approach, and the distance in centimeters from the spot. A spot landing earns maximum points. In addition, a dead stop-feet only landing will be given bonus points. "Run-in" landings that touch down before the spot will be scored at the point of 1st touchdown. "Overshoots" will be marked where motion stops. Keel or wingtip touches lose the bonus. Fall down, control bar, or nose plate landings will have points subtracted.

B. Duration-Time Judgement: with proper winds, Brunick-Kronplatz is very soarable. Under these conditions, a maximum time limit of 20 minutes will be set with no more than 4 gliders aloft at once. Takeoff to touchdown will be timed at exactly 20 minutes. Every second over or under will cost one point. On non-soarable days, a normal flight time will be set...determined by a flyer on the jury. Again, points will be subtracted for each second above or below the norm. In all cases, 1,000 points will be maximum.

C. Figures-Aerial Ballet: Cortina D'Ampezzo. Each figure will have a point value, and a point list will be provided before the contest. Every competitor must make out a preflight point run and figure series plan and turn it in to the judges before the flight. If the pilot does exactly as planned—no more—no less—a 20% bonus will be awarded. The landing area is 30 meters in diameter. A 10% bonus will be awarded for dead stop-standup landings in the 2 meter bull's-eye.

D. Please send in suggestions on possible figures.

E. No stunt flying will be allowed, such as: standing in the control bar, backwards, no hands, or flying upside down from the harness, etc.

13. Other events: These events will have as much variety as possible, with skill and judgement the determining factor.

A. Parallel Flights: Pilots will draw starting numbers 1-50. There will be 2 of each number, and like numbers will fly against each other. The hill will be non-soarable. Both pilots are free to look for lift, but must fly around a distance marker and return to parallel landing areas. The last one down advances in the fly-offs.

All flyers making stand up landings in the landing area after rounding the pylons will be given base points. Each round has a base point worth: 1st round-500, 2nd round-600, 3rd round-700, 4th round-800, 5th round-900, and the final winner-1,000.

B. Safety in parallel flights. Ridge soaring rules apply. That is, lower pilot has the right of way, no crowding, keep minimum distance, etc. Sailing rules will apply where necessary.

C. Balloon Slalom. There will be an even, clear slope with balloons 10 to 20 meters above the terrain. Pilots must maneuver between the balloons. The distance between the balloons decreases as the pilot nears the landing area. The last four will be increasingly difficult to round. The balloon will only count if the pilot's body has passed to the outside and then cuts back across the fall line. Pilot or glider may touch the balloon. Score 50 points for each of the 9 rounded, and 50 points for a stand up landing in the 10 meter circle. The slalom will be run twice. It is mathematically possible for all 100 flyers to score 1,000 points. Ties may be broken by the fastest elapsed time during the slalom.

14. All events in the World Cup Tour are to be judged by an international jury. All organization and contest rules will be the responsibility of the Hang Glider Flyers Association in the country sponsoring the event. All final decisions will be made by the World Cup organizers and the World Cup director.

15. Team Competition and Show. On the final day of each event, there will be a team competition. Each 5-man team will have 10 minutes to put on a show of formation or individual flying. Audience participation

will determine the winner by filling out a program ballot, international jury will count the ballots, and a prize will be awarded to the winning team. The hosting national team may fly, but will not be judged in the contest.

16. Women's Event. The World Cup qualification rounds are open to female participation, and if qualified, will make the tour with their team. Negotiations are under way to sponsor a special Women's Tour with separate competitions.

## THE WORLD CUP STANDARD

Because of the variety of the contests—accuracy, duration, distance, figures, parallel starts, grace of flight, etc., the contest is designed to test pilot skill. So, a standard type of hang glider will be designed to perform these maneuvers in a safe but high performance manner. Standards have been set, and all competitors must be in compliance. They are general enough to allow designers and manufacturers to apply new technology and ideas in producing the World Cup Standard Rogallo Delta Flexible Wing.

1. General. The World Cup is a contest between Delta Hang Gliders of nearly the same performance characteristics where consistent pilot skill will determine the winner.

2. Flyers may use only one glider throughout the entire World Cup Tour. Each tube, nose plate, and sail will be marked.

3. In case of damage, minor repairs may be made. If the entire glider is destroyed or stolen, a reserve glider may be used. Reserve gliders must be registered before the World Cup Tour begins.

4. Glider design must take into consideration the usage the World Cup Tour will require: a glider that can be flown safely under all conditions. It should have good dive recovery, make easy turns, consistent 360s, and figures, have stable parachuting tendencies for spot landings, high speed/low speed capability, high L/D, low sink rate, and hands off stability. All new design or

construction techniques that may be questionable or protested at the time of registration will require World Cup Headquarters approval by the given deadline.

5. Materials must conform to HMA (US Hang Glider Manufacturer's Association) standards as of 1 January 1976. A copy will be sent on request.

6. The frame must have the following specifications:

90° nose angle or less.

Not more than four structural tubes will be allowed, 2 leading edges, 1 keel, and 1 cross. Tubes shall be circular with parallel walls and straight throughout the entire length. No preformed tube curve permitted. The maximum diameter will be 5 cm (2″).

Because of container and cable car limitations, all gliders must break down to 3.3 meters maximum.

7. Bracing is required as follows:

Only cable bracing may be used.

Control bar cables are limited to six. Two cables to the nose plate (a single cable from the control bar to a nose eye bolt and back is considered as two), two cables to the keel behind the base line, and one cable to each side at the cross tube-leading edge junction.

The king post must be connected to the keel with the heart bolt, or no more than 15 cm behind the heart bolt. A J-wire between the CX and nose plate will be allowed, but can not bow the keel more than 2 1/2 cm.

King post cables will be limited to four, connected to the nose plate, each leading edge cross tube, and to the keel behind the base line.

Deflexers are not recommended, but may be used at the pilot's discretion. Deflexers will only be used to keep the leading edge tube from bending during flight. Under normal flying tension, the leading edge tube must be straight or not more than 5 cm (tube diameter) down and out from a straight line.

Turning and adjusting on the ground of the keel (straight or positive upward flex), and the deflexers may be made. There will be no slack cables or negative reflex. Adjustment from prone to seat may be made.

There will be no mechanical adjustment of any cables in the air.

There will be no other cables or tensioning devices in the system.

There will be no streamlining in the entire flying system, including the pilot. Exception—nose plates.

There will be no instruments used in flight other than a timing device (watch).

8. The sail specifications are as follows:

The sail must be one complete unit without openings or divisions. The material must be the same grade throughout and conform to HMA requirements.

Sail cut must be a least 7° more than the frame angle.

Example: 90° frame—minimum, 97° sail = 3.5° billow.

No cambered sails. Dogleg cuts limited to 10 cm.

A maximum of 4 battens per side may be used. They must be straight, unsupported, and not penetrate sail pockets, of constant cross section, and homogeneous material.

Sails should be as colorful as possible and individually decorated. Somewhere on the sail should be a 50 cm circle for the contestant's World Cup number.

Wing loading will follow a straight line graph based on 4.4 kg per square meter (.9 lb/sq ft). Pilots may not fly a wing larger than the graph maximum. Pilots, glider, and harness, will be weighed at registration. They may be spot-checked at any time.

Aspect ratio may be no higher than 3.5 (wing span$^2$/area projected). Sail area is measured from the projected nose (apex) to the end of the sail on the assembled frame.

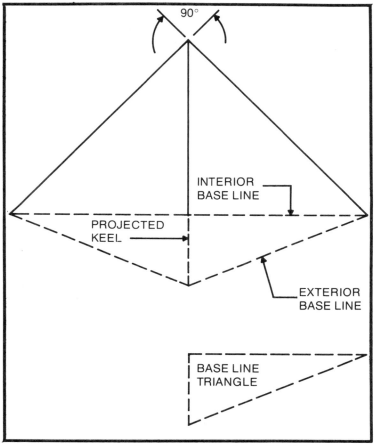

Fig. A-1. A graph detailing what was done for the World Cup tour.

Base line triangle. Shortened keel, scalloped sail, swallowtail cut, and all other performance designs may be used, provided they fall within the base line triangle.

A graph of what was done and the area removed from the triangle accompanies the glider during the World Cup events (see Fig. A-1).

The base line triangle is an area made up of straight lines from wing tip to wing tip of the sail, and the wing tip to projected keel tip. The projected keel length is where the tip of the keel would come if it were the same length as the leading edge of the sail. No part of the sail may be cut into the interior base line,.and no part of the sail or battens may protrude beyond the exterior base line measured with the sail fully extended off the frame.

## OPEN CLASS COMPETITION

1. Because there should be a continuing flow of new technology and aeronautical advancement in the sport of hang gliding, there will be an open class of competition during the World Cup.
2. There will be no World Cup points given in this class, but each event will be a part of the overall open competition.
3. Any type of hang glider that is weight shift controlled (no pilot movable surfaces) and has an unsupported-untethered trailing edge may compete.
4. The glider must be collapsible (3.3 m maximum) for easy transportation, and able to be set up in a reasonable length of time.
5. The competition will be a combination of duration (soaring) to a maximum limit, distance over a pre-scribed course, and area landing—crossing a base line, and bonus points for accuracy. Maneuverability, 360s, and other figures, will gain bonus points.
6. Only pilots on a World Cup team may compete in the Open. Instruments and streamlining will be allowed.

## SAFETY

1. Helmets. An approved safety helmet must be worn, not WWI leather ear warmers or children's plastic kayak rock bumpers. Helmets may be decorated to suit the pilot's individual taste (clouds, birds, flowers, etc. No advertising).
2. During the week long events, only team pilots may fly the area. No other flyers will be allowed in the air.

## SPONSORSHIP

Because of the magnitude of the World Cup Tour with so many nationalities traveling through many different countries over a five-week period, financial assistance and sponsorship will be welcomed.

1. Unsponsored teams are recommended. They will have all expenses paid for the duration of the World Cup by the Flyers Pool. This will include hotels, most meals, transportation between events, and entry fees. Personal expenses will not be included. Team members must fly with no advertising of any kind on sail or clothing except that manufacturers may display their logo on the sail and frame, once, provided that the total area does not exceed 15 × 30 cm.

2. Individual sponsorship will not be allowed due to the unique team structure of the World Cup.

3. Team Sponsors. There will be twenty teams of five men during the competition. A team may have one sponsor for the World Cup, but that sponsor must pay the entire expense of the team throughout the tour, including transportation, hotels, meals, and a predetermined amount of advertising money into the Sponsor Pool.

4. Qualification Round Sponsor. The same Team Sponsor may also sponsor the qualification round in the team's area.

5. With Sponsored teams, the advertising space will be limited to $2^2$ meters on the sails, and 2 logos of not more than 10 × 15 cm on the pilot's jump suit. Helmets may also carry the sponsor's logo. The Contest Program will list the team sponsors, and Team Vans may carry advertising of the sponsor.

## TRANSPORTATION DURING THE WORLD CUP

1. Flyers. The ten teams outside of Europe will have the use of a transit type van. The 5 members of the team and a 6th person, either a team leader, sponsor's representative, journalist, or driver, will be able to transport all of the team's equipment and gliders to each event. A limited amount of sightseeing will be permitted.

2. The driver (team member or other) must have an international driver's license and experience driving buses or vans. The minimum age for drivers will be 25 years. The van will be signed out to the driver, and a daily kilometer log book must be kept.

   Warning: between each event there will be an international border crossed. Keep your passport at all times. There will be absolutely no drinking of alcoholic beverages during travel, and no drugs. Border inspections are thorough.
3. The ten teams from Europe should be provided with a van from their own country.
4. Journalists. International journalists invited from outside Europe will be provided with the same type of automobile as offered for 1st prize in the World Cup. Four journalists per car, and five cars. European journalists will provide their own transportation or use the contest buses.
5. Family and guests. A special, all inclusive package is being worked out to include air and ground transportation, hotels, meals, and sightseeing during the World Cup Tour. A two-month advance booking is necessary.
6. During the travel days, there will be a travel information packet provided by the tourist office with a map of the area, the exact road and markings that should be followed, and the many interesting historical and scenic landmarks. The travel route will not be the most direct. It will be set up as a rally with check points and stops at points of interest. Border crossings will be preplanned to speed up inspections. The sponsoring petroleum company will have a list of authorized fill-up stations for team vans and journalists.

## PRIZES

1. To be a contestant alone is a prize. There will be contingency prizes from various sporting goods manufacturers. All contestants will receive a cut

crystal trophy created by Joseph Nalepa, world famous Czech designer. Competitors from outside of Europe will have special low rate flights. It will be a paid 5-week tour of famous European holiday resorts and flying sites in 4 different countries, including transportation, hotels, most meals, lifts, entrance fees to Flyers Balls, and other functions. All of this, plus worldwide publicity.

2. Cash Prizes. There will be a minimum $10,000 in prize money broken down to the top 10 winners.
3. For the World Cup Winner, there will be a brand new sports car.
4. The top 5 win automatic places on the World Cup Tour for the next year.

## HMA CATEGORY 1 SPECIFICATIONS
## FOR ROGALLO TYPE HANG GLIDERS

The following paragraphs give the specifications for the Rogallo type hang gliders.

### SPECIFICATION 1—BOLTS

All Category 1 aircraft shall be equipped with aircraft type grade 5 or better bolts for all fastening applications. Grade 8 bolts are recommended. All bolts must be of proper length for design application, i.e., unthreaded portion of shaft should take all loads. Threads should not extend below washer and nut. At least 1 1/2 threads must show above locknut when fastener is in position and ready for flight. All bolts using wing nuts with secondary safety systems should have hole in bolt for safety pin, at least 1 thread above fastener when in position ready for flight. Corrosion resistant plating must be used on all bolts and fastening hardware. A 1/4″ minimum bolt size is required for all main structural joints. A 5/16″ bolt size is recommended for the heart bolt at cross structure.

## SPECIFICATION 2—NUTS

Locking type fasteners are required on all critical, i.e., necessary for flight, single system joints. Nylon type or plastic filled locknuts are acceptable, however all metal locking types are recommended. Nylon type nuts are to be used only on singular operations, i.e., where a fastener is used once for the life of the airframe. A secondary safety system, i.e., safety ring, or safety pin, is required on all non-locknut systems. In any case, a secondary system is recommended at any high use disconnect joint, such as a wing spar to cross bar junction.

## SPECIFICATION 3—CABLES

All flying wire cables must have a minimum pull breaking strength of 920 pounds, i.e., equivalent to 7 × 7, 3/32″ stainless cable. Should cable used not be in accordance with current state of the art, cable with equivalent characteristics to 7 × 7, 3/32″ stainless wire rope shall apply. Any cable other than stainless must be of a corrosion resistant type. Landing wires, i.e., cables to king post, must be at least 2/3 strength of those cables used for flying wires.

## SPECIFICATION 4—CABLE ENDS

Both roll swaged and nico press fittings are HMA approved provided they are installed in accordance with FAA's manual AC 43.13-1A, Chapter four, i.e., single nico sleeve application at cable loop is approved, however, cable must protrude through sleeve after swaging. In this event some sort of covering similar to plastic heat shrink tubing is recommended to prevent open cable ends from cutting or tearing the sail. Thimbles of corrosion resistant material are required on all cable end loops. Note: For home built kits where proper nico press swaging tools are not available, it is recommended that two nico sleeves be used on all cables rigged with hand operated thread swaging type devices.

## SINGLE LOOP CABLES

Single loop flying wires of continuous strand are acceptable to both front and rear mounting points provided a properly swaged nico sleeve is used to locate the flying wires at midpoint in the cable. A twist in the wires is recommended at the nico sleeve mounting point to prevent undue load at the sleeve.

## SPECIFICATION 6—TURNBUCKLES

No turnbuckle shall be installed on any flying wire without an approved secondary system being permanently attached. Such secondary systems must be as strong or stronger than the primary system. Approval for such designs must be secured in writing by the HMA Technical Committee. Standard hardware quality turnbuckles are not permitted on any airframe anywhere. Only aircraft quality or specially designed tensioning devices of corrosion resistant material will be permitted. It is recommended that turnbuckles or tensioning devices be used only on the upper cables, i.e., landing wires.

## SPECIFICATION 7—ATTACH POINTS

Tangs or other such specially designed mounting hardware must sustain at least three times the pull strength of the attached cable or flying wire. It is recommended that all attached systems be made of corrosion resistant materials.

## SPECIFICATION 8—BALL LOCK PINS

All quick release mechanisms or quick pin devices are acceptable only when used in a shear load type application. Ball lock pins are not acceptable at any time where the locking device must carry load, i.e., shaft must take the entire load. A recommended visual distance between the locking balls and the locking surface shall be 1/16" minimum. Any hole next to the locking balls must be within the designed tolerance practices of the ball lock pin's manufacturer. All ball locks must lock against steel or steel lock rims, i.e., no pin can be used in a nonferrous application without use of a hardened steel safety washer. Safety wires or lanyards are recommended to locate quick pins near their appropriate mounting point.

## SPECIFICATION 9—SAIL MATERIAL

Any wing or membrane material should be comparable in strength and wear characteristics to at least 3.0 oz "fleet boat"

Dacron sail cloth material, this eliminates monofilm polyethelene sails. Other comparable characteristics should include stretch, weathering resistance, and long term durability as well as rip strength when damaged. Other materials may be submitted to the HMA Technical Committee for approval in writing before use in production. Current state of the art shows that the best material for production use at the time these specifications were approved is 3.8 oz stabilized Dacron.

## SPECIFICATION 10—STITCHING FOR SAIL MATERIALS

Thread and needle size must correspond with sail material manufacturer's recommendation. Either straight or zigzag stitching is approved. Double stitching is recommended where necessary. Alternate methods of fastening sail materials are acceptable provided they meet the same standards for strength, wear and durability as conventional methods and are approved in writing by the HMA Technical Committee.

## SPECIFICATION 11—TUBING

The minimum material size in 6061-T6 or 6063-T832 for gliders over 14 feet shall be 1-1/2 inch diameter aluminum with .049 wall thickness. Other sizes of similar or different material can be approved by the HMA Technical Committee upon submission of adequate test data for the use required. A minimum yield strength of 35,000 pounds per square inch with characteristics comparable or exceeding 6063-T832 or 6061-T6 aluminum is recommended.

## SPECIFICATION 12—SLEEVES

At any point where a connecting or fastening load is imparted to the airframe, i.e., wing spar to cross bar or cross joined by the heart bolt, an outer sleeve of similar material plus an internal crush resistant material such as wooden dowel or bushing is required. At any point on the airframe where a fastener is used for locating other structural hardware, e.g., nose plate, tangs, etc., an internal bushing is required and a dowel is recommended. Wing spars are to comply at the junction point with both sleeving and internal bushing or dowels. Cross bar end holes must have crush resistant bushings or dowels or the equivalent. Alternate systems can be submitted to the HMA Technical Committee for approval in writing.

## SPECIFICATION 13—KING POSTS

Some sort of vertical structure above and connected to the airframe is required to triangulate the airframe's main structure by use of landing wires. Such structure or king post shall have triangulating wires coming to the nose to tail longitudinally and from wing spar junction to wing spar junction transversely. It is recommended that king post or landing wires do not interfere with the sail when glider is in flight.

## SPECIFICATION 14—CONTROL BARS

Because of size variations on different models, control bars do not have definite specifications other than the following. The minimum tubing size permitted in any control bar design shall be 6061-T6 1"OD × .065 wall or equivalent. Such tubing can be used only provided all flying wires are attached to specially designed fittings that can import the flying wire loads equally into the tubing, i.e., no holes can be drilled for eye bolts or flying wire shackle mounts in 1"OD × .065 wall 6061-T6 or equivalent. A minimum of 1"OD × .083 wall 6061-T6 or equivalent material is recommended for most control bars. In any case, flying wires can not attach to the control bar more than 6 inches above the base bar unless some additional structure is used to effectively double the wall thickness at that point, i.e., on single piece control bars it is not permitted to mount a shackle or similar purpose flying wire mounting device by drilling a mounting hole in the tube, unless that hole is less than 6 inches from the center of the base bar. It is recommended that all bars be reinforced at the mounting points with additional internal or external sleeve of equal or greater wall thichness. On multi-section control bars all connecting devices must be structurally stronger than the control bar material itself. The attachment systems on the base bar to the down tube structure must be such that a shear load of at least 750 pounds can be applied to that junction without visual signs of stress.

Furthermore, any control bar base tube must be capable of withstanding a 750 pound bending load. Bars are to be tested by mounting the bar at the point where the flying wires are attached and a 750 pound weight shall be suspended in the center of the control bar. No visible deformation should be evident after the test weight is removed.

## SPECIFICATION 15—PILOT SUPPORT SYSTEMS

Any and all parts of any pilot support systems used on any category 1 hang glider must support at least four times the intended flier's weight. Swing seats—in the case of swing seat support systems, a continuous strand of the support system's material, i.e., webbing, nylon rope, etc. must pass under the seat to insure the flyer's safety in the event of seat breakage. All swing seats must have a quick release type lap belt with buckle of metal to metal type. Chest and/or back straps are recommended to prevent the flyer from falling out of the seat. Should such a seat system possibly interfere with the flyer's wearing a helmet, a spreader bar above the pilot's head is highly recommended. Prone harness—variations in harness design preclude any definite specifications, however it is required that the vertical straps supporting the pilot from the mounting point on the glider be of continuous strand design around and under the flyer to prevent the flyer from being disconnected from the glider in the event of some harness failure. In general it is recommended that any system used to support the flyer have some sort of "easy release," i.e., carabiner type attachment system to enable the pilot to quickly detach himself from the airframe in any emergency. Furthermore, such a system should operate easily and in any altitude whether a load is being placed on it or not. Should a real "quick release," i.e., instantaneous pull release device, system be used, it should have some sort of positive secondary safety system to prevent the flyer from becoming totally unattached inadvertently.

## SPECIFICATION 16—SPECIFICATION PLATE

All gliders meeting HMA Category 1 Specs must be equipped with a plate so stating the fact. Such "HMA plate" should be affixed to the glider's airframe where it can be easily seen by any flier or meet inspector. It is further recommended that each glider have affixed to it a disclaimer, clearly stating the potential hazards of flight in Rogallo type aircraft.

The disclaimer wording as of August 11, 1974, is as follows:

Warning

Hang gliding is a dangerous activity and can result in serious injury or death even when engaged in under ideal circumstances. This equipment is manufactured in accordance with the safety, material, construction and flight standards established by The Hang Glider Manufacturer's Association, Inc. This equipment should be used only under proper conditions after properly supervised instruction and practice from an experienced hang gliding instructor. The manufacturer has no control over the use and maintainence of this equipment and all persons using this equipment assume all risks for damage or injury. The manufacturer and the HMA, Inc., disclaim any liability or responsibility for damages or injury resulting from the use of this equipment.

## HANG GLIDER CARE, MAINTAINANCE AND PREFLIGHT INSPECTION

It is suggested that all flying wires be replaced ever fifty (50) flying hours or after six (6) months of flying and normal ground handling. Replace all worn components regularly and damaged parts immediately. Flying wires should be replaced after any crash, as should any bent or damaged fasteners or hardware. Inspect entire airframe before every flight. Check all spars, sail, cables and their attachment points. Inspect all fasteners, hardware and secondary systems. Check control bar and pilot support systems for proper rigging relationship and wear. Be sure hang glider is in correct trim per manufacturer's specifications. Do not fly if the hang glider does not pass preflight inspection or conditions are unsafe. Wear an HMA approved crash helmet.

## SPECIFICATION 17—INSTRUCTION BOOKLET

All gliders sold by HMA members must be delivered with an HMA approved instruction booklet covering the basics of Rogallo flight. The list of such approved booklets is available from the HMA. Furthermore, it is recommended that each manufacturer supply a list of readings with the booklet to further instruct the buyer in improving his flight techniques. The approved list of readings is available from the HMA and shall be updated from time to time.

## DEMONSTRATED FLIGHT CONTROL REQUIREMENTS FOR HMA CATEGORY 1 ROGALLO TYPE HANG GLIDERS

The following maneuvers can be performed by either factory fliers or assigned fliers. In any case, no glider shall receive HMA Category 1 approval without performing these maneuvers:

1. Demonstrated control by fliers both at high and low end of manufacturer's recommended weight range for the glider.
2. Achieve a minimum glide ratio of 3 to 1 over 100 yards distance with the heaviest recommended pilot.
3. Demonstrate stall and recovery.
4. Demonstrate steep dive and recovery (sail flap induced with forward portion of sail in lift condition).
5. Perform two consecutive 90° turns in opposite directions.
6. Perform two 360° turns in opposite directions.
7. Demonstrate parachuting ability of glider by landing on a 6 foot circle. One out of three tries from takeoff altitude of 300 feet.
8. Demonstrate 8 seconds of hands-off flight with no radical changes in altitude.

## SPECIFICATION 18—FLYER PROFICIENCY LEVEL

All gliders submitted to the HMA must be classified according to a flyer proficiency level which will relate to the USHGA and PFA flight proficiency level or "hang badge" rating. A glider may be classified in more than one classification if the HMA Technical Committee feels it qualifies. The manufacturer will submit the glider in the classification he feels it conforms to, but final approval and classification may be changed by the HMA Technical Committee. The three classifications in ascending order of flyer proficiency level are: (A) Beginning to Intermediate, (B) Intermediate to Advanced, and (C) Advanced to Expert.

## HMA FULL MEMBERS

SKY SPORTS, INC.
P O Box 441
Whitman, Mass. 02382
Ed Vickery, Pres.

ZEPHYR AIRCRAFT CORP.
25 Mill Street
Glastonbury, Conn. 06066
Al Mulazzi, Pres.

CHUCK'S GLIDER SUPPLY
4200 Royalton Road
Brecksville, Ohio 44141
Chuck Clusarczyk, Prop.

FOOT-LAUNCHED FLYERS
1411 Hyne
Brighton, Mich. 48116
Dale Frey, Pres.

APOLLO
722 Barrington Road
Streamwood, Ill. 60103

PLIABLE MOOSE DELTA
WINGS, INC.
1382 Caddy Lane
Wichita, Kansas 67212
Gary Osaba, Pres.

KONDOR KITE CO.
P O Box 603
Lewisville, Texas 75067

SUN SAIL CORP.
6753 E. 47th Avenue Dr.
Denver, Colo. 80216
Ted Schmiedeke, Pres.

SAILBIRD FLYING
MACHINES
3123A N. El Paso
Colorado Springs, Colo. 80907
Joe Sullivan, Pres.

DYNA-SOAR, INC.
3518 Cahuenga Blvd. West
Hollywood, Calif. 90068
Jim Sommers, Pres.

ULTRALITE PRODUCTS,
INC
137 Oregon Street
El Segundo, Calif. 90245
Peter Brock, Pres.

SEAGULL AIRCRAFT, INC.
1554 5th Street
Santa Monica, Calif. 90401
Michael Riggs, Pres.

OMEGA HANG GLIDERS
P O Box 1671
Santa Monica, Calif. 90406
Joseph Faust, Pres.

EIPPER-FORMANCE, INC.
1840 Oak Street
Torrance, Calif. 90501
David Cronk, Pres.

SUNBIRD GLIDERS
1411 Chase Street No. 7
Canoga Park, Calif. 91304
Gary Valle, Pres.

FREE FLIGHT SYSTEMS, INC.
12424 Gladstone Avenue
Sylmar, Calif. 91342
Gerald M. Albiston, Pres.

DELTA WING KITES &
    GLIDERS, INC.
P O Box 483
Van Nuys, Calif. 91408
Bill Bennett, Pres.

HAWK INDUSTRIES
5111 Santa Fe Street
San Diego, Calif. 92109
Burke Ewing III, Pres.

SOLO FLIGHT
930 West Hoover Avenue
Orange, Calif. 92667

SPORT KITES, INC.
1202 C.E. Walnut
Santa Ana, Calif. 92704
Chris Wills, Pres.

J.L. ENTERPRISES
1150 Old Country Road
Belmont, Calif. 94022
Jim Lynn, Pres.

MANTA PRODUCTS
1647 E. 14th Street
Oakland, Calif. 94606
Kent Trimble, Pres.

TRUE FLIGHT
1719 Hillsdale Avenue
San Jose, Calif. 95124
Herman Rice, Pres.

THE NEST AIRPLANE
    WORKS
1445½ W. 11th Avenue
Eugene, Oregon 97402
Bernard Nolfard

SUN VALLEY KITE SCHOOL
17360 Beach Drive, N.E.
Seattle, Wash. 98155

MULLER KITES, LTD
P O Box 4063, Postal Station C
Calgary, Alberta T2T5M9
Canada
Willi Muller, Pres.

**HMA ASSOCIATE MEMBERS**
Dan Poynter
P O Box 4232
Santa Barbara, Calif. 93130

Victor F. Musser
c/o Foremost Dairies
2842 North Hacienda
Fresno, Calif. 93705

Gary D. Daniel
10441 South Vultee
Downey, Calif. 90241

W.B. Products
560 Sourth Helberta
Redondo Beach, Calif. 90277

L. Gabriels
4 Thornlea Avenue
Hollonwood, Oldham,
Lancaster OL8 3PX England

Kartway Park Ltd.
9102 51 Avenue
Edmonton, Alberta, Canada
Ralph E. Clark

Emory Gliders
409 South Dawson Street
Raleigh, N.C. 27601

Pacific Gull
1321 Calle Valley No. 7
San Clemente, Calif. 92672

Delta Wing Kites, Inc.
P O Box 144
Monroe, Wash. 98272
Bill Jopin, Pres.

Walt Wilson
122 Crestwood Circle
Pacific, Calif. 94044

Tod Mountain Flying School
749 Victoria Street
Kamloops, B.C., Canada
Niel S. Smith, Pres.

Flight Realities
1945 Adams
San Diego, Calif. 92116
Bob Skinner

Sutton Brothers
222 Verbeke Street
Marysville, Penna. 17053
Allen P. Sutton

Howe & Bainbridge
816 Production Place
Newport Beach, Calif. 92660

A & A Flight Systems
10 North Barton
New Buffalo, Mich. 49117
Tom Arbanas

Bird Feathers Sails
3021 Airport Avenue
Santa Monica, Calif. 90405
Bob Pence

Colver Soaring Instruments
3076 Roanoke Lane
Costa Mesa, Calif. 92626
Frank W. Colver

Feather Sky Sails
P O Box 0172
San Diego, Calif. 92115

Aircraft Unlimited, Inc.
1845 Stinson Blvd, N.E., Suite 213
Minneapolis, Minn. 55418
Eugene Comfort

S. A. Aviation Centre (PTY) Ltd.
P O Box 33191
Jeddedtown Transaal 2043
South Africa

The Cloudman Glidercraft Co.
905 Church Street
Nashville, Tenn. 37203
John Burkhalter

Aerolab
P O Box 4168
Milwaukee, Wisc. 53210
Mark Hays

Aero-Glider Airfoil Co.
P O Box 4108
Hamden, Conn. 06514
Martin R. Goldfarb

The Hangliding Store
Ridge Road R.D. No. 1, Box 57
Marlboro, N.Y. 12542
Dan Chapman

Hang Gliders Northwest
312 N.E. 84th
Portland, Ore. 97220
John Ford

Wings West, Delta Wing Kites, Inc.
2608 N.E. 62nd
Seattle, Washington 98115
Dick Boone

S & F Tool Co.
P O Box 1546
Costa Mesa, Calif. 92626
Frank Shaffer

Sky Sails, Inc.
3432 Dalworth
Arlington, Tex. 76011
Ted Winberg

Skysails, Inc.
1110 East Pike
Seattle, Wash. 98122
Bill Fundy

Emerald Pacific Co.
P O Box 5080
Eugene, Ore. 97405
John Foster

Albatross Sails
11545 Sorrento Valley Road
No. 304
San Diego, Calif. 92121
Tom Price

HMA CERTIFICATION SHEET

MANUFACTURER_____

DATE____/____/____

NAME OF MANUFACTURER'S REPRESENTATIVE
SUBMITTING GLIDER_____

HMA REPRESENTATIVES RECEIVING GLIDER

MANUFACTURER'S REPRESENTATIVE WHO WILL FLY
GLIDER_____

1._____

2._____

PFA MEMBER  YES /_7  NO /_7

3._____

MANUFACTURER'S ADDRESS_____

GLIDER NAME_____AIR FRAME SIZE_____AIR FRAME SAIL AREA_____

APEX ANGLE AT NOSE_____SERIAL NUMBER OF GLIDER_____

IS THIS GLIDER SUITABLE FOR PRONE?_____SEATED?_____BOTH?_____

HEAVIEST FLIER RECOMMENDED BY MFR. LBS-KGS_____

LIGHTEST FLIER RECOMMENDED BY MFR. LBS-KGS_____

(1)  KEELSPAR

    LENGTH_____DIAMETER & WALL THICKNESS_____MATERIAL_____

    SLEEVE  YES /_7  NO /_7  LENGTH & WALL THICKNESS_____MATERIAL_____

    DOWELING  YES /_7  NO /_7  LENGTH & POSITIONS - NOSE_____CG POINT_____TAIL_____

    BUSHING  YES /_7  NO /_7  POSITION - NOSE_____CG POINT_____TAIL_____

        BUSHING MATERIAL_____FLARED?  YES /_7  NO /_7

    SPECIAL FEATURES_____

_____

(2)  WINGSPAR

    LENGTH_____DIAMETER & WALL THICKNESS_____MATERIAL_____

    SLEEVE  YES /_7  NO /_7  LENGTH & WALL THICKNESS_____MATERIAL_____

    DOWELING  YES /_7  NO /_7  LENGTH & POSITIONS - NOSE_____WING JOINT_____

    BUSHING  YES /_7  NO /_7  POSITION_____

        BUSHING MATERIAL_____FLARED?  YES /_7  NO /_7

    SPECIAL FEATURES_____

_____

_____

_____

(3)  CROSSPAR

    DIAMETER & WALL THICKNESS_____MATERIAL_____

    SLEEVE  YES /_7  NO /_7  LENGTH & WALL THICKNESS_____MATERIAL_____

    DOWELING  YES /_7  NO /_7  LENGTH & POSITION_____

    BUSHING  YES /_7  NO /_7  POSITION_____SPLIT?  YES /_7  NO /_7

        BUSHING MATERIAL_____FLARED?  YES /_7  NO /_7

    SPECIAL FEATURES_____

417

(4) A.  NOSEPLATE - MATERIAL_____DESCRIPTION_____PHOTO:  APPX. "A"

B.  NOSEPLATE FASTENERS - SIZE, GRADE, & NUMBER_____

(5) HEART ASSY. FASTENERS - SIZE & GRADE_____PHOTO:  APPX. "B"

(6) CONTROL BAR MOUNT BRACKET

MATERIAL_____WALL THICKNESS_____PHOTO:  APPX. "C"

SPECIAL FEATURES_____

_____

(7) KING POST ASSEMBLY

KING POST LENGTH_____DIAMETER_____WALL THICKNESS_____

MATERIAL_____METHOD OF LOCATING LANDING WIRES AT TOP OF MAST_____

SPECIAL FEATURES_____

_____

(8) CONTROL BAR

OVERALL HEIGHT_____

OVERALL WIDTH_____

HOW MANY SECTIONS_____

DOWNTUBE DIAMETER_____WALL THICKNESS_____MATERIAL_____

BASETUBE DIAMETER_____WALL THICKNESS_____MATERIAL_____

FASTENERS_____

HOW FAR ABOVE LOWEST PORTION OF BASETUBE DO FLYING WIRES ATTACH?_____

REINFORCEMENT AT ATTACHMENT POINT OF FLYING WIRES?_____

TOTAL WEIGHT SUPPORTED BY BASETUBE BEFORE DEFORMATION_____
(Must support 750 pounds.  Wt. may be distributed 9" on either side of center of
basetube)

SPECIAL FEATURES_____

_____

(9) FLYING WIRES

A. FRONT CABLES - SEPARATE OR SINGLE ATTACHMENT TO NOSEPLATE_____

MATERIAL_____SIZE____STRANDING_____TEST_____

COATED_____CLEAR_____OPAQUE_____

METHOD OF ATTACHMENT - NOSEPLATE _____CONTROL BAR_____

THIMBLES AT ALL LOOPED ENDS?_____

B. REAR CABLES - SEPARATE OR SINGLE ATTACHMENT_____

MATERIAL_____SIZE____STRANDING_____TEST_____

COATED_____CLEAR_____OPAQUE_____

METHOD OF ATTACHMENT - KEELSPAR_____CONTROL BAR_____

THIMBLES AT ALL LOOPED ENDS?_____

418

C. SIDE CABLES - MATERIAL_____ SIZE_____ STRANDING_____ TEST_____

COATED_____ CLEAR_____ OPAQUE_____

METHOD OF ATTACHMENT - CROSSPAR_____ CONTROL BAR_____

THIMBLES AT ALL LOOPED ENDS?_____

.SPECIAL FEATURES_____

_____


(10) RIGGING

ARE FLYING & LANDING WIRES TENSIONED AFTER ASSEMBLY?_____

METHOD OF TENSIONING - TURNBUCKLE, KING POST, ETC._____

HAS TENSIONING DEVICE BEEN TESTED TO THREE TIMES CABLE STRENGTH?_____

DATA ATTACHED?_____


KEELSPAR:

KEEL REFLEX BEHIND C.G. POINT? YES /‾/ NO /‾/   POS /‾/ NEG /‾/   MAX."___MIN."__

METHOD OF INDUCING REFLEX: MECHANICALLY BENT, FLYING WIRE, CABLE TENSION

DEVICE, ETC._____

HAS REFLEX INDUCING HARDWARE BEEN TESTED TO THREE TIMES CABLE STRENGTH?_____

DATA ATTACHED?_____

KEEL REFLEX AHEAD OF C.G. POINT? YES /‾/ NO /‾/ POS /‾/ NEG /‾/ MAX."___MIN."____

METHOD OF INDUCING REFLEX: MECHANICALLY BENT, FLYING WIRE, CABLE TENSION

DEVICE, ETC._____

HAS REFLEX INDUCING HARDWARE BEEN TESTED TO THREE TIMES CABLE STRENGTH?_____

DATA ATTACHED?_____

WING SPAR:

SPECIAL RIGGING TO CONTROL WING SPAR SHAPE?_____

METHOD OF INDUCING OR CHANGING SHAPE?_____ PHOTO APPX. "WS"

CROSSPAR:

SPECIAL RIGGING TO CONTROL CROSSPAR SHAPE?_____

METHOD OF INDUCING OR CONTROLLING SHAPE OF CROSSPAR_____

PHOTO APPX. "CS"

HAS A PROFESSIONAL STRUCTURAL ANALYSIS OF YOUR GLIDER DESIGN BEEN PERFORMED BY A

RECOGNIZED STRUCTURAL ANALYSIST? YES /‾/ NO /‾/ APPENDIX "S" DATA

WHAT STATIC LEAD TESTS HAVE BEEN PERFORMED ON TAIL AIR FRAME:_____

_____

**419**

## APPENDIX C
## USHGA HANG RATING PROGRAM

Remember, the hang rating program is based on witnessed tasks and it is not a system of awards. Some may seem to require excessive precision or attention to details, but the practice preparing for them will prove beneficial. Remember also, it is up to a local site to decide who flies there. A pilot may fly a hill if the local people feel that he is capable of it. The Hang Rating is to introduce pilots at strange sites. Think of it this way: a non-rated beginner has to fly a hill to learn, but there can't be less than a Hang One hill. However, the possession of a Hang One tells other sites that the pilot can set up his glider and generally get off the ground, but there is no assurance he can do more.

### HANG ONE

1. Unassisted takeoff: Just that—no keel push. Shouldn't jump onto the glider.

2. Safe, straight flight:
    A. Minor corrections in flight so that pilot lands into wind on his feet.
    B. Should control the airspeed without undue over-control.
3. Knows material in "Guide to Rogallo Flight—Basic", excluding turns. The observer should be convinced that the pilot understands it.
4. Flys beginner hills in gentle conditions with a ground clearance of up to 20 feet.
5. Should feel confident that he can fly another beginner hill without causing troubles for others.
6. Should be able to set up and check his own glider.

## HANG TWO

1. Planned flight paths with "S" turns of at least 90 degrees azimuth over points preselected by the pilot. These must be alternating turns and should be smooth and without very much speed change. The pilot should never have to roll out of a turn because of either too much or too little airspeed.
2. Landing within 40 feet of a spot.
3. Ground clearance of at least 40 feet.
4. Flight in smooth winds to 18 mph, gusty to 11 mph.
5. Knows all material in "Guide to Rogallo Flight—Basic."

## HANG THREE

1. Must have held Hang Two Rating for at least two months and have at least 30 flying days and a total of at least 90 flights. For applicants with 200 hours of flight experience in other aircraft these time and flight requirements may be waived upon endorsement of two observers, one of whom must be a qualified instructor. However, in no case may the time be less than one month or less than 30 flights.
2. Demonstrates precison gentle and steep linked 180° "S" turns along an applicant predetermined track.
3. Three spot landings in a row must be within 30 feet apart.

4. Depending on the terrain, the pilot will fly what is considered a standard task for the site to provide assurance that he differentiates between airspeed and groundspeed, as well as between flight path and ground track.
5. Demonstrates precise 180° entry turns as follows:

   A. These are 180° turns which are entered from a slight dive.
   B. A given turn rate is established and held.
   C. The airspeed is reduced at a constant rate throughout the turn so that, as the glider is rolled to level at the 180° mark, the airspeed is approximately that of minimum sink.
   D. The bank angle should be smoothly reduced throughout the turn so that, as the airspeed drops, the turn rate is constant.
   E. No stall should be evident.
   F. The maneuver should be witnessed in both directions.
   G. The entire demonstration should leave no doubts in the mind of the observer.
6. Pass oral quiz which will be published with answers in *Ground Skimmer*.
7. Ground clearance of 75 feet in at least ten flights.
8. It will not be assumed that a Hang Three pilot has flown in smooth winds greater than 20 mph or mildly gusty winds greater than 15 mph.

## HANG FOUR

1. Must hold a Hang Three Rating for at least four months during which he will have made at least 60 one-minute flights. Pilot must make five flights at each of five different Hang Three sites of which at least three will have been inland.
2. Must make five 5-minute flights.
3. Must soar above a low point for at least five minutes on three different flights.
4. Ground clearance of at least 250 feet on five different flights.

5. Demonstrates figure eights:

    A. The pilot will choose two points which are across the wind. The wind must be sufficient to cause definite ground drift. The pilot will fly towards the midpoint between the pylons; at the proper time he will turn across the wind to enter the figure eight with an upwind turn. The crosswind leg is used to help establish ground drift information.

    B. The turns in the eight will be gentle to medium as required to fly the turns so that they describe a constant radius ground track around the pylons.

    C. The turns must be altered smoothly as they are flown around the pylons.

    D. The cross in the eight should consist of straight line segments which should be entered confidently and require only very minor corrections for drift changes so that the entry to the second turn of the eight is at the same radius as the other turn.

    E. The important points to consider are precision of correction for wind drift and the smoothness shown while turning.

    F. Height will reduce the accuracy possible in judging distance around the turn and should be allowed for, both from the point of view of the pilot and observer.

6. Must demonstrate three consecutive landings within 20 feet of a spot after flights of at least one minute.

7. Must fly over an imaginary 15 foot high barrier and land no more than 30 feet past the barrier and within ten feet of a center line.

8. Must pass oral quiz.

9. The log available as part of the rating card may be used to substantiate portions of these tasks as they are individually signed by an observer.

## HANG FIVE

After possessing a Hang Four for at least one year and after having been witnessed for all the special skills, a pilot may receive a Hang Five Rating. The rating will indicate that the pilot is skilled and has indicated the maturity and judgement to act prudently so as to not be a hazard to himself or the sites which he visits.

## SPECIAL SKILLS

(Allowed with Hang Three and Four—not to be witnessed until pilot holds a Hang Three at least 2 months.)

1. Turbulence: Controlled and unpanicked flight in conditions resulting in multiple sail inversions and requiring quick, deliberate, correct, and substantial control applications.
2. High Altitude:

   A. Flights in which terrain clearance exceeds at least 1,000 feet for at least three minutes.
   B. During such altitude conditions, 720-degree turns are accomplished in both directions.
   C. The pilot will have flown flights of over ten minutes.
   D. Balloon-launched flights over flat terrain are not to be used as evidence for this skill.
3. Cliff Launches (2 categories):

   A. Cliffs to be precipitous and over 100 feet high.
   B. Launches must be either:

      i. Unassisted in near-calm conditions, or
      ii. Assisted in windy conditions with strong lift right at takeoff.
4. Cross Country:

   A. Demonstrated ability to recognize landing areas previously visited on the ground, but not visible at take off or during the first few minutes of flight.
   B. Must be able to determine wind direction from natural sources while in flight.
   C. Must be able to set up conservative planned approaches to strange landing areas allowing for possible surprises.
   D. Must be able to explain various means of determining possible locations of wires, fences, poles, etc.
   E. Must be able to discuss wind and lift in various regions such as canyons.

F. Must be able to explain the correct use of airspeed in striving for maximum distance traveled over the ground in various conditions of wind and lift or sink.

5. 360° Turns: The following forms of the 360 must be witnessed:

   A. Basic 360°:
      i. Left and right; gentle and steep.
      ii. Precise pitch and lateral control must be witnessed. Just "banking and cranking" will not suffice.
   B. Enter turn so flown as to be a 360° instead of a 180°. The turn should be entered from a crosswind leg so that the first portion is downwind.
   C. Enter turn that begins at minimum sink airspeed, smoothly increase airspeed, maintaining maximum safe turning rate, so that at the 180° mark the airspeed is near the maximum L/D airspeed or slightly greater. Maintain this airspeed and maximum safe turning rate to completion. The roll out should not exhibit marked pitch up.
   D. Enter turn that must have at least maximum L/D airspeed to a medium bank. At the 90° mark, decisively roll to a maximum safe turn rate without pitching obviously up or down. Resume the original bank and turn rate at the 270° mark until completion of 360°. Each demonstration will be to the left and right without noticeable slipping or skidding.

NOTE:

A significant cost will be involved in the Hang Rating System because of printing, clerical work and mail. Hang One and Two will be a problem of the schools and instructors, so any fee will be up to them. The cards will be supplied as a service by the USHGA. For Hang Three and Four Ratings, as well as for the special skills, there will be a fee of $1.00 for each card mailed. For non-USHGA members, the fee will be $2.00. There will be no fee in the case of Hang Five.

Observers will issue temporary slips to pilots earning Hang Three and Four Ratings. The observer will keep a copy and send one to USHGA which in turn will mail the pilot his permanent card.

## APPENDIX D
## USHGA CHAPTERS (CLUB ORGANIZATION)

To implement the affiliation article of the USHGA bylaws, the USHGA Board of Directors has made provision for USHGA Chapters. The object is to encourage a close relationship between the national association and the various hang gliding clubs and regional organizations, in order to maximize the distribution of safety information and news, and promote the growth of the activity.

Chapters are those member-controlled organizations approved by USHGA which maintain a certain percentage of their members as USHGA members. The percentage is the same as that required to amend the organization's bylaws, but not less than 50%.

Chapters remain autonomous organizations, financially independent from USHGA, and self-governing.

To minimize administrative matters, USHGA dues for members of Chapters will ordinarily be paid on an individual basis directly to USHGA, although the Chapter may collect and submit them for new members to help insure that the membership percentage requirement is met. Renewal dues will be solicited by USHGA directly from the members. Chapters must submit rosters of their members to USHGA twice each year, in June and December, so they may be checked for conformity to the membership percentage requirement. If the percentage falls below the requirement, the Chapter will be advised and allowed a month to have more of their members join USHGA to correct the situation. A list of Chapters will be published in *Hang Gliding* from time to time, showing the number of members in each and percentage of USHGA members.

Initial tangible benefits of USHGA Chapter status are as follows:

1. Insurance. USGHA members of Chapters may purchase liability insurance to cover their hang glider flying, through a special program developed with Trident Insurance Services, 315 Montgomery Street, #1120, San Francisco, Calif. 94104. The premium is $8.50 per year for $300,000 single-limit coverage. Application for this insurance must be made directly with Trident.
2. The Chapter is given a subscription to *Ground Skimmer* for its library or to use for promotional purposes.
3. Chapters may purchase addressed mailing labels for USHGA members for any area of the U.S. desired, for only 1¢ each (minimum order must be for 100, or $1.00).
4. Chapters will receive preferential news coverage in *Hang Gliding* and be specially noted in USHGA lists of hang gliding organizations.
5. Chapters may purchase designated items that USHGA sells, at special discount prices, in minimum quantities.

Other tangible benefits will be added as they are developed. Intangible benefits are numerous and, being subjective, depend on the person considering them; however, most significant is the effectiveness that results from the unity of a large Chapter membership. The more enthusiasts and organizations that support USHGA, the more USHGA will be able to do for them.

Application for USHGA Chapter status should be made by letter from an officer of the organization, indicating intent to maintain the Chapter qualification requirement. The letter should also give the address to which the Chapter's subscription to *Hang Gliding* should be mailed, and be accompanied by three items:

1. A roster of the names and addresses of all members of the organization. (If known, indicate which are USHGA members and give their membership numbers.)
2. A copy of the organization bylaws.
3. A copy of the organization's membership application form (it is recommended that it have a space for the applicant's USHGA membership number).

Approval of Chapter applications will be by letter after qualifications has been confirmed.


## USHGA SANCTION REQUIREMENTS FOR HANG GLIDING MEETS

The following are the conditions required for a hang gliding contest (other than the National Championships) to be sanctioned by USHGA. They represent minimum standards established by the USHGA Directors to help ensure safe, fair competitions for the best interests of hang gliding and the pilots concerned.

1. Pilots will be required to wear protective headgear.
2. An ambulance must be in the landing areas during all official flying. If only one ambulance is provided and it is used on an emergency run, then flying must cease until it returns.
3. Minimum USHGA Hang Rating requirements for all entrants must be set by representatives of the sponsors who are at least USHGA Hang 4 pilots themselves.

4. Two copies of the proposed rules for the contest must be submitted to USHGA Contest Committee at least 90 days prior to the contest. The rules must not contain any maneuvers or tasks that are inherently hazardous.
5. A written report and score table for all contests must be submitted to USHGA within a month after the close of the event, to provide information for publication in *Ground Skimmer* magazine and for the Association's permanent files.
6. The sanction fee for hang gliding contests other than the National Championships has been set at $150.00. The fee should accompany a short letter applying for sanction which indicates that the conditions of sanction (USHGA Item #9, 7/75 edition) are understood and will be adhered to, signed by a representative of the sponsor.
7. Champions declared in USHGA-sanctioned events will be recognized by USHGA and published as such in *Hang Gliding*.
8. Top-scoring participants in USHGA-sanctioned Regional Hang Gliding Championships conducted according to standards established by the USHGA Contest Committee will be qualified to enter the subsequent year's National Championships without further demonstration of ability.

## STANDARD ROGALLO CLASS

1. Purpose: To provide a class of flexible-wing hang gliders of comparable performance controlled by weight shift only, which can be flown safely by inexperienced pilots.
2. Airworthiness: The hang glider must conform to the structural requirements established by the Hang Glider Manufacturers Association (HMA).
3. Obligatory Requirements:

   A. Nose Angle. The nose angle of the leading-edge tubes shall not exceed 90°.
   B. Tubes. There will be 4 structural tubes only (2 leading edge tubes, 1 keel tube and 1 cross tube). Tubes shall be circular in cross section with parallel walls and straight throughout their total length. No preformed curvature of tubes is permitted.

C. Bracing. Bracing cables must run from the extremities of the keel and cross tube to a king post on top and a control bar below. No additional bracing arrangements are permitted, such as leading edge tensioners or deflexers.

D. Sail. The sail must be continuous, without openings or divisions. The billow of the sail shall not be less than 3.5° per side (nose angle of sail laid flat, in excess of leading edge/keel angle). The trailing edge of the sail must be unsupported and untethered, and may not be roached forward of a line from wing tip to wing tip.

E. Battens. Flat battens of constant cross section that do not exceed half the sail chord in length are permitted. They must be removable and aligned between radial and parallel to the keel. The may not be preformed.

F. Ratio of Leading Edge to Keel. The ratio of leading edge-to-keel sail length must not exceed plus or minus 10%.

G. Wing Loading. The minimum wing loading shall be 0.9 lb/sq ft in flying trim with pilot. If necessary, ballast must be added to correct.

H. Reflex. There must be no less than 1″ positive reflex in the keel. The airframe must be non-adjustable except for CG trim devices.

I. Additional Surfaces. There shall be no external-stabilizing devices other than dive-recovery devices.

J. Permitted. Streamlining of cross tube, control frame and king post of no more than 4 to 1 fineness ratio, landing wheels, sail windows, seat or prone harness, variometer, airspeed indicator, altimeter.

K. Prohibited. Aerodynamic controls, capsule or partial capsule fairing of the pilot.

L. Manufacturers. Specifications and measurement data for production models should be submitted to USHGA for its files.

M. Conformity Check. All gliders are subject to a conformity check prior to and after competition.

## SELF-LAUNCH OPEN CLASS

Any type of hang glider capable of being folded up and carried to the launch site by the pilot only. Must be foot-launched without assistance.

## OPEN CLASS

Any type of hang glider capable of being foot-launched with help from no more than one assistant, and landed using the pilot's legs. May be taken to launch site by any means.

## RECOMMENDED SAFETY
## PARAMETERS FOR OPERATION OF HANG GLIDERS

Department of Transportation, Federal Aviation Administration Advisory Circular, AC NO: 60-10

1. **Purpose.** Since the sport of "hang gliding" or "sky sailing" has become popular, numerous questions have arisen as to the FAA position on the regulation and operation of these vehicles. The purpose of this Advisory Circular is to suggest safety parameters for the operation of "hang gliders" and to present the current FAA intent with respect to the regulation and operation of those vehicles.

2. **Definition.** For purposes of this Advisory Circular, "hang glider" means an unpowered, single place vehicle whose launch and landing capability depends entirely on the legs of the occupant and whose ability to remain in flight is generated by natural air currents only.

3. Background. There has been a recent revival of popular interest in the almost forgotten art of powerless flight. This is now being accomplished by very light vehicles that are self-launched and unpowered. The sport is referred to as "hang gliding" or "sky sailing." New materials, modern construction techniques, improved knowledge of stability and control requirements, and imaginative configurations have all been applied. Coupled with low cost and an aviation adventure that has attracted both young and old, this increasingly popular sport is expected to grow dramatically in the near future. The revival of early Lilienthal days is being conducted primarily in open unpopulated areas where favorable wind conditions exist and terrain features provide an acceptable glide ratio clearance. The glide ratio of most of these vehicles is 4 to 1 or less. In a few instances, a higher glide ratio has been obtained through a hard wing construction; however, they still retain the feature of being self-launched and landed. Several corporations have been formed to manufacture these craft, along with a manufacturer's association that intends to provide minimum materials criteria to ensure safe construction. Numerous clubs have been formed, and many more may be formed in the future, which will provide safety guidance through both operational control and educational media.

4. Regulatory Information. The FAA is interested in this activity, but at this time does not have sufficient data and information with respect to "hang glider" design and operational capabilities to make any determination as to the need for new specific action. It is the FAA's intent to observe the growth and safety status of this activity as it progresses and to continually assess the need for FAA involvement. The following, however are certain regulatory areas of which "hang glider" operators should take cognizance:

   a. Federal Aviation Regulations, Part 101. Part 101 specifies rules applicable to kite operations. Those rules are applicable to any vehicle intended to be flown at the end of a rope, having as its only means of support the force of the wind moving past its surfaces, and that is not capable of sustained flight when released from its tether. No person should operate a "hang glider" at the end of a surface towline without first becoming fully familiar with Part 101.

b. Federal Aviation Regulations, Sections 91.17 and 91.18. Section 91.17 provides rules applicable to the towing by an aircraft of gliders as that term is defined in FAR Part 1. Section 91.18 (a) provides, in part, that no pilot of a civil aircraft (other than under 91.17) shall operate except in accordance with the terms of a certificate of waiver issued by the Administrator.

5. Safety Suggestions. The following guidelines are suggested for the use of all participants in "hang gliding," manufacturers of "hang gliders" and operating clubs:

a. Suggestions relating to operation of the vehicle:

(1) Limit altitude to 500 feet above the general terrain. It must be remembered, however, that there are certain aircraft operations conducted below 500 feet above the terrain and "hang glider" operators should be alert to this.

(2) Do not fly them within controlled airspace, specifically a control zone, airport traffic area, or within five miles of the boundary of an uncontrolled airport unless authorized by airport authorities.

(3) Do not fly them within any prohibited or restricted area without prior permission from the controlling or using agency, as appropriate.

(4) Do not fly them within 100 feet horizontally of, or at any altitude over, buildings, populated places, or assemblages of persons.

(5) Remain clear of clouds.

(6) Questions regarding operations in conflict with the above recommended safety parameters should be discussed with the nearest FAA district office.

b. Suggestions to manufacturers and clubs.

(1) Develop criteria and construction techniques. (It is recommended that aircraft quality hardware and materials be utilized in construction as appropriate.)

(2) Ensure that adequate quality control procedures are utilized during manufacture of the vehicle.

(3) Pay particular attention to ensure that a good training program is established. (The United States Hang Glider Association can be helpful in this area.) Students should be taught early to recognize their individual limitations as well as the limitations of the "hang glider."

(4) Provide adequate instructions in "do-it-yourself" kits so that proper hardware is utilized and good construction techniques are employed.

(5) Coordinate with local municipalities and property owners for recognized flying sites.

(6) Establish strong safety programs and distribute safety related materials to clubs, associations, and operators of "hang gliders".

(7) Develop close coordination with the Federal Aviation Administration.

(8) Operators of "hang gliders" should be encouraged to wear protective clothing, including a helmet.

6. Conclusion. The Federal Aviation Administration is willing to devote time and effort, within reason, to assist manufacturers and clubs during this developmental period. District offices are encouraged to work with manufacturers and clubs so that the sport is conducted in a safe manner. Safety related materials developed by clubs and manufacturer' associations

will be disseminated to all regions as it is developed. Appropriate material coming to the attention of field offices should be forwarded to headquarters as well as related safety information developed by local FAA personnel. The "hang glider" community should, on the other hand, make a vigorous effort to develop safety criteria and instructions usable in the manufacture and operation of "hang gliders".

7. Distribution. This Advisory Circular should be given the widest distribution possible by district offices to ensure that all persons interested in this activity are aware of the information contained in this document.

signed: James F. Rudolph
Director, Flight Standards Service

# ACCIDENT REPORT FORM

Complete and forward to USHGA, P.O. Box 66306, Los Angeles, CA 90066, immediately.

Date of Accident_____     Flyer's Name_____

Place of Accident_____     Flyer's Address_____

_____     _____
<u>Nearest City          State</u>                    City        and        State
Height of Hill_____                       _____
Time of Accident_____A.M. _____P.M.            AGE            Phone Number
Individuals who actually witnessed the         Weather Conditions_____
flight and/or impact (include address and                          (Clear, fog, haze,...)
phone number):_____      Wind speed estimate_____mph
_____      Gusty?_____Steady?_____
_____      Wind direction vs. flight direction:
_____            Directly into wind?_____
                                                     Cross wind angle?_____

Experience of the flyer having accident_____
                                           (months, years, or # of flights) Badge rating?
Type of kite flown_____
                         (Manufacturer)                (Keel length or type)
Type of suspension gear:  Seat only_____  Prone harness_____  Combination_____

Protective gear worn by flyer:  Helmet_____  Boots_____  Gloves_____  Other_____

Condition of kite after accident:  Total wreck_____  Bent or broken leading edge_____
                                   Bent or broken control bar_____
                                   Torn sail_____  Bent keel_____  Other_____

Injuries:  Fatal_____  Non-fatal_____
           Hospitalized overnight?  Yes_____     No_____
           Head_____  Back_____  Legs_____  Arms_____  Other_____
           Describe apparent injuries_____
           _____
           _____

Describe flight and apparent cause of accident_____

_____

Other members of flying party who did not witness the accident itself (include address &
phone number):

_____
_____

Photographs taken by anyone at scene?  Yes____  No____  If so, by whom? _____
Who has kite remains?_____

SUPPLY ANY OTHER PERTINENT INFORMATION ON REVERSE.
Please attach newspaper clippings or other data pertaining to accident.
Date of this report:_____     Name of Reporter_____
                                              Flying Experience_____
ITEM #15 (12/74)                                       (mos., yrs., # flights)

**440**

# APPENDIX G
## SOURCES FOR ULTRALIGHT GLIDERS, ORGANIZATIONS, AND PUBLICATIONS

Compiled and Published by the United States Hang Gliding Assn., Inc., Box 66306, Los Angeles, Calif. 90066, phone (213) 390-3065. Additions and corrections are solicited. This list is of, to the best of USHGA's knowledge, the sources for ultralight gliders, organizations, and publications in the region defined below. There are many other manufacturers, many of which advertise in USHGA's publication, *Hang Gliding*, for those who desire to shop for hang gliders nationally. For sources in other areas, write or phone USHGA, specifying states desired. Items listed below are in zip order.

## REGION ONE

### Manufacturers

**Crown Enterprises**, c/o Jerry Sanderson, 40 E Idaho St., Kalispell, Mt. 59901   (406) 756-9377

**Freedom Wings**, c/o Mike Mylnar, Box 201, Ketchum, Id. 83340 (208) 726-5835

**Glider Sports International**, 2045 SE Hawthorne Blvd., Portland, Or. 97214

**Beamways Flying Machines**, Box 22524, Milwaukie, Or. 97222 (503) 654-8530

**Sailbird of Oregon**, c/o David Miller, 829 NE Imperial, Portland, Or. 97232

**Jobe Wings, Mfg.**, 2844 W Lake Sammamish Rd NE, Redmond, Wa. 98052 (206) 885-5539

**Free Flight Dynamics**, 1915 Island View Pl., Anacortes, Wa. 98221 (206) 273-7202

**Dealers And Schools**

**Free Flight of Moorhead**, The Escape Hatch, 1815 N 11th St., Moorhead, Mt. 56560

**Free Flight of Montana**, 221 Jackson St., Billings, Mt. 59101 248-6717

**George V. Nilson, NFT Inc.**, Box 2367, Great Falls, Mt. 59103 (406) 453-5183

**Free Flight of Poplar**, Box 35, Poplar, Mt. 59255

**Jack Olson**, Box 1139, Great Falls, Mt. 59403 (406) 453-4377

**Free Flight of Helena**, 718 Broadway, Helena, Mt. 59601

**Big Sky Delta Wing Kites**, 201 E Central, Missoula, Mt. 59801

**Hanger Nine**, c/o Jay Raser, RT 2, Mullan Rd, Missoula, Mt. 59801

**Upward Bound**, Box 2009, Missoula, Mt. 59801 (406) 549-5076

**Upward Bound South**, 110 N 2nd Ave, Pocatello, Id. 83201 (208) 233-8127

**Free Flight of Twin Falls**, 259 Main Ave E, Twin Falls, Id. 83301

**Chandelle of Idaho**, Box 1221, Sun Valley, Id. 83353

**Sun Valley Kite School**, Box 781, Sun Valley, Id. 83353 (208) 622-3511

**Soaring Sports**, Box 2764, Idaho Falls, Id. 83401 (208) 523-1677

**Free Flight of Caldwell**, Rt 3, Caldwell, Id. 83605

**Hang Glider Shop**, 2901 State St., Boise, Id. 83702 (208) 342-9549

**Mike Hester**, 3051 Rowland Ln., Boise, Id. 83703

**Millers Marina & Pro Shop**, 1710 S Roosevelt St., Boise, Id. 83705 (208) 343-2830

**Pegasus Aeronautics**, 636-5 Ave, Lewiston, Id. 85501 (208) 743-8341

**Aeron Indtr.**, 9985 SE Eastmont Dr., Gresham, Or. 97030 (503) 665-8560

**Delta Wing Gliders of Mt Hood**, 2604 NE 61 Ave, Portland, Or. 97213 (503) 281-1484

**Hawk of Oregon**, c/o Lynn Sanders, 2270 SE 39th, Portland, Or. 97214

**Hang Gliders Northwest**, c/o John Ford, 312 NE 84 St, Portland, Or. 97220 (503) 253-6631

**Ben Franklin's Kite Shop**, 11430 SE Reedway, Portland, Or. 97266 (503) 771-3147

**Pacific Hang Gliders**, 1729 La Bona Dr, Eugene, Or. 97401 (503) 484-9900

**Rex Miller**, 634-A E 8 Ave, Eugene, Or. 97403

**Oregon Manta**, 350 W 4th Ave, Eugene, Or. 97403

**Southern Oregon Manta**, Box 37, Phoenix, Or. 97535 (503) 535-2396

**Cascade Free Flight**, Box 176, Duvall, Wa. 98010 (206) 788-1002

**Hawk of Seattle**, c/o Mike Peterson, 26-21st Pl, Kirkland, Wa. 98033

**Pacific Northwest Hang Gliding Sch**, 10831 NE 112 Ave, Kirkland, Wa. 98033

**Chandelle Northwest**, 77 Madison St, Seattle, Wa. 98104 (206) 682-4655

**H & H Water Sports, Inc**, 1006 S 198 Pl, Seattle, Wa. 98148 (206) 824-2668

**Region** #1-Alaska, Idaho, Montana, Oregon, and Washington

**Bruce Barr**, 17360 Beach Dr NE, Seattle, Wa. 98155 (206) 363-0900

**J-Bird Hang Gliders**, Rt 5, Box 234-A, SP 2, Arlington, Wa. 98223

Fairhaven Kite Co, 1200 Harris St, Bellingham, Wa. 98225

Delta Wing Kites, Inc, 20928 133 St SE, Monroe, Wa. 98272 (206) 794-6540

Hang In There Baby, c/o Derco, Box 11, Keyport, Wa. 98345

Jerry Bain, 309 N 19 St. Kelso, Wa. 98626 (206) 425-5211

Wright Flight, 126 E Peter's St, Wenatchee, Wa. 98801

Sport Flight, N 4922 Market, Spokane, Wa. 99207 (509) 487-5676

Sport Kites Spokane, c/o Bob Bird, Box 7400, Spokane, Wa. 99207

George Gregor, 1425 Marshall, Richland, Wa. 99325 (509) 943-3951

Gary King, Jr., 308 E Northern Lights Blvd, Anchorage, Ak. 99503

Two Wheel Taxi & Ski Shop, 2917 Spenard Rd, Anchorage, Ak. 99503 (907) 272-4431

Klean Fun Kites, Box 4-2990, Anchorage, Ak. 99509 (907) 274-4120

Falcon Air, 4049 Mallard, Fairbanks, Ak. 99701

## Organizations

Missoula Hang Glider Assn, 444 Stevens #1, Missoula, Mt. 59801

Oregon Hang Glider Assn, Box 3815, Portland, Or. 97208

Pacific Northwest Hang Glider Assn, c/o Vern Roundtree, 30003 112th SE, Auburn, Wa. 98002

Robert Lockhart, 604 N 20 Ave, Yakima, Wa. 98902

Inland Empire Hang Gliders, c/o Conrad Agte, E 3904 Courtland, Spokane, Wa. 99207

Eastern Washington Hang Gliding Assn, c/o George Gregor, 1425 Marshall, Richland, Wa. 99352

Alaska Sky Sailors, Box 78, Palmer, Ak. 99045

## Publications

OHGA Newsletter ($5/Yr), Box 3815, Portland, Or. 97208

Pacific Northwestern Hang Glider Assn.; Newsletter, c/o Vern Roundtree, 30003 112 SE, Auburn, Wa. 98002

Ragwings Newsletter, c/o Conrad Agte, Inland Empire Hang Gliders Assn., E 3904 Courtland, Spokane, Wa. 99207

## Sources For Ultralight Hang Gliders, Organizations, And Publications

### REGION TWO

## Manufacturers

**J. L. Enterprises**, Box 802, Belmont, Ca. 94002  345-5935

**Phantom Wing Inc.**, 110 2nd Ave S, Pacheco, Ca. 94553  (415) 798-7350

**Manta Products**, 1647 E 14 St, Oakland, Ca. 94606  (415) 536-1500

**Ultralight Flying Machines**, Box 59, Cupertino, Ca. 95014

**True Flight**, 1719 Hillsdale Ave, San Jose, Ca. 95142

## Dealers And Schools

**Gull Wing Flight Sch**, Box 893, Morro Bay, Ca. 93442  (805) 772-3794

**Jim Green**, 3726 N Van Ness Blvd, Fresno, Ca. 93704  (209) 222-6025

**Tic Musser**, 2842 N Hacienda, Fresno, Ca. 93705  (209) 227-2282

**Chandelle Fresno**, c/o Alpine Shop, 4777 Blackstone, Fresno, Ca. 93726  (209) 299-9591

**Monarch Skysails**, 136 E Olive, Fresno, Ca. 93728

**Free Flight of Monterey Pen.**, 2201 Fremont Blvd, Monterey, Ca. 93904

**Seagull Soaring**, Box 5474, Carmel, Ca. 93921  (408) 394-3347

**Hawk of Monterey**, c/o Ed Holder, 880 Ocean St #D, Monterey, Ca. 93940

**Lee Gardener**, 2201 Fremont Blvd, Monterey, Ca. 93940

**Golden Gliders**, c/o Larry Wolf/training off., 451 Dela Vina Ave, Monterey, Ca. 93940

**Chandelle San Francisco**, 2123 Junipero Serra Blvd, Daly City, Ca. 94015  (415) 756-0650

**Come Fly a Kite**, 900 North Point, San Francisco, Ca. 94109

**Boat & Motor Mart**, 3250 Army St, San Francisco, Ca. 94110  (415) 824-3545

445

**Cyngus Sky School**, c/o Youmans, 3868 California St, #5, San Francisco, Ca. 94118

**Wings West**, 300 H Nimitz Dr, Yerba Buena, San Francisco, Ca. 94130

**Free Flight of Fresno**, Box 589, Fresno, Ca. 94509

**Sport Kites Pleasanton**, c/o Tom Drengacz, 1642 Harvest Rd, Pleasanton, Ca. 94566

**Hang Gliders West**, 906 Sir Francis Drake Rd, Kentfield, Ca. 94904   (415) 453-7664

**Northern Calif. Sun**, Box 1624, Sausalito, Ca. 94965   (415) 388-2923

**Angel Wing Kite Sales & Sch.**, 236 Santa Cruz Ave, Aptos, Ca. 95003   (408) 688-3045

**Aeolus Hang Gliders**, 529 Capitola Ave, Capitola, Ca. 95010

**Pacific Pantry**, c/o Mike Barcelo, 110 Cooper St, Santa Cruz, Ca. 95060

**Portola Surf Shop**, 1709 Portola Dr, Santa Cruz, Ca. 95060   (408) 475-9882

**Bill Johnson**, 2211 Vera Cruz, Modesto, Ca. 95350   (207) 521-5289

**Thunder Chicken Enterprises**, 1431 Angie, Modesto, Ca. 95351   (209) 537-8033

**Free Flight of Manteca**, 17810 Kram, Manteca, Ca. 95366

**Bruce Shade**, 4817 Forrectal St, Fair Oaks, Ca. 95628   (916) 961-1472

**Ron Rupp**, Homewood Resort, Box 165, Homewood, Ca. 95718   (916) 525-7256

**Tahoe Hang Glider Specialists**, Box 2366, Olympic Valley, Ca. 95730   (916) 583-2700

**Sacramento Valley Hang Gliders**, 3210 Bulmoral Dr, Sacramento, Ca. 95821   (916)  489-0476  967-9731  487-9003

**Free Flight Systems**, 125 Parmac Rd #17, Chico, Ca. 95926

**Dave Thomas**, Quiksilver Mtn, 1022 Mangrove, Chico, Ca. 95926

**Sail Wing Sky School North**, 2631-A Rancho Rd, Redding, Ca. 96001

**Region** #2-Northern California

**Halls Hawks Hang Glider Plans** (Only, 2446 Roosevelt, Berkeley, Ca. 94703   (415) 841-4508

## Accesories And Parts

**Dungar Sails**, c/o E.B. Dunbar, Grove St, Pier Bldg. A, Oakland, Ca. 94607

## Organizations

**Slo Soaring Assn**, c/o Dave Malis, Box 93, Avila Beach, Ca. 93424

**Fellow Feathers of San Francisco**, 2123 Junipero Serra Blvd, Daly City, Ca. 94015

**Wings of Rogallo**, 502 Barkentine Ln, Redwood City, Ca. 94065

**Sierra Hang Gliding Assn**, c/o Bob Russell, Box 443, Sutter Creek, Ca. 95685

## Publications

**Fellow Feathers**, Self-Launched Pilots Of San Francisco, 2123 Junipero Serra Blvd, Daly City, Ca. 94015

**Wings of Rogallo Newsletter**, 502 Barkentine Ln, Redwood City, Ca. 94065

## REGION THREE

## Manufacturers

**Ultralight Products**, 137 Oregon St, El Segundo, Ca. 90245   (213) 322-7171

**Seagull Aircraft**, 3021 Airport Ave, Santa Monica, Ca. 90405   (213) 394-1151

**Conquest Hang Gliders**,   554-0877

**Glider Kites**, 13836 Cornuta, Bellflower, Ca. 90706   (213) 866-4976

**Eipper-Formance Inc.**, Box 246-GS, Lomita, Ca. 90717   328-9100

**Velderrain Hang Gliders**, Box 314, Lomita, Ca. 90717   676-7214

**Cliffhanger**, 3603 Fairman St, Lakewood, Ca. 90712

**Sunbird Gliders**, 21420 Chase St 7B, Canoga Park, Ca. 91304 (213) 882-3177

**DSK Aircraft**, 11031 Glen Oaks, Ca. 91331 833-7393

**Free Flight Systems**, 12424 Gladstone Ave, Sylmar, Ca. 91342 (213)365-5607

**The Bird People**, Box 943, Sun Valley, Ca. 91352

**Delta Wing Kites**, Box 483, Van Nuys, Ca. 91408 (213) 785-2471

**Hang Gliders San Diego**, c/o Britt Reynolds, 4531 Mission Bay, San Diego, Ca. 92109

**Hawk Industries**, 8566 Sugarman Dr, La Jolla, Ca. 92137

**Volmer Aircraft**, Box 5222, Glendale, Ca. 92201 (213) 247-8718

**Solo Flight Inc.**, 1411 N Citrus Ave, Orange, Ca. 92667 (714) 538-9768 and 639-0331

**Pacific Gull**, 1321 Calle Valle #F, San Clemente, Ca. 92672

**Sports Kites, Inc.**, 1202-C E Walnut, Santa Ana, Ca. 92701 (714) 547-1344

## Dealers And Schools

**Flex-O-Kite Ski Co.**, c/o Floyd Music, 13618 Catalina Ave. Gardena, Ca. 90247

**Bird Builders**, 22225½ Pacific Coast Hwy, Malibu, Ca. 90265 (213) 456-6946

**Sail Wing Sales & Service Center**, 1116 8th St, Manhattan Bch, Ca. 90266

**West Wind Sch. of Hang Gliding**, Box 331, Manhattan Bch, Ca. 90266

**Astro Flight Inc.**, 13377 Beach Ave, Venice, Ca. 90291

**Air Supply**, 2230 Michigan Ave, Santa Monica, Ca. 90404

**Seagull Flight School**, 3021 Airport Ave, Santa Monica, Ca. 90405 (213) 679-2064

**Condor Kites**, 5507 Calle Mayor, Torrance, Ca. 90505

**PRN Systems**, c/o Dave Clement, 6580 Capers Way, Cypress, Ca. 90630

**Hang Glider Shop**, 1351 S Beach Blvd, La Habra, Ca. 90631

**Bob Velzy**, 13077 E Rosecrans Blvd, Santa Fe Springs, Ca. 90670 (213) 921-4111

**Pat Jackson**, 4819 Trimble Ct, Long Beach, Ca. 90814 (213) 434-3057

**Aero Crafts**, Box 8175 A, La Crescenta, Ca. 91214

**Free Flight Systems Hang Gliding Sch.**, 12424 Gladstone Ave, Sylmar, Ca. 91242

**So. California Sch. of Hang Gliding**, 7537 Alabama, Cunoga Park, Ca. 91303 (213) 347-0390

**Delta Ray Kites**, 16603 Covello St, Van Nuys, Ca. 91406

**Delta Wing Flight School**, Box 483, Van Nuys, Ca. 91408 (213) 785-2472

**Windways**, c/o Mike Turchen, 1368 Max Ave, Chula Vista, Ca. 92011 (714) 427-8514

**Pacific Ultralight**, c/o Doug Fronius, 100 Stoney Knoll Rd, El Cajon, Ca. 92021 (714) 444-8389

Region #3-Southern California and Hawaii

**Hawk of Lakeside**, c/o Harry and Margie, 10028 Maine, Lakeside, Ca. 92040

**Keen Things Enterprises**, 9489 Mission Park Pl, Santee, Ca. 92017

**John Dunham**, Box 6211, San Diego, Ca. 92106 (714) 222-1183

**Hang Gliders of San Diego**, 163 Turquoise St, San Diego, Ca. 92109 (714) 488-0722

**Jim Rusing**, c/o Sea World, 1720 S Shores Rd, San Diego, Ca. 92109 (714) 222-6363

**Westerly Sails**, c/o Dale Braegger, 3912 W Pt. Loma Blvd, San Diego, Ca. 92110

**Feather Sky Sails**, Box 0172, San Diego, Ca. 92115

**Free Flight of San Diego**, Box 15722, 7848 Convoy Ct, San Diego, Ca. 92115

**Flight Realities**, 1945-C Adams Ave, San Diego, Ca. 92116 (714) 298-1962

**Cal-Gliders**, 11545 Sorrento Valley Rd, Bldg 3, Suite 303, San Diego, Ca. 92121 452-0351

**USA Hang Gliders**, 2722 Murray Ridge Rd, San Diego, Ca. 92123 (714) 560-9301

**Fly Me Kites**, Box 444-4, Running Springs, Ca. 92382

**Hang-Gliders**, 24523 Monterey, San Bernardino, Ca. 92410

**Fly High Sails**, 12702 Lorna St #B, Garden Grove, Ca. 92641

**Speed & Marine Assn.**, 401 W Chapman, Orange, Ca. 92666

**Escape Country**, Robinson Ranch, Trabuco Canyon, Ca. 92678 (714) 856-7964

**Sky King Enterprises**, 1101 W Stevens #47, Santa Ana, Ca. 92707

**Free Flight of Ventura**, Ultralight Hang Gliders, Box 2094, Ventura, Ca. 93001 (805) 648-6687

**Windsong/School**, 27 N Garden, Ventura, Ca. 93001

**Casa de Motor Homes**, 2605 Wagon Wheel Dr, Oxnard, Ca. 93030 (805) 485-1818

**Free Flight of Santa Barbara**, 1806-J Cliff Dr, Santa Barbara, Ca. 93109 (805) 965-3733

**Flight Realities**, 2414 Park Way, Bakersfield, Ca. 93304 (805) 323-9759

**Ray Shannon**, 512 Jefferson, Bakersfield, Ca. 93305 (805) 327-2054

**William Wooley, Jr.**, 3801 Allen Rd, Bakersfield, Ca. 93307 (805) 589-2555

**Gull Wing Flight School**, Box 893, Morro Bay, Ca. 93442

**David Rachubka**, 3121 Coral St, Morro Bay, Ca. 93442 (805) 772-3794

**Aero Specialities Co.**, 1205 W Main St, Santa Maria, Ca. 93454

**Don Partridge**, Box 404, Bishop, Ca. 93514 (714) 873-5070

**Monarch Skysails**, 136 E Olive, Fresno, Ca. 93728 (209) 264-6880

**Sport Kites Kauai**, Box 337, Lawai, Kauai, Hi. 96765

**Dick Eipper**, Box 244, Kula Maui, Hi, 96790

**Stan Truett**, Box 7, Kula Maui, Hi, 96790

**Dove Hang Gliders of Hawaii**, 41-049 E Hukai St, Waimanolo, Hi, 96795

**Sport Kites Oahu**, c/o Mike Dorn, 5283 Kulanianaole Hwy, Honolulu, Hi, 96812 373-9312

**Air Performance Hawaii**, 217 Prospect, Honolulu, Hi. 96813

**Manta Hawaii**, 762 S Queen St, Honolulu, Hi. 96813 (808) 533-7254

**Ultralight Flying Machines of Hawaii**, c/o Dave Bettencourt, Suite 1401, 841 Bishop St, Honolulu, Hi. 96813 523-2451

**O'Brien Kites**, c/o Larry D. Smith, 1637 Kapiolani Blvd, Honolulu, Hi. 96816 955-5880

**Ed Cesar**, 83 Niuiki Circle, Honolulu, Hi. 96821

## Organizations

**United States Hang Gliding Assn., Inc.,** Box 66306, Los Angeles, Ca. 90066  (213) 390-3065

**Self-Soar Assn., Inc.,** Box 1860, Santa Monica, Ca. 90406  (213) 390-3423

**La Hang Glider Assn.,** Malibu Self-Soarers, Box 1860, Santa Monica, Ca. 90406  (213) 395-4991

**Ultralight Flight Organization,** Box 81665, San Diego, Ca. 92138

**Orange County Sky Sailing Club,** c/o Gail Montgomery, 916 Delaware, Huntington Beach, Ca. 92648  (714) 960-1676

**Escape Country Sky Surfing Club,** c/o Escape Country, Trabuco Canyon, Ca. 92678  586-7964

**Kydid Flyer Club,** 323 N Euclid #140, Santa Ana, Ca. 92703  (714) 554-0877

**Central Calif. Hang Gliding Assn.,** 1505 E Magill, Fresno, Ca. 93710

**Sierra Hang Gliding Assn.,** Box 443, Sutter Creek, Ca. 95685

**Pacific Tradewinds Skysailors, Ltd.,** Suite 1401, 841 Bishop St, Honolulu, Hi. 96813

## Accessories And Parts

**Mehil Enterprises,** 5900 Canterbury Dr A-121, Culver City, Ca. 90203  (213) 340-3138

**Helmets, Hang Gliding Helmets,** 1331 Berea Pl, Pacific Palisades, Ca. 90272

**Sailrite Kits,** 2010 Lincoln Blvd, Venice, Ca. 90291

**Bird Feathers,** 1554-5th Ave, Santa Monica. Ca. 90401

**Supplies, Kits, and Plans,** 5042 Malaga Dr., La Palma, Ca. 90623

**Wollard Products,** Box 268, Sunland, Ca. 91040  322-2509

**Taras Kiceniuk, Jr.,** Palomar Observatory, Palomar Mtn, Ca. 92060

**Frank Colver,** 3076 Roanoke Ln, Costa Mesa, Ca. 92626

**Hall's Hawks,** 12561 Pearce St, Garden Grove, Ca. 92643  (714) 530-3515

**BWB Enterprises,** Box 5575, Inglewood, Ca. 93010

## PUBLICATIONS

**Ground Skimmer Magazine**, c/o USHGA, BOX 66306, Los Angeles, Ca. 90066  (213) 390-3065

**Hang Glider Weekly/Low & Slow**, Box 1671, Santa Monica, Ca. 90406

**Hang Glider Magazine**, 3333 Pacific Ave, San Pedro, Ca. 90731

**Delta Kite Flyer News**, Box 483, Van Nuys, Ca. 91408  (213) 785-2474

**The Flyer**, San Diego UFO, Box 81665, San Diego, Ca. 92138

**Skysailors Poopsheet**, c/o Tradewinds Skysailors, Ltd., Suite 1401, 841 Bishop St, Honolulu, Hi. 96813

### Additions (CLUBS)

**Southland Hang Gliding Assn.**, c/o 13419 Kornblum Ave, Hawthorne, Ca. 90250  (213) 679-2064

**Channel Island Hang Gliding Assn.**, 380 Elwood Beach Dr #11, Goleta, Ca. 93017

## REGION FOUR

### Manufacturers

**Sun Sail Ltd.**, c/o Ted Schiedeke, 6753 E 47th Ave,, Denver, Co. 80216  (303) 321-8482

**Sports Aloft, Inc.**, Box 26, New Castle, Wy. 82701

**Mountain Green Sailwing**, Box 711, Morgan, Ut. 84050  (801) 829-6590

**Sky Bird Enterprises**, c/o Bob Williams, Box 12938, Las Vegas, Nv. 89112  (702) 452-4257

### Dealers And Schools

**Cal-Gliders, Colorado**, c/o Gary Rolkers, 4301 Stuart, Denver, Co. 80212  (303) 477-0169

**Hi Country Bicycle Works**, 515 Humboldt St, Denver, Co. 80218

**Alpine Haus**, 1600-8th Ave, Greeley, Co. 80221

**Rocky Mountain Marine**, 5411 Leetsdale Dr. Denver, Co. 80222  (303) 355-9477

Mike Larsen, 775 Merry Ln, Boulder, Co. 80302 (303) 494-6318

Summit Flight, Box 1485, 3001 S Glencoe, Denver, Co. 80222

C. B. Jensen Group, Box 22, Hideaway Park, Co. 80450 (303) 726-5969

Naturally High Flight Systems, Box 5218, Steamboat Vlg, Co. 80477 (303) 879-0303

Alpine Haus, 628, S College, Fort Collins, Co. 80521

Leading Edge Air Foils, 1508 Newcastle, Colorado Springs, Co. 80907

Free Flight of Alamosa, c/o George Guerin, 3 Bellwood Dr, Alamosa, Co. 81101

Free Flight of Canon City, Fremont Sales & Service, Box 70, Canon City, Co. 81212

Blue Mesa Aeronautics, 717 W Virginia Ave, Gunnison, Co. 81230 (303) 641-3566

Jerry Riggle, 282 Little Park Ct, Grand Junction, Co. 81501

Get High, Inc., c/o Jon Totman, Box 4551, Aspen, Co. 81611 (303) 925-3275

Colorado Manta, Box 122, Snowmass, Co. 81654 (303) 927-4104

Alpine Haus, 111 W 17th, Cheyenne, Wy. 82001

Life Cycle, 1224 15 St, Denver, Co. 82020 (303) 572-0405

Alpine Haus, 17th and Grand Ave, Laramie, Wy. 82070

Snow King Sky School, Box R, Jackson, Wy. 83001

Hawk of Wyoming, c/o Ken Bird, Box R, Jackson, Wy. 83001

Delta Ray Kits, 1704 N Valley View Dr, Layton, Ut. 84041

Miller Ski & Cycle Haus, 834 Washington Blvd, Ogden, Ut. 84041 (801) 392-3911

Sail Bird of Utah, c/o Sherman Savage, 847 N 750 E, Layton, Ut. 84041

Bob Bills, Jr., 695 E 1600 N, Orem, Ut. 84057

Hang Gliding School, c/o Larry Matson, 1507 S 1600 E, Salt Lake City, Ut. 84105

Free Flight of Salt Lake City, 6073 S 530 W, Murray, Ut. 84107

Cal-Gliders, Utah, c/o Bruce Brown, 1736 E 4050 S #5, Holiday, Ut. 84117 (801) 278-7118

Sunset Sport Center, 2909 Washington Blvd, Ogden, Ut. 84401 (801) 487-3586

**Chandelle Utah/Sky School**, 3698 E 7000 S, Salt Lake City, Ut. 84117 (801) 272-4236

**Cal-Gliders, Utah**, c/o Kent Warren, 240 E 850 S. Springville, Ut. 84663 (801) 489-4006

**Robertson Marine**, 97 S Main St, Springville, Ut. 84663

**Chandelle Phoenix**, Ski Haus Action Sports, 2501 E Indian School Rd, Phoenix, Az. 85016

**Flying Fox**, 3147 N 31 Ave, Phoenix, Az. 85017 (602) 269-8222

**U.S. Gliders**, 11024 N 22nd Ave. #5, Phoenix, Az. 85029 (602) 944-1655

**Genesis II Inc.**, Box 3526, Phoenix, Az. 85030 (602) 257-1261

**Sport-Air**, 4313 E University, Phoenix, Az. 85040

**Arizona Sun Hang Gliding Sch.**, 5438 E Voltaire, Scottsdale, Az. 85254 996-3904

**Free Flight of Arizona**, Star Route, Box 5, Winkelman, Az. 85292

**Icarus II**, 2762 N Stone, Tucson, Ax. 85705

**Hang Gliders Inc.**, 1300 E Valencia, Tucson, Az. 85706

**Ski Haus Action Sports**, 2823 E Speedway, Tucson, Az. 85716 (602) 881-4544

**Flight Inc.**, Village Apts. #159, Flagstaff, Az. 86001

**New Mexico Sky School**, c/o Don Marshall, 4007 Central NE, Albuquerque, NM 81708

**Cal-Gliders, New Mexico**, c/o Neal Bakkum, 7208 Arroyo Del Oro NE, Albuquerque, NM 87109 (505) 296-2943

**Sky Sailors Sales & Service**, 7208 Arroyo Del Oro NE, Albuquerque, Nm. 87109 292-1533

**Base Camp**, c/o Peter Hayes, 121 W San Francisco St, Sante Fe, NM 87501 (505) 982-9707

**Sierra Wings**, Box 710, Verdi, NV 89439

**Sierra Hang Gliding Sch.**, Box 4557, Stateline, NV 89449 (702) 583-3910

**Sierra Wings**, 253 E Arroyo, Reno, Nv. 89502 (702) 825-7740

Wings, c/o Bill Duca, 906 S 4th St #3, Las Vegas, Nv. 89101 (702) 384-4358

## Organizations

**Fellow Feathers of Denver**, 344 St. Paul St, Denver, Co. 80206 (303) 355-1697

**Pike's Peak Hang Gliders Club**, 4955 El Camino Dr C-4, Colorado Springs, Co. 80918

**Arizona Hang Glider Assn.**, Box 21755, Phoenix, Az. 85036

**Southern Arizona Hang Gliding Assn.**, 826 E Holoway, Tucson, Az. 85719

**Northern New Mexico Free Air Force**, c/o G.A. Barker, Box 438, Chimayo, NM 87522

## Publications

**Fellow Feathers Flocker**, 344 St. Paul St, Denver, Co. 80206 (303) 355-1697

## REGION FIVE

## Manufacturers

**Bede Development**, Box 12128, Wichita, Ks. 67212

**Pliable Moose Delta Wings**, 243 Matthewson, Wichita, Ks, 67214 (316) 262-2664

## Dealers And Schools

**Stanley E. Samuelson**, Osceola, Ia. 50213 (515) 342-2789

**Boag Chumley**, 8219 Lista Ln, and 1323 Park Ave, Des Moines, Ia. 50315 (515) 285-8594

**John F. Rademacher**, 101 2nd S, Fargo, ND 58102

**Peter Hadley**, 6901 W 194, Stillwell, Ks. 66085 (913) 432-4766

**D. W. Kites Sales & Service**, 200 W 30, STE #102, Topeka, Ks. 66611

**Trailwinds Gliders, Inc.**, Box 275, Wichita, Ks, 67201

**Prairie Skimmer Hang Gliders**, 308 E Pine #3, Wichita, Ks. 67214 (316) 262-2592

**Midwest Wings**, 202 S Fourth, Osborne, Ks. 67473

Benny Jumper, Country Estates 12 B, Hays, Ks.
67601 (913) 625-7576

City Lock and Marine, 2031 St. Marys Ave, Omaha, Ne.
68102 (402) 341-9672

Buzz's Body Shop & Marine Supply, RR Ave, E Box 72,
Kearney, Ne. 68847 (402) 237-2624

Midwest Free Flight, Box 205, Fairfield, Ne. 68938

## Publications

Wings Unlimited, 4155 E Jewell, Suite No. 301, Denver,
Co. 80222

## REGION SIX

## Dealers and Schools

Hunt's Kites Inc., 11959 Glenvalley Dr, Maryland Hts, Mo.
63043 (314) 739-3456

Ray Wall's Delta Wing Kites, Rt 1, Wappapello Lake, Mo.
63966

Mike Calagari, 6647 Holmes, Kansas City, Mo. 64131

Sky Unlimited, Hang Glider Supply, 122 McConnell, Joplin,
Mo. 64801

Ark-La-Tek Diver Supply, 9118 Blom, Shreveport, La.
71108

General Wings Inc., 3117 N Portland, Oklahoma City,
Ok. 73112

Thunder Electronics, 1305 N MacArthur, Oklahoma City,
Ok. 73127 (405) 947-8854

## Organizations

Midwest Hang Glider Assn., 11959 Glenvalley Dr,
Maryland Hts, Mo. 63043 (314) 739-3456

## Publications

The Flatland Flyer, c/o Midwest Hang Glider Assn., 11959
Glenvalley Dr, Maryland Hts, Missouri 63043 Editor:
Al Signorino

# REGION SEVEN

## Manufacturers

**Dyna Soar Mfg. Co.**, Box 236, Carmel, In. 46032

**Marske Aircraft Corp.**, 130 Crestwood Dr, Michigan City, In. 46360 (219) 897-7039

**Sport Wings Inc.**, Box 1647, Lafayette, In. 47902 (317) 423-2646

**Sky Sails of Michigan**, 1611 S Woodward, Royal Oak, Mi. 48067 (313) 545-0051

**Foot Launched Flyers**, 1200 Dani, Brighton, Mi. 48116

**Delta Wing Kites**, 8620 W Auer, Milwaukee, Wi. 53222 (414) 476-8125

**Aspen Enterprises**, Box 423, Neenah, Wi. 54956

**Delta Sail Wing Gliders**, 501 Westview Dr, Hastings Mn. 55033 (612) 437-2685

**Aircraft Unlimited**, Box 1616, Minneapolis Int'l Airport, Minneapolis, Mn. 55111 (612) 483-3765

**Firecraft, Inc.**, c/o Dan Johnson, 4904 N Pulaski Rd, Chicago, Ill. 60630 (312) 736-7050

**Icarus II**, Box 1155, Battle Creek, Mi. 49016

## Dealers and Schools

**Free Flight of Indianapolis**, Box 297, Fishers, In. 46060

**Hoosier Hang Gliders**, c/o Greg Rector, 707 Highwood, Greencastle, In. 46135 653-4039

**Olympic Cyclery**, 1016 Franklin, Michigan, In. 46360 (219) 872-1411

**Oxbow Airsports**, Rt 1, Box 323A, Elkhart, In. 46514 (219) 533-1868

**Robert Newcombe Mfg's Rep.**, 30000 Southfield B-52, Southfield, Mi. (313) 644-4039

**Thomas Drewek**, 27073 Bonnie Dr, Warren, Mi. 48093

**Eco-Flight Systems Inc.**, 2275 S State, Ann Arbor, Mi. 48104 (313) 994-9020

**Rudolph Kishazy**, 1460 Junction #3, Plymouth, Mi. 48170 (313) 455-7920

**Free Flight of Ann Arbor**, 8778 Main St, Whitmore Lake, Mi. 48189

**Free Flight of Detroit**, 19366 Kelly Rd, Harper Woods, Mi. 48225

**William Hutchinson**, 409 E Buttles, Midland, Mi. 48460 (517) 835-6608

**Tom Dunn**, 3568 Alamando Rd, Rt 2, Coleman, Mi. 48618 (517) 465-6504

**Great Lakes Sky Sails Inc.**, 5125 N River Rd, Freeland, Mi. 48623 (517) 695-5607

**Hutch's Hang Gliders**, 425½ S Saginaw Rd, Midland, Mi. 48640 (517) 835-8771

**Great Lakes Sky Sails**, c/o Brad Boese & Larry Bender, 837 Grand River E, Lansing, Mi. 48823 (517) 351-1325

**Sports Meister**, 213 E Grand River, E Lansing, Mi. 48823 (517) 349-3531

**Prime Time Products Inc.**, Box 244, Sarmac, Mi. 48881

**Aero Float Flights**, Box 1155, Battle Creek, Mi. 49016 (616) 965-6455

**Delta Wing Kites**, c/o Jim Laure, 7844 Shaver Rd, Portage, Mi. 49081 (616) 375-1159

**Flight Systems**, 10 N Barton, New Buffalo, Mi. 49117 (219) 879-6756

**Sky School**, c/o Larry Nedry, 728 Buth Dr, Comstock Park, Mi. 49321 (616) 364-4912

**Felix Marine**, 14023 Green, Grand Haven, Mi. 49417 (161) 842-3680

**Chandelle of West Michigan**, 25 W 9th St, Holland, Mi. 49423

**Skyscape Sports**, 25 W 9th St, Holland, Mi. 48423

**D & D Skysailing**, 987 Fennwood, No Muskegon, Mi. 49445 (616) 744-4288

**Custom Displays**, 1530 Monroe Ave NW, Grand Rapids,Mi. 49505 (616) 364-4510

**Delta Wing of Michigan**, c/o Dave V'Dovick, 1434 Lake Dr SE, Grand Rapids Mi. 49506 (616) 458-4078

**Region** #7-Illinois, Indiana, Michigan, Minnesota, and Wisconsin.

**Gar's Sports Center**, c/o Gary J. Meernik, 2531 S Division Ave, Grand Rapids, Mi. 49507

**Sailboat Center**, 22 44th St, Grand Rapids, Mi. 49508 (616) 534-0015

**Sugarloaf Sky School**, RR 1, Cedar, Mi. 49621

**Manta Michigan**, 327 Man St, Frankfort, Mi. 49635 (616) 352-9312

**Kim Wilson**, 216 Birchwood St, Traverse City, Mi. 49684 (616) 946-4663

**Chandelle of Harbor Springs**, c/o Ned Keys, RR 1, State Rd. Harbor Springs. Mi. 49740 (616) 526-5051

**Dave Tiemeyer**, Star Rt 550, Box 334, Marquette, Mi. 49855

**Free Flight of Watertown**, Geogoire Specialties, 857 Silver Lake St, Oconomowoc, Wi. 53066

**Gordie Quick**, 2023 E Milwaukee, Janesville, Wi. 53545

**H & H Petrie's Sports**, Box 5427, Madison, Wi. 53703 (608) 256-1347

**Eau Claire Hang Glider Shop**, 3038 Irene Dr, Eau Clair, Wi. 54701 (715) 835-8811

**Tommy Bartlett Water Shows**, Box 65, Wisconsin Dells, Wi. 53965 (608) 253-3031

**Free Flight of St. Paul**, c/o Norcat Col, 2210 Whitebear, Maplewood, Mn. 55109

**Northwestern Hang Gliders Inc.**, c/o Fred Tiemens, 1215 Washington Ave S, Minneapolis, Mn. 55404 (612) 341-3322

**Midwest Hang Glider**, c/o Mike Reincke, 2002 Garfield S #24, Minneapolis, Mn. 55404

**Delta Sports**, 3325 Park Ave S, Minneapolis, Mn. 55407

**Midwest Hang Gliders**, 2002 Garfield Ave S #24, Minneapolis, Mn. 55404 (612) 874-9868

**Mornes Inc.**, 1022 W. 4th St, Grand Rapids, Mn. 55744

**Arrow Marine**, Hwy 14 W & 7th St NW, Rochester, Mn. 55901

**Midwest Sports Center**, Fairmont, Mn. 56031

**Alpine Imports Ltd.**, Box 97, Crystal Lake, Ill. 60014 (815) 459-1816

**Apollo Sky Sailing Centers**, 222 Waukegan Rd, Glenview, Ill. 60025

**Joe Meboe**, 337 Prairie Ln, Lake Zurich, Ill. 60047

**Chandelle of Chicago**, Div. of Four Winds Sports Ltd., 109 W Prospect, Mt. Prospect, Ill. 60056   (312) 398-3451

**Munson Marine Inc.**, Box 538 RFD 1, Round Lake, Ill. 60073   (815) 358-2720

**Apollo Sky Sailing Centers**, 722 Barrington Rd, Streamwood, Ill. 60103

**Apollo Skysailing Center**, Schaumburg Flight Center, 700 E Higgins Rd, Schaumburg, Ill. 60172   (312) 885-0958

**Sailbird of Chicago**, c/o John Prescott, 305 S Wright, Naperville, Ill. 60540

**Ben Heck**, 7191 W Grand, Chicago, Ill. 60635   (312) 637-1007

**Arthur R Koch**, 9702 Shore Dr, Rockford, Ill. 61111   (815) 654-0080

**Harold W. Lewis**, 139 S Center St, E Alton, Ill. 62024   (618) 259-4737

**Easy Traveling Corp.**, 12173 E D Ave, Richland, Mi. 79083   (616) 343-1480

## Organizations

**Ultralight Flight Orgn. of Southeastern Michigan**, c/o John Holden, 1863 Royal, Berkley, Mi. 48072

**Wisconsin Self-Soaring Assn.**, 151 Milwaukee Ave, S Milwaukee, Wi. 53172   (414) 762-2751

**Wisconsin Ultralight Pilots SCC.**, c/o Bill Schauder, 545, W 22360 Quinn Rd, Waukesha, Wi. 53186   (414) 542-5583

**Madison Sky Sailors**, c/o Connie Robinson, 2925 Sachs St, Madison, Wi. 53704   (608) 249-1668

**Northern Sun**, 240 N McCarrons Blvd, St. Paul, Mn. 55113   (621) 489-8300

## Publications

**Wind Free**, c/o Madison Sky Sailors, 2925 Sachs St, Madison, Wi. 53704 ($2 per yr.)

**Hanging In There**, 6301 Knox Ave, Richfield, Mn. 55423

## REGION EIGHT

## Manufacturers

**Sky Sports Inc.**, Rt 83, Ellington, Ct. 60629   (203) 872-7317

**Zepher Aircraft Corp.**, 25 Mil St, Glastonbury, Ct. 06033   (203) 633-9074

**New York Hang Gliders Inc.**, 144-45 35th Ave, Flushing, NY 11354 (212) 762-1280

**Dixxon Hang Glider Supplies**, 4 Arden Ln, Farmingville, NY 11738 (516) 588-7562

**Sky Sports Inc.**, Box 441, Whitman, Ma. 02382 (617) 447-3773

## Dealers and Schools

**Eco Flight**, 151 N Valley Rd, Amherst, Ma. 01002 (413) 253-5852

**Mountainview Glider Sports Inc.**, 300 Pleasant St, Northampton, Ma. 01060 (413) 584-7233

**Venus Hang Glider Co.**, Box 87, Wilbraham, Ma. 01095

**Brodie Mtn. Kite Sch**, c/o Brokie Mtn. Ski Area, Rt 7, New Ashford, Ma. 01237 (413) 443-4752

**Cal-Gliders, Mass.**, Neimi Manufacturers, 25 Willow St, Fitchburg, Ma. 01420 345-7337

**ACME Kite Co., Inc.**, box 303, Maynard, Ma. 01754

**Pliable Moose Delta Sky Sails of Wichita, Kansas**, c/o G.J. Goulet, 17 Norfolk St, Haverhill, Ma. 01841 (617) 372-6601

**Stan Smith**, Box 131, E Orleans, Ma. 02643

**The Base Camp**, c/o Phil Purvis, 401 Kingstown Rd, Wakefield, RI 02879 (401) 783-1245

**Northwest Manta**, Box 481, Locania, NH 03246 (603) 524-6837

**Winnipesaukee Wings Hang Glider Club**, Box 481, Laconia, NH 03246

**Terry Sweeney**, RFD 2, Concord, Nh. 03301 (603) 774-4700

**The Hanger,** Mittersill Ski Area, Franconia, NH 03580 823-8150

**Sky People,** Box 898, North Conway, NH 03860 (603) 356-5544

**Eastern Sky Hang Gliders**, Kenyan King, North Fryeburg, Me. 04058

**Adventurer Hang Gliders**, Box 518, Loring AFB, Limestone, Me. 04750

**Patrick Mouligne**, Sugarloaf Ski School, Sugarloaf, Me. 04947

**Sky Truckin' Inc.**, Box 142, Kingfield, Me. 04947

**Green Mtn. Sky Sports**, Box 169-A, Newbury, Vt. 05051 (603) 787-6315

**Eastern Seagull Sales & Service**, Magic Mtn. Ski Area, Londonderry, Vt. 05148 824-5566

**Post Skis**, Box 977, Stowe, Vt. 05672

**Connecticut Hang Glider Assn.**, 58 Gail Rd, E Hartford, Ct. 06108

**Free Flight of Main**, Snoops Sales, 63 Union St, Bangor, Me. 04401

**Fuji Industries**, 26 Broadway, New York, NY 10004 (212) 943-4435

**Go Fly a Kite**, 1434 3rd Ave, New York, NY 10028

**Free Flight of Hicksville**, 77 E End Ave, Hicksville, Long Island, NY 11801

**Long Island Kite Dist.**, 5 Bethpage Rd, Hicksville, NY 11801 (516) 681-8738

**Wind & Sea**, 5419 Merrick Rd, Massapequa, NY 11783 (516) 798-9887

**Ultralight Wings**, Kenmore Sta. Box 384, Boston, Ma. 12215 (617) 536-2497

**The Hang Glider Store**, Ridge Rd, Marlboro, NY 12542 (914) 236-7994

**Arturo Lebron Flying Machines**, Divison Lebron-Krawec, Box 119, Mountaindale, NY 12763

**Surf Bird Hang Gliding School**, West Mtn., Glens Falls, NY 12801 (518) 436-7731

**McCarron Aero Corp.**, 17 Vichy, Saratoga Springs, NY 12866 (518) 587-1957

**Syracuse Sky Sports**, Hoag Ln, Fayetteville, NY 13066 (315) 637-8990

**The Soaring Emporium**, c/o Shane Connors, Malone Rd, Rd 2, Syracuse, NY 13215

**Windworld**, c/o James McLaughlin, 401 Breakspear Rd, Syracuse, NY 13219

Free Flight of New York, c/o Mark J. Senit, Herkimer, NY 13350

Wind Riders Ltd., 12 Whig St, Newark, NY 13811 (607) 542-8822

Free Flight of Buffalo, 3973 Harlem Rd, Amherst, NY 14226 (716) 839-3231

Zepher Aircraft, c/o Bill Tucker, Rd 3, Warsaw, NY 14569

Southern Tier Flight Shop, Rt 99, Osceola Rd, Woodhull, NY 14898

## Organizations

Windward Kite and Glider Club, 25 Willow St, Fitchburg, Ma. 01420

Boston Sky Club, Box 375, Marlboro, Ma. 01752

New England Hang Gliding Assn., Box 356, Stoughton, Ma. 02072

Connecticut Hang Gliders, 27 Clear St, Enfield, Ct. 06082 749-6340

Clarkson College Hang Glider Club, c/o Robert S. Murphy, Star Rt, Potsdam, Ny. 13676

Wind Riders LYD, 12 Whig St. Newark, NY 13811 (607) 642-8822

Hang Gliders of Western New York, c/o Paul Suozzi, 2643 Union Rd, Cheektowaga, NY 14227

## Publications

Windward Newsletter, 25 Willow St. Fitchburg, Ma. 01420

Boston Skysurfer, Box 375, Marlboro, Ma. 01752

## REGION NINE

## Manufacturers

Deltrasoarus Inc., Box 361, Wharton, NJ 07885 (201) 386-0925

Free Flight of Eastern Penn., 620 Walnut St. Reading, Pa. 19601

Chuck's Glider Supplies, 4200 Royalton Rd, Brecksville, Oh. 44141 (216) 526-5436

Franklin Mfg. Corp., Rd 2, Glen Rock, Pa. 17327

## Dealers And Schools

**Phila. Hang Glider Sales**, c/o Eric Sigel, 363 Overlook Dr, Downingtown, Pa. 19335

**Bennett Delta Kites and Gliders-East**, Box 74, Holmdel, Nj. 07733 (201) 542-8536

**Free Flight of Lebanon**, 1 Lynwood Dr, Lebanon, NJ. 08833

**Action Sport Cycles**, 108 Essex Ave, Metuchen, NJ 08840 (201) 494-5555

**Pennsylvania Sport Kites**, c/o Richard Wilson, 6052 Dalmation Dr, Bethel Park, Pa. 15102

**Free Flight of Greenburg,** Rd1, Greenburg, Pa. 15601 523-3788

**Clean Air Aviation**, 355 W Aaron Dr, State College, Pa. 16801 (814) 234-1967

**Lancaster County Marine**, Rt 222, 4 Lauber Rd, Akron, Pa. 17501 (171)859-1121

**Clean Air Aviation**, 175 Hollywood Dr, Middletown, Pa. 17057 (717) 939-0084

**Ed Skovish**, RR1, Homlock Creek, Pa. 18612

**Icarus Inc.**, Box 51, Broomall, Pa. 19008

**Clean Air Aviation**, 300 Hatboro Pike G-3, Hatboro, Pa. 19040 (215) 627-3227

**Free Flight of Reading Inc.**, 620 Walnut St, Reading, Pa. 19601 (215)- 376-6669

**Maryland Manta**, 5603 McKinley St, Bethesda, Md. 20034 (301) 530-8612

**East Coast Hang Gliders Ltd.**, Box 961 Washington, DC 20044

**Ferranti's Phoenix Hang Glider Co.**, 2209 Pecan Ln, Bowie, Md.

**Sport Flight**, 3305 Ferndale, Kensington, Md. 20795 (301) 942-6737

**Jeffair**, 1107 Primrose Ct #30, Annapolis, Md. 21403

**The Kite Exchange**, 7358 Shenandoah Ave, Annadale, Va. 22003

**Delta Wing Kites**, c/o Larry Davis, Rt 6, Box 94, Martinsville, Va. 24112 (703) 673-1596

**J. J. Sky Surfing Inc.**, c/o John L. Sleely Jr., Box 1181, Martinsburg, WV. 25401

Derby City Kite Sales, 8400 Blue Lick Rd, Louisville, Ky. 40219 (502) 969-6295

Cal-Gliders Ohio, Freedom Wings Inc., 33 Actou Rd, Columbus, Oh. 43214 (614) 263-1333

Recreational Flying Machines, Airport Rd, Rt 3, St. Clairsville, Oh. 43950

Troyer Kite Supply, 4299 Kent Rd, Stow, Oh. 44224

Free Flight of Mansfield, 2499 Panonia Rd, Mansfield, Oh. 44903

## Organizations

Pittsburgh Hang Glider Assn., Box 67, Trafford, Pa. 15085

Nittany Valley Hang Gliders, c/o Dennis Pagen, 355 W Aaron Dr, State College, Pa. 16801

Garden Spot Hang Glider Flyers, c/o Steve Bucher, 338 E Cedar St, New England, Pa. 17557

Eastern Penn., Hang Glider Assn., Box 524, Reading, Pa. 19603

Glide on Assn., 323 Bradley Ave, Rockville, Md. 20851

Capitol Hang Glider Assn., 7358 Shenandoah Ave, Annadale, Va. 22003

Tidewater Hang Glider Club., c/o Otto Horton Jr., 5624 Hampshire Ln #102, Virginia Beach, Va. 23462

The Hang Glider Club of Virginia, c/o Davis Smith, Red House, Va. 23963

Ohio Hang Glider Assn., c/o Tony Mittelo, 26815 Bagley, Cleveland, Oh. 44138 235-2445

Cincinnati Hang Glider Assn., 5725 Dragon Way #400, Cincinnati, Oh. 45227 (513) 272-1476

## Publications

Skyline Newsletter, 7358 Shenandoah Ave, Annadale, Va. 22003

Ohio Hang Glider News Flyer, 26875 Bagley Rd, Cleveland, Oh. 44138 235-2445 .

## Additions

Sky Actions Sports Inc., 16 Weir Pl., Ringwood, NJ 07456 (201) 962-6554

## REGION TEN

### Manufacturers

Flight Dynamics, Inc., Box 5070, Raleigh, NC 27607

Kitty Hawk Kites, Box 386, Nags Head, NC 27959 (919) 441-6247

WDM Enterprises, 2770 Bufordi Dr, Marietta, Ga. 30060

Johnson Flex-Wing Kites, Box 91, Cypress Gardens, Fl. 33880

Cloudmen Glidercraft, Co., 905 Church St, Nashville, Tn. 32703 (615) 256-6221

Butterfly Ind., Inc., 1911½ W Cumberland Ave, Knoxville, Tn. 37916 (615) 522-0202

### Dealers and Schools

Doss & Sons, 434 Brookstown Ave, Winston Salem, NC 27101

Free Flight of Greensboro, c/o Frank J. Howard, 2300 Phoenix Dr, Greensboro, NC 27406

Marshall & Shuck, 7005 Tanbaric Way, Raleigh, NC 27609 (919) 876-6300

Scott's Marine and Water Ski Supply, 908 Lexington Ave, Charlotte, NC 28203 (704) 376-7348

Hawk of Fayetteville, c/o James Brink, Box 3734, Fayetteville, NC 28303

Land, Air & Sea Ventures, Box 275, Wrightsville Beach, NC 28480

Fly Cataloochee, c/o Paula J. Prentice, Rt 1, Box 500, Maggie Valley, NC 28751

Patton Motor Homes, Inc., 4809 Wilkinson Blvd, Charlotte, NC 29208

B & H Sales, 380 N Four Lane Hwy, Marietta, Ga. 30062 (404) 428-0037

Appalachian Mountaineering, 5725 Buford Hwy NE, Atlanta, Ga. 30340

California East Hang Gliders & Parasails, Box 109, Daytona Bch, Fl. 32015   252-6335

Island Park Bayfront, Box 2868, Sarasota, Fl. 32629   (813) 366-6659

Freeform, Inc., c/o Peter Larsen, 1201 N Highland Ave, Clearwater, Fl. 33515

Hal Elgin's Holiday Water Sports, 6639 Emerson Ave S, Petersburgh, Fl. 33707   345-3697

Jim McCormick Ski School, Box 84, Cypress Gardens, Fl. 33880

Mountain High, Inc., Box 911, Clarksville, Tn. 37040   (615) 552-1962

Flying Contraptions, Ltd., Box 17463, Nashville, Tn. 37217   (615) 834-7251

J & P Distributors, 860 Murfreesboro Rd, Nashville, Tn. 37217

Hazel Stro, 4513 Brummond Dr, Chattanooga, Tn. 37401

Free Flight of Greenville, c/o Formex, Co., 100 Austin St, Box 254, Greenville, Tn. 37743

## Organizations

North Carolina Hang Glider Soc., c/o Tommy Thompson, 104 Wright St, Lewisville, Nc. 27023   (919) 945-5260

Atlanta Ultralight Assn., c/o Dyches Boddiford, 18 Peachtree Ave #B-7, Atlanta, Ba. 30305

## Publications

The Albatross, c/o North Carolina Hang Glider Assn., 104 Wright St, Lewisville, NC 27023   (919) 945-5260

## REGION ELEVEN

## Manufacturers

Kondor Kite Co., Box 603, Lewsville, Tx. 75067

Jack Hinson, 6205 Shadybrook #153, Dallas, Tx. 75206

## Dealers and Schools

**David Broyles**, 1403 Austin, Irving, Tx. 75061 (214) 357-1779

**Gentle Earth**, 6723 Snider Plaza, Dallas, Tx. 75205

**Hawk of Dallas**, 13508 Maham St #217, Dallas, Tx. 75240

**Sky Sails, Inc.**, 2432 Dalworth, Arlington, Tx. 76011 (817) 261-3462

**Free Flight of Temple**, 719 S 25 St, Temple, Tx. 76501

**Crow Flite**, 1803 Branard, Houston, Tx. 77006 (713) 528-6867

**Laudar Aerial**, c/o John Tyson, 2120 S Post Oak Rd #6, Houston, Tx. 77027

**Natural High Sports**, 11817 Chimney Rock Rd, Houston, Tx. 77035 (713) 721-2765

**Houston Delta Wing**, c/o George P. Lasko Jr., 10614 Plainfield, Tx. 77071

**Free Flight of Corpus Christi**, Dockside, 315 Beach St, Box 772, Port Arkansas, Tx. 78373 (512) 749-6141

**Gill Enterprises**, 2004 Spring Glen Rd, Mission, Tx. 78572

**Sport Haus**, 2309 Broadway, Lubbock, Tx. 79401 (314) 744-2121

**The Sky Surfer**, 6460 Regal Crest, El Paso, Tx. 79904 (915) 566-8734

## Organizations

**South Central Hang Gliding Soc.**, 2722 San Jose, Dallas, Tx. 75211 (214) 331-5383

**Hill Country Gliders Club & Site**, Rt 1, Box 326, Wimberly, Tx. 78678

# REGION TWELVE

## Canada

### Manufacturers

**B & T Enterprises,** Box 1874, Calgary, Alb., Canada T2P 2L8

**Muller Kite Ltd.,** Box 4063 Postal St 'C', Calgary, Alb., Canada T2T 5M9 (403) 266-1446

**Birdman Enterprises,** 8011 Argyll Rd, Edmonton, Alb., Canada 466-5370

## Dealers And Schools

**Kartway Park Ltd.,** 9102 41 Ave, Edmonton, Alb., Canada 435-2333

**(Al) Linkewich Hang Gliding Sch.,** Box 857, Red Deer, Edmonton, Alb., Canada

**Mountain Flying Ltd.,** Box 613, Cambridge, Calgary, Alb., Canada

**The Werner Kausche Co. & Kite Workshop,** 215, 11 Ave SW, Calgary, Alb., Canada 264-7926

**Eagle Delta,** c/o Barry Howie, Box 11, Invermere, B.C., Canada

**Tod Mountain Flying School,** 749 Victoria, Kamloops, B.C., Canada

**Big Whit Ski Development,** RR 3, Hall Rd, Kelowna, B.C., Canada

**Delta Wing Displays,** c/o Bob Jones, Box 892, Kelowna, B.C., Canada

**Tip's Up,** 918 Vernon St, Nelson, B.C., Canada V1L 4G6 (604) 352-6224

**Bob Conners,** 5711 Blue Bell, W Vancouver, B.C., Canada

**Kitslinno Marine Lumber Ltd.,** 1502 W 2nd Ave, Vancouver, B.C., Canada (604) 736-0166

**Ture Flight Hang Gliders Ltd.,** 4509 Rupert St, Vancouver, B.C., Canada (604) 438-3255

**Robert Henderson,** 235 Baseline Rd W, London, Ont., Canada N6J 1V9

**Free Flight of Midland,** Midland Mike's Special Sports, Box 614, Midland, Ont., Canada

**Mesle Canada Reg'G,** Box 610 RR 5, Ottawa, Ont., Canada K1G 3N3

**Skysurfing Unlimited,** 621 Redwood Ave, Ottawa, Ont., Canada K2A 3E8

## Organizations

**Alberta Hang Glider Assn.,** 2425 3 Ave NW, Calgary, Alb., Canada

Rocky Mountain Hang Gliding Club, 366 Ritchie St, Kimberley, B.C., Canada   (604) 427-4

Southern Ontario Hang Glider Assn., c/o John D. Forman, c/o Minisport, 10 Governors Rd, Dundas, Ontario, . Canada

Southwestern Ontario Air Riders, 33 Plymouth Ave, London, Ont., Canada

## Publications

The Flypaper, c/o The Alberta Hang Glider Assn., 2001 22 Ave SW, Calgary, Alb., Canada.

## Foreign

## Manufacturers

South African Aviation Centre, Box 33191, Jeppestown, Transvaal, Burco Hs, 17 Error St, New Doornfont, Johannesburg, South Africa   23 2385-46

Breen Hang Gliders, New Road, Crickhowell, Powys, S. Wales, U.K.

## REGION #12-Canada and Foreign

Ultralight Flight Systems, c/o Steven Cohen, 15 Grand Parade, Brighton Le Sands, N.S.W. 2216, Australia

Sky Craft Pty Ltd., 138 Bellevue Parade, Suite 122, Carlton, N.S.W. 2218, Australia

Bill Moyes, 173 Bronte St, Waverley, Sydney, Australia 2024

Delta Wings Kites & Gliders, Wing Works, Elland Rd, Brighouse, Yorkshire, England

Hi Kites, c/o David Walling, 20 Aldsworth Close, Fairford GISO, England GL7 4LB

Mc Broom Sailwings Ltd., 12 Manor Ct Dr, Horfield, Common Bristol, England GS7 OXF

Manufature De Cerfs-volants, 2/30 Sq. Hector-Berloiz, 94700 Malsons-Alfort 207-63.21

Scot-Kites, 19 Camphill Ave, Glasgow, Scotland G41 3A⅞

Chandelle Europs A.G., Post Fach 26, 8640 Rapperswil, Switzerland

Swiss Delta, 7550 Schuls, Switzerland

Delta Glider, 7021 Stetten' Filder, Bernhauser STR 31, West Germany

**Mike Harker Delta Glider,** CH-7550 Schuls, Swiss Delta
FFA, West Germany   084-91381

## Dealers And Schools

**Wings Hang Gliders,** 125 Melville Rd, W. Brunswick,
Victoria 3055, Australia 362638

**Free Flight of Ecuador,** Titan Cia Ltd., 10 De Agusto, 608
Of Casilla 3140, Quito, Ecuador

**Critchley-Hugh S Co.,** c/o Edmond Critchley, 8 Oak Tree
Close, Virginia Water, Surrey, England

**Champfort-Sports,** c/o Mike Wyer, Rte. Du Mont d Arbvis,
74120 Megeve, France

**Aquilone Delts,** Corvara' Badia, Italy

**Flipper Scow Italia,** c/o Peter Skaarup, Casella Postale
113, 22100 Como, Italy

**Flipper Scow Italia,** Icaro 2000, c/o Punto Mare, Via Arco,
2, 20121 Milano, Italy

**Free Flight of Japan,** 4-2-3 Chuo, Nakanoku, Tokyo, Japan

**Mike Harker Delta Glider,** 81 Garmisch, Postfach 123,
West Germany   (088) 215*6726

**Pacific Kites Ltd.,** Box 45-087, Te Atatu, New Zealand

**New Zealand Gliding KIWI,** Box 545, Tauranga, New
Zealand

## Organizations

**Australian Self-Soar Assn.,** 42 Lansdowne Parade, Oatley,
N.S.W., Australia 2223

**Wings!,** British Hang Gliding Assn., Monksilver, Taunton,
Sommerset, England

**Societe Delta,** 18 Rue D'Armenonville, 92200 Neuilly,
France   722-7065

**Delta Flight Club,** c/o Gerard Gourion, 49 Blvd. St. Michel
Paris, 5, France

**Hang Gliding Group,** Holland P/A Frederiksoord, (dr)
9517, Holland

**Japan Hang Gliders Inc.,** 5-12-18 Yagumo Meguro-Ku,
Tokyo, Japan 152   (03) 724-1201

**Mike Harker Delta Glider,** 1-39033 Corvara, Drachenflug
Club, West Germany   421-83128

**Canterbury Hang Glider Club,** Box 22481, Christchurch, New Zealand

## Publications

**New Zealand Gliding KIWI,** c/o New Zealand H.G. Assn., Box 451, Wellington, New Zealand

### BIBLIOGRAPHY FOR THE HANG GLIDER'S BIBLE.

(1)  Abbot, Ira H. and Albert E. Von Doenhoff, "Theory of Wing Sections", Dover Publications, N.Y., NY.

(2)  Adelson, Joe and Bill Williams, "Hang Flight", Eco-Nautics, Redlands, CA.

(3)  Batchelor, B. K., "An Introduction To Fluid Dynamics", Cambridge University Press, Cambridge

(4)  Bisplinghoff, R.L., Holt Ashley and Robert L. Hoffmann, "Aeroelasticity", Addison-Wesley Publishing Co., Inc. Reading, MA.

(5)  Brimm, D.J., Jr. and H. Edward Boggess, "Aircraft Maintenance" Pittman Publishing Corp., N.Y., NY.

(6)  Bungay, Stanley and Stuart Leavell, "Standard Aircraft Handbook", Aero Publishers, Inc. Fallbrook, CA.

(7)  Carrier, Rick, "Fly. The Complete Book of Sky Sailing", McGraw-Hill Book Company, N.Y., NY.

(8)  Chanute, Octave, "Progress In Flying Machines", Lorenz and Herweg Publishers, Long Beach, CA.

(9)  Dedera, Don, "Hang Gliding. The Flyingest Flying", Northland Press, Flagstaff, AZ.

(10)  Dohm, John, "The New Private Pilot", Pan American Navigation Service, No. Hollywood, CA.

(11)  Duke, Neville and Edward Lanchberry, "The Saga of Flight", Avon Books, N.Y., NY.

(12)  Dzik, Stanley J., "Aircraft Hardware Standards Manual and Engineering Reference", Aviation Publications, Milwaukee, WI.

(13)  East, Omega B., "Wright Brothers", National Park Service Historical Handbook Series No. 34, Washington, DC.

(14)  Etkin, Bernard, "Dynamics of Flight", John Wiley and Sons, Inc., N.Y., NY.

(15)  Federal Aviation Agency, "Basic Glider Criteria Handbook," U.S. Government Printing Office, Washington, DC.

(16)  Halacy, D.C., Jr., "The Complete Book of Hang Gliding", Hawthorn Books, Inc., N.Y., NY.

(17)  Harper, Harry, "The Evolution of the Flying Machine", David McKay Co., Philadelphia, PA.

(18)  Lilienthal, Otto, "Birdflight As The Basis Of Aviation", Longmans, Green And Co., N.Y., NY.

(19)  Lougheed, Victor, "Vehicles Of The Air"

(20)  Marin, Joseph, "Mechanical Behavior Of Engineering Materials", Prentice-Hall, Inc., Englewood, CA.

(21)  McCormick, Barnes W., Jr., "Aerodynamics Of V/STOL Flight", Academic Press, N.Y., NY.

(22)  McFarland, Marvin W., "The Papers of Wilbur and Orville Wright", McGraw-Hill Book Co., Inc., N.Y., NY.

(23)  McKinley, James C. and Ralph D. Bent, "Maintenance and Repair of Aerospace Vehicles", McGraw-Hill Book Co., Inc. N.Y. NY.

(24)  Means, James, "The Aeronautical Annual" (1895, 1896, 1897) W. B. Clarke and Co., Boston, MA.

(25)  Peery, D.J., "Aircraft Structures", McGraw-Hill Book Co., Inc., N.Y., NY.

(26)  Perkins, C.D. and Robert E. Hage, "Airplane Performance, Stability and Control", John Wiley and Sons, Inc., N.Y., NY.

(27)  Pope, Francis and Arthur S. Otis, "Elements of Aeronautics", World Book Co., Inc., NY., NY.

(28)  Poynter, Dan, "Hang Gliding. The Basic Handbook of Skysurfing", Santa Barbara, CA.

(29)  Pritchard, J.L., "Sir George Cayley", Parrish, London.

(30)  Rauscher, Manfred, "Introduction To Aeronautical Dynamics", John Wiley and Sons, Inc., N.Y., NY.

(31)  Roughley, T.C., "The Aeronautical Work of Lawrence Hargrave", Americana Archives Publishing, Topsfield, MA.

(32)  Siposs, George, "Hang Gliding Handbook. Fly Like A Bird", Tab Books, Inc., Blue Ridge Summit, PA.

(33)  Sherwin, Keith, "Man-Powered Flight", Model and Allied Publications, LTD, Herts, England.

(34)  Smithsonian Institution, "The Wright Brothers", Information Leaflet 8 (rev), Washington, DC.

(35)  Tietjens, O.B., "Fundamentals of Hydro- and Aeromechanics", Dover Publications, Inc., N.Y., NY.

(36)  USHGA, *Ground Skimmer* magazine, Los Angeles, Ca.

(37)  Von Mises, Richard, "Theory of Flight", Dover Publications, N.Y., NY.

(36)  Welch, Ann and Lorne, "New Soaring Pilot", John Murray, London.

(37)  Wood, K.D., "Aircraft Design", Johnson Publishing Co., Boulder, CO.

(38)  Hoerner, Dr. S.F., "Fluid Dynamic Drag", N.J.

# Index

**479**